P9-AFQ-484

AMERICAN
SPIES

AMERICAN

SPIES

ESPIONAGE AGAINST THE
UNITED STATES
FROM THE COLD WAR
TO THE PRESENT

MICHAEL J. SULICK

Georgetown University Press

Washington, DC

Library of Congress Cataloging-in-Publication Data

Sulick, Michael J.
  American spies : espionage against the United States from the Cold War to the present / Michael J. Sulick.
     pages cm
  Includes bibliographical references and index.
  ISBN 978-1-62616-008-8 (hbk. : alk. paper)
1. Espionage—United States—Case studies. 2. Espionage—United States—History—20th century. 3. Espionage—United States—History—21st century. 4. Spies—United States—Biography. 5. Spies—United States—History. 6. Spies—Communist countries—Biography. 7. Intelligence service—United States—History—20th century. 8. Cold War. I. Title. II. Title: Espionage against the United States from the Cold War to the present.
  UB271.U5S852 2013
  327.120973—dc23
                          2013000035

∞ This book is printed on acid-free paper meeting the requirements of the American National Standard for Permanence in Paper for Printed Library Materials.

15 14 13   9 8 7 6 5 4 3 2 First printing

Printed in the United States of America

To my wife Shirley and all the
other intelligence community members,
former and current,
for their contributions to
our national security.

Contents

Preface

My first book, *Spying in America,* covered a long period of US history, about 180 years from the nation's birth to the dawn of the Cold War. This second book follows the first and covers a far briefer time, about sixty years from the Cold War to the present day, but spying by Americans escalated significantly after World War II. Once the United States became a superpower after the war, the nation became a prime espionage target not only for its Soviet adversary in the Cold War but also for a host of other nations.

Considering this increased espionage activity, this volume can serve as little more than an introduction to the history of spying against America during and after the Cold War. A discussion of all the spy cases in the past sixty years would be well beyond the scope of this broad review. As in *Spying in America*, my selections were based on the importance of the particular case or its relevance to other issues associated with espionage in American history. Most important, my goal is to encourage laypeople, students, and general readers interested in intelligence to delve more deeply into the threats to national security from espionage.

I express my thanks to those who encouraged me to complete and publish both volumes and assisted me in doing so, especially Doug Hubbard, Mark Lowenthal, David Major, Keith Melton, and Jim Olson. I would also like to thank Burton Gerber and Hayden Peake for their insights and suggestions, and for their corrections to the manuscript. Most of all, I would like to thank my colleagues at the Central Intelligence Agency (CIA) and in the intelligence community for their unheralded dedication and tireless devotion to protecting this nation.

All statements of fact, opinion, or analysis expressed are those of the author and do not reflect the official positions or views of the CIA or any other US government agency. Nothing in the contents should be construed as asserting or implying US government authentication of information or the CIA's endorsement of the author's views. The material has been reviewed by the CIA to prevent the disclosure of classified information.

Abbreviations

CIA   US Central Intelligence Agency

COINTELPRO   Counterintelligence Program, conducted by the Federal Bureau of Investigation between 1956 and 1971 to disrupt the activities of the Communist Party of the United States of America and to monitor, penetrate, discredit, and disrupt the activities of certain domestic political organizations.

CPUSA   Communist Party of the United States of America

DIA   US Defense Intelligence Agency

DOD   US Department of Defense

DOE   US Department of Energy

DOJ   US Department of Justice

FBI   US Federal Bureau of Investigation

FISA   Foreign Intelligence Surveillance Act, a federal law enacted in 1978 that prescribes procedures for the judicial authorization of physical and electronic surveillance for the collection of foreign intelligence and counterintelligence information

FSB   Federal Security Service (Federal'naya sluzhba bezopasnosti), Russia. The FSB, which was established after the collapse of the Soviet Union and dissolution of the KGB, is the primary internal security service of the Russian Federation and is responsible for counterterrorism, counterespionage, and border security.

GRU Main Intelligence Directorate (Glavnoe razvedyvatel'noe upravlenie), Russia. The GRU, the foreign military intelligence directorate of the General Staff of the Armed Forces of the Russian Federation, collects intelligence overseas on military issues related to Russian national security. During the Soviet era, the GRU belonged to the Soviet Army's General Staff.

KGB Soviet Committee of State Security (Komitet gosudarstvennoy bezopasnosti); primary national security agency of the Soviet Union, 1954–91, responsible for internal security, foreign intelligence collection, counterintelligence, border protection, and electronic surveillance.

NCIX National Counterintelligence Executive. NCIX was established in January 2001 by presidential directive to coordinate and oversee national counterintelligence for the US government. NCIX reports to the director of national intelligence and replaced the National Counterintelligence Center, which was established in 1994 after the arrest of CIA spy Aldrich Ames.

NIS US Naval Investigative Service, responsible for investigating and countering crime, terrorism, and espionage against the US Navy and Marine Corps; renamed the Naval Criminal Investigative Service in 1992.

NSA US National Security Agency

PERSEREC Personnel Security Research Center; a DOD organization responsible for improving the effectiveness and fairness of DOD's suitability and security systems. PERSEREC has published considerable historical information on past US espionage cases.

PFIAB President's Foreign Intelligence Advisory Board advising the president on the quality and effectiveness of intelli-

gence collection, analysis, and counterintelligence; renamed the President's Intelligence Advisory Board in
2008.

PRC   People's Republic of China

SVR   Foreign Intelligence Service (Sluzhba vneshney razvedki);
Russia's civilian foreign intelligence service, formed from
the First Chief Directorate of the KGB at its dissolution.

Introduction

Coca-Cola has kept its formula a secret since the 1800s.
Kentucky Fried Chicken has never let the competition get its hands
on Colonel Sanders' original recipe. So why has the US government
lost its most sensitive secrets to foreign spies?

J. MICHAEL WALLER, "Espionage and National Security"

The first major spy against America, Benjamin Church, was one of the leading patriots in Massachusetts during the Revolutionary War. Church, a physician by profession, tended to wounded colonists at the Battle of Bunker Hill. George Washington later appointed him chief surgeon of the army, and his compatriots elected him to the Massachusetts Continental Congress, where he was chosen to represent it in relations with the other colonies.

Church also kept a mistress and enjoyed a lavish lifestyle beyond his meager salary as a doctor. To maintain this standard of living, he was paid by the British to provide information from the inner councils of the revolutionaries. Although he was spotted consorting with British general Thomas Gage and his friends knew that he was living beyond his means, his revolutionary credentials were impeccable and he was beyond suspicion. His spying was only discovered because he foolishly entrusted his mistress with a letter to his British spymasters. Instead of delivering the letter directly, the mistress left it with someone who passed it to the Continental Army. The woman was detained, questioned by Washington himself, and finally identified Church as the author of the damning letter.

Church was arrested and claimed that he was feeding false information to the enemy by inflating troop strengths in hopes of persuading the British to abandon their cause. This feeble argument failed to convince Washington, who convened a council that found Church guilty. But because the colonies had enacted no law regarding espionage, Church could not be tried for the crime. To recommend an espionage law, the Continental Congress quickly appointed a committee that included two future US presidents, John Adams and Thomas Jefferson. Congress approved their recommendation, mandating the death sentence for espionage, but Church could not be tried retroactively. Instead, he was banished to the West Indies, and his ship sunk at sea en route to his new home.

The Benjamin Church affair included many of the elements of espionage cases that would plague US national security throughout American history: spying for money; the failure of the spy's colleagues to recognize indicators of his espionage; unfettered access to valuable national security information; the spy's rationalization of espionage when caught; exposure resulting from the spy's shoddy security practices; and finally, the impact of an individual spy case on the development of espionage legislation.

The companion volume of this book, *Spying in America*, traces the history of espionage against the United States from the Benjamin Church case until the onset of the Cold War.[1] America remained particularly vulnerable to espionage in those 175 years because of a chronic disbelief that those like Benjamin Church who were entrusted with the nation's secrets would betray them. By the start of the Cold War, the United States had established institutions and capabilities to combat espionage; yet this disbelief persisted. The intent of this study is to examine the history of this disbelief through the stories of individual spies and to provide the reader with insights into the unique nature of espionage against America, its successes, failures, and consequences for national security. "To counter espionage," as one intelligence historian put it, "you must first understand it. To do this, you must be aware of its history."[2]

American disbelief in espionage reached its heights in the decades preceding World War II. A century and a half after the Church case, the Soviet Union ran the most significant espionage penetration of the United States in its history. Americans disenchanted with capitalism flocked to the ranks of the Communist Party of the United States (CPUSA), and the Soviets exploited the opportunity to form an underground network of spies in almost all key agencies in the administration of Franklin D. Roosevelt and in the Manhattan Project, the nation's most secret military venture of World War II.

The Soviet effort was aptly dubbed the "Golden Age" of espionage by two historians of the era, Allen Weinstein and Alexander Vassiliev.[3] The Soviet network included spies from all walks of life, from inside and outside the government, from the highest levels to low-ranking clerks. The network included couriers like Elizabeth Bentley, a Vassar graduate from an established New England family who became the lover of her spy handler, Jacob Golos, and ran his extensive network after his death. It also included Harry Dexter White, the assistant secretary of the Treasury, one of the most senior US government officials in history to become a spy.

Inside the Manhattan Project, the Soviets' ring included David Greenglass, a junior mechanic at the Los Alamos National Laboratory, and his brother-in-law, Julius Rosenberg, whose own network of spies passed the Soviets secrets on a broad spectrum of US conventional weapons besides the atomic bomb. And finally, it included one of the youngest American spies in its history, Theodore Hall, a brilliant scientist in his twenties when he worked on implosion, one of the key elements in detonating the atomic bomb.

Because of the Soviet dictator Joseph Stalin's purges and the USSR's surprising nonaggression pact with Nazi Germany, some of these spies later became disillusioned with communism. One of them, Bentley, was among the first to alert the US government to the Soviet espionage networks. A few years later, the Venona Project, one of America's greatest counterespionage achievements, enabled identification of a large number of spies after American cryptographers decrypted Soviet message traffic between the United States and Moscow.[4] Despite the irrefutable proof of widespread espionage that eventually surfaced, officials at the highest levels of the US government could not believe that their wartime ally would spy against the United States and that top government officials would betray the nation's secrets.

The United States was more vigilant about espionage after the revelations about vast Soviet networks, but national disbelief still persisted throughout the Cold War as Americans continued to spy for the USSR. By the time the Cold War ended, every agency involved in national security and every branch of the armed forces except the US Coast Guard had suffered spies in its midst.[5] Even officials of the agencies responsible for gathering intelligence and thwarting foreign espionage, the Central Intelligence Agency (CIA) and Federal Bureau of Investigation (FBI), refused to believe that one of their own would commit espionage. As a result, both organizations overlooked major spies in their ranks. Just as American colonists ignored the signs of Church's espionage, his association with known Tories and his unexplained wealth, their twentieth-century counterparts would fail to see similar indicators.

Americans not only disbelieved that their fellow citizens would betray the nation's secrets but were also wary of government efforts to catch spies. A bedrock of American democracy since its birth has been the guarantee of civil liberties. Throughout American history, the inherent friction between guaranteeing these liberties and ensuring national security has influenced counterespionage, that is, the thwarting of foreign espionage and protection of the nation's secrets. Americans grew highly suspicious of counterespionage, and some regarded it as at best an unwarranted invasion of privacy and at worst outright persecution. Their suspicions were justified at various times in the nation's history when overeager zealots who saw spies everywhere crippled American counterespionage as much as disbelievers who refused to see spies anywhere. These zealots aggravated suspicion of counterespionage by violating civil liberties in the name of national security and committing the very excesses many Americans feared.

The abuse of civil liberties dates back to the Civil War, when Lafayette Baker, chief of one of the two Union security services, detained hundreds of alleged Confederate subversives without legal basis but caught few real spies in the process. Baker's excesses would be repeated in the future when Americans overreacted to foreign threats by arbitrarily abusing the rights of selected citizens. After World War I, one such wave of spy mania occurred when Attorney General Mitchell Palmer launched his notorious Red Raids against alleged communists and anarchists. Like Baker, Palmer ordered the detention of hundreds of suspects without legal basis, again apprehending few real spies and subversives. Although subversives had organized labor strikes and engaged in even more violent protests, Palmer, who fancied himself a presidential candidate, had grossly exaggerated the extent of foreign sedition and eventually his hopes for the White House were dashed.

Revelations of massive Soviet espionage before and during World War II fueled both zealotry and suspicion of counterespionage in the early days of the Cold War. Senator Joseph McCarthy's shrill allegations of pervasive communist infiltration of the US government denigrated scores of civil servants but again surfaced no real spies. Like Palmer, McCarthy was discredited, but his misguided crusade raised American suspicions of government efforts to prevent foreign espionage. These suspicions were reawakened during the political turmoil of the 1960s and 1970s as opponents of the Vietnam War increased and minority groups clamored for recognition of their civil rights. The FBI's director, J. Edgar Hoover, initiated its Counterintelligence Program (COINTELPRO) to investigate possible associations between foreign adversaries and civil rights and antiwar activists. No spies were discovered, and COINTELPRO, once revealed, was itself investigated and condemned by Congress for its abuse of civil liberties.

The inherent tension between guaranteeing civil liberties and preserving national security has continued to the present day. More than a decade has passed since the terrorist attacks of September 11, 2001, and the US government is still wrestling with the dilemma of defending the nation from terrorism while upholding civil liberties. This dilemma is reflected in debate over policies regarding the treatment of captured terrorists and government programs to monitor communications to identify potential terrorists and prevent future attacks.

After World War I, concerns about possible abuses of civil liberties resulted in a significant decrease in many counterespionage activities and personnel. From the end of the Revolutionary War to the onset of World War II, the United States created organizations to gather intelligence and combat espionage only to confront wartime threats. Once the wars ended, the organizations were disbanded, and succeeding generations confronted espionage threats anew in the next conflict.

The establishment of these capabilities was often marked by interagency rivalries that also hampered American efforts to combat espionage. During the Civil War, the Union at one time had two rival organizations to catch Confederate spies, one headed by the infamous Lafayette Baker and the other by Allan Pinkerton, who would later establish the nation's foremost detective agency. By the end of the war, both agencies had disappeared. As World War I loomed fifty years later, a mishmash of federal agencies competed for counterespionage authority. The State Department, Department of Justice (DOJ), Secret Service, and military services at various points each conducted counterespionage activities on their own and squabbled among themselves over jurisdiction. With World War II on the horizon in 1939, Franklin D. Roosevelt finally invested central counterespionage authority in the FBI, which had proven to be the most effective agency for the task and already had the legal authority to investigate federal crimes such as espionage.

The exposure of vast Soviet spy networks in the United States and the onset of the Cold War dramatically transformed America's counterespionage bureaucracy. The Cold War rivalry between the United States and the Soviet Union affected every facet of America's interaction with the rest of the world—bilateral relationships, diplomacy, foreign aid, and military strategy—and espionage, an essential element of national security, was no exception. The FBI significantly increased its counterespionage efforts against the Soviets in the United States and, almost two decades after its birth, the nation finally created a peacetime intelligence service with the establishment of the CIA in 1947.

Although these institutional capabilities were established and refined both during and after the Cold War, interagency rivalries persisted and would increase America's vulnerability to espionage threats. Institutional conflicts between the FBI and CIA, in particular, would impede the sharing of information and result in spies inside the intelligence community operating undetected for years. Frustrated with this interagency bickering, both the executive branch and legislative branch finally took measures to ensure that both agencies cooperated in the future.

In 1995, Congress enacted a provision mandating that all federal agencies, not just the CIA, alert the FBI whenever they have indications that classified information may have been disclosed without authorization to a foreign nation.[6] This legislation and other reforms eventually fostered the unprecedented cooperation between the two agencies that led to the exposure and arrest of key spies deep inside America's national security establishment.

This study presents the stories of those people who have spied against America from the onset of the Cold War to the present. As in *Spying in America*, the stories here focus on six fundamental elements of their espionage: the motivations that drove Americans to spy; their access and the secrets they betrayed; the tradecraft used by the intelligence services that controlled them—that is, the techniques of concealing their espionage; the exposure of the spy operations; the punishment meted out to the spies; and finally, the damage these espionage operations inflicted on America's national security.

Although the Cold War rivalry between the United States and Soviet Union produced some dramatic changes in spying against America, the motives that drove American citizens to spy remained the same as in the past: money, ego, revenge, romance, simple thrills, ideological sympathy, and dual loyalties. Like Benjamin Church, many spied out of greed, whereas others spied out of loyalty to a cause, like those people who joined the Soviet networks of the 1930s and 1940s.

One striking difference in the Cold War, however, was that the vast majority of Americans who spied for the Soviets and their bloc allies betrayed secrets primarily for financial motives. In the early years after World War II, Soviet aggression in seizing Eastern Europe, revelations about its oppressive regime, its acquisition of the atomic bomb, and subsequent fears of nuclear warfare all crushed America's idealistic flirtation with the communist utopia. Ironically, Americans who spied for the Soviets in the Cold War were no exception; few betrayed US secrets to the Soviets out of sympathy with communist ideology. One of America's most damaging spies, US Navy warrant officer John Walker, laughed at his Soviet handlers when they tried to proselytize him about the marvels of communism and his contributions to world peace.[7]

By the 1980s, even as Cold War espionage between the superpowers was at its height, a new trend emerged when increasing numbers of Americans were caught spying for nations other than those that belonged to the Soviet bloc. According to a study by the Personnel Research and Security Center (PERSEREC) of the Department of Defense (DOD), almost one-third of the American spies arrested during the 1980s committed espionage for other countries besides the Soviet Union.[8] By 2007, the then–national counterintelligence executive, Joel Brenner, claimed that "there are now 140 foreign intelligence services that try to penetrate the United States or US organizations abroad, and for many of them, we are their number one target."[9]

Besides the increasing number of nations spying against the United States, another new trend directly affected motivations for espionage. Globalization, the socioeconomic and cultural interdependence of peoples and corporations, increasingly affected traditional concepts of loyalty to one nation-state, and a larger number of Americans spied not for money or ideological beliefs but because of foreign attachments and dual allegiances. According to the PERSEREC study, half the spies exposed in the 1990s claimed that dual allegiance drove them to cooperate with foreign powers.[10]

The 1990s marked a momentous transformation in the world order that influenced espionage and every other aspect of national security. The fall of the Berlin Wall at the dawn of the 1990s was rapidly followed by the toppling of communist regimes in Eastern Europe, the reunification of Germany, and the dissolution of the USSR. The superpower conflict that had defined the world order since the end of World War II was over, but new threats to US national security eventually emerged. As CIA director James Woolsey noted in his Senate confirmation hearing, "We have slain a large dragon. But we live now in a jungle with a bewildering variety of poisonous snakes."[11] During the decade, the United States confronted that "bewildering variety of snakes" by deploying troops across continents in Somalia, Iraq, Serbia, and Haiti. By the end of the decade, attacks against the World Trade Center in New York (1993) and US embassies in Africa (1998) elevated terrorism on the list of the gravest national security threats to the nation. After 9/11, terrorism topped the list.

Although the new world order changed spying against America, espionage in some respects remained the same. The Soviet Union had disappeared, but the newly established Russian Federation continued to run sources inside the US government, even during the brief honeymoon in US–Russian cooperation in the early years after the end of Soviet communism.

In the 1990s, however, the Russian espionage threat was eventually overshadowed by Chinese spying. Communist China had been an adversary of the United States for decades, but since the formal opening of diplomatic relations with Beijing in 1979, thousands of students, scientists, and businesspeople traveled to the United States, many of whom actively collected and provided information to Chinese intelligence. By 2010 Chinese espionage had eclipsed Russian spying in the United States.[12]

Whatever the motives of American spies during and after the Cold War, the Soviet and other intelligence services were primarily concerned with the access offered by Americans interested in trading secrets. Although the USSR and United States never engaged in direct conflict during the Cold War, critical intelligence questions for both sides concerned strategic military plans, tactical deployments, and gauging the capabilities of the other side's weaponry, especially its nuclear arsenal, to determine if it had a decisive advantage on the battlefield. To answer these questions, the Soviets were quite successful in enlisting US military personnel as spies throughout the Cold War. In the 1970s, the Soviets and their bloc allies also achieved considerable success in finding spies who worked for US defense firms involved in classified weapons projects.

In some instances, their successes were extraordinary. John Walker, a naval warrant officer who offered his services to the Komitet gosudarstvennoy bezopasnosti (KGB), the Committee for State Security, provided the Soviet Union with information on the nation's entire naval defense, especially nuclear submarines and their movements, that could have had "potential . . . war-winning implications for the Soviet side," according to then–director of naval intelligence William Studeman.[13] On the army side, Sergeant Clyde Conrad passed the war plans of NATO to a Soviet surrogate, the Hungarian intelligence service, including information about US tactical nuclear capabilities, the deployment of armor and aircraft, and the location of missile sites.

The Chinese pursued similar access. In their quest to modernize the People's Liberation Army, the Chinese accelerated their development of advanced weapon systems by simply stealing the technology through espionage. The majority of Chinese espionage cases in the past twenty years have involved the theft of US military technology.

Another new development in spying against America involved access not only to government but also to corporate secrets. In the increasingly globalized economy, commercial information about a corporation's products and strategies was crucial to competitors. The United States, the only remaining superpower after the Cold War, became the main target. Some surveys estimate that economic espionage costs US business from $45 billion to as much as $250 billion annually.[14] In response to the increasing theft of corporate secrets, in 1996 Congress passed the Economic Espionage Act, which made the theft or misappropriation of trade secrets a federal crime.

To ensure the continued flow of secrets and to communicate with their spies, the Soviets and their allies employed tradecraft—the full range of techniques to hide clandestine intelligence operations from the enemy, including codes, secret writing, and "dead drops," that is, concealed caches of information planted in areas where they are not likely to be found by passers-by. The Soviets had learned from their past mistakes operating in America and had developed more secure and sophisticated tradecraft to ensure the safety and longevity of their Cold War sources. In the 1930s and 1940s, the Soviets' underground espionage networks in the CPUSA evolved from Marxist discussion groups and maintained this clubby approach in their espionage activity. Members of a spy ring often knew the identities of their fellow spies, met and telephoned them quite openly, and shared knowledge about their respective spying tasks—all rudimentary breaches of secure clandestine tradecraft. The Soviets eventually tried to exercise better control over their CPUSA spies and impose better security measures, but by then it was too late. Defectors from the cause like Elizabeth Bentley and others, thanks to these poor security practices, knew scores of agents and revealed all their identities to the FBI.

Aside from the poor security practices of the CPUSA network, once the Cold War started, Soviet intelligence services also confronted far more scrutiny from the FBI. To counter FBI monitoring, the Soviets often met their US sources outside the United States and, when that was impossible, inside the country they used "impersonal communications," clandestine techniques to avoid risky face-to-face contact that often employed methods such as dead drops and elaborate systems of signaling readiness to send and receive those caches of information. This system had been used successfully by intelligence services for centuries. During the Revolutionary War, the British routinely exchanged information through dead drops in Paris with Edward Bancroft, a spy who worked as an aide to Benjamin Franklin, then the colonial liaison to France.

In spite of all the security precautions the Soviets took, spies are human beings, often flawed ones, and thus make mistakes. Often the very motives that drive one to spy lead to their exposure. The person who spies for the thrill of it takes unnecessary risks and is caught. The person who spies out of ego believes that he should follow his own rules, and his arrogance leads to costly mistakes and eventual exposure. And the one who spies for money, in spite of warnings by his handlers, will spend beyond his means; and his sudden, unexplained wealth will raise suspicions and lead to his demise. Americans during the Cold War spied for all these motives, and many were eventually unmasked precisely because of such blunders.

At the same time, many Cold War spies were exposed not only because of their security mistakes. The one significant difference from the past in American counterespionage during the Cold War was the US government's active pursuit of foreign intelligence officers with information about American spies. America had finally realized that the best way to catch spies is to have spies of your own in the adversary's intelligence service. This counterespionage tactic dates back centuries—as the Chinese military strategist and philosopher Sun Tzu noted in the *Art of War*, "It is essential to seek out enemy agents who have come to conduct espionage against you, . . . give them instructions, and care for them. Thus double agents are recruited and used."[15]

Before the Cold War, US counterespionage services made little effort to recruit spies in enemy intelligence services with information about their own espionage work in America. During the height of Soviet spying in the United States in the 1930s and 1940s, the FBI was more focused on countering the spread of Soviet communism in American society by infiltrating the CPUSA instead of pursuing Soviet intelligence officers. The FBI had missed an excellent opportunity because the time for approaching Soviet intelligence officers was particularly ripe. Stalinist purges had eliminated officials both in the military and intelligence services, and a summons for an officer in the United States to return home may have been a pretext to lure him to prison or his execution. The FBI made few attempts to recruit these officers and offered an alternative: Identify American spies in return for a safe haven in the United States.

The situation changed dramatically with the onset of the Cold War, when the FBI intensively sought to recruit officers serving in the United States from both Soviet intelligence services, the civilian KGB and the military Glavnoe razvedyvatel'noe upravlenie (GRU), the Main Intelligence Directorate of the Armed Forces. The CIA, although its primary duty was the collection of intelligence, was also responsible overseas for the recruitment of officers in foreign intelligence services who could reveal their countries' spies in the US government. Its highest priority was the recruitment of Soviet intelligence officers.

A large number of the American spies discussed in this study were caught thanks to US sources inside the espionage departments of the KGB and GRU and other intelligence services.[16] At the same time, unfortunately, some of these same sources were betrayed by Soviet penetrations of the FBI and CIA. As Viktor Cherkashin, one of the KGB's leading spy handlers, notes in his memoirs, "Almost all spies in the Cold War were exposed by other spies."[17]

Once these spies were caught, the punishments meted out to them varied. The United States had made legislative progress since the Revolutionary War, when Benjamin Church was caught but the young colonies had enacted no espionage laws to enable them to try him in court. The United States eventually enacted espionage laws but still faced a thorny dilemma prosecuting spies, which was epitomized by the Venona Project. The messages revealed the vast extent of Soviet espionage in the United States, and painstaking analysis enabled investigators to identify many of the American spies. However, this irrefutable evidence could not be used in open court without revealing the existence of the project. As the PERSEREC study notes, spies like William Weisband, who actually revealed the Venona Project to the Soviets, and Theodore Hall, the brilliant, young physicist in the Manhattan Project, largely escaped justice—Weisband received a one-year sentence for contempt of court and was not tried for espionage; Hall was never tried at all. Prosecutors would face the same dilemma throughout the Cold War.[18]

In the early decades of the Cold War, spies were at times eased out of their positions quietly and were not prosecuted if classified information might be revealed in a court trial. DOJ and the CIA secretly agreed that any accused spies inside the CIA would not be prosecuted if the agency determined that a prosecution would damage national security.[19] In the mid-1970s, congressional investigations of reported civil liberties abuses by the CIA and FBI spotlighted the practice of avoiding prosecutions to preserve secrets.[20] As a result, President Gerald Ford abolished the secret agreement between DOJ and the CIA.

In 1977, President Jimmy Carter's attorney general, Griffin Bell, abandoned the policy of "letting the spy go and keeping the secret" and urged a balanced approach that would enable prosecution without revealing classified information and endangering valuable sources.[21] A year later, Congress passed the Foreign Intelligence Surveillance Act (known by its acronym, FISA), which established a special court that could grant warrants in national security cases but would deliberate requests in secret to preserve classified information. DOJ is required by the law to demonstrate to the FISA court probable cause that the suspect is an agent of or cooperating with a foreign power.

In 1980, Congress passed further legislation, the Classified Information Procedures Act (CIPA), which established a process for determining at the early stage of a prosecution whether issues regarding the disclosure of secrets might affect the case.[22] CIPA facilitated discussions of issues regarding the relevance and admissibility of classified information but could not completely resolve the dilemma. In many cases, both prosecutors and defense attorneys would need to use classified evidence to make their arguments in court.

To avoid court trials, the US government in some major cases reached plea bargains with the accused spies in which prosecutors agreed to the lesser sentence of life imprisonment rather than the death sentence. In these major cases the plea bargains also stipulated that the spy had to cooperate fully in debriefings about his espionage activity, which enabled the government to determine the extent of information passed along with the names of foreign handlers and modus operandi, all of which might enhance US counterespionage capabilities in the future. Because of these plea bargain agreements, some major spies avoided the fate of Julius Rosenberg and Ethel Rosenberg, the last American civilians executed for espionage.

Both FISA and CIPA contributed to increased convictions of American spies by the 1980s, when more than sixty Americans were arrested for spying. The increased number of convictions finally punished spies for the considerable harm they have inflicted on US national security. Ironically, however, the overall damage to national security from espionage has fueled America's complacency. Although the United States has been riddled with spies throughout its history, the republic still stands. The espionage activities of Benjamin Church and Benedict Arnold, America's most infamous traitor, did not prevent the colonies from winning their independence. The Union was preserved after the Civil War despite Confederate spying, and the United States emerged victorious in two world wars despite enemy espionage. Although the nation's most closely guarded secrets—its atomic bomb, defense plans, and intelligence networks—fell into Soviet hands during the Cold War, the USSR has nonetheless been cast into the dustbin of history. Despite American vulnerability to espionage, a host of other political, economic, and military factors have proven far more decisive than espionage in resolving the nation's conflicts with foreign enemies.

Although espionage alone may not tip the scales of victory in the struggle between nations, the loss of secrets takes its toll in other costly ways. Whenever spies were discovered during the Cold War, the United States was compelled to devise countermeasures to offset the military, scientific, and economic advantages that the Soviet bloc gained from stolen secrets. John Walker's compromising of US naval capabilities cost the government millions of dollars to develop countermeasures. The tax dollars spent on all these measures could have been devoted to building roads, hospitals, and schools throughout the country.

Moreover, the damage caused by espionage cannot be calculated only in dollars. When Walker spied for the KGB, he had access to information about US bombing raids against North Vietnam. He passed that information to the Soviets, who in turn passed it to their North Vietnamese allies. In various towns and cities across the United States, a father lost a child, a son lost a father, or a sister lost a brother who was a pilot shot down over Vietnam because of a spy's betrayal.

American spies also cause other incalculable losses. Spies exposed inside the US intelligence services and the military have eroded the trust of foreign counterparts whose cooperation, especially in today's fight against terrorism, are critical to the United States' defense. In the post-9/11 world, if a foreign intelligence service refrains from sharing counterterrorist information with the United States because of concerns about American spies, the results could be catastrophic.

The extensive damage done by American spies—millions of taxpayer dollars in countermeasures, loss of life, and the erosion of national credibility—has been inflicted by an infinitesimally small percentage of the population. At the peak of Soviet espionage in the 1930s and 1940s, the Venona Project transcripts and other sources revealed that more than five hundred Americans spied for the Soviets, undoubtedly the highest number in US history but a mere fraction of the American population of about 132 million at the time.[23] The number of spies is also paltry compared to the figures for other criminals. In 1936 alone there were more than 3,500 homicides in the United States, seven times the number of Soviet spies. In the 1980s sixty-two Americans were arrested for espionage, about half the number of homicides in 1985 alone for the state of Oregon.[24] By these measures, espionage is truly one of the rarest of crimes in the United States—yet one of the costliest.

Many of the stories presented here tell of spies who operated for years before they were discovered. During the Cold War, some of these spies passed information that could have given the Soviet Union significant military advantages if war had then erupted between the superpowers. Fortunately, both sides realized the risks of nuclear devastation in unleashing a war, and the United States had time to repair the damage done by spies.

Today, the United States no longer has that luxury in fighting the war on terrorism. A terrorist spy who penetrates the US government could acquire secrets that would enable a devastating terrorist attack on American citizens that would cause Cold War espionage losses to pale by comparison. The United States can no longer afford complacency about espionage in a world where stolen secrets could result in imminent danger to its citizens.

Aside from the imminent threat of terrorist spies, another emerging threat that could prove equally damaging to US national security is cyberespionage. Computer hacking—that is, the unauthorized access to and manipulation of information systems—was once the province of mischief makers and thieves but has rapidly evolved into a sophisticated tool used by foreign intelligence services to steal American government and commercial secrets.

This development is certainly no surprise. Spy services have exploited technological advances for centuries to facilitate the acquisition of secrets. Computer technology is particularly well suited to espionage and has significantly enhanced many of the essential elements of clandestinity. Massive amounts of data can now be acquired and transmitted at increasingly faster speeds through easily concealed portable devices like computer flash drives and memory cards. At the same time, the perpetrator is protected by the anonymity of cyberspace and his theft at times remains undetected.

Foreign adversaries, especially China and Russia, have capitalized on these advantages to penetrate both US government and industry information systems. In 2011 a report to Congress by the National Counterintelligence Executive (NCIX) noted that "the computer networks of a broad array of US government agencies, private companies, and other institutions—all holding large volumes of sensitive economic information—were targeted by cyberespionage."[25]

The NCIX report emphasized that computer attacks are increasing exponentially, especially against US government classified information systems. In 2008 alone the Department of Homeland Security reported a 40 percent increase in intrusions into US government computer systems from the previous year.[26] Security industry experts expect the frequency of cyberespionage to rise even more dramatically in coming years, especially with the development of more advanced malware.[27] However, despite these disturbing omens, Shawn Henry, once the FBI's senior cyber official, warned that many American organizations continue to ignore the threat: "Either they don't recognize it, they don't understand it, or they don't care."[28]

Perhaps America's chronic disbelief in the threat of espionage still prevails. Hopefully, this historical review of espionage in America will assist the public in recognizing, understanding, and caring about this threat.

PART **1**

THE COLD WAR: 1950–70

1

The KGB Rebuilds

Despite some low- and middle-level Soviet penetrations in postwar Washington, there have been no successors to agents of the caliber of Hiss at the State Department, Harry Dexter White of Treasury, Duncan C. Lee of the intelligence community, or Lauchlin Currie of the White House.

OLEG GORDIEVSKY *on the state of the KGB in the 1950s;
quoted by Andrew and Gordievsky,* KGB, *375*

During the 1950s, hostility toward Soviet communism was ingrained in the everyday lives of Americans. Communist aggression and subterfuge dominated the news, and fallout shelters and air raid drills became routine precautions against the threat of a Soviet attack. At the end of the 1940s, such Hollywood films as *The Red Menace, I Married a Communist,* and *The Iron Curtain* epitomized the anticommunist mood of the next ten years. Nightly television fare included weekly series like *I Led Three Lives,* the exploits of Herbert Philbrick, an FBI infiltrator in a network of the CPUSA. Science fiction films also proliferated in the 1950s, but even the strange aliens from outer space were curiously similar to Soviet aggressors. And a children's comic strip hero, Captain America, sounded alarms of the communist menace: "Beware, commies, spies, traitors and foreign agents! Captain America is looking for you."[1]

Senator Joseph McCarthy fanned the flames of anticommunism with his allegations of widespread communist subversion in the US government.

His allegations initially appeared plausible given the revelations of communist defectors and the trials of Soviet spies like Julius and Ethel Rosenberg. He claimed he had a list of 205 State Department employees who were CPUSA members and, as chairman of the Senate's Permanent Subcommittee on Investigations, he also launched a probe of alleged spy rings in the US Army. McCarthy's efforts ultimately uncovered not a single spy.

Even after McCarthy was eventually discredited, his fiercest critics condemned him not for his rabid anticommunism but for his excesses. Ardent liberals like Senator Hubert Humphrey censured McCarthy at the same time as they loudly voiced their opposition to the Soviet Union. Their anticommunist fears were justified by communist actions around the globe. Vietnamese communists under Ho Chi Minh drove the French out of their country in 1954, the new communist government in China was rattling sabers against Taiwan, and the Soviets brutally crushed a Hungarian dissident uprising in 1956. By the end of the decade, communism had almost reached American shores when Fidel Castro seized power in Cuba and forged a close relationship with the Soviet Union.

The Soviets also challenged the technological supremacy that America had established in World War II. The Soviets had not only developed their own atomic bomb but had also outraced the United States to the new frontier, outer space. In 1957, the Soviets launched the world's first satellite into space, and four years later the Soviet cosmonaut Yuriy Gagarin became the first human being to orbit the Earth.

To a stunned America, the Soviet Union seemed to be trouncing the United States on a number of fronts. In espionage, however, the situation was different. The Golden Age of Soviet espionage in America was followed by a dark age. The KGB's networks from the 1930s and 1940s were in tatters, and the pool of potential recruits had dried up in a nation that was openly hostile to communism. Finding communist sympathizers in the 1950s, much less recruiting them as spies, was a daunting task in a country where the Soviets were portrayed as devils with horns and cloven hooves and where the FBI now scrutinized their every move.

The KGB had already abandoned the American communists for espionage work because of defector revelations and the abysmal tradecraft of their American spies. The CPUSA still offered some potential for future recruits, but the KGB had to be cautious about FBI infiltration. By the end of the 1950s, the FBI had riddled the CPUSA with so many informants that agents joked that the party would be bankrupt without dues paid from the FBI's coffers. CPUSA membership plummeted from 75,000 to 10,000 by the end of the decade, and the party could not collect enough dues to fund its newspaper, *The Daily Worker*.

The trial of KGB officer Rudolf Abel in 1957 highlighted the problems of Soviet intelligence and its evolving approach to spying in the hostile US environment. Abel was born William Fisher to a family of Russian revolutionary émigrés who had fled the tsar's oppression for England in 1901. The family returned to Russia after the Revolution, and Fisher, a native English speaker, was recruited by the KGB as an "illegal."[2]

In 1948, Fisher was dispatched to the United States as the KGB's new chief of illegals to rebuild the Soviets' shattered espionage network. Abel joined a long Soviet tradition by operating in the United States as an illegal officer. During the heyday of Soviet espionage in the 1930s and 1940s, Soviet intelligence officers worked as diplomats under cover of official government facilities in the United States. Their efforts were supplemented by a parallel illegal network of officers who lived and worked in foreign countries without ostensible affiliation with official Soviet establishments so they would not invite scrutiny by local security services. Illegals were responsible for recruiting and handling some of the Soviets' best penetrations of the US government in the 1930s and 1940s.

As the Soviet defector Vassili Mitrokhin later claimed, the KGB radically reformed its approach to espionage in the United States by placing "a renewed emphasis" on illegal operations.[3] Abel established a low profile as an artist and photographer who was self-employed so he could forgo record checks by prospective employers. He also had absolutely no contact with the CPUSA. He shaped the prototype of the future Soviet illegal in America: the little "gray man" with solid cover and documentation who could pass as a Westerner and melt quietly into the fabric of American life to spy against the United States.

Abel collected some intelligence from the remnants of the atomic spy ring, including the former Los Alamos National Laboratory scientist Theodore Hall. Hall was a child prodigy who received a degree in physics from Harvard as a teenager and then had volunteered to the Soviets and provided them with information on the implosion method of detonating the American atom bomb. The network, however, was disrupted after the arrest of the Rosenbergs and the FBI's questioning of Hall, who was suspected of espionage but never prosecuted.[4]

Abel lasted eight years as the illegal chief until he was compromised by his own radio operator, Reino Hayhanen, another illegal who had been assigned to the United States under cover as a Finnish immigrant to communicate Abel's intelligence back to Moscow. Abel's ascetic self-discipline and meticulous attention to tradecraft were equally matched by Hayhanen's carelessness, alcoholism, and spousal abuse.[5]

Hayhanen was not only arrested for drunken driving and beating his wife but also misplaced a KGB concealment device in 1953, a hollowed-out nickel with microfilm inside, and may have used it to buy a paper from a Brooklyn newsboy. The newsboy dropped the nickel, which split in half to reveal its suspicious contents, and the boy gave it to the New York City police, which in turn handed it over to the FBI. The FBI correctly assumed the coin belonged to a Soviet agent somewhere in New York and began the hunt.

The hunt ended in 1957 when Hayhanen, en route home to meet his KGB masters, defected to the US Embassy in Paris and ratted out Abel. The FBI arrested Abel and hailed the unmasking of a Soviet spy as a major coup against the KGB. In fact, although Abel had collected some intelligence during his time in the United States, no major American spy was identified as a result of the arrest. As Mitrokhin and Andrew note, "Fisher never came close to rivaling the achievement of his wartime predecessor, Itzhak Akhmerov. During eight years as an illegal resident, he appears never to have identified, let alone recruited, a single promising potential agent."[6]

The prosecution presented an array of spy paraphernalia found in Abel's apartment, photographs of which were splashed across the nation's newspapers. Abel was convicted in November 1957 and sentenced to thirty years in prison, but five years later he was exchanged in a spy trade for Francis Gary Powers, the pilot of the U-2 reconnaissance aircraft shot down over the USSR. Abel was publicly lionized as a master spy in the Soviet press when he died in 1971. Although the propaganda about Abel was intended to enhance the KGB's image, the Soviet intelligence service "was well aware that in reality he had achieved nothing of significance."[7] Though Abel was a competent officer, FBI scrutiny and the absence of a CPUSA underground complicated his chances of achieving the earlier successes of his comrades.

The Soviets also faced other counterespionage concerns. Besides FBI scrutiny inside the United States, the newly established CIA was hunting the KGB abroad. One hundred seventy years after the birth of the republic, the United States had finally established an institution to collect intelligence, and now it was almost exclusively focused on the USSR.

Unfortunately, some of the CIA's fledgling attempts to spy on the Soviets failed abysmally. In 1956 a glaring example was its first officer in Moscow, Edward Ellis Smith.[8] In a ham-fisted attempt to protect his cover, Smith never advised American ambassador Charles Bohlen of his CIA affiliation and pretended he was a security officer. Smith eventually informed the ambassador of his true affiliation. Unfortunately, he also advised Bohlen at the same time that he had been seduced by his comely Soviet maid and that the KGB had tried to blackmail him into spying for them. The angry ambassador sent Smith back home.[9]

On a trip back to the States, Bohlen, a longtime friend of President Dwight D. Eisenhower, was playing golf with the president and told him that "the CIA placed a man in my embassy without telling me, and he got involved with a Russian girl and they took pictures of them in the nude!" Eisenhower reportedly stopped playing to make an immediate call to the secretary of state.[10] Any CIA officer would cringe on hearing this tale; alienating an ambassador is serious enough, but angering the president of the United States dims any career prospects, no matter how bright.

The CIA eventually scored its first espionage success against the Soviets from a "walk-in," an unexpected offer of intelligence that would recur throughout the Cold War among Soviets disaffected with the communist regime. In January 1953, Pyotr Popov, a GRU major stationed in Austria, threw a note into the slightly open window of a US intelligence officer's parked car. In the note Popov offered secret military information in return for money. Aside from money, Popov wanted revenge for the Soviets' mistreatment of their peasantry. He gained that revenge by delivering mounds of Soviet secrets to the CIA. According to Harry Rositzke, the chief of the CIA's Soviet Division at the time, "this one man's reporting saved the Pentagon at least half a billion dollars in its research-and-development program."[11] Although Popov represented the CIA's first major penetration of the Soviet intelligence services, he was also, unfortunately, the first of many American spies in the KGB and GRU who were eventually caught and executed.

Another penetration of the GRU proved to be the most productive long-term source of US intelligence on the Soviet Union. Dmitriy Polyakov was recruited by the FBI in January 1962 while serving undercover at the United Nations and handled by the CIA in Moscow and overseas posts for more than two decades.[12] He rose through GRU ranks to major general, the highest-ranking Soviet spy in the US network. He also fell victim to the spy wars between the superpowers when he was betrayed by Aldrich Ames, a spy in the heart of the CIA's Soviet operations who is discussed in chapter 18.

Polyakov himself had compromised GRU spies in the US military.[13] Without his cooperation, some of the enlisted military men who spied for quick cash in the 1950s and 1960s might never have been caught.

Spies in the Enlisted Ranks

Once global threats had been avoided, the time for national missions and civic loyalties had returned and the great idealistic spies finally disappeared from the scene. . . . After that, payment became the norm.

ALEXANDER FEKLISOV, *the Rosenbergs' case officer, quoted in Alexander Feklisov,* Man behind the Rosenbergs, *59*

Both Soviet intelligence agencies, the KGB and GRU, moved quickly to find a new generation of American spies. Prospects of recruiting the bonanza of well-placed spies in policy circles from the previous two decades were dim, but American policy toward the Soviet Union was hardly a secret. The policy was openly adversarial, and the key question for the Soviets was when and if tensions would flare up in a military clash. As a result, the Soviet intelligence services shifted their emphasis to stealing American military secrets to give the Red Army an advantage in the event that an armed conflict erupted.

The KGB and GRU found a new pool of potential recruits among America's enlisted military. The Soviet intelligence services realized they would find few with communist sympathies and instead focused on character flaws and vulnerabilities that might be exploited to lure military personnel to spy. In the consumer society of the 1950s, the enlisted military man could scarcely afford the car, the home, the leisure time diversions, and the new time-saving gadgets that were now staples of the average civilian's lifestyle. Unlike the spies of the Soviets' Golden Age, the new generation of American traitors was predominantly military and overwhelmingly motivated by money. Paradoxically, some of these uniformed spies would still profess love for their country and rationalized their espionage as a petty crime, a quick business deal little more than selling stolen goods from a military commissary on the black market. The heavy post–World War II US military presence in Europe also offered the Soviets a distinct advantage because the KGB and GRU could spot and cultivate targets far from the FBI's intense monitoring of their activities on American soil.

Nelson Drummond

Nelson Drummond, an African American navy yeoman, was just the kind of recruit the Soviets hunted in Europe. Drummond was assigned to a US Navy base outside London in 1958 when a GRU officer approached him on the street in a classic recruitment operation.[1] The Soviets had learned that the twenty-seven-year-old sailor from Baltimore was a drinker, gambler, and hustler who had incurred heavy debts since arriving in the United Kingdom. More important, the Soviets knew that Drummond was a clerk with access to classified documents on US weapons systems and NATO defenses. The GRU officer developed the case slowly, first offering the debt-ridden Drummond money in exchange for a US Navy pass to shop in the commissary. Soon Drummond was persuaded to pass secret documents to the GRU. By then, he was dependent on his GRU cash supplements.

When his tour ended in London, Drummond was assigned to a Mobile Electronic Technical Unit at Naval Station Newport in Rhode Island, where he continued to have access to military secrets. He began to exhibit behavior that is typical of many American spies flush with newfound cash from spying. On his yeoman's monthly salary of about $120, he was able to buy two cars and his own business, a bar outside the naval base. Aside from flaunting his unexplained wealth, he also got into scrapes with the law. Between 1960 and 1961, he was arrested for drunken driving, illegal gambling, and twice on assault charges, hardly the low-profile behavior expected of a spy.

Drummond was among the four American spies identified by Dmitriy Polyakov in the early 1960s.[2] The FBI could not use the information from a productive spy like Polyakov to make the case, but Drummond's unexplained wealth and careless tradecraft provided enough evidence to catch him in the act of passing secrets. The FBI began to follow Drummond to New York City, where he met his GRU contacts once a month and where agents discovered bank accounts with inordinately high balances. In 1962, the FBI trailed Drummond to a diner in Westchester County and arrested him and two GRU officers in the middle of a clandestine meeting. In August 1963, Drummond was convicted and sentenced to life imprisonment. His espionage reportedly required $200 million to revise the plans, procedures, and manuals he had compromised.[3]

Drummond was the first African American convicted of espionage.[4] Throughout the Cold War, Soviet intelligence services pursued potential spy recruits among African Americans and other minorities, hoping to exploit their sense of racial discrimination to lure them into espionage. This tactic ultimately failed. As the PERSEREC study on American espionage indicates, "Seen as a whole, espionage by Americans has been a young white man's crime."[5] Soviet recruitment efforts targeting minorities resulted in few spies, undoubtedly because of the Soviets' own inherent racism. Espionage relationships often depend on personal bonds between a spy and his or her case officer. Russians, the predominant force in the Soviet Union, scorned non-Russians and were especially prejudiced against darker-skinned minorities, routinely denigrating them with the slur *chernozhopy* ("black asses"). The barely disguised prejudices of Soviet intelligence officers undoubtedly disillusioned many would-be spies among minority Americans.

Robert Lee Johnson

The Soviets searched for other alienated Americans among the military but most often benefited from volunteers. In February 1953, Robert Lee Johnson, a young army sergeant stationed in West Berlin, crossed into East Berlin with his girlfriend Hedy, a German prostitute, and requested political asylum. He bitterly resented the army for not promoting him. Like other military spies of the era, he also needed money to support his vices. Like Drummond, Johnson was a heavy drinker and inveterate gambler.[6]

KGB officers persuaded Johnson that he could better exact his revenge against the military by "working in place," that is, by continuing in his job rather than defecting and spying under the Americans' nose, also earning far more money in the process.[7] Johnson agreed, and he embarked upon a twelve-year espionage career. Eager to please, he not only filched documents from his job in army intelligence but also, on his own initiative, enticed a fellow soldier into espionage. His KGB contacts were initially upset that Johnson had recruited James Allen Mintkenbaugh without consulting them, but they quickly changed their minds when they learned that the new recruit was a homosexual. Mintkenbaugh felt that his sexual orientation made him a pariah in the mainstream military. This visceral motivation would ensure his continued cooperation with the KGB and offer the Soviets a potential mechanism to spot other homosexuals in the army whose resentment could lead them into espionage.

Johnson produced low-level intelligence and, given his serious character defects, he was a difficult agent to control.[8] In 1956, he left the army and the KGB to try to win a fortune gambling in Las Vegas and write a novel. Predictably, he failed at both efforts and sank into poverty, drinking heavily and forcing his wife back into prostitution.

Suddenly, Mintkenbaugh recontacted Johnson on behalf of the KGB and threw him the life preserver of renewed spying. Johnson rejoined the army, and from 1957 to 1959 he was a guard at missile installations in Texas and California, where he stole classified documents and photographs on America's nuclear arsenal. At one point, he even managed to steal a sample of rocket fuel for the KGB—but his best was yet to come.

In 1961, Johnson was assigned as a guard to a military courier facility outside Paris responsible for transporting sensitive materials to bases throughout Europe. Inside a triple-locked vault in the facility were operational plans for US and NATO forces in Europe and information about US nuclear weapons and cryptographic systems.[9] Johnson initially rifled through the sealed pouches and passed the contents to the KGB, but his Soviet masters wanted to exploit his unique access to the utmost.

Johnson arranged to stand weekend duty alone inside the facility, a procedure considered secure because the duty guard had no access to the impregnable vault. With the help of KGB surreptitious entry experts, Johnson worked his way past each of the three locks. He first made a wax impression of one lock, found the combination of the second one misplaced in a desk drawer, and used a KGB X-ray device to penetrate the remaining lock.[10] Armed with easy access to the secrets inside, Johnson routinely emptied the contents of the vault and passed them to KGB officers waiting nearby. After the Soviets photographed the materials and resealed the pouches, they returned the stolen documents to Johnson, who would lock them back up in the vault.

Johnson repeated the procedure several times over a two-year span. Judging by the comments of the Soviet defector Oleg Gordievsky, his espionage was among the most highly valued in KGB history. KGB officers proudly informed Johnson that he was appointed a major in the Red Army and passed on to him Premier Nikita Khrushchev's personal congratulations.[11] According to Gordievsky, by April 1963 Johnson had stuffed seventeen flight bags full of America's most precious military secrets for the KGB. The spy careers of Johnson and Mintkenbaugh came to an end because of information from Yuriy Nosenko, a KGB defector who became embroiled in a bizarre counterespionage scandal that involved one of the lingering mysteries in American history, the assassination of President John F. Kennedy.[12]

Johnson and Mintkenbaugh were arrested in November 1964. By then Johnson's life was in shambles, and his wife had suffered a mental breakdown under the stress of her husband's espionage. Both spies were sentenced to twenty-five years in prison, but Johnson only served seven years of his term. In 1972, his son Robert visited him in his cell at the Lewisburg federal penitentiary. Robert, shamed by his father's crime, plunged a knife into Johnson's heart and killed him.

Among the secrets that Johnson delivered to the KGB were military cryptographic materials. The KGB was well aware that there was no better way to learn US military plans and intentions than by reading its communications. In addition to the military services, the KGB made concerted efforts to recruit spies in the newly established National Security Agency (NSA), the heart of America's secret communications and intercept capabilities. Unfortunately, their efforts met with some success.

NSA was established in November 1952 to unite all US military and civilian cryptological activities under one roof. NSA inherited a proud cryptographic tradition that included Herbert O. Yardley's Black Chamber, the breaking of Japanese codes in World War II, and the Venona Project. President Dwight Eisenhower, a firm believer in signals intelligence because of his wartime experience, poured considerable resources into the agency.[13] By 1957 NSA had built a multi-million-dollar facility in Fort Meade, Maryland, with the most sophisticated computer complex in the world. The KGB was still smarting from the damage to its spy networks inflicted by the Venona cryptographers, but it exacted revenge when a handful of volunteers appeared on its doorstep offering NSA secrets.

Bernon Mitchell and William Martin

Two of the more eccentric spies in US espionage history were rare exceptions in the era: defectors driven not by greed but by a murky brew of motivations—politically naive communist sympathies, arrogance bred of intellectual brilliance, and resentment against a system that frowned on their sexual mores.

Bernon Mitchell and William Martin were both mathematical geniuses but seriously flawed human beings. But as the Cold War intensified in the 1950s, NSA sorely needed their talent and hired them despite glaring indicators of their unsuitability for sensitive positions. Mitchell, the older of the pair, was born into a middle-class family in Depression-era San Francisco, and early in his youth he became obsessed with mathematics and science, much like atomic bomb spy Theodore Hall.

Beneath this passion for science, however, were hints of psychopathic behavior. Mitchell at times applied his scientific skills to playing pranks against his classmates, on one occasion filling balloons with hydrogen and bursting them in midair to scare them. According to one study of his case, Mitchell also devised a bizarre device to cause neurosis in cats.[14] His most deviant behavior involved a six-year-long sexual experiment as a teenager with chickens and dogs.[15] Shockingly, he recounted these barnyard experiences to security investigators but was still hired by NSA.

William Martin was born and raised in Columbus, Georgia, and, like his friend and co-conspirator, showed keen talent for math at an early age. Like many mathematicians, Martin, described as an "insufferable egotist," was fascinated by and excelled at chess, but he also betrayed an unsportsman-like contempt for the opponents he easily defeated.[16]

Mitchell and Martin both joined the US Navy during the Korean War and were assigned to the Naval Radio Intercept Station at Kamiseya, Japan. The misfits quickly became friends, undoubtedly because their peers considered them quirky outsiders. During their time in the navy, the two friends proved to be gifted mathematicians, chess enthusiasts, and introverts who displayed "unusual sexual behavior patterns."[17] Despite this behavior, Mitchell and Martin were hired by NSA in 1957 because of their superior mathematic talents and their navy experience in cryptography.

During the next two years, Mitchell's and Martin's resentment against US policies quietly festered. Initially, Mitchell and Martin were outraged that US aircraft intentionally penetrated Soviet airspace to trigger radar and thus collect signals intelligence, an activity that the pair believed could spark a war. In 1959 the pair complained to Representative Wayne Hays about these provocative American airborne violations of Soviet airspace, but Hays ignored the two whistleblowers. Mitchell was the first to take a more drastic measure to vent his resentment. In December 1959 he went secretly to Mexico City and requested asylum at the Soviet Embassy. According to files smuggled out of the USSR by the Soviet defector Vassili Mitrokhin, the KGB pled with Mitchell to work in place at NSA but he steadfastly refused, though he promised to cooperate fully once ensconced in the USSR.[18] The pair also secretly traveled to Cuba the same month. The following June, while ostensibly on leave, Mitchell and Martin traveled together to Mexico City and from there to Cuba, where they were exfiltrated to the Soviet Union.

Intelligence community agencies would normally have some twinge of security concern when an employee failed to report back to work after a vacation. Shockingly, NSA did not begin to track the pair down until eight days after they were due back to work. In Mitchell's house, security officers found a safe deposit box that contained a written denunciation of US foreign policy and an incoherent tribute to the Soviet Union. NSA's worst fears were now justified, but it had still not fathomed the extent of the betrayal.

A few months later, in September 1960, Mitchell and Martin suddenly appeared at a Moscow press conference to denounce the United States and, in particular, NSA. The most embarrassing statement in their interview was Martin's claim that NSA had intercepted the communications of US allies, including Italy, France, the United Arab Emirates, Uruguay, and Indonesia.[19] Coming on the heels of the U-2's shooting down over Soviet airspace, the revelation told the world that the United States spied as actively as the Soviet Union.

According to Gordievsky, the KGB was disappointed by their new defectors' knowledge of American cryptographic secrets. Their most important information was their assurance to the Soviets that NSA was still unable to break their codes.[20] Because Mitchell and Martin had no further access and their prior knowledge had been squeezed out by KGB debriefers, their only remaining value to the USSR was to serve as propaganda tools to embarrass the United States, which the pair did quite effectively.

Mitchell and Martin both grew disillusioned with life in the USSR, but they eventually abandoned any hope of return to the United States after the KGB devised a variety of ruses to ensure that they stayed. After all, their abandonment of a life in the USSR would have been as embarrassing to the Soviets as their denunciation of the United States had been to the Americans.

Jack Dunlap

Meanwhile, the Soviets were running a more valuable spy inside NSA who, ironically, was not a mathematician but a chauffeur. At first glance US Army sergeant Jack Dunlap seemed an unlikely candidate to become a Soviet spy. Dunlap had served for eight years in the US Merchant Marine before joining the army, where he was awarded a Bronze Star and Purple Heart in Korean War combat.[21] However, like the other military spies of the era, he suffered from a tragic character flaw. He was an incurable womanizer, and the financial burden of supporting his philandering while raising seven children drained his enlisted man's bank account.

Dunlap found a way out of his predicament when he was assigned as a chauffeur to the Fort Meade chief of staff in 1958. The financially strapped sergeant transported top-secret documents around the base as part of his duties, and this unique access could boost his rapidly dwindling savings. He walked into the Soviet Embassy to offer information for money and, over a three-year period, provided the GRU with NSA manuals and design plans for cipher machines and CIA estimates regarding the Soviet armed forces.[22]

Like other financially motivated spies, Dunlap made the cardinal security mistake of flaunting his sudden infusion of cash: He bought a new Jaguar, two Cadillacs, and a cabin cruiser and joined a yacht club. Amazingly, his purchases aroused not an iota of suspicion at NSA, even when the agency dispatched an ambulance to his yacht club after he received a minor injury in a regatta incident.[23] It was simply inconceivable that a decorated war veteran could be a spy.

Once again, the CIA's spy in the GRU, Polyakov, supplied a lead that the inconceivable was happening inside NSA. During the FBI's hunt for the spy, Dunlap set off alarm bells when he decided to leave the army and join NSA as a civilian employee. He had to submit to a polygraph test as a routine part of the application process, and the needles jumped off the charts at his innocent responses to questions about foreign contacts and handling classified information. Dunlap admitted to petty theft but not to espionage. As the FBI closed in on him, he drove to a remote spot, left his car running, attached one end of a hose to the exhaust pipe, and put the other end in the front window. Moments later, the sergeant who had received about $40,000 from the GRU for betraying his country died of asphyxiation.

Summing Up

The cases of Mitchell and Martin and Dunlap highlight serious flaws in NSA's security system. In its quest to hire skilled mathematicians, NSA turned a blind eye to security reviews that contained unfavorable comments from peers about Mitchell and Martin and ignored Mitchell's own admission of deviant sexual behavior.[24] NSA repeated the same mistakes made by the Manhattan Project, which hired physicists and engineers despite their communist beliefs because the need for mission expertise outweighed security risks.

In Dunlap's case, NSA ignored glaring signs of suddenly unexplained affluence. NSA's oversight, however, reflected a broader US government security issue. The lingering influence of loyalty checks and McCarthy's allegations about communists in government continued to have a negative impact on counterespionage. The FBI and other investigative agencies focused their background investigations on an employee's communist sympathies instead of his or her overall suitability for work in sensitive positions. Following the defection of Mitchell and Martin, NSA broadened investigations to search for similar sexual deviants in its ranks, but Dunlap did not fit that profile.

NSA's security staff paid no attention to Jack Dunlap, a sergeant who made little more than $120 a month but owned two cars and a cabin cruiser, but its antennae would have been raised if he had been found reading *The Communist Manifesto*. The majority of spies who betrayed their country for money in the 1950s and 1960s cared more about Cadillacs than communism. American counterespionage was living in a bygone past, searching for communists ideologically motivated to spy. The Soviet intelligence services, conversely, had managed to stay a step ahead of their American adversaries. A flurry of soldiers and sailors who volunteered to spy for cash convinced the KGB and GRU that dollars and not doctrine were the key to stealing America's secrets. The trend of financially motivated espionage continued in the 1960s, but dramatic upheavals in the United States offered possibilities for the KGB to find spies among a new generation of Americans who were becoming increasingly disillusioned with their government.

Vietnam and the 1960s

The United States is confronted with a new style in conspiracy—conspiracy that is extremely subtle and devious and hence difficult to understand; . . . a conspiracy reflected by questionable moods and attitudes, by unrestrained individualism, by non-conformism in dress and speech, even by obscene language, rather than by formal membership in specific organizations.

J. EDGAR HOOVER, PTA Magazine, *1966; quoted in "History of the FBI"*

NSA defectors Mitchell and Martin made headlines with their denunciation of the United States, but their story quickly disappeared from the front pages. When they appeared at their Moscow press conference in September 1960, America was in the throes of a heated presidential campaign that would mark the transition between the 1950s and 1960s. By a razor-thin margin, voters rejected the candidate of the past decade, Eisenhower's vice president, Richard Nixon, in favor of John F. Kennedy, a youthful war hero and senator bred in the rough-and-tumble schoolyard of Boston politics. Kennedy epitomized the shifting American population of the 1960s, a decade dominated by youth, a new generation of 70 million teens and young adults born during the postwar baby boom.

But the youthful exuberance and optimism symbolized by the Kennedy administration only lasted a short time. Three years after his election, President Kennedy was assassinated. A shocked nation grieved throughout the late November weekend of 1963, glued to their television sets, watching the images of unfolding events—the swearing-in of a new president with Kennedy's widow by his side, her stylish pink suit grotesquely stained with her husband's blood; the capture of the suspected assassin with shadowy Soviet and Cuban links; the shooting of the suspect by a Dallas nightclub owner; and thousands of mourners streaming in silence past Kennedy's coffin in the Capitol Rotunda.

In the years after that tragic weekend, America experienced a revolution that polarized the nation by the end of the 1960s. A decade that had started with optimism ended in turmoil. The turbulent changes in America shook the status quo in virtually every walk of life. The crew cuts of the 1950s were abandoned for shoulder-length hair and bushy sideburns. Gray flannel suits and prim, flowered skirts were discarded for bell-bottom jeans and granny dresses. Crooning soloists like Bobby Darin and Pat Boone were driven off the pop charts by bands like Jefferson Airplane and the Grateful Dead that blared the jarring rhythms of psychedelic rock.

America's status quo was shattered most of all in the political arena. Minorities organized to demand their long-denied civil rights. Martin Luther King Jr. emerged as the charismatic spokesman for African Americans and crystallized their hopes for racial harmony in his "I Have a Dream" speech on the steps of the Lincoln Memorial. Gloria Steinem and Betty Friedan ridiculed the 1950s stereotype of the happy homemaker and aggressively advocated equal treatment for women.

One of the primary catalysts of the 1960s' political revolution was the Vietnam War. The US military presence in Vietnam had mushroomed from a handful of advisers in the early 1960s to more than half a million troops by 1968, and America's disillusionment with the war gradually developed into the greatest antiwar movement in US history. Protests were initially limited to student activists on campuses across the nation, but in just a few years they were joined by millions of other Americans as the Vietnam conflict continued with no end in sight.

In 1970, 65 percent of the respondents to a Gallup poll expressed their belief that the United States should withdraw from Vietnam.[1] In November 1969, half a million Americans marched in an antiwar demonstration in the nation's capital, chanting "Hey, hey, LBJ, how many kids have you killed today?" Symbols of patriotism were trampled and desecrated. Students set their draft cards ablaze. The American flag was burned, stomped on, or embroidered on the seats of tattered jeans.

The youth of the 1960s found a host of ways to vent their frustration with the US government and opposition to the war. Some sought escape to an alternate universe through hallucinogenic drugs, while others fled to hippie communes where they farmed their own food and set up makeshift governments. Still others channeled their opposition through political activism, some even engaging in violent acts of sabotage. Espionage would certainly have been another way to vent the generation's opposition to the government.

As protests swelled in the 1960s, the Soviets must have been rubbing their hands together in gleeful anticipation of expanding their spy networks in America. If the 1930s and 1940s had been the Golden Age of Soviet espionage, then surely the 1960s would be its Renaissance. American disenchantment with the US government had skyrocketed and even surpassed Depression-era levels, when thousands were lured by an idealized Soviet communism. America was again ripe for exploitation by the Soviet intelligence services.

The KGB's hopes, however, were dashed. Despite broad dissatisfaction with the government and heated opposition to the war, the turmoil of the 1960s did not produce any known major spy who betrayed his country because of antiwar or antigovernment sentiments. Unlike the communist sympathizers and spies of decades before, the 1960s generation shouted its protest from the rooftops instead of huddling in small cells to philosophize about the ills of American capitalism. The 1960s generation marched and chanted in mass rallies instead of skulking alone through government corridors to sniff out secrets for the Soviets. The communist spies of the 1930s and 1940s were nurtured by an alien philosophy, an import from a land where centuries of oppression had made intrigue and conspiracy commonplace. The opposition of the 1960s generation was homegrown and American to the core—open, boisterous, and unrestrained.

American campuses illustrated the stark contrast between the generations. Universities that had been breeding grounds for Soviet spies in the 1930s were now the scenes of mass demonstrations, sit-ins, and even seizure of campus buildings by force. At Columbia University in New York—

which counted Whittaker Chambers, Elizabeth Bentley, and Judith Coplon among its communist spy alumni—more than a thousand students occupied campus buildings in 1968 until the police were called in to eject them by force.[2] A year later, students at Julius Rosenberg's alma mater, the City College of New York, briefly shut down the school in protest against the Vietnam War. And at Harvard—where Theodore Hall, Harry Dexter White, and Lauchlin Currie were lured by the communist experiment—students seized control of the university's main hall to protest the Reserve Officers Training Corps (ROTC) program until policemen stormed the building.

Opposition to the war even intensified in the US military, which had been a primary source of financially motivated spies in the 1950s. However, antiwar sentiments in the military produced no bonanza of spies for the Soviets. Protest was expressed in other ways. Some soldiers simply deserted. By the end of the 1960s, more than 65,000 army soldiers had deserted, almost the equivalent of four infantry divisions.[3] Others voiced their protests through political activism instead of spying for the enemy. In the late 1960s antiwar publications such as Left Face! sprung up at US military bases around the country.[4] A very small minority protested by more violent means. A particularly heinous method of protest was known as "fragging," the slang term derived from the M-26 fragmentation grenades that an angry enlisted man would roll or pitch into a tent to kill a superior. Although most of these lethal attacks were triggered more from personal animosity, some were violent expressions of opposition to the war.

The Soviets could also no longer rely on the communist ideology that produced the vast network of spies in the 1930s and 1940s. Although the Communist Party was emasculated by the 1960s, a New Left movement emerged in opposition to the government and the Vietnam War. This New Left, however, rejected the Soviet brand of communism and often criticized the US government by comparing it to the oppressive totalitarianism of the Soviet Union. New Left activists dismissed the Soviet Union as the center of international communism and looked to agrarian communists like Mao Zedong and Ho Chi Minh as models.

Communist front groups tried unsuccessfully to engage New Left organizations like Students for a Democratic Society (SDS). A handful of avowed pro-Soviet radicals like Angela Davis courted African American organizations, but these groups scorned communism as "a white man's thing." The majority of the 1960s leftists embraced Henry David Thoreau's civil disobedience more than Vladimir Lenin's political terrorism.

The US government responded to the barrage of antiwar protests. Presidents Lyndon Johnson and Richard Nixon believed that hostile foreign powers were covertly fomenting the widespread unrest in the country, and J. Edgar Hoover continued the FBI's tradition dating back to the Palmer Raids of the early 1920s by focusing on subversion rather than espionage. In 1956 he established COINTELPRO, an acronym for the Counterintelligence Program, which was designed to disrupt political dissident organizations more than catch spies.

COINTELPRO targeted a host of antiwar and civil rights organizations in the 1960s, including SDS, the Black Panthers, and Martin Luther King Jr.'s Southern Christian Leadership Conference. At Hoover's direction, FBI agents infiltrated informants, planted false media stories about the groups, harassed them, and investigated them with warrantless wiretaps and surreptitious break-ins. FBI agents bugged Martin Luther King Jr.'s phones but surfaced not a shred of evidence that King or his followers were spying for or were supported by foreign powers.

Hoover terminated COINTELPRO in 1971 after political activists burglarized an FBI office in Pennsylvania and leaked files about the program to the media. In 1975 a Senate committee investigating US intelligence activities (the so-called Church Committee, chaired by Idaho senator Frank Church) lambasted the FBI's program: "Many of the techniques used would be intolerable in a democratic society even if all of the targets had been involved in violent activity, but COINTELPRO went far beyond that. . . . The Bureau conducted a sophisticated vigilante operation aimed squarely at preventing the exercise of First Amendment rights of speech and association, on the theory that preventing the growth of dangerous groups and the propagation of dangerous ideas would protect the national security and deter violence."[5]

Hoover's concerns, however, were justified to some degree. Some ultraradical fringe groups advocated the violent overthrow of the US government. The Weather Underground was an SDS splinter group that was impatient with the SDS's peaceful protests and broke away to change the government by violent means. The Weathermen, as they were also known, orchestrated thirty bombings of government and corporate targets, including the US Capitol, the Pentagon, police stations, and monuments. In 1970, the Weathermen planned to bomb a dance at Fort Dix in New Jersey, but three of its members assembling the device in their Greenwich Village apartment accidentally blew themselves to smithereens. The Weathermen's leaders went underground after that explosion, and the radical group gradually disintegrated. Although COINTELPRO was effective in preventing this type of sabotage, the program uncovered not a single spy working for a foreign power in its fifteen years.

Although COINTELPRO found no spies, the Soviets were still stealing American secrets, even if they were unable to exploit antiwar protests to launch another Golden Age of espionage. The vast majority of American spies in the 1960s were not political activists but, as in the previous decade, military personnel simply lining their pockets in exchange for US secrets. The Soviets shared some of these spies' information with the North Vietnamese in order to hamper US military efforts in Southeast Asia.[6]

A typical spy of this stripe was William Whalen, an army lieutenant colonel on the Joint Chiefs of Staff who was paid more than $5,000 for passing the GRU's plans on US troop deployments and Strategic Air Command plans for nuclear retaliatory strikes.[7] He was recruited in 1959, and he retired from the army the next year after suffering a heart attack but continued to walk the Pentagon's corridors in retirement to ferret out military secrets. However, he eventually fell under suspicion. After Polyakov alerted the FBI, Whalen was investigated, arrested in July 1966, and sentenced to fifteen years' imprisonment the following year.

Another military spy, US Air Force staff sergeant Herbert Boeckenhaupt, bought a new Avanti sports car with his illicit earnings from the GRU in return for top-secret cryptographic data. Polyakov supplied the lead to Boeckenhaupt, whose unexplained wealth provided ample grist for the prosecution's mill.[8] Boeckenhaupt was arrested in 1966 and, only twenty-four years old, was sentenced to thirty years in jail.

The only espionage case directly related to the Vietnam War occurred after the United States withdrew from Vietnam. This spy saga began as a wartime romance. On April 30, 1975, the last helicopter evacuating Americans and South Vietnamese took off from the roof of the US Embassy in Saigon. America's war was over, but peace talks still continued in Paris over postwar reparations and future relations with the Ho Chi Minh government. The North Vietnamese had planted no known spies inside the US government during the years of conflict, but they found one during the talks.

Ronald Humphrey, a married US Information Agency officer assigned to Saigon in 1969, fell in love with his Vietnamese neighbor, Nguyen Chi Thieu. Humphrey also believed that she saved his life when she warned him about a land mine attack along a road he planned to travel. He decided against the trip and was horrified to learn that the attack had occurred as his mistress had warned.[9] She was later arrested by the North Vietnamese authorities, and Humphrey struggled to secure her release and bring her and her five children to the United States. In 1976, desperate over her fate, the lovelorn Humphrey began to provide a North Vietnamese intelligence contact, David Truong, with classified information about the United States' intentions toward Vietnam, believing that Truong had influential contacts that could secure Thieu's freedom. The North Vietnamese kept their part of the devil's bargain; in July 1977 they allowed Humphrey's mistress and four of her children to emigrate.

David Truong was a Vietnamese American antiwar activist whose father had run for the South Vietnamese presidency. Truong lobbied Congress to end the conflict, and he founded the American-Vietnamese Reconciliation Center at Stanford University to support his efforts. To complement his lobbying activities, Truong also spied for the North Vietnamese. His principal task was to acquire information from Humphrey and in turn pass it to Yung Krall, a Vietnamese American courier, who then carried the booty to the North Vietnamese in Paris.

Yung Krall appeared to possess solid credentials to serve as a courier because her father was then North Vietnam's ambassador to the Soviet Union. Krall, however, was married to a US Navy officer, and she agreed in 1977 to serve her adopted country as a double agent for the CIA.[10] Code-named "Keyseat," Yung Krall showed the CIA all the documents she was ferrying to Paris for Truong, which clearly showed that the Vietnamese had a penetration in the State Department. The CIA notified the FBI, which appealed to the new attorney general, Griffin Bell, to use the president's "inherent power" in national security matters to tap Truong's telephone without a court warrant.

Bell agreed and, only a few days after the tap was in place, the FBI pinpointed the spy. Truong was not a professional intelligence officer, and he made a cardinal tradecraft blunder by using the telephone to contact his agent. FBI eavesdroppers heard Truong ask "Ron" to drop by his apartment in a few days. After "Ron" left the apartment, FBI agents trailed him back to the US Information Agency and obtained his full name from the register in the lobby he signed before going to his office.

The Humphrey case set an investigative precedent—it was the first time the bureau installed concealed video in a suspect's office, which enabled agents in this case to observe the precise documents that Humphrey was pilfering for his North Vietnamese handlers.[11] After gathering this mountain of evidence, the FBI arrested Humphrey and Truong on January 31, 1978, for conspiracy to deliver classified information to a foreign power.

The Humphrey espionage case set another important precedent. The CIA objected to the prosecution of Humphrey and Truong because its classified information would need to be revealed in open court proceedings. The CIA refused to let Yung Krall testify based on a long-standing agreement with DOJ to forgo prosecutions of arrested spies if agency secrets might surface in court.

Attorney General Bell scuttled this agreement because he believed that spies should be prosecuted as the law required. After obtaining President Carter's approval, Bell decided to prosecute the case and compelled CIA director Stansfield Turner to allow Krall's testimony. Four months after the trial, Carter, uncomfortable with authorizing the Truong wiretap without a warrant, signed groundbreaking legislation, the Foreign Intelligence Surveillance Act (known by its acronym "FISA"), which established a special court that would grant warrants in national security cases but would deliberate requests in secret to preserve classified information. DOJ is required by this law to demonstrate probable cause to the FISA court that the suspect is an agent of or cooperating with a foreign power.[12]

At the trial Truong denied passing secrets to the Vietnamese and claimed that he had given Humphrey's information only to academics and members of Congress. Humphrey tearfully recounted his romantic motives for passing the information to Truong, but he denied the espionage charges: "I'm a proud, loyal American despite what has happened here. I disgraced myself and family by some bad judgment. With God as my witness, I am not a spy."[13] Humphrey assessed his actions as mere security violations, not a crime. The documents, he claimed, were merely innocuous messages about US–Vietnamese relations.

Government witnesses at the trial disputed Humphrey's self-serving assessment. According to their testimony, the State Department information passed to the Vietnamese in Paris betrayed US negotiating positions throughout the Paris peace talks. Initially, the talks had gone well and the Vietnamese were identifying the remains of American servicemen slain in the war, but they were stiffening demands for reparations allegedly promised by President Nixon, perhaps based on Humphrey's documents.[14]

Humphrey's attorney closed his arguments by appealing to the jury's sympathy: "My client's case is that of a man who loved too much and trusted too much."[15] The tale of Humphrey's noble but misguided attempt to free his lover may have tugged at some jurors' heartstrings, but after fourteen hours of deliberation they declared both defendants guilty. In July 1978 Humphrey and Truong were sentenced to fifteen years in prison in the only known case of Vietnamese recruitment of a spy in the US government.

Humphrey's case was unique among the American spies of the 1970s. He spied solely because of a wartime love and a sense of obligation, no matter how misplaced. The other major spies of the 1970s were perhaps motivated primarily by money, but money was only one strand in the intricate web of motivations that drove them to spy against America.

PART

DECADE OF TURMOIL: THE 1970s

Espionage and the 1970s

> People no longer felt the same obligation to obey those whom
> they had previously considered superior to themselves in age, rank,
> status, expertise, character, or talents.
>
> *The political scientist* **SAMUEL HUNTINGTON** *on America in the 1970s, in*
> The Crisis of Democracy; *quoted by Zinn,* People's History, *559*

As Huntington's comments illustrate, loyalty to the US government plummeted in America in the 1970s, and the Soviet intelligence services found more fertile ground to find American spies in a decade marked by heightened disenchantment with the US government and a sluggish economy. A Harris poll in July 1975 showed that in the decade from 1966 to 1975, public confidence in the presidency and Congress fell from 42 percent to 13 percent.[1] A series of scandals rocked America's faith in its democratic institutions and created a national malaise that affected the country throughout the decade.

The Vietnam War seemed increasingly unwinnable as the North Vietnamese Army and Viet Cong insurgents overcame superior American forces and military technology. Protests against the war escalated; in the first year of the decade, students on campuses around the nation opposed the war in more than 1,800 demonstrations. American society was polarized over Vietnam, and disillusionment with the government turned into cynicism and outright anger as a result of subsequent events in the 1970s.

In 1972, a burglary of the Democratic National Committee headquarters in Washington's posh Watergate office-hotel-apartment complex blew the lid off a presidential domestic spying program against political opponents. During the next two years, President Nixon's closest aides were indicted, and Vice President Spiro Agnew resigned in 1973 after pleading no contest to charges of tax evasion and money laundering while he was governor of Maryland. In July 1974, the House of Representatives Judiciary Committee recommended the impeachment of Nixon over the Watergate scandal, and in August of that same year, he became the first American president to resign from office.

Gerald Ford, whom Nixon had named vice president after Agnew's resignation, entered the White House as the first unelected president in US history. Although he wanted to heal the nation, the avalanche of government woes gathered more momentum. In 1975, Saigon fell to Ho Chi Minh's forces after 58,000 Americans died to prevent a communist takeover. In the wake of revelations about FBI illegalities in COINTELPRO, congressional committees reviewing US intelligence activities released evidence that the CIA had opened mail illegally, overthrown foreign governments, and planned to assassinate foreign leaders.

The impact of these political scandals was exacerbated by severe blows to the economy. Oil prices soared and lines at gas stations stretched for blocks after the Organization of the Petroleum Exporting Countries dramatically escalated prices and reduced supplies to nations that supported Israel in the Yom Kippur War in 1973. In the United States, the impact of high fuel prices rippled throughout the economy, sparking increased prices for petroleum-based products, 10 to 15 percent annual inflation increases, and an overall decline in America's standard of living.

The national malaise was reflected in movies about the lingering trauma of Vietnam. In *Coming Home* Jon Voight played a handicapped Vietnam veteran whose difficulties coping with civilian life reflected the struggles of the nation. *The Deer Hunter* explored the darker side of the Vietnam experience and the lasting psychological wounds of its combat veterans. Americans increasingly abandoned mainstream religion to seek the new spiritual bromides offered by television evangelists. Divorce rates, drug use, and crime, especially juvenile delinquency, increased. The American dream was becoming the American nightmare.

Meanwhile, one ostensible ray of hope amid these woes was an easing of superpower tensions. The United States had become wary of foreign adventures after more than a decade of war in Vietnam, and Soviet leader Leonid Brezhnev also needed a respite, confronted with a struggling economy and strains inside his Eastern European satellites. As a symbol of new Cold War détente, the United States and the Soviet Union reached agreement in the Strategic Arms Limitation Treaty (known as SALT) in 1972 to limit anti–ballistic missile systems. The superpowers also agreed to conduct joint experiments in space, and Apollo Flight 18 and Soyuz Flight 19 met over the Earth on July 17, 1975.

In the same month that the Soviet cosmonauts met their American counterparts in space, the KGB met a young American citizen, Andrew Daulton Lee, in Mexico City and tasked him to obtain a manual on a highly classified satellite communications system from his partner in espionage, Christopher Boyce. Despite détente, the KGB was still relentlessly gathering secrets from American spies. The Soviet intelligence services exploited Americans' disillusionment with the government in the 1970s but, as in the preceding decade, Americans remained impervious to the lure of Soviet communism. Money, not ideology, remained the predominant motive for Americans to spy against their country—but money would still be only one factor in the tangled web of motives driving the major spies of the decade.

Although spies of the previous two decades were often driven by pure greed, some major spies of the economically starved 1970s desperately needed money to survive financial crises. David Barnett was a classic example. After a few years as a CIA contract employee, Barnett joined the CIA as an operations officer and served in Korea and Indonesia before resigning in 1970. For the next six years, he struggled to eke out a living as an expatriate American in Indonesia. After a seafood-processing venture he pursued collapsed, he approached a Soviet cultural attaché in Jakarta with a note offering to sell CIA secrets for $70,000.[2]

Barnett's information may have been dated, but it was still of value to the Soviets. In a February 1977 meeting with the KGB in Vienna, Barnett betrayed his former colleagues and his obligations to agents by divulging the identities of CIA operations officers and their sources in Indonesia.

But his true value to the Soviets was his revelation of a CIA program code-named HABRINK.[3]

Barnett unraveled a mystery that had haunted the Soviet military during the Vietnam War. The Soviets had provided their North Vietnamese allies with SA-2 surface-to-air missiles, which had shot down American planes over Vietnam. But squadrons of American B-52 bombers eventually began to fly across the country and drop their payloads without suffering a hit. The Americans clearly had found some way to evade the Soviet missiles.

The Soviets also provided the missile to other countries where they sought to extend influence, including Indonesia. Although control over such weapons was extremely tight at Soviet military bases, their developing-world clients guarded them with security that was less than airtight.

The CIA obtained the SA-2 guidance system, which enabled the US military to jam the radio frequencies directing the missile and save the lives of American bomber crews.[4] And HABRINK was not limited to surface-to-air missiles. The CIA also acquired Soviet manuals and equipment for surface-to-surface naval missiles, submarines, patrol boats, and destroyers. Knowledge of the HABRINK program allowed the Soviets to modify their weapons systems to defeat America's newly developed countermeasures. Any tactical advantage the United States may have gained through HABRINK was destroyed by Barnett's spying.

The KGB persuaded Barnett to continue spying for it by reentering the world of American secrets. The KGB tasked him to explore job opportunities in the State Department's Bureau of Intelligence and Research, the Defense Intelligence Agency (DIA), the CIA, or congressional intelligence oversight committees. Barnett returned to the United States in 1978, and a year later he was hired as a contractor by his old employer, the CIA, to train a new generation of operations officers.

As happened in many other cases throughout the Cold War, Barnett was unmasked by a Soviet spy working for the CIA. The source was stationed at the KGB residency in Jakarta and fingered Barnett to his CIA handlers.[5] When Barnett entered his CIA classroom on March 18, 1980, he was confronted by FBI agents. He confessed immediately and was arrested. During the next three weeks, he detailed his spying activities in twelve interviews with the FBI.[6]

Barnett's case also illustrated Attorney General Griffin Bell's new approach to handling espionage cases. The CIA again argued against prosecution because secrets such as HABRINK would need to be revealed in court, but Bell overruled the CIA as he had in the Humphrey case. The CIA secrets betrayed by Barnett, in Bell's view, were already known to the Soviets, so the prosecution of a spy outweighed any potential damage to national security. Barnett pled guilty and was sentenced to eighteen years in prison.

The damage done by Barnett paled in comparison with the treasure trove of secrets betrayed by contractors spying inside major US defense firms. An emerging trend in the 1970s was an increase in espionage by government contractors that were entrusted with developing America's most sophisticated weapons systems but showed a woeful disregard for elemental security practices.

Soviet Science and Technology Espionage

The value of the data stolen each year by the
Scientific and Technical Directorate is much greater than
the annual costs of operating the entire KGB.

STANISLAV LEVCHENKO, *KGB defector,*
quoted by Barron, KGB Today, *196*

Soviet theft of American technology had been a priority of the KGB and GRU since both services began stealing industrial secrets in the 1920s, and it reached its height with the concerted espionage effort against the atomic bomb in the 1940s. In the 1970s, the Soviet bloc's intelligence services significantly expanded their spying efforts to steal military technology in order to whittle away the US edge over the Warsaw Pact. Among their primary targets were the aerospace industry in southern California and Silicon Valley, the corridor of high-technology firms in northern California working on multimillion-dollar defense contracts.

William Bell

An engineer at one of these aerospace companies proved to be one of the most damaging spies of the decade. William Bell had spent his career at the

Hughes Aircraft Company, which developed the latest generation of military radar, electronics, and missile systems. His motivations were complex, though money was clearly the dominant force that drove him to spy. He was born in 1920, grew up in Depression-era Seattle, and joined the US Navy when he was eighteen years old. He served on a minesweeper at Pearl Harbor and was wounded twice at Iwo Jima. After the war, he received a degree in physics from the University of California, married, and had two sons and a daughter. In 1952, he began a lifelong career as a military radar expert at Hughes.

According to DOD's PERSEREC study of Cold War espionage, more than a quarter of American spies experienced a life crisis before they crossed the line into spying.[1] Bell experienced a series of traumatic crises before he decided to spy. After working on a Hughes project in Belgium, he divorced his wife and married a Belgian airline attendant. Saddled with heavy alimony payments, he returned to the United States only to face overdue taxes he had not paid while stationed in Europe. Aside from the mounting financial pressures, his career was at a standstill as younger counterparts at Hughes leapfrogged ahead of him. Then family tragedy struck. While on a camping trip in Mexico, his eighteen-year-old son died in an accident.[2]

Almost bankrupt, his career at a dead end, and grieving from the loss of his child, Bell was at the lowest point in his life when he and his family decided to make a fresh start by moving into the Cross Creek Apartments in Playa del Rey, California, in 1976. After a few months living in the complex, he began playing tennis with a young neighbor who was about to reverse the engineer's run of bad luck.

Bell's neighbor, Marian Zacharski, was an aggressive and extremely competent tennis player. Zacharski was the West Coast representative of Polamco, the Polish American Machinery Corporation, which marketed industrial machines in the United States. He was also a Polish intelligence officer.

The Bell case illustrates the advantages that the Soviets enjoyed in Cold War espionage because of assistance from their Eastern European counterparts. Eastern Europeans enjoyed more freedom of movement around the United States and aroused less suspicion among Americans than the Soviets did, and Poles possessed the special advantage of being able to blend in among the country's large Polish American population.

Zacharski was a particularly adept operations officer. He was described as "handsome, charming and mannerly."[3] He spoke flawless English and was thoroughly immersed in American culture. He was disarmingly affable but also cocky and self-assured.

Zacharski was operating in the United States as an illegal. Illegals do not enjoy diplomatic immunity and can be imprisoned and even executed if caught. At every meeting with Bell, Zacharski had to gauge his target's reactions, take his pulse to determine if Bell might have gotten cold feet, whether he had been pushed too far or too fast at any step along the road to recruitment, or, more important, if he had gone to the FBI and was luring Zacharski into a trap.

Zacharski did a masterful job. His approach was slow and patient, and he carefully assessed his target before making a recruitment pitch. Zacharski first became Bell's tennis partner and then his friend. Later Zacharski admitted that, although he is a fierce competitor, he let Bell beat him at tennis to stroke his target's ego.[4] After all, Zacharski knew that the real victory would not be on the tennis court.

Zacharski went beyond friendship. As he elicited information about Bell's work and his financial problems, Zacharski realized that his prey needed something more. About half Bell's age, the twenty-six-year-old Zacharski eventually became like a son to his target, filling the emotional vacuum left in the wake of his real son's untimely death. After that, filling the financial vacuum in Bell's life was simple.

After a year of forging a personal relationship, Zacharski made his first subtle move toward recruitment. Zacharski's cover job for Polamco was a perfect vehicle to ease his target into spying. The job required Zacharski to market Polish machinery, and the American aircraft industry was a potentially huge client. Zacharski asked his father figure for a list of potential buyers, and Bell took the bait. In return for the favor, Zacharski paid Bell $5,000.[5]

Bell had still not crossed the line into espionage, but even if he did not yet know it, he was accepting money from a foreign intelligence officer. Zacharski's next step was to pay Bell $5,000 for receiving unclassified Hughes documents. To bait the hook more deeply, Zacharski persuaded Bell to accept a "consulting" agreement that would guarantee regular payments. When the Cross Creek complex was converted to condominiums, Bell told Zacharski that he could not afford the down payment to buy his apartment, and his surrogate son passed him $7,000 to cover the expense. Soon after receiving this payment, Bell did not flinch when Zacharski gave him a camera to begin photographing classified US information at Hughes. Whether Bell rationalized his "consulting" or not, he now had become a full-fledged spy.

In September 1979, Bell traveled to Austria for the first of a series of meetings in Europe with Zacharski's colleagues. By this stage, the flimsy veneer of business had disappeared and the relationship bore all the earmarks of espionage. Bell arrived at his first meeting after taking a circuitous route from Geneva, made contact with shadowy figures who used only first names, and handed them rolls of filmed secret documents during long walks in the Austrian woods.

During these meetings in Europe, the Poles made subtle threats about Bell's family that convinced him he could not extricate himself from the illicit relationship without dire consequences. Despite the threats, Bell was still addicted to the fruits of his consulting career. Thanks to his side business, he had erased his debts and had bought a $2,000 necklace for his wife, a new Cadillac for himself, and a trip for both of them to Rio de Janeiro.[6]

In exchange for these luxuries, Bell passed the Poles a candy store full of secrets, information about America's most highly classified military systems, which the Poles dutifully conveyed to their Soviet masters. As a specialist in radar, Bell himself had worked on some of the programs he betrayed, especially the "quiet" radar system whose emissions would remain undetected by enemy sensors and were to be used on B-1 and new "Stealth" generation bombers. A CIA estimate of the damage done by Bell revealed that he had also passed to the Poles documents on the F-15 fighter jet's "lookdown–shootdown" radar system that enabled the planes to spot low-flying enemy aircraft or missiles from above.[7]

Bell looted more than radar systems. At later meetings, he passed documentary information about the Phoenix air-to-air missile, the Patriot and Hawk surface-to-air missiles, the Cruise missile, and antitank missile systems.[8] The litany of America's most modern offensive and defensive weapons was catalogued in a CIA damage estimate, which concluded that Bell saved the Soviet bloc "hundreds of millions of dollars in R&D efforts by permitting them to implement proven designs and by fielding operational counterpart systems in a much shorter time period. Specifications will enable them to develop defensive countermeasures systems."[9] If the Cold War had suddenly erupted into a military conflict, the Soviets would have had a surprising advantage that could have cost American lives.

Bell, increasingly worried about the Poles' subtle threats, may have breathed a sigh of relief when he was confronted by the FBI on June 23, 1981. As FBI agents later testified in court, they showed Bell a news article about the defection of a Polish official at the United Nations and his revelations about his country's espionage activities in the United States.[10] When confronted, some spies confess immediately, but others, like the Rosenbergs, maintain their innocence even when presented with overwhelming evidence of their guilt. Bell did not take a second. As soon as he heard about the Polish defector, he blurted out, "Did he mention me?"

Bell not only confessed but, in yet another betrayal, turned against his surrogate son and agreed to entrap him. With a listening device taped to his body, Bell met Zacharski to discuss the next steps in their spying conspiracy. Zacharski was arrested after the meeting, and Bell, in return for his cooperation, received only eight years in prison and a $10,000 fine, a relatively light punishment considering the extensive damage he had done to national security. Zacharski was sentenced to life. The FBI had caught a rare fish, an illegal without diplomatic immunity, and the stiff sentence was designed to give the Soviet bloc pause about using illegals in the United States.

Zacharski's future reflected the shifting tides of history after the Cold War. After almost four years in a Tennessee federal penitentiary, he was released in a spy exchange and returned to his homeland. Under the terms of his release, Zacharski was prohibited from ever returning to the United States, an unlikely prospect in the heyday of the Cold War. After the dissolution of the Warsaw Pact, the new postcommunist Polish government defended Zacharski and argued that he should get a US visa. The Polish minister of the interior, Andrzej Milczanowski, who had spent time in communist jails for dissident activity, argued that Zacharski was simply a patriotic intelligence officer doing his job and, with the Cold War over, his travel to the United States should no longer be an issue.

Milczanowski even appealed directly to FBI director Louis Freeh, but he was refused. Freeh was under considerable pressure from Israel to release one of its spies, Jonathan Pollard, who had been sentenced to life imprisonment in 1987. Allowing Zacharski to travel to the United States would have diluted Freeh's argument against Pollard. Besides, FBI counterintelligence bitterly opposed any such deal. During his years in jail, Zacharski had been repeatedly interrogated by the FBI about his knowledge of Polish intelligence activities but had steadfastly refused to talk.

In one of the ironic twists of the post–Cold War era, Milczanowski decided to appoint Zacharski chief of Polish foreign intelligence in August 1994. This nomination set off a furor on both sides of the Atlantic. Virulently anticommunist Poles were outraged that an officer of the repressive communist era would head their country's intelligence service. Some people in the United States shared their views. Because the appointment might affect Poland's entry into NATO, Zacharski resigned four days after starting the job.[11] The incident proved the extent to which memories of Cold War espionage still lingered on both sides of the divide.

The Zacharski–Bell case also underscored the incredibly lax security in defense firms. After his arrest, Bell himself admitted that he had displayed all the classic signs of a spy—extreme debt offset by suddenly unexplained wealth, disgruntlement with his job, and open contact with a Soviet bloc national, all indicators that went unnoticed by his employer.[12]

At the same time Bell was passing American secrets from Hughes Aircraft, an espionage case with remarkable similarities was progressing at another defense firm. Like Bell, the spy was an engineer and worked on the West Coast. Like Bell, the spy needed money. And, like Bell, the spy was recruited and run by Polish intelligence.

James Durward Harper

James Durward Harper was like Bell in many ways—a veteran, middle-aged, deeply in debt, his career at a standstill. He had been trained in electronics while in the US Marine Corps and had worked for a number of companies before starting his own consulting firm. Through a business associate, he first met Polish intelligence officers in 1975 and agreed to acquire information on a wish list of high-technology items. Although Harper had no security clearance or access to classified documents, he managed to elicit enough information to merit a handsome payment in a Geneva meeting with the Poles.

By 1979, Harper's business was failing and he was divorced and flat broke. He was middle-aged, and with thinning brown hair and a paunch was hardly a lothario. He still had no access but found a girlfriend who did—Ruby Shuler, an executive secretary to the president of Systems Control Inc. (SCI) in Palo Alto, California. SCI conducted research on the Minuteman missile for the US Army's Ballistic Missile Defense Center in Alabama. The Minuteman was a key pillar of America's arsenal, and efforts to ensure that it could withstand Soviet missile attacks were crucial to US strategic defense.[13]

Harper and Shuler got married in a whirlwind romance built on espionage. The Shuler–Harper relationship was not the close father–son bond of Bell and Zacharski or the love spawned by the Rosenbergs' devotion to communism. Their marriage was inspired by espionage and nurtured by booze and greed. Harper drank considerably, but his wife was an alcoholic. Ruby always kept a pint of vodka in her purse and would slip out into the ladies' room for a nip throughout the day.[14] In her alcoholic haze, she first abetted Harper's espionage by stealing documents from her boss's safe. Soon she was letting Harper into her office at night and on weekends so the pair could copy stacks of classified information to sell to the Poles.

Initially, the greedy Harper tried to squeeze $1 million from his Polish handler, Zdislaw Przychodzien. The haggling erupted into a shouting match and caused a temporary rift in the relationship. Harper recontacted Przychodzien in Warsaw to patch up the rift in May 1980. A month later he smuggled out more than 100 pounds of secret documents on US ballistic missile defenses, still damp from the riverbank where he had stashed them. Twenty KGB specialists rushed to Warsaw to review this material. Later, KGB chief Yuriy Andropov awarded medals to Przychodzien and the other Polish officers who had been involved in the case.[15]

Harper walked away with a hefty payment of $100,000, an unusually high amount for the notoriously stingy Soviet bloc services. Later, Harper delivered them a list of the documents that were stored in the SCI safe so that Przychodzien could order them as if shopping from a department store catalogue. Harper toted piles of documents on subsequent trips abroad that netted him tens of thousands of dollars more each time. In eight years of espionage, Harper earned about $250,000.[16]

But this gravy train came to an abrupt halt in August 1981. Ruby Shuler Harper lost her access after SCI was bought by a British firm and she was shuffled off to another job that did not require a security clearance. Ironically, her behavior in the office had never aroused any suspicion among her coworkers. None of them raised any concerns about her heavy drinking. One of them even accompanied her to the bank one day and was apparently unfazed when he noticed her stuffing wads of hundred dollar bills into a safe deposit box.[17]

After earning $250,000 from spying, Harper decided that it was time to retire. Just as Bell had turned against Zacharski, Harper thought he would extricate himself by betraying his Polish buyers. He anonymously contacted an attorney and arranged to meet him at a piano bar. Over a few cocktails, "Jay," as Harper identified himself, revealed tidbits of his espionage over the years, proposing to reveal all and serve as a double agent against the Poles in return for immunity from prosecution. In other words, Harper would get off scot-free, wealthy from selling secrets to the Poles and exonerated for betraying them.

The attorney opened negotiations with the US government on behalf of his anonymous client. Unknown to the attorney and Harper, the CIA had their own spy inside the Polish intelligence service who had picked up corridor gossip about awards meted out to a few of his colleagues in a big case.[18] At a reception, Polish officers with tongues loosened by vodka boasted, and the mole overheard the words "missile research" and "California."[19]

On the basis of this information from the Polish source and the comments from the lawyer's anonymous client, the FBI was able to narrow down the list of suspects.[20] Harper was the anonymous client, and Harper was also a spy against America. The only vexing question arose from Harper's lack of access, but the search for his subsource was easy. The source had revealed the contents of the information now in Polish hands, and they matched documents kept at SCI, where Harper's wife Ruby worked.

The FBI still needed evidence that would stand up in court. Information from the Polish source ultimately led to Harper, but introducing this information in court would compromise a well-placed agent who might learn of other spies. The FBI received approval from the newly established FISA court for the electronic surveillance of Harper. FBI agents listening to his phone conversations heard him bragging about his wealth and planning a trip to Europe, supporting evidence that could be used in a trial.

One of the most telling calls the FBI intercepted was a conversation between Ruby and a friend that summed up their spy marriage. "There was a reason Jim and I got married that only he and I know," she confessed. "I can't tell you or anyone else, and I never will."[21] Ruby kept her vow. Less than three weeks after the call, dissipated from a lifetime of alcohol, she died of cirrhosis of the liver. As testimony to their marriage of convenience, Harper accelerated his mourning period and remarried two months later.

The newlyweds' honeymoon did not last long. In October 1983 the FBI arrested Harper and confronted him with the weight of evidence. Startled by the mountain of detail, Harper cried out, "Oh, my God! They know everything about it!"[22] He was sentenced in May 1984 to life imprisonment without possibility of parole.

US ballistic missile experts estimated that Harper's treason "could impair the nation's defense program into the twenty-first century," an amazing accomplishment for a spy who had no direct access to secrets.[23] The spy who had betrayed America's defenses admitted that he had done it for "the money and the thrill of it."[24]

The Soviets targeted American high technology besides weaponry. Satellite technology was a primary KGB target because the Strategic Arms Limitation Treaty (SALT) of 1972 included strict compliance and verification measures to ensure that both superpowers would honor their promises. The Soviets had never signed a treaty they did not intend to violate; but to evade verification of their missile reduction obligations, they had to counter America's sophisticated satellite reconnaissance capabilities. To divine the highly classified capabilities of America's spies in the skies, the KGB was tasked to find spies on the ground to steal the information. The KGB leapt at the opportunity when a pair of young Americans volunteered information about US satellite communications in 1975.

Christopher Boyce and Andrew Daulton Lee

Christopher Boyce and Andrew Daulton Lee were born and raised in an affluent community in southern California. The two youngsters seemed unlikely spy candidates. Their friendship dated back to the Catholic grammar school they had attended, and both had then also been altar boys. Boyce's father was a former FBI agent and a security director for an aircraft manufacturer. Christopher, the eldest of nine children, scored high on IQ tests as a boy and finished grammar school as class president. Lee was adopted, and his adoptive father, who was a decorated B-24 pilot in World War II, ran a successful pathology practice.

Boyce and Lee were products of the 1970s, though in different ways. Boyce's disillusionment over the Vietnam War, the bombing of Cambodia, and the CIA's role in overthrowing the Allende government in Chile festered into rebellion against his parents' generation and ended in his abandonment of the Catholic Church and dropping out of college. Lee, conversely, vented his generation's disenchantment by becoming immersed in the drug culture. He began to sell drugs and eventually did jail time for a series of narcotics violations. Lee sought escape from the problems of the 1970s in a haze of narcotics; Boyce found comfort in the curious hobby of falconry. Years after their arrest, the spies' story would be memorialized in a book and film titled *The Falcon and the Snowman*.[25]

In 1974 Boyce's father, frustrated by his son's indolence, used his contacts to obtain an entry-level job for Christopher at TRW Systems, one of the area's largest defense contractors. Starting at a $140 weekly salary as a clerk, within six months Christopher received a top-secret clearance for a job in TRW's "black vault," the heart of the company's most sensitive US government project. The project, code-named Rhyolite, was a US government covert satellite surveillance system, and the vault was the center for TRW communications and a satellite ground station in Australia.[26]

Background checks on Boyce for the top-secret clearance yielded glowing reports from his parents' friends and teachers who still remembered the devout altar boy. Interviews with his peers, as Boyce himself later admitted, would have surfaced his drug use, festering antigovernment views, and close friendship with a known narcotics dealer, Andrew Lee.[27] As a result of the background check, a young, low-paid, immature college dropout obtained more access than the average intelligence community veteran possessed, including clearances for DOD top-secret materials, CIA compartmented projects, and NSA cryptographic information.

Security at TRW was as shoddy as at the defense contractors plundered by Bell and Harper. Boyce and his coworkers partied inside the top-secret vault, sometimes putting a cipher destruction machine to dual use as a blender to mix daiquiris and margaritas. On one occasion, Boyce's boss pasted a photo of a monkey's face on his access badge as a joke and walked undisturbed in and out of the highly classified facility.[28] Funny, perhaps, but also a sad reflection on TRW's security practices.

Boyce, more intellectual than his confederate Lee, drew an insidious lesson from his observations of TRW security and concocted the espionage scheme. He easily removed NSA computer cards and tape from two cryptographic machines in the vault and passed the items to Lee, who ferried the materials to the Soviet Embassy in Mexico City in March 1975. Given FBI scrutiny of Soviet facilities in the United States, Mexico City had long been a haven for the KGB and GRU to meet American spies safely.

Lee also had a pattern of traveling to Mexico to smuggle drugs back into the United States, hardly a low-profile cover for a spy. Still, he managed to avoid arrest before embarking on a few more trips to Mexico to deliver Boyce's materials. In the next eighteen months he would pass the Soviets information about Rhyolite and other spy satellite programs. In return he received a few thousand dollars, well short of the value of the material to the parsimonious KGB.

Not surprisingly, Lee wasted his share of the spy loot to buy cocaine and fund his drug-running operation. Despite Boyce's warning to conceal his identity from the KGB, Lee succumbed to KGB pressure and related his friend's entire biography. Lee's slips of the tongue were not limited to the KGB. High on cocaine, he blurted out first to his sister and then to a girlfriend that Boyce and he were swindling the Russians and passing doctored information to mislead them. Because Lee was always spinning tall tales, both of them ignored his boasts.[29]

In November 1975 Lee, again numbed from snorting cocaine, went haywire when the Soviets failed to appear at a scheduled meeting in Mexico. He went directly to the Soviet Embassy to find his KGB collaborators, even though they had sternly warned him never to return to the heavily monitored facility. The KGB was visibly rankled when he came, and their annoyance turned to outrage when they developed the rolls of film he brought.

Pictures of classified material were out of focus, and some of the shots were porno flicks inserted by Boyce as a joke. Chastened by a KGB tongue lashing, Lee left with $5,000, a paltry sum compared with the $50,000 he had expected for the film.[30]

Sinking further into drug addiction, Lee began cheating the unsuspecting Boyce out of their espionage payments, sharing only a quarter of their booty with his partner in crime. Boyce was already nervous about his friend's growing addiction, and independently set up a channel to the KGB through coded phone calls. When the KGB alluded to a $60,000 payment in one call, Boyce realized that Lee was bilking him. Lee had only given him $15,000 and had told him that the total was $30,000. In almost two years of passing on America's most precious satellite secrets to the Soviets, Boyce received only $20,000.

Boyce then decided he would meet directly with the KGB and accompanied Lee to their next scheduled meeting in Mexico. Lee, even in his drug-induced haze, realized he would no longer be of value in the conspiracy once Boyce was in direct contact, but he had no choice. At the meeting Boyce and the KGB learned that Lee was deceiving them both. The KGB contacts were furious when they raised with Boyce their need for satellite operating frequencies. Boyce told the KGB he never had access to the information, never would, and had so informed Lee, who had lied to his Soviet paymasters about his partner's access. After the meeting, Lee's future role was in serious doubt.

Frantic that he would be cut out of his spy cash, Lee went to the Soviet Embassy after Boyce returned home. This time the KGB, never known for their bedside manner with unruly agents, taught him a lesson. They whisked Lee out of the embassy in a darkened car and, once they confirmed they were not under surveillance, abruptly stopped the car and threw him out onto the pavement. Lee was no longer merely unnecessary for the operation; he had become a liability.

The KGB never had a chance after that to remove Lee from the operation. In January 1977 Lee's atrocious tradecraft, his disregard of KGB warnings, and his drug use all finally compromised the operation. Lee was becoming more and more desperate for ready cash to support his habit, and he dispensed with his KGB communications plan by rushing again to the embassy to get a quick payment. To get the KGB's attention, he put a note into a cigarette pack and threw the package over the embassy wall. He was spotted by the Mexican police guarding the embassy, who assumed he was a terrorist or engaged in some kind of criminal act. After a silly attempt to bribe the police, Lee compounded his growing problem when an American diplomat passing by on the street stopped to check out the ruckus. Lee shouted that he was an American citizen and needed help. The diplomat contacted a consular officer who, according to established procedures when American citizens are arrested abroad, went to the police station where Lee had been taken.

The police had already found marijuana on Lee and told him to empty out his pockets at the station. Out came an envelope with three strips of microfilm. A Mexican policeman held one of the strips up to the light and knew enough English to understand what he read. He handed the strip over to the American consular officer, whose eyes opened wide with shock when he read the first words, "Top Secret."

After a few days of Mexican-style interrogation, Lee confessed that Boyce was his partner but claimed that they were working for the CIA by feeding false information to the Soviets. This feeble tactic had been used for centuries by spies when they were caught. America's first spy, Benjamin Church, had claimed that he was giving disinformation to the British when confronted with his incriminating letter full of information on revolutionary forces.

The Mexican police handed Lee over to the FBI. He repeated his story to the FBI agents, who then arrested him on espionage charges. Boyce was arrested a few days later. The two young men, still in their twenties, were indicted for espionage on January 26, 1977.

The friendship of the two former altar boys was finished. Lee wasted no time implicating Boyce when he was caught, and Boyce quickly countered by accusing Lee of blackmailing him into providing secrets to the KGB. Boyce claimed that he had once written a letter about classified CIA activities and Lee had promised to get it published but instead had used it to force Boyce into espionage. This lame defense failed. After separate trials, Boyce was sentenced to forty years in prison and Lee to life.[31]

Lee committed espionage to fund a drug habit that enhanced his self-image. Boyce, whose motives were more complex, enjoyed his KGB payments but spied to strike back at a system that he believed had failed his entire generation. In the process of seeking this revenge, Boyce, along with his partner, had given away secrets that damaged national security at a critical time in the Cold War. The accumulated weight of information on the Rhyolite and similar programs provided the USSR with a unique window into America's ability to verify and monitor Soviet compliance with a treaty limiting the most lethal weapons aimed at the US heartland. To round out this knowledge, all the Soviets needed was information about the satellites themselves.

William Kampiles

Another volunteer with a different set of motives filled the gap. William Kampiles was twenty-three years old and bored. When he was hired by the CIA in March 1977, he imagined a glamorous James Bond existence that would involve traveling abroad, using his fluent knowledge of Greek, lurking in back alleys in far-off lands, and recruiting spies whose reports would be rushed to the president of the United States. Instead, day in and day out he endured twelve hours of drudgery in the CIA Watch Center, where he read incoming reports from overseas, routed them around the Washington intelligence community, and occasionally alerted policymakers to unfolding crises in which he played no part. Other watch center analysts worked the dreary shifts at the CIA, but they did not commit espionage because of the tedium. William Kampiles did.

Kampiles yearned for the thrills and excitement of a career in the CIA's Directorate of Operations (DO), in which operations officers recruited spies and acquired enemy secrets on the front lines of the Cold War. But he was rejected for work as an operations officer in the DO, and his resentment began to smolder. If the CIA would not satisfy his ambitions, he would teach it a lesson. He would become an operative on his own to exact revenge against the CIA and prove its misjudgment of his potential. Revenge and thrills, a dangerous combination, drove Kampiles to take the fateful step into espionage.[32]

When he joined the CIA, Kampiles appeared an unlikely candidate for espionage. He grew up in a Slavic and Greek ethnic neighborhood on Chicago's South Side. As a Greek American, he could have been part of the long and proud tradition of his compatriots at the CIA. One Greek American, Thomas Karamessines, was a veteran of the Office of Strategic Services and became the director of clandestine operations. Another, George Tenet, would become CIA director twenty years after Kampiles resigned from the agency.

Chicago's South Side, as one journalist said after Kampiles's arrest, was "an improbable breeding ground for spies."[33] Poor but patriotic, families on these Chicago streets produced military men and public servants. Kampiles joined their ranks after his family struggled to eke out a living. His father died when he was nine years old, and his mother slaved for a lifetime in the Ford Motor Company's cafeteria to enable her children to pursue the American dream. Kampiles, like Boyce, was an altar boy. He also had a paper route as a boy to supplement his mother's meager salary, and he worked his way through Indiana University by delivering groceries and toiling at a steel mill.

After graduating from Indiana, Kampiles was hired by the CIA to work in the Watch Center. In November 1977, after only eight months at the CIA, he resigned after he was rejected by the DO and received a negative performance evaluation from the Watch Center. Before he walked out of CIA headquarters, he pilfered a copy of the manual for the KH-11, the CIA's most sensitive spy satellite.

In February 1978, Kampiles acted out his fantasy. He traveled to Athens and walked into the Soviet Embassy, where he presented the local KGB with the KH-11 manual. But the KGB officers in Athens apparently were not in a position to appreciate the golden nugget Kampiles had just dropped in their lap, so Kampiles was told to return a few days later while Moscow evaluated his information.[34]

The KH-11 was the CIA's latest-generation spy in the sky. The satellite transmitted its photographs back to Earth in real time. Previous satellites had dropped their cameras, which had to be snatched in midair by specially equipped planes or retrieved on the ground and whisked to special labs where the film was developed. The resolution of the KH-11's cameras was also amazingly detailed. From hundreds of miles above Earth, a KH-11 photograph plainly showed the numbers on the license plates of cars in Soviet parking lots.[35] Thanks to the KH-11, if a Soviet leader decided to cheat on the missile treaty, the president of the United States would know about it immediately.

Moscow realized the significance of the walk-in's gift. However, stingy as always, the KGB paid Kampiles a measly $3,000 for the manual.

Kampiles had now satisfied his need for revenge and thrills, but he had still not proven to the CIA his mettle as a self-styled operations officer. His dual motives, however, were inherently at odds. A spy cannot take revenge on his government and then tell it he has done so. Kampiles, however, did just that. He contacted a friend, Anastasia Thanakos, and spun a yarn to her about conning the Soviets in Athens.[36] Bill Kampiles was always telling tall tales, Thanakos thought. But considering the nature of his story, she agreed with his request to pass the information on to George Joannides, a friend of hers at the CIA, who met with Kampiles and asked him to write a letter about his activities that would be passed on to appropriate agency officials. Kampiles wrote the self-incriminating explanation, but, as in the stories he told his friends, he omitted the single most relevant detail: the theft and sale of the KH-11 manual. Amazingly, he asked the CIA in his letter whether there would be interest in continuing his self-initiated double agent operation against the Soviets.

On August 17, 1978, Kampiles was interviewed by the FBI in Hammond, Indiana, and was then arrested after confessing that he had passed the manual to the KGB. As it turned out, the FBI already knew about Kampiles's contact with the Soviets. The Soviet officer who first met Kampiles when he entered the embassy in Athens was Sergey Bokhan, a GRU officer who was spying for the CIA. Bokhan reported Kampiles's approach to his CIA handler.[37] Kampiles's own conversations with his former CIA colleagues about his flirtation with the KGB in Athens sealed his fate. He had provided sufficient self-incriminating evidence, so Bokhan's information would not have to be used in court.

After ten hours of deliberation, the jury at Kampiles's trial found him guilty. On December 22, 1978, he was sentenced to forty years in prison. The CIA had again tried to argue that revealing KH-11 secrets in court would harm national security but was overruled. Testimony by CIA experts, in fact, convinced the jury of the damage done by Kampiles. The CIA's deputy director of science and technology, Leslie Dirks, told the court that the theft could jeopardize SALT. The manual showed the Soviets the quality of photographic images, which would enable them to construct better camouflage for their missiles. The manual also revealed the geographical limits of the KH-11's coverage, which would help the Soviets evade monitoring of their compliance with the treaty.[38] In effect, America's eyes in the sky were blinded and its ability to monitor Soviet promises under the treaty was blunted. One young, disgruntled, thrill-seeking spy was able to tip the scales of superpower rivalry in the Soviets' favor.[39]

Kampiles heralded the American spies who were to come in the following decades. His reasons for spying were complex and sometimes inherently contradictory, and this witches' brew of conflicting motives would prove to be a trend among spies in the years to come. As his defense attorney claimed at the trial, "Bill Kampiles is a young, patriotic boy that got involved in a bizarre notion."[40] The same could be said of the spies in the 1980s and 1990s. And there were many of them.

Before William Kampiles betrayed the KH-11 satellite, the CIA believed there were far more damaging Soviet spies in its midst. For more than two decades, one man dominated CIA counterintelligence and, unbeknownst to the American public at the time, he ran the most intensive hunt for spies in the nation's history.

James Angleton and the Spy Hunt in the CIA

I think, if asked to single out one specific group of men, one type,
one category as being the most suspicious, unbelieving, unreasonable,
petty, inhuman, sadistic, double-crossing set of bastards in any language,
I would say without any hesitation the people who run
counterespionage departments.

A character in the novel by **ERIC AMBLER,** Light of Day, *52*

One of the most notorious "bastards" in American counterespionage history, some would say, was James Jesus Angleton, the longest-serving chief of CIA counterintelligence. During his twenty-year stewardship, he was suspicious of almost every Soviet agent, volunteer, and defector except one. He was equally suspicious of his colleagues, some of whom undoubtedly thought him to be petty, inhuman, sadistic, and double-crossing. The Angleton legacy would haunt the CIA and provoke a backlash that would irreparably damage the spy agency. Angleton was discredited, and his warnings were ignored. Twenty years later, this repudiation of Angleton would blind the CIA to a spy in its midst.

Angleton embodied the enigmatic figure of a master counterspy. He reportedly dubbed the world of counterespionage "a wilderness of mirrors," and he proved to be its foremost denizen. Tall, gaunt, with slumped shoulders and sunken cheeks, he chain-smoked cigarettes in his dimly lit office as he avidly hunted Soviet moles by poring over files through the thick lenses of his black, horn-rimmed glasses. He was brilliant, a Renaissance man of eclectic interests, champion fly fisherman, cultivator of exotic orchids, and lover of English poetry.

Angleton was born in Boise, Idaho, but his father moved the family to Dayton, Ohio, where he worked as an executive at the National Cash Register Company. The family resettled to Italy after the elder Angleton bought the company franchise there. Angleton alternated between living with his parents in Italy and studying in England in his early years, and he eventually returned home to study at Yale. He began his long government service by joining the army in 1943 and, given his Italian fluency, he was assigned to the Office of Strategic Services (OSS). By the end of the war, the twenty-eight-year-old Angleton was the OSS counterintelligence chief in Italy.

Angleton was among the first wave of OSS veterans who joined the newly established CIA in 1948. As part of his early duties, he was in official contact with MI-6, the British foreign intelligence service, and quickly forged a solid working relationship with its new representative in Washington, Kim Philby, whom he had known during an earlier OSS assignment in London. Angleton and Philby shared two passions: long, martini-laced lunches; and espionage. At the behest of their governments, they also shared secrets. Unbeknownst to Angleton, Philby was sharing those secrets with the KGB.

In 1951 Philby resigned under a cloud of suspicion after two of his close colleagues, Donald Maclean and Guy Burgess, defected to the Soviet Union. Philby, who had access to the Venona Project messages regarding HOMER, Maclean's code name, had warned him and Burgess, fellow spies in the "Cambridge Five" espionage ring. In addition to Philby, Maclean, and Burgess, the other two members of the ring were Anthony Blunt and John Cairncross. The five were sterling examples of so-called seeding operations, in which an intelligence service recruits a young spy with the potential background and education to enter government service. The advantage of this tactic is the ability of the intelligence service to guide the spy's career and direct him to agencies and even specific positions where he will have maximum access to valuable intelligence.

The five spy ring members were all attracted to communism while studying at Cambridge University in the 1930s, and all later found government jobs tailor made for Soviet espionage purposes.[1] Maclean and Burgess were Foreign Office diplomats who served in the British Embassy in Washington. Blunt worked for MI-5, the British internal security service, and later received a knighthood for his career as a prominent art historian. Cairncross worked at the British decryption headquarters in Bletchley Park and later for MI-6. Philby perhaps enjoyed the best access of all and was able to save a number of British and American spies for the Soviets because of his insider's knowledge of US–UK counterespionage investigations.

Angleton was shaken by Philby's betrayal. The counterspy's innate sense of conspiracy would evolve into an obsession to find spies who he was convinced must be lurking somewhere in the CIA. Angleton would trust few in the future. Ironically, the next intelligence officer Angleton dared to trust would be a KGB defector, and once again he would make a grave miscalculation that would have enormously damaging repercussions.

In September 1954, Angleton was appointed by CIA director Allen Dulles as chief of the CIA's Counterintelligence Staff.[2] He was only thirty-seven years old, and he remains today the youngest head of CIA counterintelligence. He served in the job for twenty years, longer than any of his successors. He also enjoyed far more authority than they did. He controlled liaison with the Israeli Mossad and other allied intelligence services, and he reported straight to the CIA director instead of through the chief of clandestine operations as other chiefs of operational components did. No one except the CIA director knew more secrets than Angleton, and his influence with a row of directors was unsurpassed.

Angleton built the Counterintelligence Staff from a handful of researchers to a robust unit of more than a hundred officers.[3] He also infused counterintelligence with new discipline. Catching spies and determining the reliability of agents and defectors required patience and painstaking analysis. He also believed that counterintelligence analysis required a careful study of history, an immersion in the adversary's past to discern espionage patterns that would unmask deception in the present. As Mark Riebling noted, "To Angleton, catching spies was much like landing trout. It was all about patience, research, deception. . . . Angleton felt too much of the country's conception of CI [counterintelligence], as promoted by detective entertainments and the FBI's own actions, was 'spy versus spy.'"[4]

Angleton was convinced that the Soviet Union was an implacable enemy that would salt its spies throughout the government just as it had done in the 1930s and 1940s. For the FBI, the arrest of illegal Rudolf Abel was a triumph; for Angleton, it was only the tip of the KGB iceberg, the first inkling that Soviet espionage was still alive and well in the United States. Angleton believed his suspicions were justified when a KGB officer defected and revealed startling secrets about the scope of Soviet espionage.

In December 1961, Anatoliy Golitsyn, a KGB officer in Helsinki, requested asylum and the CIA immediately whisked him and his family out of Finland to the safety of the United States.[5] Golitsyn was an unremarkable KGB officer who had been born in the Ukraine in 1926. Until his defection, his career had followed a typical path of training, assignments at KGB headquarters, and, before Helsinki, one overseas assignment in Vienna. He provided solid leads to penetrations of NATO countries but he did not have a single lead to any major American spies.

Golitsyn, however, had a monumental ego. Dealing with defectors has always been a task requiring delicacy and tact by CIA handlers. Most defectors already suffer from psychological problems once they have severed all ties to their native land, but even by these standards, Golitsyn was a challenging client. Arrogant and inflated with a sense of his importance, he insisted on an array of special privileges and even demanded a meeting with President John F. Kennedy to present his information, a proposal flatly rejected by his CIA handlers.

An earlier defector, Peter Deriabin, had earlier told the CIA that Golitsyn was a worthwhile recruitment target because he would be susceptible to flattery, had an "overblown notion of his expertise and was unpopular with his fellow officers."[6] Despite Golitsyn's inflated self-importance, Angleton was intrigued by some of the Russian's initial comments about the Soviets' master plan for strategic deception. When Golitsyn, unsatisfied that his demands remained unmet, refused to cooperate with the Soviet Bloc Division responsible for debriefing him, the unit gladly handed him over to Angleton.

Golitsyn revealed to Angleton the Soviets' master plan to dominate the planet. Any "thaw" in relations with the free world would merely be a clever stratagem designed to lull the West into letting down its guard as the

KGB covertly destabilized Western governments. Golitsyn even convinced Angleton that the Sino/Soviet rift was a cunning ruse to persuade the West of serious fissures in the international communist movement, even though every overt sign showed that the two communist giants had become bitter adversaries.

Golitsyn's ramblings now proved to Angleton that his suspicions were on the mark. Angleton enabled Golitsyn to untangle the strands in this Soviet spider web by allowing the defector to read CIA files, a gross violation of basic security practice.[7] Golitsyn, after all, had become a US citizen and as such was free at any time to return to the USSR and reveal the secrets in those files to his former employers in the KGB. For a CIA officer to permit this access either mistakenly or intentionally would have been a major lapse. For the chief of CIA counterintelligence, it was madness.

Golitsyn told Angleton that his former employers in the KGB would go to incredible lengths to prove that he was lying about the conspiracy. According to the CIA's Rasputin, any Soviet defector, any spy who followed him would be a double agent directed by the KGB to discredit his revelations of the Soviet plot. This tactic ensured that Golitsyn's theory would remain unchallenged by any Soviet agent who just might have more access and better intelligence that he no longer possessed.

Angleton, however, believed his guru. As counterintelligence chief, Angleton had significant influence in determining the reliability and veracity of the CIA's spies, and he put thumbs down on potential Soviet spies or defectors whose information might contradict Golitsyn's view. Potential new sources were pronounced to be a sham and only proved Golitsyn's predictions. The master plan now became a self-fulfilling prophecy. CIA operations to recruit spies or debrief volunteers were seriously impeded at a time of heightened crisis in the Cold War when policymakers craved intelligence to divine Soviet plans and intentions.

The most important Soviet source whom Angleton dismissed as a double agent was Yuriy Nosenko, who became a tragic victim of Golitsyn's claim that all future defectors would be KGB provocateurs. Nosenko was a member of a delegation to a disarmament conference in Geneva in 1962 when he first approached the CIA. He was a potentially informative source because he had worked in the America Department of the Second Chief Directorate (SCD) of the KGB, the internal security arm responsible for monitoring Americans in the Soviet Union and orchestrating recruitment operations against them.

SCD officers worked almost exclusively inside the USSR's borders and rarely had an opportunity to travel to the West, unlike their First Chief Directorate counterparts like Golitsyn, who lived overseas and could contact the CIA away from the prying eyes of the KGB. If any SCD officer harbored thoughts of spying or defecting to the Americans, he would have to patiently await a rare opportunity to travel abroad and contact the CIA in a Western country. SCD officers knew better than any other Soviet the danger of doing so inside the USSR, where Western embassies were in a fishbowl, their citizens were surveilled on the streets, and their apartments and offices were laced with listening devices. Nosenko could prove to be a unique source.

Nosenko offered intriguing information right from the start. He informed the CIA of a spy supplying the KGB with military secrets from a courier center, which resulted in the arrests of Robert Lee Johnson and Allen Mintkenbaugh. He also reported that Pyotr Popov, the CIA's first key mole inside the GRU, was caught by KGB surveillance, which discovered an American Embassy officer mailing a letter to the Russian source.[8] Besides that, Nosenko revealed that the KGB used chemical substances to track the movement of Americans, especially suspect CIA officers, around Moscow. According to Nosenko, the KGB would apply the invisible substances to the clothing pockets and shoes of targets to trace envelopes or other materials passed to agents and to follow their movements.

Angleton doubted Nosenko from the start. He suspected that Popov had been compromised by a mole in CIA. Another possibility for the compromise was the FBI's clumsily overt surveillance of Margarita Tairova, an illegal trained by Popov for dispatch to the United States. But for Angleton, Nosenko's version served two purposes: diverting attention from a mole in the CIA; and fostering a myth of the KGB's invincibility in Moscow, that is, that the KGB had a quiver full of magic arrows like spy dust and no Soviet spying for the CIA was safe. The Johnson lead was dismissed as "throwaway" information, that is, information that was accurate but could be sacrificed because the KGB operation had been suspended due to security concerns about Johnson's erratic behavior. All this inside information, however, was trivial compared with the bombshell that Nosenko would later divulge to his CIA contacts.

In 1964, Nosenko met the CIA contacts again and surprised them with the news that he had to defect, a course he earlier had claimed he would never follow. Since the last time the CIA contacts had met him, President Kennedy had been assassinated while traveling in a motorcade in Dallas. A nation gripped by sorrow watched as the FBI and police feverishly sought the assassin. They arrested a suspect, Lee Harvey Oswald, and were confident he was the killer. Two days after the arrest, Oswald was gunned down in a police station by a Dallas strip club owner named Jack Ruby. As the facts about Oswald seeped out, the glimmer of a heinous international conspiracy emerged.

Oswald had carried placards on American streets in support of Fidel Castro. He was a former marine, and every marine is a rifleman. And he had lived in the USSR and had a Russian bride. The ominous links pointed to a Soviet-Cuban plot. If the Soviets had conspired to kill the US president, an outraged nation could not stand by idly and war could be imminent. The Soviet Union vehemently denied any involvement in Kennedy's assassination, but America remained skeptical.

Nosenko became a key actor in the tense drama. As an officer of the KGB's America Department, he was the best prospect for inside information about Oswald. Nosenko told the CIA that the KGB indeed had met with Oswald but had dismissed him as a potential agent because he was mentally unstable.[9] For Angleton and Golitsyn, the story proved beyond any doubt that Nosenko was a KGB fabricator dispatched to prove that the Soviets had played no role in Kennedy's assassination.

Angleton's suspicions were justified. Oswald had served in the US Marine Corps at a U-2 reconnaissance plane base in Japan, surely a juicy intelligence target of interest to the Soviets. Nosenko also cast doubt on his credibility because of constant discrepancies in the information he provided, even about his own biography. He admitted that his rank was lower than he had originally claimed, and he also insisted that he was under suspicion and had been recalled to Moscow, although this, too, was a lie.

The determination of a defector or agent's bona fides, the verification of their truthfulness, is critical to the assessment of the information they provide. In few other cases in American espionage history was this determination as important as in the Nosenko case. If Nosenko was telling the truth about Oswald, the Soviets had not been involved in the Kennedy assassination. If he had been directed by the Soviets to lie about Oswald, then the Soviets may have been involved, with all the attendant consequences. Another possible theory was that the Soviets did not conspire to kill Kennedy but, frightened that the Americans would believe they did, had dispatched Nosenko because a spy would be more convincing than their official denials.[10]

Despite his interrogators' efforts to rattle him, Nosenko unflinchingly stood by his story. Without any concrete evidence of Soviet involvement, the Warren Commission on the assassination concluded that President Kennedy had been murdered by a lone gunman. Some observers at the CIA remained unconvinced and decided to force the truth from Nosenko. On April 4, 1964, Nosenko began 1,277 days of solitary confinement in miserable conditions first in the attic of a CIA safehouse and then at an isolated CIA training facility.[11] In spite of this harsh treatment and relentless questioning, Nosenko still insisted that he was telling the truth.

After forty-two months in captivity, Nosenko was released in October 1967 when pressure from within the CIA forced a review of his case.[12] A critical issue in the review was an earlier examination of Nosenko by a CIA psychologist that had been debunked by the conspiracy theorists. The psychologist had concluded that Nosenko "was not the type to be chosen for a mission that could have changed the course of history; . . . nor, frankly, was he the kind of man who could be trusted to run the kind of cover-up operation on Kennedy's assassination where failure might mean the outbreak of World War III."[13]

Even without an expert psychological opinion, the notion that the Soviets would entrust their fate to a single double agent seems highly improbable. If they had, the KGB would have ensured that the details of Nosenko's story would have been airtight to convince the Americans. There would have been no lies about military rank or recall to Moscow or the many other discrepancies and alterations that riddled his debriefings. Besides that, the Soviet intelligence services often operated like the Soviet military, and Soviet military doctrine relied on the massive use of force. Reliance on one lone defector, rather than an overwhelming number of such ruses, hardly fit Soviet intelligence doctrine.

Years later, the KGB arrested a number of CIA sources thanks to information from its spy in the agency, Aldrich Ames. To protect him, the Soviets flooded the CIA with red herrings suggesting that the compromises were attributable to other factors rather than a mole in the organization.[14] The KGB would surely have dispatched an even stronger fleet of double agents to reinforce a deception scheme to prevent the potentially catastrophic fallout over the Kennedy assassination.

Even if Nosenko had been a master deceiver, it is difficult to believe that the KGB would have allowed him to go to America. Any double agent, no matter how effective, would face challenges sticking to a bogus tale when under full control of the opposition and confronted for hours every day by a relentless barrage of questions designed to trip him up. The Soviets were also convinced that their American counterparts were fully capable of using and willing to use mind-altering drugs, truth serums, torture, or any other method that would eventually extract the truth from a provocateur. Given these odds, would the Soviets have gambled their national security on a sole agent in the hands of the Americans? Doubtful.

The CIA eventually deemed that Nosenko was not a double agent. More than two decades later, the agency's conclusion was corroborated by another Soviet defector. Vassili Mitrokhin, a senior KGB archivist, defected to the British in 1992 with a treasure trove of notes extracted from Soviet files. Mitrokhin's information included leads to and identification of KGB spies that subsequently proved the accuracy of his materials. Among these materials were a damage assessment on Nosenko's defection and information indicating that the KGB, unaware of Nosenko's plight in the United States, was plotting to assassinate him, hardly a just reward for his role as a double agent.[15]

In spite of these revelations, skeptics still remain. Tennent "Pete" Bagley, the first CIA officer to debrief Nosenko, eventually doubted the defector's information. Bagley believed that Nosenko had been dispatched by the KGB first to protect moles inside the CIA and then to convince the US government that Oswald had no relationship with the KGB. In his book *Spy Wars*, Bagley launched a passionate defense of the conspiracy theory in which he provided a comprehensive list of the many discrepancies in Nosenko's information that were ultimately exposed.[16] Bagley's defense, however, raises the same issue about the Soviets' choice of Nosenko to deceive the United States.

As Bagley convincingly notes, Nosenko's information was full of inconsistencies and fabrications, and he did not even appear well versed in his own job duties. Would the KGB have entrusted a double agent mission vital to Soviet national security to someone as inconsistent in his stories, ill prepared, and unconvincing as Nosenko? Again, this is highly doubtful. Bagley's theory ironically reinforces the view that Nosenko would not have been tasked by the KGB to misinform the Americans about Oswald.

Angleton's suspicions about the Soviets were not limited to agents and defectors like Nosenko. As counterintelligence chief, he was responsible for uncovering penetrations of the CIA, and his own experience in the Philby affair had intensified his fears of betrayal from within. Golitsyn fueled these fears, telling Angleton that the CIA had indeed been penetrated by a spy. As Golitsyn claimed to recall from KGB files, the spy was code-named SASHA, was of Slavic descent, had a surname beginning with the letter "K" and possibly ending in "ski," and may have served in Germany. Golitsyn's revelation launched Angleton and his mole hunters on a forced march through CIA personnel rolls to find SASHA.[17]

SASHA, in fact, did exist, and was eventually identified from Golitsyn's information as a CIA contract agent named Igor Orlov, a native Russian who had spied for the Soviets behind Nazi lines in World War II and defected after the war.[18] He worked for the CIA in Germany as a principal controller of a network of low-level agents tasked with gathering information on Soviet military personnel. The FBI investigated Orlov but found insufficient evidence to prosecute before their suspect died of cancer. Orlov's career with the CIA was already over by the time Golitsyn fingered him, and he hardly had the access of a highly placed mole. Undeterred, Golitsyn then claimed that the mole must be one of the CIA staff officers who supervised Orlov.

Golitsyn's new allegation sparked Angleton's search for the Soviet penetration of the CIA. During Angleton's mole hunt, code-named HONETOL, about forty CIA officers were suspected of spying for the Soviets and fourteen of them were fully investigated and subjected to FBI electronic and physical surveillance.[19] Leonard McCoy, a CIA officer familiar with the project, wryly commented that "at the height of HONETOL, the FBI seemed to be following more suspect CIA officers in the United States than they were following KGB officers."[20]

The project officially lasted for a brief period, November 1964 to April 1965, but officers were investigated before that and scrutiny of others lingered beyond 1965. Most of the officers worked in the Soviet Division of the Directorate of Operations (DO), where their primary duty was engaging Soviets around the world to recruit them as spies, a mission that placed them high on Angleton's list of suspects. Even though the FBI found nothing remotely hinting at espionage in any of the cases, suspicions about the officers lingered. As a result, assignments were lost, promotions were stalled, careers were at a standstill, and none of the suspects knew the reason. Even after they were cleared, whispered rumors in the corridors of the small, elite CIA directorate persisted, and the officers remained in a Kafkaesque limbo.

After Jimmy Carter was elected president, his new CIA director, Stansfield Turner, learned of the spurious allegations and ruined careers and advised Congress of the issue. On October 14, 1980, Congress enacted special legislation to compensate the HONETOL victims and restore their lost honor. It was too little and too late, but the law ended an appalling chapter in American counterespionage history. Not a single spy had been unmasked through the HONETOL project. Instead, the careers of CIA officers were shattered at the height of the Cold War when policymakers sorely needed the Soviet spies they could have recruited and the intelligence they could have provided. CIA officer McCoy claimed that HONETOL "removed about 75 percent of the most qualified and experienced officers from the Soviet Division. So, at a stroke, we lost our most capable and linguistically qualified staff."[21]

Angleton's mole hunt finally turned into a Frankenstein that attacked its creator. One of Angleton's officers, Clare Petty, a fanatic believer in the mole hunt, concluded that Golitsyn was a double agent. The Soviet defector, however, could not have done so much damage without a highly placed spy inside CIA. And that spy, Petty asserted, had to be James Jesus Angleton, who had supported Golitsyn, fostered his theories, and sidelined a generation of agents and operations officers—all to benefit his KGB masters. Petty's allegations were dismissed, but, as Tom Mangold notes, "the sorcerer would have been proud of his apprentice."[22]

After two decades as head of counterintelligence, Angleton's career came to an end. Once William Colby was appointed CIA director in 1973, he began edging Angleton out of his job by gradually stripping away his extraordinary authorities.[23] Colby took the Israeli liaison account from Angleton and declared that his Counterintelligence Staff would no longer be the deciding voice on the reliability of agents. He also ordered CIA field stations to be more aggressive in handling Soviet "walk-ins," intelligence volunteers rejected out of hand by Angleton as disinformation-feeding double agents.

The new director also found Angleton's master plan theory cumbersome and incomprehensible and, more important, believed that Angleton's actions had needlessly destroyed careers, paralyzed Soviet operations, and damaged relations with key foreign intelligence services. As Colby said in his autobiography, he was even disappointed in Angleton's performance in counterintelligence: "I looked in vain for some tangible results in the counterintelligence field and found little or none."[24]

Colby was trying to ease Angleton out slowly, hoping that the "Gray Ghost" would realize that he should retire, but the obsessive counterintelligence chief ignored the hint. Finally, in December 1974 *New York Times* reporter Seymour Hersh advised Colby that the newspaper would be publishing his story about the CIA's illegal domestic activities and that Angleton would be exposed as the architect of MHCHAOS, a program in which the CIA monitored American political activists, and HTLINGUAL, the intercept and review of mail sent to and from the USSR.[25] Colby summoned Angleton to his office and told him "You will now leave, period."[26]

Almost forty years have passed since Angleton's departure. Although Angleton initially had his defenders in the first years after his retirement, subsequent literature—books by Martin, Mangold, and Wise—harshly criticized his tenure for paranoia, naive faith in Golitsyn, and damage to the CIA's Soviet operations. Golitsyn himself was discredited by KGB colleagues who later defected. In his history of the KGB, Oleg Gordievsky claimed that Golitsyn demonstrated little understanding of the KGB's incapability in the 1960s to orchestrate the grand plans he ascribed to them. Gordievsky added that Golitsyn himself, as a midlevel supervisor, had devised his own plan to reorganize the KGB and was disenchanted when his recommendations were summarily rejected.[27]

Angleton was also discredited by his colleagues in the CIA. In the late 1970s and early 1980s, senior officers in the Soviet Division who had lived through the mole hunt held sessions with new officers to brief them on the excesses of the Angleton era.[28] The lesson drummed home to the young officers was clear: Arbitrary accusations of trusted colleagues in the elite DO ruined operations and the careers of good men. Suspecting a fellow CIA officer of espionage was tantamount to believing that the Earth was flat.

CIA counterintelligence would overcompensate for the excesses of the Angleton era by refusing to even conceive that a CIA officer from the DO could be a spy. The intense reaction to Angleton's spy hunt would lead the CIA to dismiss any possibility that one of its own would betray his country.

That overreaction would have dire consequences. The anti-Angleton mindset would later condition the DO to dismiss the possibility of a mole inside its ranks to explain the mysterious compromises of one Soviet agent after another in the 1980s. That overreaction would also render the CIA incapable of ferreting out Aldrich Ames, the spy who burrowed into the heart of Soviet operations for nine years and betrayed those agents to the KGB. Through his passion for counterespionage, Angleton had ironically discredited it.

However, the controversy over Angleton's mole hunt and blind embrace of Golitsyn obscured the rich legacy of the CIA's longest-serving counterintelligence chief. As CIA veteran William Hood pointed out, Angleton strengthened counterintelligence as an independent discipline in the espionage profession and established the basic principle that intelligence collection and covert action cannot succeed without the support of solid counterintelligence.[29] If the spies providing intelligence are not assessed for reliability and accuracy, then the intelligence is not only worthless for the policymaker; it can lead to uninformed and, at times, disastrous policy decisions. Thirty years after Angleton's retirement, faulty intelligence about Saddam Hussein's weapons of mass destruction proved him correct.

Angleton was ultimately right about moles in the CIA. Unfortunately, he looked for them in the wrong place. Another decade would pass before dozens of spies were discovered in the US government, and some of them had operated undisturbed during Angleton's reign over CIA counterintelligence.

PART  III

THE DECADE
OF THE SPY:
SOVIET SPIES
OF THE 1980s

Espionage in the 1980s

The 1980s became the "Me! Me! Me!" Generation of status seekers.

"American Cultural History" website, Lone Star College–Kingwood

In the 1980s, America turned away from the liberal idealism and social consciousness of the previous two decades and toward self-centered materialism and conservatism. After the economic downturn of the 1970s, national income rose 20 percent and Americans spent their newfound wealth on clothing, cars, and gadgets that proclaimed their social status. A study by the University of California and the American Council on Education in 1980 epitomized the goals of the Me Generation. According to the survey, college freshmen in America were more interested in status, power, and money than at any time during the past fifteen years, and business management was the most popular major.[1] The materialist individualism of the Me Generation was captured in a poster that showed a fashionably dressed young man with a champagne glass in hand standing in front of a shiny Bentley sports car. The poster was captioned "Poverty Sucks."

The unabashed materialism of the decade was paralleled by a resurgence of unabashed patriotism after a decade that ended on a sour note for American prestige abroad. In 1979, Islamic revolutionaries overthrew the shah of Iran, a key US ally in the volatile Middle East, and Iranian students seized the US Embassy in Tehran in November 1979. The students, backed by Ayatollah Khomeini's new fundamentalist regime, held fifty-two hostages in a humiliating saga that was splashed across the nation's television screens daily during the fourteen-month crisis. As Americans celebrated the Christmas holidays the following month, the Soviet Union ended the détente that marked superpower relations in the 1970s by invading Afghanistan.

Frustrated by negotiations to end the Iran hostage crisis, President Jimmy Carter approved a secret rescue mission that failed and contributed to his loss of a second term in the White House. President Ronald Reagan capitalized on America's gloomy mood over its declining global prestige to defeat Carter in the first presidential election of the 1980s. As a final blow to Carter, the Iranians released the hostages minutes after Reagan's inauguration in January 1981.

Reagan ushered in an era of patriotic conservatism when traditional values of hard work, patriotism, and faith in God that were once scorned as "establishment" virtues in the 1960s counterculture were back in vogue. The earlier rebellion of the nation's youth came full circle. Young Americans raised the flag instead of desecrating it, military enlistments increased, and, according to a Gallup poll, 81 percent of teenagers were "very proud" to be Americans.[2]

Reagan vowed to restore American prestige around the world and confront the Soviet Union, which had taken advantage of US problems overseas to expand its influence. Reagan declared the Soviet Union to be an "Evil Empire" and took stronger measures to resist the Soviet threat than any previous president, vastly increasing defense spending and countering communist influence in every corner of the globe.

Reagan's aggressive policies aggravated the swelling problems of the "Evil Empire" in the 1980s. The Soviets were combating a well-armed insurgency in Afghanistan and confronting increasingly rebellious Eastern European satellites on their doorstep. As the Solidarity labor movement grew more strident, Polish communist leaders imposed martial law in 1981 as an alternative to a Soviet invasion. Soviet prestige suffered other embarrassing setbacks during the decade. The vaunted Soviet air defense mistakenly shot down a civilian Korean Airlines plane in 1983, and four years later failed to track a small airplane that a nineteen-year-old German pilot landed near Red Square in Moscow. In 1986 the Chernobyl nuclear reactor exploded in Ukraine with disastrous consequences, the contamination of vast areas of the USSR, the evacuation and resettlement of thousands, and the spread of radioactive fallout over almost half the globe.

By the mid-1980s, the Soviets had also endured geriatric leadership for decades. After eighteen years of rule by Leonid Brezhnev and his aging coterie, the Soviet Union experienced three rapid leadership changes. KGB chief Yuriy Andropov assumed the mantle after Brezhnev's death, but died after fifteen short months on the job. His successor, Konstantin Chernenko, was, at seventy-three, the oldest leader in the USSR's history, and he died after a year in office. In an abrupt change, the Politburo named a far younger leader, Mikhail Gorbachev, who was only fifty-four years old when he became general secretary of the Communist Party in 1985.

Gorbachev introduced daring reforms, which were interpreted by many in the West as a breath of fresh air after seventy years of stifling Soviet communism. Gorbachev had little choice because the stagnant Soviet economy was unable to compete with Reagan's accelerated military spending. "Star Wars," in particular, the media's term for Reagan's Strategic Defense Initiative, envisioned a costly space-based shield against a nuclear attack, which the worried Soviets interpreted as a US tactic to enable a first strike without fear of retaliation. The Soviet Union was already cracking apart at the seams, and competing with Star Wars could be the final blow.

Despite their declining fortunes in the 1980s, the Soviets achieved considerable success in the espionage arena. Ironically, in the 1950s, when the Soviets were outpacing their American adversary on a number of fronts, their espionage efforts lagged far behind as they recovered from the loss of extensive spy networks from previous decades. The reverse occurred in the 1980s. In spite of a disintegrating economy, a quagmire in Afghanistan, and a row of humiliating international embarrassments, the Soviets obtained critical information from some of the most damaging spies in American history. If the 1930s and 1940s had been the Golden Age of Soviet espionage in America, then the 1980s were its Renaissance. Though more Americans spied for the Soviet Union in the Golden Age, the quality of penetration of the US government in the 1980s rivaled, and in some cases surpassed, the Soviets' earlier achievements.

According to DOD's PERSEREC study, sixty-two Americans were arrested for espionage in the 1980s, and almost half were caught in the two-year period from 1984 to 1986.[3] In 1985, dubbed by the media "the Year of the Spy," eleven were arrested. In a span of five days in November of that year, three major spies were caught. The spies of the 1980s betrayed secrets in a dazzling array of agencies—the CIA, FBI, NSA, US Army, US Navy, US Marine Corps, and US Air Force. As in the past, the overwhelming majority of these spies were enlisted military men motivated by the desire to score quick cash. Spies from the military and other agencies were prey to the same sleek Madison Avenue ads featuring shiny sports cars, designer clothes, and the latest electronic gadgets. Young enlisted men on low salaries used their access to secrets to enjoy the good life symbolized by the fashionable gentleman in the Bentley poster.

The primacy of financial motivations for spying was not the only pattern that continued in American espionage in the 1980s. Another that persisted in the 1980s and beyond was Americans' disbelief in espionage by their fellow citizens. For example, no one suspected that Glenn Michael Souther, a US Navy photographer's mate, was betraying top-secret satellite reconnaissance information to the Soviets, even though he did little to conceal his spying from his wife and numerous girlfriends. Souther volunteered to the KGB in 1980 while stationed in Italy. His Italian wife grew suspicious of his behavior, and he confessed his espionage to her. As their marriage fell apart, she tried to alert a Naval Investigative Service (NIS) agent about her husband, but her report was ignored.

After abandoning his wife, Souther went through a succession of girlfriends. He openly discussed his pro-Soviet views with them, and they also observed him preparing coded letters and caches and conducting other espionage activities.[4] One of his paramours was suspicious but only realized the nature of his activities after seeing *The Falcon and the Snowman* in a movie theater.[5] She tried to notify the FBI but gave up after she received recorded messages at the local office. Another girlfriend was a navy colleague who received routine security briefings, but even she was unsure that Souther's suspicious behavior was related to espionage.[6] After the FBI, unaware of these observations over the years, interviewed Souther, he defected to the Soviet Union in 1986, where he committed suicide three years later. The case was not unique; others would ignore or dismiss signs of espionage throughout the decade and beyond, including some with far more experience in the national security arena than Souther's wife and girlfriends.

Souther was among the two-thirds of the decade's spies who were from the military. A high number came from the ranks of the US Navy, including one of the most notorious networks of the century, the John Walker spy ring. Navy security was incredibly lax and underwent a vast overhaul after revelations that Walker and his ring had easily smuggled America's most cherished cryptographic secrets out of ships and naval bases.

Although the Walker ring stole volumes of secrets for eighteen years, more than half the decade's spies were caught before their espionage careers were launched. As was wryly noted in the PERSEREC study, the interceptions of these prospective traitors made the 1980s "less the 'Decade of the Spy,' as has been claimed, so much as the 'Decade of the Unsuccessful Spy.'"[7] The quick arrests resulted from a combination of increased FBI counterintelligence scrutiny of Soviet bloc intelligence officers and the glaring ineptitude of the budding spies. Young military spies, in particular, had no training in intelligence and no conception of the FBI's surveillance capabilities against Soviet bloc facilities.

No budding spy illustrated this more than Michael Tobias, a navy petty officer aboard the USS *Peoria* in San Diego. Tobias filched top-secret cryptographic key cards from the ship and, along with his nephew, drove to the Soviet Consulate in San Francisco to sell the material for $100,000. They arrived at the consulate before it opened and decided to return to San Diego. The hapless pair then began calling the US Secret Service, admitting they were planning to sell secrets to the Soviets and offering instead to return the materials to the government in exchange for money and amnesty. The FBI swiftly traced the callers, and Tobias was arrested. He was sentenced to twenty years in prison in one of the most inane espionage approaches in US history.[8]

During the 1980s, 80 percent of American spies passed their secrets to the Soviet Union and its allies. As in past decades, the Soviet intelligence services were ably aided by the USSR's Eastern European satellites. Echoing Polish triumphs of the 1970s, Hungarian intelligence ran a spy ring that betrayed NATO's entire defense against the Warsaw Pact, and the Czech intelligence service infiltrated an illegal into the CIA who compromised one of America's most productive sources inside the Soviet Union.

A new trend in espionage emerged in the decade as more Americans were arrested for spying on behalf of countries unaffiliated with the Soviet bloc. The trend would increase in the 1990s and, by the end of the century, seventeen nations outside the Soviet bloc had run spies inside the US government.

Even the tiny African nation of Ghana, hardly an espionage superpower, managed to penetrate the CIA. Sharon Scranage, a CIA support assistant assigned to Accra, was convinced by her Ghanaian lover, Michael Soussoudis, to provide identities of CIA officers and their sources. The head of Ghanaian intelligence service at the time was a Marxist sympathizer who presumably shared Scranage's information with the Cubans. Scranage, after failing a polygraph test and admitting to espionage, agreed to entrap Soussoudis, who was arrested and deported to Ghana in exchange for eight agents compromised as a result of her betrayal. Scranage was arrested in July 1985 and sentenced to five years imprisonment.[9]

The spies of the 1980s not only worked for a wide range of US agencies and conspired with a number of countries. They also included a broad spectrum in age, length of time spying, and motivations. In age they ranged from Michael Walker, a twenty-two-year-old US Navy enlisted man, to Larry Wu-tai Chin, a sixty-three-year-old Chinese translator at the CIA. Although the majority spied for a short period before they were caught, the Walker ring supplied secrets to the Soviets for eighteen years, and a Hungarian ring under Army Sergeant Clyde Conrad went undetected for fourteen years. The record, however, belongs to Wu-tai Chin, whose espionage cooperation with the Chinese spanned more than three decades.

Like their predecessors, many of the decade's spies betrayed secrets for money and earned a paltry sum for their crimes. In the 1980s, however, three of the five spies who earned more than $1 million for their treachery were arrested: John Walker, Larry Wu-tai Chin, and Clyde Conrad.[10] The most damaging spies of the decade, including the three members of the million dollar club, were paid well for their secrets but some committed espionage for a number of motivations besides money. Some spied out of resentment against wrongs real or imagined, and others because of dual loyalties. One spy fell victim to sexual entrapment and betrayed his country because of a romance with a young woman under KGB control. But the most damaging of them all was John Walker.

Evil Spy for the Evil Empire

JOHN WALKER

All happy families are like one another;
each unhappy family is unhappy in its own way.

Opening line of **LEO TOLSTOY'S** Anna Karenina, *17*

The unhappy family of John Walker was unhappy because he was evil incarnate. He was an abusive, philandering husband; a neglectful father; a cold, manipulative son; and an exploiting brother. He had no redeeming qualities except one. John Walker was an exceptional spy.

During eighteen years of spying for the Soviet Union, Walker betrayed secrets so vital that they cost American lives in Vietnam and would have jeopardized national defense in the event of war with the USSR. During those eighteen years, he also ruined his dysfunctional family. His wife became an alcoholic and carried on a ten-year romance with his brother. His brother and son were lured by Walker into his espionage ring and imprisoned as a result. His son was a drug user. One of his daughters spent time in juvenile detention, and the other two were frequent runaways in their youth.

As a husband, Walker habitually cheated on his wife Barbara and bragged of his sexual exploits to his male pals. When a tavern he bought lost money, he tried to force Barbara into prostitution to support their family. When she discovered that Walker was a spy and protested, he beat her to a pulp. When the couple got divorced, he paid a pittance in alimony and child support and left her and their children in abject poverty. When he feared that his ex-wife might betray his spying out of spite, he asked the Soviets to kill her. After his arrest, he said "I should have killed Barbara."[1]

As a son, Walker took his mother along on a trip to Europe where, unbeknownst to her, he met with his Soviet spymasters and received thousands of dollars for US secrets. When they returned to the United States, Walker convinced his mother to carry a concealed money belt strapped to her waist without telling her what the contents were. The cash in the belt far exceeded the amount that American citizens were allowed to bring in under law. Walker made his own mother an unwitting accomplice to his crime and exposed her to possible arrest.[2]

As a father, Walker convinced his impressionable son Michael to join the US Navy and recruited him as a spy. Michael was sentenced to twenty-five years in prison as a result. Walker also tried to persuade his daughter Laura to remain in the army and spy with him. When she balked because she was pregnant, Walker told her to get an abortion, apparently needing another source more than a grandchild. As a sibling, Walker also recruited his brother, Art, into the ring. As a result Art Walker was sentenced to life imprisonment.

Benedict Arnold and Julius Rosenberg were spies, but they loved and cared for their wives and children. John Walker cared for no one but himself. At his sentencing, the disgusted judge remarked: "I look in vain for some redeeming aspect of your character. One is seized with the overwhelming feeling of revulsion that a human being could be as unprincipled as you."[3]

Walker ended up in that courtroom because of the wife he had abused for years. As Chapman Pincher noted in his study of espionage, "Probably the most hazardous complication . . . for the traitor who fears exposure is the danger of a woman scorned."[4] At his very first meeting with the KGB, its Washington chief, Boris Solomatin, advised Walker that, "if your wife finds out, she will be the weak link in the chain."[5] His warning turned out to be prophetic.

Barbara Walker's knowledge of her husband's espionage gnawed at her for sixteen years. She had reached for the phone in the past to tell the authorities but was too afraid of her husband to do it. Finally, in November

1984 she contacted the FBI and, her voice slurred from the vodka she constantly drank, revealed John Walker's treason. The FBI was initially skeptical that her story was only the drunken ramblings of a bitter ex-wife, but experienced counterintelligence agents recognized her tales of retrieving dead drops with her husband as more than fantasy. They became convinced when Walker's daughter, Laura, corroborated her mother's story and agreed to cooperate with the FBI to ensnare her abusive father.

The FBI was granted a warrant for full surveillance of John Walker. In May 1985 FBI surveillance revealed that Walker was telling various people that he would be out of town a certain weekend that month, but strangely he told each of them different destinations. The FBI suspected that Walker was planning contact with the KGB and launched massive mobile and aircraft surveillance to monitor his travel north toward Washington on May 19. The hunch proved correct. FBI agents spotted Walker leaving a cache with secret documents for the Soviets in a wooded Maryland suburb. Spending the night in a nearby hotel, Walker was called in the wee hours of the next morning by an FBI agent posing as the hotel manager, who tricked the spy into leaving his room because someone had supposedly hit his car in the parking lot. Agents cornered Walker by the elevator near his room and ended an eighteen-year espionage nightmare for the United States.

John Walker earned more than $1 million in nearly two decades of spying, enormous wealth for a man who had grown up in poverty. Born in July 1937 in Washington, Walker grew up in a family broken by a debt-ridden, alcoholic father who first lost his house and then his wife. The family moved to New York City, then Richmond, and finally settled in Scranton. During these early years of his life, Walker already showed glimmers of his innate evil. He was raised as a Catholic but practiced his religion in odd ways, throwing rocks through church windows, robbing from the poor box, and even stealing a tin of hosts intended for Holy Communion.[6]

By his teens, Walker was a high school dropout who was arrested for a series of burglaries. His older brother, Art, was a naval officer by then and convinced a judge to give the juvenile delinquent a choice: jail or military service. Walker followed his brother's advice and joined the US Navy in 1956. For a while, it seemed that Walker had found his niche in life. As a communications officer on submarines, he received the US Navy's equivalent of high school and college degrees and quickly ascended in the ranks, receiving seven promotions in nine years.[7]

In 1957, Walker married Barbara Crowley, one of seven children from a poor Boston family. The couple eventually had four children and, on a meager navy salary, they were so financially strapped that the family lived in a cramped trailer. Walker decided to supplement his income by buying the House of Bamboo bar near the Norfolk naval base, but the business rapidly lost money and only aggravated an already serious financial situation.

Walker was desperate. He was also the communications watch officer of the Atlantic Fleet's submarine command. In that job he managed coded message traffic and had access to the cryptographic systems of US nuclear submarines, which were considered the most invulnerable leg of the nation's triad of land, sea, and air missiles. The combination of desperation and access proved to be a volatile mixture.

In December 1967, Walker slipped into the Soviet Embassy in Washington unnoticed by nearby FBI observation posts. He put his offer bluntly to an embassy security officer: "I'm a naval officer. I'd like to make some money, and I'll give you genuine stuff in return."[8] His offer was probably one of the few honest statements Walker made in his life. To back up his claim, he handed over key settings for a US Navy cryptographic machine.[9]

Oleg Kalugin, the KGB officer who was chief of the political intelligence section at the time, reviewed the materials with Boris Solomatin, the KGB resident. Kalugin later resettled to the United States, where he recounted Walker's approach in a book about his KGB career. According to Kalugin, "Solomatin's eyes widened as he leafed through Walker's papers." "'I want this,' Solomatin cried." Walker, they agreed, was the kind of spy who turns up once in a lifetime.[10]

Moscow agreed with their assessment. At a second meeting in February 1968, the normally stingy Soviets passed Walker $5,000, a testimony to the value of his information. Because of Walker's potential, the KGB would not risk further face-to-face meetings in the United States. Instead, Walker was given a plan for "impersonal communications" consisting of dead drops where he would cache his secrets and an elaborate set of signals for spy and handler to communicate. His personal meetings with the KGB would be rare and occur years later only outside the United States in Casablanca and Vienna.

During his first decade as a spy, Walker allowed the Soviets to read America's national defense playbook. Walker was given a special rotor device that enabled him to pass the KGB the wiring pattern for cryptographic machines.[11] Along with technical manuals that Walker also provided, the Soviets were then able to reconstruct the machines. Their knock-off versions, however, still could not decipher communications without the keylists, information changed on a daily basis that enabled encryption and decryption of messages. Walker accommodated the KGB on that score as well. As he later confessed, "If it [a secret] was within my grasp, color it gone."[12] Thanks to Walker, the Soviets had unfettered access to ship movements, contingency attack plans in the event of war, and launch procedures for America's nuclear submarine fleet.

Walker was a once-in-a-lifetime spy not only because of the information he provided but also because of his attention to tradecraft procedures. He followed the KGB's impersonal communications plan religiously. The plan was a carefully choreographed espionage ballet. Walker would check for any surveillance along a serpentine route in the Washington suburbs. Once he was sure that no one was following him, he and his Soviet handlers would leave empty soda cans at predesignated locations indicating that both sides were ready for an exchange. At another predesignated site in the woods, he would leave a package with his stolen secrets hidden in a trash bag (he estimated that he passed the KGB six to eight rolls of film every three months in these caches).[13] The KGB, in turn, would leave a package at another site with wads of cash, instructions, new questions, and an occasional personal note designed to compensate for the lack of personal contact in the unorthodox relationship.

Walker also lived the cover of a dedicated naval officer and patriot to avoid suspicion. He was a vocal conservative and belonged to the virulently anticommunist John Birch Society. Ironically, the long hours he spent at work, while he was secretly photographing American secrets, were interpreted by his superiors as devotion to duty. In a 1972 performance review, when he had already been selling secrets for four years, his commanding officer described him as "intensely loyal, taking great pride in himself and the naval service, fiercely supporting its principles and traditions. He possesses a fine sense of personal honor and integrity, coupled with a great sense of humor."[14]

But even the best spies make mistakes. The paradox of espionage is that the money often motivating spies also triggers their downfall. In 1968 Walker's wife, Barbara, noticed that their financial situation was improving, but she was brushed off when she asked Walker about the money. She rifled his desk drawers one day and discovered a metal box with cash, sketches of dead drop sites, and KGB notes. Barbara immediately knew the source of Walker's newfound wealth and confronted him; she received a savage beating in return. Because she was now aware of his spying, he brought her along on two occasions when he exchanged materials with the Soviets. Her description of these outings years later would convince an initially skeptical FBI that her husband really was a spy.

Walker violated another tradecraft principle in his eagerness for more cash. The KGB, as normal practice, asked him to spot colleagues who they could target for recruitment as spies. Given their experience with agents recruiting other new spies in the 1930s and 1940s, the KGB preferred that their own trained professionals assess and cultivate potential recruits that were identified by their spies. Walker decided to take the initiative to recruit a new spy on his own.

Walker needed a new spy because he was facing a dilemma. In 1976 he would be due for a periodic reinvestigation and a polygraph test to maintain his top-secret clearance. Walker feared that he would be unable to pass the polygraph test and decided that he would retire rather than risk exposure. Still, he had become addicted to his secret income. So he decided to recruit a replacement with continuing access to top-secret US Navy materials.

Walker was blessed with the natural instincts of a professional intelligence officer to assess candidates for recruitment as spies. He had a demonic ability to sense a person's vulnerabilities and "an ability to bend others to his will."[15] He also had no qualms about exploiting people for personal gain, which, in fact, had been the key feature of all his personal relationships, even with his own family.

Walker's cultivation of Jerry Whitworth was a textbook recruitment. Walker and Whitworth became friends when they were both instructors at a naval communications school in San Diego. The two were both divorced hedonists and spent hours aboard Walker's boat, aptly named the *Dirty Old Man,* with lady friends and cases of liquor. Walker realized that Whitworth shared his love for the good life, but he was patient in sizing up and manipulating his new target before making a recruitment pitch.

Their personal bond was strong because they shared similar backgrounds. Just two years younger than Walker, Whitworth had been born in Oklahoma, abandoned by his father at birth, and grown up hating his stepfather. In 1956, he joined the US Navy after high school and left after his first hitch to attend college. But he flunked out and reenlisted in the navy, where, like Walker, he turned in a solid performance over the years as a communications specialist.

Walker gradually elicited information from Whitworth to evaluate his prospects as a spy. Whitworth confided that he had never informed the navy about his divorce so he could continue to receive his wife's allotments in his salary. Whitworth was defrauding the government. If Whitworth was willing to commit one crime for money, Walker reasoned, he might be ready to commit a more profitable one. Walker already noticed that Whitworth envied his comfortable financial status, so he began dropping vague hints about his side business to entice his target.

Walker crafted a subtle recruitment pitch. He never asked Whitworth to spy and never mentioned the Soviets. Walker framed the offer as a business consultancy and remained vague about his clients. Knowing that Whitworth was an ardent supporter of Israel, Walker hinted that the Israelis would be among the recipients of his information. If Whitworth had needed a rationale to cloak his greed, Walker had given it to him. In 1974 Whitworth took the bait and agreed to pass secrets to John Walker, somehow rationalizing to himself that he was aiding the Israeli cause.

Walker's KGB handlers were angry when he presented them Whitworth's recruitment as a fait accompli, but they soon changed their opinion once they began receiving the new recruit's information. For the KGB, Whitworth was a clone of Walker—he served in similar assignments and could supply the same steady stream of keylists. But Whitworth offered even more. He was trained in satellite communications just at the time DOD was updating its worldwide military communications and launching new satellites as the linchpin of the new network.[16] Whitworth quickly proved his value by passing a manual for a new tactical satellite communications system.

In 1976, with Whitworth now in place, John Walker retired from the navy and divorced his wife. He formed his own private detective agency, partly to cover his KGB payments and partly to learn a trade that would improve the security of his spying. Thanks to Whitworth, Walker was still earning enough money from the Soviets to support his lavish lifestyle. Whitworth provided the Soviets with a gold mine in 1982 when he participated in a huge fleet exercise involving the NATO allies. Whitworth's information revealed to the Soviets the military's operational plans and coordination among the allies and between US ships and air elements. Naval experts later claimed that this information "saved the Soviets at least fifty man-years of analytic labor."[17]

Whitworth was meeting Walker between two and four times a year to pass up to fifty rolls of filmed secrets, and his monthly spy salary had jumped from $2,000 to $6,000. By the time he was arrested, Whitworth had garnered about $335,000 from the KGB. Unlike Walker, however, Whitworth wavered in his commitment to espionage. Increasingly worried that he would be caught, Whitworth told Walker in 1979 that he was retiring from the navy. Walker again proved to be an effective intelligence officer by playing on his friend's avarice to dissuade him from quitting the trade.

Walker, however, only convinced his friend for a few years. In 1983 Whitworth retired from the navy without advising Walker. But his worries still gnawed at him, and he decided to confess and seek immunity from prosecution. In 1984, he sent an anonymous letter to the FBI, signed Rus, in which he admitted his espionage activities. He specified that he was giving away cryptographic information but claimed he had not realized at first that the information went to the KGB. The FBI fulfilled his request to place newspapers ads in response to his overtures. Whitworth, realizing that he would probably not receive the immunity for which he had bargained, got cold feet and signed off.[18] A year would pass before he would be arrested.

Whitworth's fears had persuaded Walker to find other sources, so he began to cultivate his own brother, Art, for possible recruitment. Art was the closest the dysfunctional Walker family had come to a success story. After graduating from the University of Scranton, Art had enlisted in the navy and risen through the ranks as an antisubmarine warfare specialist to lieutenant commander. After retiring from the navy in 1973, he set up a radio repair business that his brother John bankrolled.

Art's business failed and, like many retired military officers, he found work with a defense contractor. In 1980, he was hired for his naval experience by the VSE Corporation of Chesapeake, Maryland, and worked on classified DOD contracts.[19] John manipulated his own brother just as he had Whitworth. Art felt that he owed John for settling the debts from his failed business and soon agreed to provide unclassified VSE documents for cash. Besides, Art decided that he deserved his brother's lifestyle: "Arthur had played it straight all his life, worked hard and no one seemed to care. What had he gotten in return?"[20]

In 1981, Art passed John a classified VSE report about the maintenance and repair of amphibious assault ships.[21] John, now that he was retired, traveled to Vienna twice a year to meet his KGB contacts and brought them Art's documents. But compared with the cryptographic treasures that John Walker and Whitworth fed to the KGB, Art's information was thin gruel, and the KGB dismissed the reports as "very low-level junk."[22] In exchange for this "junk," Art Walker received a measly $2,000 and life imprisonment.

Walker even cultivated his own children for espionage, as if his criminal career was a family business that they would someday inherit. He had flirted with the idea of persuading his two eldest daughters, Margaret and Cynthia, to join the military so they could become his spies. His youngest daughter, Laura, joined the army in 1978 on her own initiative after graduating from high school, and, as luck would have it, she was trained in communications. Walker smelled fresh blood for the spy ring and made his move. After years of neglect, he began to visit Laura and shower on her the paternal love she had craved.

Laura Walker married an army colleague who became a habitual drug user. As bills began to plague the newlyweds, John Walker decided that his daughter was ripe for recruitment. When Laura informed him that she was leaving the army because she was pregnant, Walker snapped "Jeez, Laura, why don't you just get an abortion? I mean, you can always have more kids later."[23] Laura, who had a strong independent streak, was horrified and rebuffed the offer. Eight years later, she repeated the story to the FBI and confirmed the details of her mother's story about Walker.

Walker's youngest child, his son Michael, was far weaker than his sister. Early on, Michael repeated the mistakes of his father's childhood, dropping out of high school and experimenting with drugs. After he eventually graduated, Michael moved in with his father and began to idolize him. John Walker was "cool"; he had money, girls, a boat, and an airplane; and his son longed to please his dad and emulate him. And Walker needed a replacement for Whitworth, who was proving less and less committed to the spy game.

Following in his father's footsteps, Michael enlisted in the navy. John Walker was delighted by the prospect of a new spy but waited until Michael got married and grew disenchanted with navy life before making his pitch. He did not really have to recruit his son. Michael had learned years before that his father was a spy when his mother had blurted out the nasty family secret to him. When Walker made his pitch, Michael was elated: "I thought it was really cool. I mean, he finally trusted me enough to tell me what he did. He thought I was man enough to handle what he was saying."[24] Like a schoolboy eager to show his dad a good report card, Michael Walker rushed home from his navy base a few days later with his first stolen document.

In 1984, Michael Walker was assigned to the USS *Nimitz,* at that time the largest aircraft carrier in the US Navy. Although he was a low-ranking administrative clerk, he was able to burrow through bags full of classified documents to be destroyed. When the FBI opened the package John Walker had set down in the Maryland woods in May 1985, agents found 129 classified documents from the USS *Nimitz* laden with Michael's fingerprints.[25] John Walker had sealed his son's fate. Michael Walker had followed his father into the navy and into espionage, and then he followed him into jail with a twenty-five-year prison sentence.

The FBI found other incriminating evidence in Walker's last package for the KGB. Walker's scribbled notes and alphabetic designators for his sources were sufficient leads for the FBI to arrest Art Walker and Jerry Whitworth in short order. In one final act of betrayal, John Walker agreed to testify against Whitworth, his friend and recruited agent. In return, Walker was promised a lighter sentence for Michael, perhaps the only positive thing the father ever did for his son.

Whitworth was convicted in July 1986 on seven counts of espionage and one count of tax evasion. A month later, the judge sentenced him to 365 years in prison and imposed a fine of $410,000. The judge described Whitworth to the court as "a zero to the bone. He believes in nothing. His life is devoted to determining the wind direction and how he can make a profit from the coming storm."[26] Arthur Walker, despite the KGB's scathing appraisal of his information, received a life sentence; and Michael was sentenced to twenty-five years because of his father's cooperation. John Walker was sentenced to two life terms plus ten years.

On the surface, Walker's motivation for spying appeared to be pure, unadulterated greed. Walker himself confirmed that money was his only motive: "I became a spy because that is what I had access to. If I'd worked in a bank, I would have taken money. If I'd had access to dope, I would've sold drugs. The point is I became a spy because I needed money. It was as simple as that."[27]

Was money the true motive? Money intrinsically is worthless—its only value is what it can acquire. The $1 million Walker was paid for his secrets certainly bought him the luxuries he was denied in his poverty. Beyond that, however, money also bought him the status and the sense of importance that so many others would crave in the 1980s and that had been denied him.

Self-importance is one of the clinical indicators of psychopathic behavior. Robert Hunter, the FBI lead agent in the case, believed that Walker "fit the personality profile of a psychopath" based on the diagnosis of a bureau behavioral scientist.[28] Walker exhibited other indicators of the profile. He was incapable of loyalty or love, deceptive, outwardly charming, callous, predatory, promiscuous, and shallow in relationships. He took great joy in hoodwinking people, as if pulling the wool over someone's eyes gave him hidden power over the target. Postarrest interviews revealed that Walker relished cheating on his wife, fooling Whitworth about the recipient of his pilfered secrets, and deceiving his children as he slowly tried to manipulate them into espionage. Above all, he enjoyed hoodwinking the US Navy. After his arrest, he crowed that "K-Mart had better security than the navy" and boasted that he had forged his own security clearance with a rubber stamp he bought at a store for $2.97.[29]

Psychopaths are also incapable of remorse and blame others for their actions. Walker's comments to the author Peter Earley after his arrest epitomize this behavior: "What has happened to me is unfair. I've been destroyed by the government for no real reason and so have Art and Mike. Our lives have been ruined and these prison sentences are just like salt in the wounds. If they let us out now, what would we do? They've taken all our money. Do you think anyone would hire us? It's really unfair."[30]

Walker's autobiography, *My Life as a Spy*, is laced with accusations against others for all the woes of his life. He blames the US Navy's hard-drinking culture for his wife's alcoholism and blames his wife for their children's problems and his decision to spy. His enlistment of his brother in espionage and attempt to recruit his daughter were, in his distorted view, "altruistic," because both were experiencing financial problems.[31] Nowhere does he mention his abandonment of his family or his beatings and continual abuse of his wife.

Walker also blamed the US government for his espionage. Disgusted by the government's saber-rattling "deceptions," Walker followed the examples of other American spies by claiming that he betrayed US secrets for noble motives. Among the motives that impelled him to spy, he claimed that the primary one was to counter US deception and improve bilateral relations. By providing the Soviets with proof that the United States had no intentions to invade the USSR, Walker alone could reduce the prospects of war.[32] According to Walker, money was the least compelling of the motives that drove him into espionage, though his entire relationship with the KGB proved otherwise.

John Walker spied not only because he loved money and all it could buy but also because he was an incurable psychopath. Psychopaths are also delusional, and Walker's fantasies were monumental. In his autobiography, he claimed that his espionage was "changing things on a world-wide level."[33] He believed that the secrets he betrayed prompted Soviet leader Leonid Brezhnev to support a strategic arms limitation treaty, and he joked that he should have received the Nobel Peace Prize for his role in winning the Cold War.[34] Walker's concern about a future job also showed that he had lost touch regarding the reality of his plight. Considering the damage he and his fellow spies had done to national security over a span of nearly two decades, he would never have to worry about a job on the outside.

The damage caused by the Walker spy ring could have given the Soviets a significant advantage if the Cold War had suddenly erupted into a military conflict. The cryptographic information that Walker and Whitworth provided over the years enabled the Soviets to read more than 1 million encrypted messages that exposed all the tactics, operations, and capabilities of the United States' sea defenses.[35] The traffic also contained details of American missile defenses, cruise missile technology, and the vulnerabilities of spy satellites.

The secrets of America's nuclear submarines were invaluable to the Soviets. Walker spied at a time when the United States had established decisive superiority over the Soviet Union at sea. US submarines had developed measures to remain quiet and maneuver undetected far more effectively than their noisier Soviet counterparts. The nuclear missiles in these submarines were considered the most secure part of the nation's nuclear triad, less vulnerable to attack than land-based ballistic missiles and airborne missiles on aging B-52 bombers.

The cryptographic materials that the Walker ring passed to the Soviets could have also allowed them to develop measures to prevent communications during a war, which might have enabled them to prevent a first strike or massive retaliation in a counterstrike. In an affidavit submitted to the court, the director of naval intelligence at that time, William Studeman, detailed the "potential war-winning implications for the Soviet side" of the Walker ring's betrayal.[36] Walker and his fellow spies alone had upset the balance of nuclear defense in the Soviets' favor.

Walker's spying career was at its height during the Vietnam conflict. Some in the military wondered why military targets in Vietnam were either evacuated or reinforced just before B-52 bombing runs. As Oleg Kalugin confirmed, Walker and Whitworth had passed keylists specifically used in Vietnam that enabled the Soviets to read communications about targets and bombing times.[37] The Soviets undoubtedly shared this information with the North Vietnamese, even though Walker believed that he was "too valuable" for the Soviets to risk exposing such data to an ally. As a result, North Vietnamese air defenses would have been alerted and able to shoot down American planes. Walker simply rationalized away his possible role in the deaths and imprisonments of American servicemen shot down over Vietnam.

Perhaps the best testimony of Walker's importance came from Soviet intelligence officers. Oleg Kalugin called Walker "the number one agent in the history of the KGB."[38] A few months after Walker's arrest, the Soviet defector Vitaliy Yurchenko echoed Kalugin's assessment. Yurchenko told his CIA handlers that, according to corridor gossip in the KGB, the Walker case was the greatest in KGB history and even surpassed the atomic bomb spies.[39] Yurchenko claimed that he was told by a KGB colleague that, in the event of war, Soviet ability to read American messages would be "devastating."[40] According to Yurchenko, Walker, who retired from the navy as a chief warrant officer, was awarded the honorary rank of admiral of the Soviet Navy for his espionage cooperation.

Fortunately, the United States and Soviet Union did not go to war. Still, the US Navy was required to develop costly countermeasures to repair Walker's damage. The chief of naval operations, Admiral James Watkins, roughly estimated that $100 million would be required to restore that balance.[41] During the 1980s, when the gap between rich and poor grew wider, that $100 million in taxpayers' money could have built schools, hospitals, and roads for American citizens.

In an earlier era, the enormous damage done by Walker would have undoubtedly earned him the death penalty. But at the time of Walker's sentencing, life imprisonment, not the death penalty, was the maximum punishment for espionage in peacetime.[42] The advantages Walker afforded the Soviets regarding the nation's sea-based nuclear deterrent equaled the Soviet theft of atomic bomb secrets through Julius Rosenberg and the other atom bomb spies in the 1940s. Walker betrayed secrets to America's sworn enemy. Rosenberg shared secrets with an American wartime ally. Rosenberg sat in the electric chair for his crime, and Walker sits in prison for his. But the Walker case ultimately did have an impact on espionage legislation: Congress passed a law mandating the death sentence for spying by military personnel in peacetime.[43]

The parallels and differences in the Rosenberg and Walker cases illustrate the impact of historical context on espionage. The Rosenbergs were both symbols and arrested spies. Their case symbolized the sharp divide between conservatives and liberals on communism, and their trial galvanized both sides into an impassioned debate. For liberals, the Rosenbergs were iconic victims of a paranoid, right-wing witch hunt. For conservatives, they were symbols of an insidious foreign menace threatening America's way of life. The Rosenbergs were ultimately executed more because of what they represented than what they did.

The Rosenbergs spied for firmly held ideological motives; Walker spied because he was a psychopath. Walker lived only for himself and justly had no supporters. If he symbolized anything, it was lax military security and continuing complacency about the threat of espionage.

America, however, had unfortunately grown accustomed to espionage by the time of Walker's arrest. The exposure of Soviet bloc spies became as routine a part of the Cold War as arms negotiations and saber rattling at summit meetings.

John Walker was compromised by the wife he had tortured for years. Other American spies were exposed by spies and defectors in hostile intelligence services. Among them were two who were compromised by Vitaliy Yurchenko, one of the most bizarre Soviet defector cases of the Cold War.

While the Soviets were reading US Navy messages because of Walker, the Americans were reading secret Soviet military messages. Unfortunately, one of the spies revealed by Yurchenko told the Soviets all about it.

The Spy in the National Security Agency

RONALD PELTON

What man, an exile from his native soil, can flee himself?

HORACE, Odes, *Book 2, in* The Complete Works of Horace, *203*

One of the most mystifying stories in the history of Cold War espionage began on August 1, 1985, when Vitaliy Yurchenko, a high-ranking KGB officer, ambled into the US Embassy in Rome and requested asylum. CIA headquarters was elated at the initial news. Yurchenko offered a potential counterespionage gold mine because he claimed he was deputy chief of the First Department of the KGB's First Chief Directorate, which was responsible for overseeing espionage operations in the United States and Canada. Besides, Yurchenko was already known to the CIA and FBI. He had served as the security officer in the Soviet Embassy in Washington from 1975 to 1980. The defector was exactly who he claimed to be.[1]

The CIA's initial euphoria was soon tempered by information from his first debriefing. Volunteers with counterespionage information are often a double-edged sword, like an "auction prize of a double date with Michelle Pfeiffer and Typhoid Mary."[2] The good news is that volunteers from counterespionage services reveal who and where the spies are, so a government can stop the hemorrhaging of its secrets. The bad news is that they reveal how serious the hemorrhage has been.

Yurchenko's first news was difficult to bear. He revealed that there were two major spies in the US intelligence community, one a fired CIA officer and the other a former analyst from NSA.[3] The CIA needed the full details as soon as possible, so Yurchenko was immediately whisked out of Italy to the United States.

Yurchenko serenaded his CIA debriefers about a host of KGB operations directed against the United States, but he gradually grew moody and irritable. One of his fantasies was living happily ever after with his lover, the wife of a Soviet diplomat then stationed in Canada. The CIA spirited Yurchenko to Canada, where he appeared suddenly at the lady's doorstep. Instead of the joyful reunion Yurchenko had envisioned, the startled woman spurned him on the spot.

Yurchenko's despondency deepened. He complained that his CIA security officers were treating him like a prisoner. He flew into a rage over leaks to the press about his defection. He had left his family behind in the USSR and believed they would be spared the wrath of the KGB if his defection never became public. Ironically, the leaks may have been prompted by CIA director William Casey, who was bursting with joy over his new prize. As then–CIA deputy director Robert Gates noted, "Casey was like a child with a new toy with Yurchenko. . . . He couldn't help bragging about this great CIA coup."[4]

Casey's new toy was broken. On November 2, just three months after he walked into the US Embassy in Rome, Yurchenko walked away from the US government. While dining with a CIA handler at Au Pied de Cochon, a fashionable restaurant in Washington, Yurchenko excused himself and left. When he did not return to the table, the CIA and FBI scoured the area, fearing the worst. The Soviet Embassy was only a mile from the restaurant.

Those fears were realized two days later when Yurchenko surfaced at an embassy press conference. "I was forcibly abducted in Rome," Yurchenko declared to the press. "Unconscious, I was brought from Italy to the USA. . . . Here I was kept in isolation, forced to take drugs."[5] The spectacle was an embarrassment to the US government, and particularly to the CIA.

After a brief three months as a defector, Yurchenko boarded an Aeroflot jet back to his homeland. Aside from the embarrassment of his scurrilous charges, his redefection raised serious doubts in the CIA about his original intentions.[6] He had provided a wealth of information in three months, unmasked two major spies, and alerted the CIA to the compromise of key sources inside the USSR. Counterintelligence experts began to dissect Yurchenko's information to determine if he had really damaged the KGB or if he had simply passed throwaway information that was no longer of use to the Russians. Even more disturbing, they reasoned, he may have been dispatched by the KGB to cover the tracks of a mole still deeply buried in US intelligence. Doubts about him soared when he appeared in a brief West German television interview in 1986—apparently, he had not met the fate of a true betrayer of Soviet secrets.[7]

The future unmasking of Aldrich Ames in the CIA and Robert Hanssen in the FBI, which are respectively described in chapters 18 and 19, provided more grist for the mill of skeptics who were convinced that Yurchenko's defection had been a KGB-orchestrated attempt to protect the two spies. Still, a majority at the CIA concluded that Yurchenko had betrayed too much information to be a deception agent sent by the KGB.

Yurchenko was no more a double agent than Yuriy Nosenko had been two decades earlier. In those twenty years, the KGB had remained convinced that the CIA was capable of using and willing to use mind-altering drugs or other methods on an intelligence volunteer fully under its control on US territory. For the KGB, risking the possibility that a dispatched double agent would be exposed outweighed the gains of feeding some critical information to deceive their American adversaries.

The two major spies whom Yurchenko compromised, Edward Lee Howard and Ronald Pelton, were considered throwaways by some because both were former employees without current access to secrets. The KGB, however, rarely allows its spies to fade into quiet retirement if they can still steal a secret. After David Greenglass, the mechanical engineer who spied on the Manhattan Project at Los Alamos, was discharged from the army and lost his access to atomic secrets, the KGB offered to fund his college education at the University of Chicago so he could spot scientists for recruitment or obtain a job in secret government research. David Barnett was long retired from the CIA when he shared secrets with the KGB, which then directed him to find a new job in the intelligence community. Robert Lee Johnson left the army, but after he rejoined at the KGB's direction, he obtained far better access as a guard at a European courier facility.

The KGB could presumably have knocked on Pelton's door and asked him to rejoin the intelligence community. Until Yurchenko revealed the existence of a spy in NSA, Pelton had escaped suspicion. Yurchenko told the CIA that an NSA employee had called the Soviet Embassy in January 1980 and then walked in to offer his services as a spy. Although he could not recall the volunteer's name and some years had passed, Yurchenko recognized the culprit from a batch of photographs of NSA employees shown him by the FBI.[8]

The person in the photograph was retired NSA employee Pelton. He grew up in Benton Harbor, Michigan, and after high school he spent four years in the air force. Based on his military experience, he was hired by NSA in 1965 and spent six years abroad in the United Kingdom before returning to the United States. In the next few years, he specialized in NSA operations against the Soviets. Although he performed well as an analyst, he was then married with four children, and he failed miserably in managing his personal finances. He was burdened with more than $65,000 in debt and declared bankruptcy. In July 1979, after fourteen years at NSA, he resigned to seek a better-paying job outside and reverse his ailing fortunes.

Many Americans have spied for money. Some spy out of pure greed, others because of financial crises that have spun wildly out of their control. Pelton was in the latter category. His foray into the private sector lasted a few months and failed to cure his financial ills. Desperate, with only a few hundred dollars left in his dwindling bank account, he walked into the Soviet Embassy and volunteered his services as a spy.

During the next few years, Pelton met with the KGB five times in Europe to betray NSA secrets. Unlike John Walker, he did not have a single document or cryptographic card to share with his new paymasters. Pelton, however, did possess a photographic memory and encyclopedic knowledge of the Soviet operations on which he had worked at NSA. In the course of his KGB debriefings, he revealed a host of US technical collection operations to the KGB, including a costly project code-named Ivy Bells.[9]

Ivy Bells was a clandestine technical operation in which US Navy frogmen placed telephone taps on a Soviet undersea cable in the Sea of Okhotsk to intercept conversations about missile tests and military exercises in the Far East. Every six months the frogmen would return to retrieve the pods they had emplaced, now full of taped conversations. Some of the phone conversations were not encrypted because the Soviets felt confident that the undersea cable was invulnerable to interception, but they had underestimated American ingenuity and technical prowess. Eventually, US satellite reconnaissance showed unusual Soviet ship activity around the tapped cable and the frogmen swam to the site only to find that their pods had vanished.[10]

The risk of discovery had always been high because the Soviets could have checked the cable at any time for routine maintenance or for routine security checks. The real reason behind the disappearance of the pods only surfaced when Yurchenko told the CIA that an NSA volunteer had betrayed the operation to the KGB. The Ivy Bells revelation helped the FBI pinpoint Pelton among the list of suspects for Yurchenko's spy because he was among the very limited number of NSA employees with authorized access to the highly compartmented operation.

Identification of a spy did not easily lead to prosecution, as the FBI had discovered in the past. More than thirty years had passed since Judith Coplon, a DOJ employee spying for the Soviets, was arrested after her espionage surfaced in the Venona Project transcripts. Even after Coplon was arrested while passing information to a Soviet, she never spent a day in jail. Others had also slipped through the net because intelligence sources could not be compromised and other evidence could not be found.

Pelton illustrated the dilemma. By the time the FBI had sufficient grounds to move on him, Yurchenko had redefected and would hardly be released by his KGB masters to testify. All the lead information in FBI hands came from Yurchenko and could be easily discredited by a defense attorney, especially because Yurchenko's reputation as a reliable reporter was in doubt after his return to the USSR. Besides, the compromise of Ivy Bells, a risky operation on a remote seabed near Soviet territory, could have resulted from any number of glitches.

FBI agents firmly believed they had their man, but they had no evidence. So, after close coordination with DOJ attorneys who would have to try the case, they devised a strategy: They would persuade Pelton to confess. The FBI's plan was a tricky one. Agents would have to teeter on a legal tightrope, gently coaxing Pelton to talk and admit his crime, yet advising him of his rights and his option to contact an attorney at any time. If Pelton decided to call an attorney, he would be advised not to utter another word.

The FBI confronted Pelton around the Thanksgiving holiday in November 1985.[11] Divorced, Pelton was living with another woman, drinking, using drugs, and barely eking out a living on a job at an Annapolis boat company.[12] Agents casually invited Pelton to a hotel near his home for a chat and dealt with him gingerly rather than bulldoze him with a heavy-handed show of evidence. The agents calmly outlined the information from Yurchenko, whose redefection had been publicized by the time of the interview. The agents then politely asked Pelton to fill in the story from the time he entered the Soviet Embassy.

Pelton was reassured by the agents' approach. He thought the FBI might consider using him as a double agent against the Soviets and he could connive his way out of jail. The agents cajoled, elicited, and wheedled Pelton's confession from him. They advised him of his rights to an attorney—at points he wavered and pondered calling one—but the agents persuaded him to continue talking. He laid out the story of his spying, but for prosecution the FBI needed proof that he had passed classified information to a foreign power. Finally, he crossed the line and admitted revealing the Ivy Bells project to the Soviets.

Pelton was arrested on November 25 and indicted the following month on six espionage-related charges. The court assigned him the same lawyer as it did to John Walker. Despite his earlier admissions to the FBI, Pelton pled not guilty; but on June 5, 1986, a jury of his peers deemed otherwise. In December 1986 he was sentenced to three concurrent life sentences. One of Yurchenko's spies had been brought to justice. The other spy, however, would escape.

The Spy in the CIA

EDWARD LEE HOWARD

While seeking revenge, dig two graves—one for yourself.

DOUGLAS HORTON, *from the* Quotations Book

No one had to burrow through voice tapes or mug shots to identify the second spy Yurchenko fingered. In his first debriefing in Rome, Yurchenko revealed that another Soviet spy was a CIA officer who had been destined for an assignment in Moscow until he was fired for drug and alcohol abuse. According to Yurchenko, the spy had passed secrets to the KGB in Vienna in September 1984.

The CIA quickly realized who the spy was: Edward Lee Howard, who had been fired in 1983 after admitting to petty theft and drug and alcohol abuse during a polygraph test before his Moscow posting. The CIA also did not have to look far to determine the damage Howard had done. His espionage explained the loss of one of the CIA's top sources in the Cold War. Six weeks before Yurchenko defected, a CIA officer in Moscow had been apprehended by the KGB as he was about to meet the source, Adolf Tolkachev.

The CIA officer's arrest meant that Tolkachev had been compromised, which was confirmed in September 1985 when the Soviet press announced his arrest and execution for espionage. Tolkachev was an electronics engineer at the Moscow Aviation Institute, which was engaged in the highly classified research and development of the USSR's most advanced weapons systems. Institute researchers like Tolkachev worked on military projects so secret that they were not permitted to travel outside the USSR. Tolkachev, however, was not deterred, and he volunteered to spy for the CIA in Moscow under the nose of the KGB. He loathed the hypocrisy and oppression of the Soviet regime and offered to share military secrets with the CIA so he could strike back at his government.

For seven years, despite intense KGB surveillance of the US Embassy in Moscow, the CIA acquired hundreds of rolls of film from Tolkachev full of information about the latest Soviet developments in aircraft electronics, fighter aircraft, air defenses, and offensive missile systems.[1] DOD estimated that Tolkachev's information saved the US government millions of dollars in developing countermeasures against Soviet weaponry. According to one DOD memorandum, "The impact of [Tolkachev's] reporting is limitless in terms of enhancing US military systems' effectiveness, and in the potential to save lives and equipment."[2] Tolkachev's information would have given the United States a clear edge in the event of military conflict—he was America's counterweight to John Walker.

Edward Lee Howard knew about the Tolkachev operation because he was tabbed as one of the officers who would be handling the Soviet spy in Moscow. He had been trained by the CIA in surveillance detection, impersonal communications, and the Russian language—and by all accounts, he seemed to be a capable officer. However, unbeknownst to the CIA, when he felt wronged, Howard lived and breathed vengeance like others breathed air. The CIA triggered that vengeance by firing him.

On the surface Howard possessed the ideal credentials for the CIA's clandestine service: higher education, overseas experience, and a knowledge of foreign languages. He was the son of a US Air Force sergeant and had grown up in England, Germany, and Japan. After receiving a degree in international relations from the University of Texas, he volunteered for the Peace Corps in Colombia, where he met and married Mary Howard, a fellow volunteer. He then transferred to the Agency for International Development and spent three years on development projects in Peru.

Howard was hired by the CIA as an operations officer trainee in January 1981, and after training he received an assignment to Moscow, a prestigious post for a new officer. Moscow was the heart of enemy territory. KGB scrutiny of Americans was intense, but the operations were among the most important in the CIA. Running operations and beating the KGB on its own turf were the most highly rewarding achievements in the career of a CIA operations officer.

Howard had to undergo another polygraph test before he left for Moscow because of the sensitivity of the assignment. After failing four tests, he admitted that he had continued to use drugs (which he had admitted on his polygraph test as an applicant) and had stolen $40 from the purse of a female passenger on an airline flight while she went to the restroom.[3] Howard's case was submitted to a CIA review board, which voted thumbs down on his continued employment. In May 1983, after little more than two years at the CIA, he was fired.

Although Howard knew he was in trouble, he was shocked at the abrupt firing. He would later say that he was "angered by the callous way they had fired me and thrown me out on the street."[4] His resentment began to simmer immediately. The same day he was fired, he encountered a CIA colleague in the corridors and angrily related to him the harsh treatment he had just received.

The CIA faces special risks when firing employees because they leave with knowledge of classified information. The risk was particularly grave with Howard, who walked out the door with the CIA's most precious secrets about Soviet operations. To mitigate the effects of his firing, the CIA kept him on the payroll for another month and arranged interviews with a psychiatrist to gauge his level of resentment. But these efforts did not mollify Howard.

Howard's vengeance was seething below the surface. Despite routine background checks of applicants, the CIA was unaware that Howard had a history of exacting revenge for real or imagined slights. Later, after his case broke, investigators unearthed past incidents of his vengefulness. A former colleague claimed that Howard told him he had grown to hate Peruvians and, one day, just for pure spite, he approached an innocent Peruvian on the street and sprayed him with mace. His thirst for revenge continued after his CIA firing. After a brawl with some Hispanic youths in New Mexico, Howard followed them in his car and fired his .357 magnum in the air to threaten them. The incident resulted in his arrest on charges of illegal gun possession and aggravated assault, but he was released on probation.[5]

Howard was also planning his revenge against the CIA. At first he just exhibited strange behavior, making crank calls to the CIA office in Moscow and showing up unexpectedly at a CIA instructor's home to complain about his unjust dismissal. Howard had also remained friends with another CIA colleague, William Bosch, who had resigned after a tour in South America. Howard suggested to Bosch that they go to Mexico City and approach the Soviets there in order to strike back at the CIA.[6] Bosch dismissed Howard's suggestion as the angry ravings of a disgruntled ex-employee. Howard's proposal only surfaced when the FBI later interviewed Bosch. But by then it would be too late.

Howard's unexpected visit to his former CIA instructor in May 1984 disturbed Burton Gerber, then chief of the CIA's Soviet Division, who decided to dispatch the officer and a psychiatrist to New Mexico to gauge his mental state. Howard had resettled there after his firing and found a job as an economist in the state legislature. Shockingly, Howard admitted to them that, on a trip to Washington, he had loitered outside the Soviet Embassy for a while and had pondered spying for the KGB. Eventually, Howard claimed, he had come to his senses and walked away.[7]

Gerber alerted CIA security officials, and the CIA paid for psychological treatment for Howard. But these measures were not enough to prevent Howard from striking back at his former employers. Just a few months after Howard was visited in New Mexico, he exacted his revenge. In his first meeting with the KGB in Europe in September 1984, he condemned Adolf Tolkachev to death by revealing the case to the KGB. During that meeting and at a subsequent one in August 1985, he also told the KGB details about the CIA's modus operandi to elude KGB surveillance in Moscow and to meet Tolkachev and other agents. Knowledge of that modus operandi jeopardized other spies that the CIA was still running inside the USSR at the time.

When Tolkachev's arrest was announced, the CIA already knew that at least one person on the restricted access list for the highly compartmented operation, Edward Lee Howard, was embittered over his dismissal and had even hinted at thoughts of espionage. Still, the CIA did not inform the FBI about Howard until after Yurchenko's revelations.

The FBI immediately launched a full investigation of Howard. On September 19, a month after Yurchenko's revelation, the FBI decided to confront Howard after he expressed willingness to meet with them. Because

Yurchenko did not want his defection publicized, the FBI agents showed Howard a news story about the defection of a KGB officer, Oleg Gordievsky, and advised him that the new defector had fingered him as a Soviet spy.[8] Howard denied the allegation but invoked his right to an attorney. The FBI gave him twenty-four hours to find one.

Howard had been under complete physical and electronic surveillance by the FBI since the onset of the investigation, and he was trailed back to his home that night. Howard vowed he would not be caught even if he had to abandon his wife and young son.

In an ironic twist, Howard used the same techniques he had learned to defeat the KGB in Moscow to elude the FBI in New Mexico. One of those techniques was the Jack-in-the-Box. The JIB, as it was called in the CIA, appeared to be a normal attaché case, but concealed inside was a spring-loaded dummy torso. The concept was simple: While being trailed by KGB surveillance, a car with a driver and front-seat passenger would turn a corner along a preplanned route. When the car was momentarily out of sight, the passenger would jump out and escape through the streets while the driver activated the JIB. The dummy torso would pop up in the front seat to replace the departed passenger. Once surveillance caught sight of its target again, nothing would appear amiss.[9]

On September 21, Howard fashioned a dummy head out of Styrofoam and shoulders from a wire coat hanger and attached them to a cut-off broomstick. He kissed his wife and son one last time, and then she drove him in their red Oldsmobile along a winding route away from their home so he could make his escape. At a jump-off point Howard had selected earlier, he rolled out of the car onto the grass and scrambled through bushes to make his escape.

Howard's elaborate ruse proved unnecessary. A rookie FBI agent manning the observation post in a vehicle near Howard's home was blinded by the glare of the desert sun and had not even seen the couple drive away. He did not realize that the couple had left their home until Mary Howard pulled into her garage later with a makeshift dummy seated beside her. The CIA had not told the FBI about Howard soon enough; now the FBI had not watched him closely enough. Both would pay heavily for their lapses.

Howard escaped by a circuitous route through Tucson, Copenhagen, and Helsinki, where his KGB patrons presumably met him and whisked him off to Moscow. A year later, in September 1986, he was paraded before the press by the Soviets like the NSA spies Mitchell and Martin. He denied any espionage and thanked the USSR for granting him political asylum for "humane considerations."

The propaganda embarrassment of an escaped spy paled in comparison with the damage Howard had inflicted on national security. The loss of Tolkachev and the other agents he betrayed was devastating. At a time when the United States had vastly increased its defense spending in the Reagan years, Tolkachev's inside information would have provided key insights into the USSR's efforts to keep pace. The compromise was equally devastating at the CIA, where the obligation to ensure an agent's security, especially one of Tolkachev's caliber, had been broken.

The other crushing blow for the CIA was Howard's compromise of its modus operandi in Moscow: the entire arsenal of tricks and ruses that it used to evade KGB surveillance and steal secrets with impunity inside the Soviet Union. To prevent espionage by its citizens, the KGB had instituted strict security measures at classified facilities and banned foreign travel by those with top-secret access. Combined with its intensive surveillance of foreigners, especially known or suspected intelligence officers, the KGB remained confident that it operated an effective counterespionage program. But the Tolkachev operation proved that the KGB had been wrong.

Howard enabled the KGB to level the playing field. Armed with knowledge of CIA tactics developed over decades, the KGB could effectively thwart operations to gather Soviet secrets from spies in their government and military. The CIA would have to start from scratch and build new capabilities to elude the KGB that could take years, an uncomfortably long period at the height of Cold War tensions in the mid-1980s.

The Howard case also sparked a wave of embarrassing cries for CIA scalps at home. As then–CIA deputy director Robert Gates noted, "Howard was the CIA's most devastating counterintelligence setback up to that time."[10] William Casey, the CIA director, was considerably harsher in his scathing attack against his Directorate of Operations (DO). He ordered the CIA's inspector general to review the DO's handling of the case and dismissed two drafts of the report as insipid.

Casey was angered after reading a highly critical report on the case by the President's Foreign Intelligence Advisory Board (PFIAB), which lambasted the CIA for blunders in hiring a drug user and failing to track his activities after his dismissal. The PFIAB report noted that, once again, American counterespionage had failed to consider the possibility that one of its own could be a spy, noting the "fundamental inability of managers of the Soviet Division to think the unthinkable, that a DO employee would engage in espionage."[11] Casey echoed PFIAB's assessment and lashed out at the DO about "the warnings ignored, . . . the reluctance to recognize a major counterintelligence problem until too late, . . . [and] an astonishing complacency about a seeming unwillingness to accept even as a possibility that a DO officer would commit espionage for the Soviet Union."[12]

The FBI was also severely criticized for allowing Howard to escape. The FBI and CIA engaged in ferocious finger-pointing, with the FBI accusing the CIA of delays in informing it about Howard and the CIA blaming the FBI's flawed surveillance for his escape. Instead of finding constructive ways to better coordinate their operations and counter Soviet spying, the CIA and FBI simply condemned each other's shortcomings.

Meanwhile, Howard struggled to adjust to his new life as an ex-spy in the Soviet Union. He had no ideological commitment to communism and little affinity for Russian culture except for that gained during his year of language study at the CIA. He had been a binge drinker for years and had slowly descended into alcoholism. Occasional sightings of him around Moscow would provide some inkling of his habitual drinking. He would stumble over to an American at a hotel, conference, or restaurant and ask "Do you know who I am?" and ramble incoherently about his tale of woe. Reports of the sightings would reach the US Embassy, which dutifully passed them on to Washington. By the early 1990s, however, Howard's name had faded into obscurity, and even embassy officers serving in Moscow at the time no longer recognized his name.

Howard tried to resettle outside the USSR, probably with considerable aid from an exasperated KGB eager to rid themselves of a drunken, washed-up defector. He made a foray into Hungary and lived there with his family until he was discovered. The Hungarian government, which had just abandoned communism, expelled him in 1989. A few years later, he tried to settle in Sweden, where he met with the FBI but rejected its proposals to return to the United States. The Swedes arrested and then deported him.[13]

Even if Howard had been caught and brought to trial, he still could have eluded justice. The charges against him were espionage, interstate flight, and violation of his probation on the aggravated assault and weapons possession charges in New Mexico. Even if convicted on the latter two charges, he would not receive the punishment he deserved for his treachery. Espionage was difficult to prove in the best of cases, and would be especially so in a Howard trial. Since his escape, another CIA spy, Aldrich Ames, had been arrested. Ames's spying overlapped with Howard's in 1985, and they had both betrayed some of the same agents, including Tolkachev. Howard had already claimed in his memoirs that Ames had compromised the Soviet agents attributed to him, and any defense attorney would have complicated the prosecution's efforts to pin the blame on Howard.

Although Howard was beyond the reach of American justice, he was serving a prison sentence of sorts. His life was clearly miserable, and he was still drinking heavily. Although he had not been tried in American courts, justice had been served. Despite the villa in suburban Moscow where he lived and the care and feeding he received from the KGB, he was living in a prison—a permanent exile in Russia, a pariah in other countries, unable to live peacefully with his wife and son. For his espionage, he was forced to live in a land he did not love and without a family he did love.

In July 2002, Russian media reports revealed that Howard had died after breaking his neck in an accidental fall and would be cremated at the request of his family. Considering his descent into alcoholism, this explanation seems plausible. But conspiracy theories abound in the murky "wilderness of mirrors." Was Howard's death truly an accident, or was the FSB, the KGB's post–Soviet successor, simply fed up with the drunken behavior of its unruly defector? Yet another scenario is also possible. Either the FSB or Howard himself, realizing that he was unwelcome in other countries, may have decided to fake his death so that he could resettle in a new country with a new identity without fear of further pursuit by the FBI.

Despite the public pronouncement, Howard's death still remains shrouded in mystery. Another mystery surrounding the Howard case plagued the CIA in the aftermath of his escape. Tolkachev was only one of a number of CIA spies inside the USSR who, one after the other, were compromised and arrested in the 1980s.[14] Files were searched, and Howard's coworkers were interviewed to determine if he had knowledge of the cases and could thus have betrayed them to the Soviets. The CIA concluded that Howard could not have compromised most of the agents who had been unmasked by the KGB. The CIA had another problem.[15]

The knowledge of the CIA's modus operandi that the KGB learned from Howard may have led to the exposure of the agents. The agents themselves may have come under suspicion by spending money or taking risks in stealing Soviet secrets. Or was it time to "think the unthinkable"—the insidious presence of a second spy inside the CIA? A possible explanation for the compromises emerged at a Christmas party at the US Embassy in Vienna in 1986, when a young marine approached the CIA with a classic spy story.

The Spy in the US Marine Corps

CLAYTON LONETREE

Quis custodiet ipsos custodies? [Who will guard the guards?]

JUVENAL, Roman Wives, *in Juvenal,* Sixteen Satires, *45*

As the last partygoers filed out of the Vienna Embassy's 1986 Christmas party, Sergeant Clayton Lonetree of the US Marine Corps pulled aside Jim Olson, a veteran in Soviet operations at the CIA. "I served in the embassy in Moscow as a marine security guard," he told Olson, "and got into something with the KGB. I'm over my head."[1]

Lonetree's admission set off an espionage investigation that would spread throughout the US Marine Corps, ignite more interagency feuds, and launch a massive hunt through CIA files to stanch the hemorrhage in its Soviet spy network.

Lonetree had been recruited by the KGB in a classic "honey trap" operation. A lonely marine in a hostile foreign country, Lonetree was befriended by Violetta Seina, an attractive, English-speaking Soviet girl, and began a love affair with her. Violetta suddenly introduced Lonetree to her kindly "uncle," a KGB officer who toyed with the young marine's emotions in order to induce him into espionage. Lonetree, of course, was not the first to fall into a KGB trap. Thirty years before, the first CIA officer in Moscow, Edward

Ellis Smith, had an affair with his Soviet maid and was sent packing by the ambassador. The Americans had still not learned their lesson.

Unlike Smith, Lonetree was young and impressionable. Only twenty-four when he arrived in Moscow in 1984, he joined the US Marine Corps as a way out of a broken home, just as John Walker had entered the navy as a way out of juvenile delinquency. Lonetree was born into a Native American family that was plagued by his father's alcoholism and parental quarrels. His mother spirited her children away from their father, Spencer Lonetree, but he later seized them back. A rigid disciplinarian, Spencer Lonetree frequently berated his son Clayton and crushed the boy's self-esteem.[2]

Lonetree found his escape in books about spying and the Nazis. He read Hitler's *Mein Kampf*, and the German madman's self-assurance inspired Lonetree to believe that he, too, was destined for greater things. Fortunately, Lonetree was also inspired by a better role model, his deceased uncle, Mitchell Red Cloud, who had posthumously received a Medal of Honor for heroic service in Korea. Lonetree followed his uncle's example by joining the US Marine Corps.

After completing a special training course in Quantico, Lonetree entered the elite Marine Security Guard (MSG), which was then and still is responsible for protecting American embassies. The MSG performs routine security duties, controlling entry by visitors into embassies, checking that classified materials are secured after business hours, and reporting violations when classified materials are not locked in safes. The MSG, however, also does far more. In an age of increasing terrorism and anti-Americanism abroad, small cadres of marines at besieged embassies have been repeatedly called on to defend American property and personnel against local mobs that far outnumber them. A member of the MSG is also the first person a foreign visitor encounters upon entering an embassy; and in his or her neat and perfectly tailored dress blues, the guard immediately projects the image of a strong and self-confident America.

The US Embassy in Moscow was an especially challenging assignment for the MSG. Because of the KGB threat, the marines were obligated to report any contact with Soviet citizens and were forbidden from fraternizing with them. At the time of Lonetree's assignment, the rest of the embassy, from the ambassador on down, had taken a relaxed attitude toward security and scoffed at rules that, in their view, inhibited their ability to conduct effective diplomacy in the Soviet Union.

The MSG discovered more than two hundred violations in 1985, but the lax security seemed to have little impact on embassy leadership. The flouting of security rules hardly set an example for the marine guards, who wondered why they were compelled to follow the strict regimen ignored by their embassy counterparts.[3] The MSG detachment commander had alerted his superiors to increasing infractions by his own troops in Moscow, but his warnings went largely ignored because the MSG was suffering from manpower shortages.

This security negligence was exploited by the KGB's Second Chief Directorate, which was responsible for monitoring embassy personnel and identifying recruitment candidates. Lonetree was a particularly attractive target. A loner since childhood, he was not popular among his fellow marine guards. He drank too much and was often moody. And he was both naive and impudent, an unhealthy mixture from the security perspective.

Violetta Seina worked in the embassy and noticed the young sergeant's isolation. As in most American embassies, natives of the country equipped with the language and contacts were hired to perform routine administrative chores that taxed the abilities of American diplomats unfamiliar with the local bureaucracy. The helpful Soviets established UPDK, a central agency to facilitate the supply of Soviet workers to foreign embassies. UPDK was a barely disguised KGB front to pepper foreign embassies with informants. Any Soviet citizen working in a foreign embassy reported to the KGB or simply lost his or her job or suffered even worse reprisals.

Lonetree casually chatted with Violetta whenever they encountered each other in the embassy. He was clearly smitten with her and, for the KGB, he evoked memories of other guards who had betrayed American secrets. Robert Lee Johnson had been a lowly army guard who had passed sacks full of US military secrets in Europe to the KGB; and John Walker, the shipboard custodian of communications materials, had let them read the US Navy's traffic. A guard inside the enemy's embassy in Moscow could be another gold mine.

One day Violetta and Clayton met "accidentally" at a Moscow metro stop and spent two hours strolling around town and deepening their casual friendship. He never reported the incident to his superiors. Before long,

Lonetree and Seina were having a secret affair in the tiny Moscow apartment she shared with her sister. Pathetically, Lonetree played amateur spy in a futile attempt to conceal the love affair from the KGB, which had orchestrated the romance in the first place. "I would use countersurveillance techniques," he later recounted, "in leaving the embassy and going to Violetta's house—these techniques included changing modes of transportation, varying my routes, backtracking and wearing different coats and changing them. I used the countersurveillance to avoid being followed by the KGB."[4]

The KGB waited only a month after the affair started before striking. In January 1986 Lonetree agreed to meet Violetta's "Uncle Sasha," who took a friendly interest in the young marine. Violetta's kindly uncle was actually Aleksey Yefimov, a KGB officer responsible for targeting the US Embassy. Yefimov closed the jaws of the trap slowly, first asking Lonetree a few innocuous questions about the embassy for a supposed friend in the Politburo. Soon he demanded more sensitive information to reel in his prize fish. Aside from Lonetree's romance, Yefimov played on the marine's heritage by discussing prejudice against Native Americans. Afraid of losing Violetta, Lonetree began supplying her favorite uncle with floor plans of the embassy and identifying embassy personnel among mugbooks full of KGB photographs.[5]

Lonetree was scheduled to leave Moscow in March 1986 and transfer to the MSG detachment in Vienna. Although the KGB would be losing a source inside its most important Moscow target, the embassy in Vienna was an important hub for a number of international activities, including arms negotiations with the USSR. Uncle Sasha convinced Lonetree to continue his cooperation with the USSR and, more important, his romantic relationship with Violetta. In a subtle attempt to transfer Lonetree's allegiance from Violetta to the KGB, Uncle Sasha persuaded Lonetree to sign a statement affirming that "I am a friend of the Soviet Union." This signed statement could be waved in Lonetree's face as blackmail should he get cold feet about cooperating with the KGB, but it was intended more to foster in the young marine an ideological impetus for his espionage.

"Uncle Sasha" Yefimov surfaced in Vienna to meet Lonetree. The pliant, young sergeant provided his true love's uncle with a phone directory and floor plans of the US Embassy in Vienna.[6] The KGB had already paid Lonetree as another hook to ensure his cooperation, and he would receive the paltry sum of about $3,500 for his espionage. But despite his low pay as an enlisted marine, Lonetree was not motivated by cash like so many other enlisted military who spied for the Soviet Union. His primary motive for spying was Violetta Seina, but he would never meet her again.

In December 1986, Lonetree lost his only link to Violetta. Her Uncle Sasha introduced Lonetree to his new contact in Vienna, known only as "George." The KGB wanted to institutionalize the espionage relationship outside the romance with Violetta, and "George" was professional yet, in Lonetree's view, somewhat cold in his approach.

Lonetree panicked. He had been the subject of a classic "turnover" in the spy trade, the transference from one intelligence service officer to another, a turning point in a nuanced relationship that confirmed the spy was no longer a friend or colleague but simply a spy in the employ of a foreign power. Trapped in a relationship that he had begun to realize was wrong, Lonetree sought a way out and decided to confess his sins to the CIA at the Vienna Christmas party.

Lonetree was driven to confess because of the KGB's gaffe. Because of the KGB's startling successes spying against America in the Cold War, some in the intelligence community viewed them as an enemy ten feet tall who outwitted their American adversaries at will. The KGB, however, fumbled cases and suffered from the same interagency rivalries as its American counterparts. The Lonetree operation was undoubtedly a stellar example.

The bedrock of Soviet power was its communist ideology, and every school, workplace, and government agency was subjected to mandatory classes on Marxism. Ideology was embedded in every aspect of Soviet life, and intelligence work was no exception. Those CIA officers who cultivated their KGB counterparts would routinely be subjected to diatribes about the evils of American capitalism and philosophical debates about the inevitable triumph of Soviet communism, as if their arguments about a decayed system would somehow persuade these Americans to spy for the USSR. The KGB also promoted communist ideology to motivate its spies, the vast majority of whom were capitalists to the core and sought only dollars in return for their secrets. John Walker, perhaps the greediest of them all, scoffed at his KGB handlers when they applauded his service to the Soviets' struggle for world peace.[7]

Lonetree was no exception. He may have been naive, but he had no communist sympathies. Uncle Sasha's taunts about prejudice against Native Americans may have had some impact on Lonetree, but in the end it was the young marine's romance with Violetta that impelled him to share secrets with the KGB. If the KGB had arranged a tryst with his lover in Vienna or elsewhere, Lonetree might have continued to provide floor plans and documents from American embassies around the world.

The Lonetree case might have also epitomized the interagency rivalry between the KGB's First Chief Directorate (FCD) and Second Chief Directorate (SCD), a rivalry that paralleled the turf squabbles between the FBI and CIA. The SCD, much like the FBI, was responsible for espionage operations on Soviet territory, and the FCD, like the CIA, was responsible for overseas spy operations. Once Lonetree had transferred to Vienna, the SCD was most likely compelled to cede primacy to its overseas counterparts, FCD officers, who believed that they were assuming control of a recruited American spy, not a young marine in love with a girl living in Moscow. Their joint failure to comprehend the importance of Violetta to the operation turned Lonetree against the KGB and compromised a penetration in the elite unit responsible for guarding US embassies.

Because the marine corps is part of the US Navy, the Naval Investigative Service (NIS) was rushed to Vienna to deal with Lonetree. NIS agents flew Lonetree back to the United States on December 26, 1986, to begin an intensive round of interviews. The NIS, however, had a long history investigating criminal activities in the US Navy and Marine Corps but had little experience dealing with major Soviet espionage cases.[8]

Pressured because of publicity about the case, the NIS conducted a hasty investigation of Lonetree and reportedly browbeat him into an early confession.[9] Finally, he confessed to a host of NIS accusations but then recanted. The case against him was falling apart and, to make matters worse, the internecine warfare that had crippled American counterespionage for years threatened to derail it altogether. NIS criticized the State Department for failing to inform it of the incredible number of nonfraternization violations at the embassy. The CIA was lambasted for delays in notifying NIS about Lonetree. State and the CIA grumbled that NIS was botching the investigation.

NIS agents interviewed other marines about Lonetree, only to discover that three more of his colleagues may have committed espionage. One of them, Arnold Bracy, set off alarm bells. Bracy had been caught having sex with a Soviet woman who also worked for the embassy. Bracy and Lonetree had served in Moscow at the same time, raising the possibility that the pair had colluded to give the KGB free rein inside embassy offices after business hours. According to MSG procedure, two marines guarded the embassy at night, so the KGB would have required two marine spies to facilitate any surreptitious entry.

NIS agents also badgered Bracy, and ultimately he confessed that he had conspired with Lonetree to let the KGB roam unhindered through the embassy. Like Lonetree, Bracy later retracted his confession, and he was exonerated of espionage.[10]

The possibility that Lonetree and Bracy conspired to allow the KGB to ransack the Moscow Embassy's safes may have explained the growing loss of agents in the USSR that haunted the CIA. A small task force of CIA officers familiar with the compromised cases conducted a painstaking inventory of every piece of paper and every message in Moscow but ultimately concluded that the two young marines had not let the KGB into the embassy.[11] The marines eventually conducted a similar review of Moscow Embassy duty logs and found no evidence that Lonetree and Bracy had been on duty together at night in the embassy.[12] The mystery of the compromised agents remained unexplained for almost a decade until the inconceivable happened again and one of the CIA's own, Aldrich Ames, was unmasked as a spy.

Lonetree was declared guilty at his court-martial and sentenced to thirty years in the brig, later reduced by five years because of his cooperation with investigators. He was released for good behavior in February 1996. His case was more of a scandalous blot on the US Marine Corps' reputation and a sad testimony on embassy security than a blow to national security. As Ronald Kessler has noted, "Ultimately this was the most scandalous fact of all, that the security of Moscow Station and the protection of many of the CIA and NSA's most important global secrets depended on the integrity of a single, young marine stationed on the KGB's home turf."[13]

PART IV

THE DECADE OF THE SPY: OTHER SPIES OF THE 1980s

The Illegal in the CIA

KARL KOECHER

Probably the most remarkable penetration of the
Main Adversary by an illegal during the Cold War was achieved
not by the KGB but by its junior partner, the Czech STB.

VASSILI MITROKHIN, The Mitrokhin Archives; *quoted by*
Andrew and Mitrokhin, The Sword and the Shield, *199*

Almost one-third of the American spies arrested in the 1980s committed espionage for countries other than the Soviet Union, a trend that increased in subsequent years. The Soviets' Eastern European partners continued to achieve successes as they had in the previous decade, but those were their last. By the end of the 1980s, the Soviets had lost their grip over Eastern Europe, the Warsaw Pact had been dissolved, and their intelligence services had disappeared or been dramatically reformed.

Among the Warsaw Pact intelligence services that disappeared was the Czechoslovak State Security Service (STB in Czech, the acronym for Statni Bezpecnost), which pulled off one of the unique espionage coups of the Cold War when it infiltrated one of its own citizens into the heart of the CIA. Soviet bloc services had a long tradition of using illegals in America, some of whom ran the major spy rings in the Golden Age of Espionage in the 1930s and 1940s. Only one known Soviet illegal had acquired a job in the US government with access to classified information: George Koval, a

GRU staff officer born of Russian parents in the United States who was in the army and assigned to the Manhattan Project.[1]

Karl Koecher was the only known illegal who was hired, cleared, and employed as a staff officer of the CIA. He came to the United States as a Czechoslovakian citizen but trumpeted his hatred of the Soviet bloc so loudly that he was accepted as a patriotic American. By the time he applied to the CIA, his anticommunist cover was firmly established.

Koecher was born in Bratislava in 1934, and he graduated from Charles University in Prague and worked for Czechoslovak Radio, where, he later claimed, the authorities harassed and then fired him for his outspoken criticism of the communist regime. In addition to his native Czech, he was versed in French, English, and Russian. In 1963 he married a fellow translator, Hana Pardamcova.

Karl and Hana followed the path of other disaffected Eastern European émigrés during the Cold War. In 1965, while on a visit to Hana's relatives in Austria, the couple defected and resettled in New York, where Karl's linguistic skills landed him a job at Radio Free Europe. After studying philosophy at Indiana University, he and Hana moved back to New York so that he could pursue a PhD in philosophy at Columbia University, where one of his professors was Zbigniew Brzezinski, later to become President Jimmy Carter's national security adviser. In 1969, Karl was hired as a philosophy professor at Wagner College on Staten Island.

Throughout this period, Koecher was vocally anticommunist and severely critical of anyone supporting communist regimes. The couple bought an apartment in a New York luxury high-rise where, among other celebrity tenants, the film director Mel Brooks and his actress wife Anne Bancroft lived. When the Czechoslovakian tennis champion Ivan Lendl tried to buy an apartment in the building, Koecher protested to the building's board of directors because Lendl was a citizen of a communist regime.[2]

Koecher and his wife were establishing their credentials as pro-American, fervent anticommunists so they could spy against America. In 1962, Koecher had been trained as an intelligence officer by the STB to infiltrate the US government. The STB, like its Soviet counterpart, was patient, waiting for Koecher to fashion the image of a rabid anticommunist that would enable him to acquire American citizenship and, ultimately, a job inside the US national security apparatus.

This deception strategy worked. Koecher became an American citizen in 1971, and his wife was naturalized a year later. After building his cover for eight years in the United States, he made his move. In February 1973, he was hired by the CIA as a translator in the Soviet and East European Division, the heart of US spying operations against the Soviet bloc. The translation unit was made up of other Russian and Eastern European émigrés who had been screened with polygraph tests and background investigations before they were hired by the CIA. They all echoed Koecher's anticommunist views, except theirs were sincere.

Although translators like Koecher were not directly involved in operations, they were given reports from the CIA's best-placed agents in the Soviet bloc, which they could render into English far more quickly and accurately than their American-born colleagues. These translators were unaware of the agents' identities, but the Soviet bloc intelligence services would be able to pinpoint the spies if the documents fell into their hands. Koecher told the STB about Russian documents he had translated that led to the compromise of one of the CIA's best Soviet spies of the Cold War.

Alexander Ogorodnik, code-named CKTRIGON by the CIA, was a diplomat in the Soviet Embassy in Bogotá in 1973. The CIA approached him after learning that he had had an affair with a Colombian woman, and he agreed to cooperate.[3] After he returned to Moscow, Ogorodnik was posted to the Soviet Foreign Ministry's global operations watch center, where he had access to diplomatic messages from all over the world. He photographed hundreds of these messages, and at one point he was able to pass them from Moscow to Washington so quickly that the CIA sometimes read them before the Soviet ambassador did.[4] Koecher translated the CKTRIGON messages and passed them to his Czechoslovakian handlers. The STB then provided them to the Soviets, who were able to narrow down the list of suspects to Ogorodnik.

Ogorodnik always knew that an arrest could come at any time, so rather than risk undergoing KGB torture, he begged for and received a poison pill from the CIA.[5] The pill was concealed in a Mont Blanc fountain pen, and Ogorodnik seized the first opportunity to use the pen as a ruse to swallow the poison. In interviews with the journalist Ronald Kessler, Koecher admitted that he had worked on the case but felt no remorse: "The people who did him in were the CIA and he himself."[6]

While Karl was at the CIA, Hana worked as a diamond grader, a job that enabled her to travel and serve as a courier to bring her husband's information to the STB. The Koechers, however, led yet another secret life that would have made illegals like Rudolf Abel blanch. Illegals like Abel lived quiet lives so they could blend into American society and quietly spy. Abel worked at home and, aside from occasionally sharing cups of tea with his neighbors, led a gray existence in America. The Koechers found a different way to blend into American society.

Karl first introduced Hana into "swinging," the swapping of sex partners and attending orgies. Soon Hana, who was vivacious and stunningly beautiful, grew more addicted to group sex than Karl, and the couple became favorites at swinging parties, some in private homes and others in group sex establishments popular during that era like Plato's Retreat and Hellfire in New York City.[7]

The Koechers later claimed that they cavorted with CIA and Pentagon officials at the sex parties, but there is no evidence that they recruited other spies among their hedonistic partners.[8] Using an illegal inside the CIA to make a recruitment approach to these officials may have backfired and compromised Koecher, who had his own unique access to classified materials. The couple, however, could have provided information to the STB on potential targets that could have enabled other Soviet bloc officers to contact and cultivate them.

Koecher's spy career only lasted a short time. After only two years at the CIA, he resigned in 1975. He continued to work on contract while living in New York, though his access was not as significant as it had been during his days in the Soviet Division. He was only passing tidbits of information in the early 1980s when an American intelligence source in the STB compromised him to the FBI.[9] The FBI monitored the Koechers for two years to build a solid legal case and ensnare other Czechoslovakian intelligence officers. The Koechers, however, may have sniffed out the FBI's interest in them, so they decided to move back to Czechoslovakia in 1984. Faced with the possibility that the Koechers would go free, the FBI moved in.

Karl Koecher was the first major spy arrested in the 1980s, a harbinger of the espionage nightmares that were to follow in the Decade of the Spy. The FBI learned a difficult lesson from its handling of the case. FBI and CIA officers confronted Koecher with his espionage and claimed that they just wanted to "fill in some blanks."[10] The officers hinted at vague assurances of immunity from prosecution to convince Koecher to confess. Koecher interpreted the approach as a proposal to become a double agent against his Czech masters. Believing he could avoid prosecution, he admitted that he had spied for the Czechs. He was not advised of his right to an attorney for six days, which is a violation of the Miranda rule.[11] Hana, meanwhile, was interviewed separately by the FBI, and, as DOJ later noted, the FBI ignored guidelines by continuing to interview her after she had requested an attorney.[12]

Instead of any deal, the Koechers were arrested on November 27, 1984. The FBI and CIA, however, had not coordinated their activities with DOJ, which had to prosecute the case in court. DOJ was furious—the FBI had implied false promises of immunity that its agents were not authorized to make and, from a legal viewpoint, the confession was improper and would undoubtedly not hold up in court. John Martin, DOJ's expert prosecutor of espionage cases, was outraged: "I authorized the FBI to arrest the Koechers. I had no idea then how disastrously the FBI and CIA had bungled the case."[13]

The US government still managed to salvage something from the wreckage. The legal case against Koecher was in serious jeopardy, but the spy turned out to be important enough to the Soviet bloc that a trade was worked out. The Soviets agreed to swap celebrated dissident Anatoliy Shcharansky for the Koechers, a testimony to their espionage contribution to the USSR. On a wintry day in February 1986, Shcharansky crossed from East to West Germany over the Glienicke Bridge, where Rudolf Abel and the downed U-2 pilot Francis Gary Powers had walked twenty-four years before in the first Cold War spy trade. A half hour after Shcharansky crossed, Karl Koecher, bundled up in a warm black coat, and Hana, clad in mink from head to toe, ambled over the bridge to freedom.

The Koechers faded into obscurity back in their homeland.[14] Three years after their return, the Velvet Revolution catapulted Václav Havel, one of the communist regime's fiercest critics, into the country's presidency, and the STB was purged, and its officers were replaced with poets, set designers, and artists—all former dissidents—who now occupied the leading positions in Czechoslovakia's new democratic government.

The STB's unique achievement in infiltrating Koecher into the CIA was dwarfed by the work of their Hungarian comrades, who controlled the largest Soviet bloc spy ring of the Cold War.

The Army's John Walker

CLYDE CONRAD

> If war had broken out between NATO and the Warsaw Pact,
> the West would have faced certain defeat. NATO would have
> quickly been forced to choose between capitulation or the use of
> nuclear weapons on German territory.
>
> **CHIEF JUDGE FERDINAND SCHUTH** *delivering the verdict in the*
> *Clyde Conrad case, quoted by Herrington,* Traitors among Us, *388*

Clyde Conrad is perhaps one of the most unheralded spies in American history. A slew of books are devoted to Benedict Arnold, Julius Rosenberg, John Walker, Aldrich Ames, and Robert Hanssen, but not a single one to Clyde Conrad.[1] Yet, as the judge's comments quoted above indicate, Conrad was one of the most damaging spies of the Cold War. For fourteen years, he directed the largest spy ring since the heyday of Soviet espionage in the 1930s and 1940s. Unlike the networks of those years, almost all the spies in his network were US military personnel with direct access to classified information. By the time the ring was neutralized, eleven members had been arrested, of whom nine were then current or retired members of the US Army.[2]

Conrad himself was one of only five American spies who earned more than $1 million for their treachery. During his career as a spy, he betrayed NATO's war plans to the Hungarian service, which in turn passed them on to the Soviet Union. If war had erupted between NATO and the Warsaw Pact in Europe, the Soviet bloc would have gone into combat armed with knowledge of its enemy's tactical nuclear capabilities, deployment of armor and aircraft, location of its missile sites, oil supply pipelines, and ammunition dumps. Thanks to Conrad, the Soviets had as much insight into the US Army as John Walker had given them into the US Navy.

Aside from Walker, Conrad was the most damaging spy in a long line of enlisted US military personnel who conspired with the Soviet bloc. Born in 1947, he was among the first of the postwar baby boomers to spy for the Soviet bloc and spent almost his entire adult life in the US Army. He was in his late teens when he enlisted, just as the Vietnam conflict began to escalate. He served a tour in Vietnam but spent most of his career in Germany, mainly in the army's Eighth Infantry Division.

His military record was excellent. As an administrative specialist, he was dubbed by his colleagues "Mr. Plans" not only because he safeguarded the military's war plans for Europe but also because he wrote some of them. He was the quintessential support officer. He was fully conversant about any detail involving his unit and served so many years in Germany that he could cut through both army and German bureaucracy to relieve his superiors of any troublesome problems. Like John Walker, he was rewarded for his efforts by glowing performance reports. According to one superior, Conrad was "an absolutely outstanding NCO [noncommissioned officer], . . . an administrative genius, . . . leads by examples, inspires his subordinates and successfully trains them."[3] His stellar performance record prompted his commanders to ensure that he remained in Germany, where his institutional knowledge could best serve the army.

Conrad's intimate knowledge of European defense plans enabled him to choose the most vital information to sell to the Hungarians. His long service in Germany also meant that he had contacts with a broad spectrum of fellow enlisted men whom he could spot and recruit to expand his spy network. Moreover, Conrad, who was to lure some of these colleagues into espionage, was himself recruited by another spy in the US Army.

In the mid-1970s, Conrad had worked for Zoltan Szabo, a senior army noncommissioned officer of Hungarian descent. Szabo's parents had fled Hungary for the United States after the bloody uprising of 1956. After a scrape with the law, Szabo, like John Walker, opted for military service and joined the US Army in 1959. Over the course of a twenty-year career, Szabo served in Vietnam, where he won a silver star for bravery in combat, and had several assignments in Germany. His file was checkered with a number of reprimands for petty violations, but his grossest violation remained hidden until long after his retirement.

On a vacation to visit the land of his birth in 1971, Szabo was confronted by Hungarian intelligence and agreed to spy on the army. He was assigned to the Eighth Army Infantry Division's war plans staff and spied for the Hungarians for sixteen years.[4] Much like John Walker, Szabo became addicted to his spy money and began spotting successors who could keep the gravy train rolling once he retired.

Conrad fit the bill. He was an established fixture at Eighth Army headquarters with long-term prospects of continued access to the same vault of military secrets that Szabo had ransacked for years. Although he worked hard in the office, he also partied hard in off-duty hours and liked fast cars and poker games. By 1974 Conrad was also struggling on his enlisted man's pay to support his family, a German wife, and her two daughters from a previous marriage. A year later his wife gave birth to a new child whom the couple had to support.

Thanks to Szabo, Conrad was able to halt his financial slide by funneling classified war plans to the Hungarians. However, he made the same tradecraft errors of many enlisted military spies by flaunting his newfound wealth. His army colleagues were well aware that he was barely eking out a living, but suddenly he was flashing gold krugerrands around and gracing the walls of his apartment with expensive art.[5] He also beefed up his bank account with thousands of dollars in three months, all in deposits of less than $10,000. Anything more than that amount would have required the bank by law to report the deposits to the Internal Revenue Service. Despite his unexplained riches, no one raised any security concerns; nor was he ever subjected to periodic reinvestigations that might have alerted army counterintelligence to the suspicious deposits.

The US Army's security proved to be as slipshod as the US Navy's had been in the John Walker case. Besides lax organizational security, there were other striking parallels in the two cases. Both Walker and Conrad recruited colleagues who could carry on their legacy after they retired and ensure continuing payments to sustain their lavish lifestyles. Beneath their greed were similar psychological motives. Walker considered himself an ace of spies and took great pleasure in outsmarting the US Navy. And Conrad suffered from an equally bloated ego. "When someone such as Clyde looks in the mirror," one intelligence historian noted, "he sees the world's cleverest, boldest and most enterprising fellow."[6] This appraisal was corroborated by those who knew Conrad. Danny Williams, an army colleague and longtime friend of Conrad, was later used as a double agent to gather evidence on the spy and claimed that "he prides himself in his ability to read people, exploit their beliefs and con anyone. It's arrogance . . . that's driving Clyde."[7] Conrad, however, craved recognition of his perceived genius far more than Walker did. Like Andrew Daulton Lee, Conrad could not resist bragging to his friends about his spying exploits, even to Williams when he suspected his friend was trying to entrap him.[8] On another occasion, while sitting in a café with his handler and a potential recruit, Conrad asked the Hungarian to "tell my buddy here what they think of me in Hungary."[9]

Conrad's arrogance and greed drove him to harebrained schemes that infuriated his Hungarian spymasters. At one point, unbeknownst to the Hungarians, Conrad was selling information to their Czechoslovakian counterparts. He also concocted a brazen ploy with his Hungarian courier to fleece the CIA by pretending to be a Soviet bloc volunteer.[10] The courier wrote a letter in his native language to the US Embassy in Vienna claiming that he was a Hungarian intelligence officer with knowledge of an American spy working for his service, a story that could have obviously blown back against Conrad. The bait was too juicy for the CIA, which paid $10,000 to the imaginary volunteer in Switzerland. The CIA, of course, never heard from the mythical volunteer once Conrad and his accomplice scampered off with the money.

Unbeknownst to Conrad, his bizarre double agent plot piqued the CIA's interests because its sources inside the Soviet bloc were already sounding alarms that such a spy did indeed exist. As it turned out, the investigation that would unmask Conrad had already begun. In the late 1970s the CIA began receiving tips from sources inside the Soviet bloc that an army spy was passing the Hungarians reams of documents about NATO's plans to counter a Soviet attack.[11] Pinpointing the spy among the thousands of troops with access to such information was tantamount to finding the proverbial needle in the haystack. Without specific information, the investigation foundered until the mid-1980s, when two top officials of the CIA and the army reenergized the hunt.

Gus Hathaway, a CIA veteran in Soviet operations, was tabbed by the director of central intelligence, William Webster, to head the CIA's Counterintelligence Staff in 1985. Concerned by the hemorrhage of NATO's defense secrets, Hathaway decided to collaborate with Lieutenant General William Odom, the army's top intelligence officer, to smoke out the spy.[12] Meanwhile, CIA sources were gradually supplying more information to narrow down the list of army suspects. The sources had provided a precise list of documents in Soviet hands, which enabled investigators to track the leak to the war-planning staffs in Europe or army headquarters.[13] Judging from reports of sizable Hungarian payments, the spy would have far more money than an army salary would provide.

Army counterintelligence investigators from West Germany's Field Counterintelligence Activity, led by Colonel Stuart Herrington, painstakingly leafed through files of military personnel to winnow down the list of those whose assignments might fit the spy's profile. After a search that had lingered on for eight years, the army sleuths honed in on Conrad. His tours would have afforded him access to the secrets stolen by the alleged spy, and he had served on war-planning staffs both in headquarters and Germany. However, CIA sources believed that the spy was still on active duty because secrets continued to pour in to Budapest. Conrad had retired from the army in August 1985, but investigators were still unaware that he had recruited his spy replacements.

"Follow the money" has been an axiom of criminal investigators whether they are pursuing bank robbers, terrorists, or spies, and army counterintelligence agents went down that path as they pursued Conrad. Discreet investigations and interviews with his colleagues alerted the US Army to his extravagant lifestyle, and an examination of his bank account rang alarm bells once the suspicious deposits were discovered. He had also committed another cardinal tradecraft blunder in handling his spy payments that heightened the army's suspicions. A CIA source had revealed that the army spy had been rewarded with a $50,000 payment for a single document in 1978. Around the time the payment was made, Conrad had traveled to the United States and declared on his landing card that he was carrying $10,000. There are few coincidences in the world of espionage.

As Herrington noted, the discovery was practically a "financial smoking gun" in the Conrad case.[14]

The smoking gun, however, was insufficient to prosecute Conrad. The army sorely needed concrete evidence that Conrad had passed classified information to a foreign power to win a conviction. Fortunately, their investigations revealed a chink in Conrad's armor when they discovered that he was repeatedly attempting to lure army personnel into vague business schemes. Like John Walker, Conrad was hunting for new recruits to expand his spy ring and his earnings.

Walker, however, carefully assessed his potential spies before making a recruitment pitch and, except for Jerry Whitworth, all were close family members who he believed were unlikely to betray him. In yet another tradecraft blunder that jeopardized his security, Conrad cast his net wide and tried to snap up new recruits with only cursory assessments. He told his friend Danny Williams that "I never recruit. I prepare a guy until I know exactly what he will do, then I find something for him and just say, do it."[15] Conrad's preparations apparently did not include any careful vetting of his potential conspirators.

Army counterespionage exploited Conrad's careless recruitment attempts. Conrad suddenly encountered a few active duty army enlisted men who were eager to accept his proposals, but all, like his friend Williams, were double agents tasked by the army to entrap him. Conrad's vaunting ego and craving for admiration made him an easy target. Instead of compartmenting operations as a disciplined spy would, Conrad boasted to the double agents about his reputation as a Hungarian spy and admitted to Williams that he had bilked money from both the Czechoslovakians and the CIA.[16] Eventually the army's double agent operations enabled investigators to photograph Conrad meeting his Hungarian spymasters, providing conclusive evidence of his collaboration with the enemy.

In spite of the evidence against Conrad, the US government still faced an unusual quandary in bringing him to justice. After retirement, he settled with his family in Germany, close to the military secrets his confederates continued to steal for him. He would have to be lured back on some pretext to the United States to be arrested. Even then, DOJ wanted an absolutely airtight case against Conrad and expressed concern that the role of CIA sources in the case could muddy the prosecution. A second option was to summon Conrad back to active duty, then arrest and try him in a military court-martial, but the tactic was unprecedented and could have also complicated the prosecution.

The third option was to allow the Germans to prosecute.[17] Conrad was a civilian residing in Germany who had sold NATO secrets and was thus subject to prosecution under German espionage laws. The Americans, however, were wary of involving the Germans because of their traditional leniency in espionage cases and Soviet bloc penetrations of the German government. Gunther Guillaume, a top Soviet spy who had been the chief aide to German Chancellor Willy Brandt, was sentenced to only fourteen years for betraying the most secret policy deliberations of his government.

The usual bickering among US agencies soon ruled out the first two options. Because the US government was unable to reach agreement from within, it approached the Germans in June 1988. American concerns about the Germans proved to be unwarranted. The joint German–American espionage investigation built a convincing case for the German courts, and the evidence against Conrad was reinforced by two more American allies. Zoltan Szabo, now retired and living in Austria, buckled under questioning by local authorities and confirmed details of Conrad's treachery. Two Hungarian brothers, Imre and Sandor Kercsik, had served for years as couriers of Conrad's stolen secrets and were living in Sweden, where they were arrested. The pair filled in further details, including information that Hungarian intelligence was fed up with Conrad's extracurricular spying activities.

Conrad was arrested in West Germany on August 23, 1988. Hungarian intelligence may have been displeased with his freelance espionage, but the Hungarian government displayed its displeasure in a much more dramatic fashion at his trial. Between the time of Conrad's arrest in 1988 and his trial in January 1990, the Communist government of Hungary became one of the first dominos to fall in the crumbling Soviet bloc. In one of the more unusual turnabouts in espionage history, the new Hungarian government apologized to Germany for Conrad's crime, which it blamed on "the mistaken policy of the former political and military leadership of the country."[18] The startling Hungarian apology was the final blow to Conrad. The German jury found him guilty, and the judge sentenced him to life imprisonment in June 1990.

In the years following Conrad's arrest, the FBI and army scooped up other members of the ring. Szabo, who had only served part of his ten-month sentence because of cooperation with the Austrians, named three more former army enlisted men he had recruited. Conrad had enlisted Roderick Ramsay, his chief subordinate in war plans, as his inside spy for his postretirement years. Ramsay was arrested and sentenced to thirty-six years in prison. Ramsay, without telling Conrad, added two more army enlisted men of his own to the spy ring. Ramsay gave up ex-sergeants Jeffrey Rondeau and Jeffery Gregory, who were both sentenced to eighteen years. Finally, nine years after Conrad's arrest, another army protégé he had recruited, Kelly Warren, became one of the few American women arrested for spying and was sentenced to twenty-five years in prison. Conrad may have craved recognition for his exploits while he spied, but he denied any espionage from the moment of his arrest. He maintained his denials until his death in a German prison in January 1998.

Conrad and Walker were the cancerous outgrowths of a pervasive failure of military security throughout the Cold War. Military personnel with access to top-secret information were not reinvestigated periodically, and red flags of suspicious behavior largely went ignored. As a result, Conrad spied undetected for fourteen years and Walker for eighteen. In the end, military security played no role either in preventing or uncovering their espionage. Walker was betrayed by his long abused ex-wife, and Conrad was unmasked by the CIA's spies in the Soviet bloc's intelligence services and through the dogged investigation by army counterintelligence.

Conrad was not the only army spy working for Soviet bloc intelligence. Another fellow enlisted man inflicted serious damage on US national security by passing secrets to one of the most effective intelligence services of the Cold War, the East Germans.

Spies for East Germany

JAMES MICHAEL HALL AND
JEFFREY CARNEY

I'm not anti-American. I wave the flag as much as anybody else.

JAMES HALL, *East German spy; quoted by Herrington,* Traitors among Us, 323

We struck a gold mine. As long as the source is careful,
this could go on and on.

East German intelligence officer on Hall; quoted by
Wolf, Man without a Face, *328*

James Michael Hall

Army counterintelligence had little time to rest on its laurels from the Conrad case. On the very day of Conrad's arrest, the US Army's Field Counterintelligence Activity (FCA) received its first hint of another well-placed spy in army ranks. This time, however, the spy was working for the Hauptverwaltung Aufklärung (HVA; Main Reconnaissance Administration), the foreign intelligence arm of East Germany's notorious security service, the Ministry of State Security, better known by its abbreviated name, Stasi.

The Stasi was well known for its massive monitoring and repression of East German citizens to snuff out antiregime sentiment. The HVA was considered equally effective in ferreting out secrets from its main adversaries,

West Germany and the United States. Among its many successes were the recruitment of Gunther Guillaume, one of West German chancellor Willy Brandt's closest aides, and Hans Tiedge, the head of West German counter-intelligence.

Despite these successes, the HVA, like any other intelligence service, sometimes made mistakes. The HVA rarely allowed its staff officers to recruit or meet its spies inside West Germany because of the risk of compromise, capture, or, more important, defection to the West.[1] Instead, the HVA used reliable Communist Party members who were allowed to travel abroad as intermediaries to contact its spies. As often in the world of espionage, this policy involved a trade-off. Intermediaries ensured the protection of staff officers and prevented defections but also broadened knowledge of an operation outside the service. Although the policy often worked, it failed in the case of the HVA's most productive spy inside the United States' most sensitive operations in Germany, its electronic eavesdropping on the Soviet Union and Warsaw Pact.

The HVA's intermediary in the case was an East German academic who turned out to be a less-than-reliable Communist Party member. In 1986, the professor was caught shoplifting while visiting West Berlin and claimed that he had staged the incident so his arrest would enable him to contact Western intelligence. The professor, later code-named "Canna Clay" by the army's FCA, revealed that he had performed low-level operational missions for the HVA in Berlin but had become disillusioned with the regime and now sought to resettle in the West. Canna Clay had little to offer at the time, and FCA agents advised him that he would have to produce significant information to merit such a reward.[2]

Two years passed until Canna Clay suddenly contacted the army on the day Conrad was arrested. This time the information he offered was significant. Canna Clay's duties had gone beyond low-level support missions. An English speaker, Canna Clay revealed that he had served as an interpreter in 1988 for two HVA meetings with an American source code-named "Paul." In addition to a physical description of the spy, Canna Clay passed a wealth of details to identify "Paul." He knew the spy's true first name, and he advised the FCA that he was an army sergeant who had recently transferred, was married to a German woman from Bayreuth, and was a flying enthusiast.[3] Most disturbing, the spy was a specialist in signals intelligence and had passed a wealth of information to the HVA on US electronic intercept operations. In return he was paid $30,000 at each meeting, a testimony to the value of his information.

As the FCA chief, Colonel Stuart Herrington, noted, this was not the "Conrad-style needle in a haystack."[4] Army counterintelligence immediately pinpointed the spy as army warrant officer James Michael Hall. Canna Clay confirmed their conclusion by identifying Hall from a group of photos.

Hall was born in Bronx, New York, in 1957. After a year in junior college, he dropped out and joined the army in 1976. Like Clyde Conrad, he spent most of his career in Germany and married a German woman who was a waitress in a bar he frequented near the remote border outpost where he was first stationed. Also like Conrad, Hall consistently received positive performance evaluations and rose through the ranks. When the army identified him as an HVA spy, Hall was stationed in Georgia and had just been promoted from sergeant to warrant officer. Despite this promising career, in the fall of 1982, just after his daughter was born, Hall experienced financial problems supporting his growing family and decided to solve them by selling secrets.

Although Hall was identified quickly thanks to Canna Clay's information, the FCA still needed proof to support an indictment and conviction. Because Hall was paid substantial sums by the East Germans, FCA agents followed the money, as in the Conrad case. The financial investigation in Hall's case surfaced considerable circumstantial evidence of unexplained affluence.

Hall had bought a new home and two expensive vehicles, and had taken flying lessons; his purchases and investments during a five-year period exceeded his estimated available cash from his army wages. In a remarkably damning move, he listed among his assets on his mortgage application "$30,000 in a shoebox," an inordinate amount for the average soldier to stash away in his rainy-day cookie jar.[5]

Surprisingly, despite his inordinately lavish lifestyle, Hall had passed two periodic security reinvestigations since his espionage career began. At the time, he attributed his extra cash to wealthy German in-laws; but during the espionage investigation, the FCA determined that neither his own family nor his in-laws were affluent or provided him with extra income.

The FCA's investigation also included physical and technical surveillance of Hall, which produced a new twist to the case. Canna Clay had told the army that he believed the previous intermediary in the case was not a German.[6] Suspicious phone calls and surveillance revealed Hall's contact with Huseyin Yildirim, a Turkish citizen who had been drummed out of his country's military for assaulting an officer.[7]

Yildirim was earlier suspected of collaboration with the East Germans, and in fact had volunteered to spy for them in 1978. Because he had no access, Yildirim was rejected but was then recruited by the HVA a year later, when he wormed his way into a job as a mechanic in the army's auto repair shop in West Berlin. He was endowed not only with mechanical skills but also with a certain charm, so he was an ideal candidate to spot and cultivate army spies for the HVA.[8] As Markus Wolf, the longtime head of the HVA, noted, both Hall and Yildirim had "hefty financial appetites."[9] In early 1982, Yildirim seized on Hall's interest in an increased income to provide him with an opportunity to pass secrets for money.

The army had by now developed compelling circumstantial evidence of Hall's espionage, his unexplained affluence, and his meetings with a suspected East German agent. To ensure that the case was airtight, however, the army decided to fulfill its promise to resettle Canna Clay so he could testify against Hall. The army investigators then planned to strengthen the case even more by taking a page from the FBI's playbook. In a classic "sting" operation, Canna Clay, once in the United States, would contact Hall for a meeting, at which he would be introduced to a Soviet intelligence officer, in reality an FBI undercover agent, who would appeal to his greed and ego to elicit incriminating information.

The sting exceeded the army's expectations. Canna Clay, his wife, and their beloved dog were exfiltrated, and Hall immediately responded to his call for a meeting on December 20, 1988. The undercover agent told Hall that the Soviets were assuming control of his case because of the extraordinary value of his information. Once Hall's ego had been stroked, the undercover agent's promise of increased payments opened the floodgates. Hall gushed forth not only about his payments from the HVA and the secrets he had passed to the HVA but also implicated Yildirim as his intermediary.

Hall epitomized the ultimate irony of espionage—the very motives that impel a person to spy also lead to his downfall. Hall spied for money, and his greed eventually provided proof of his espionage through his unexplained wealth and expansive confession to the undercover FBI agent. After the meeting, the army had all the proof required to convict Hall, and he was immediately arrested.

Hall was cooperative from the start. He confessed that he had committed espionage because he had been financially strapped, but he claimed that he was still a patriot. "I'm not anti-American," he told the army, "I wave the flag as much as anybody else."[10] At the same time, he initially rationalized his crime by claiming that he was hurting the communist cause by forcing his spymasters to spend sorely needed funds on secrets that he did not consider damaging to US security. Eighteen years later, however, chastened by his time in prison, he said "I'm a treasonous bastard, not a Cold War spy."[11]

During his initial questioning, Hall revealed yet another new twist to the case. He admitted that he had first volunteered to spy not for the East Germans but for the Soviets by dropping a letter into the mailbox of the USSR Consulate in West Berlin in 1982. The Soviets accepted his offer and devised an impersonal communications plan for him to use once stationed back in the United States. By coincidence, Yildirim made overtures about espionage a few weeks later and, like his fellow spy Clyde Conrad, Hall decided that he could double his earnings by providing the same information to the East Germans.

The HVA, ever loyal vassals of the KGB, shared Hall's information with the Soviets, who soon realized that their army spy was working for both services. The KGB confronted Hall on his duplicity during a meeting in Vienna in June 1985 and demanded that he sever his ties with the East Germans. Despite the stern warning, Hall dropped contact with the KGB after his return to the United States in 1985. Other spies like John Walker had followed the KGB's communications plans scrupulously in the United States, but Hall found them cumbersome and time-consuming. He preferred the easier tradecraft of photocopying documents in the safe house rented at the HVA's expense and passing them to his intermediary, Yildirim. If Hall had followed Soviet instructions and cut ties with the East Germans, his new intermediary, Canna Clay, could not have betrayed him to the army and he might have continued passing secrets for many more years.

Because Hall was on active duty in the military, his case was investigated by army counterintelligence. Yildirim, as a civilian, had moved from Germany to Florida and fell under the jurisdiction of the FBI. Although initially unconvinced that the Turk was a spy, the FBI eventually agreed to arrest him simultaneously with Hall. A search of Yildirim's residence surfaced incriminating evidence, including Hall's fingerprints on money found in the Turk's vehicle.[12]

Yildirim, however, proved to be less cooperative than Hall. In a fit of self-delusion, Yildirim imagined that he would be exchanged in a spy trade. He also claimed that he was actually working on behalf of the US government to protect its secrets and, as proof, had squirreled away secrets provided by Hall in caches to prevent their passage to the HVA. Though Yildirim believed the information would be exculpatory, it had exactly the opposite effect and only provided prosecutors with further concrete evidence of his conspiracy to commit espionage. At his two-day trial, the prosecution called thirty-two witnesses to testify; the defense, none.[13] Yildirim was convicted and sentenced to life imprisonment. Yet in spite of the sentence, he was eventually released on parole in 2004 after serving fourteen years of his term.[14]

Hall was spared the death sentence for his cooperation; in March 1989 he pled guilty and received a forty-year sentence, a dishonorable discharge, and a $50,000 fine. Unlike Yildirim, he is still in prison today.

By the time of his imprisonment, Hall had been paid an estimated $300,000 and had been presented with a medal for distinguished service to the German Democratic Republic by no less a figure than Stasi chief Erich Mielke. The payments and the award testified to the value of the secrets that Hall had betrayed to his communist masters. After the collapse of East Germany, German journalists obtained a letter from HVA chief Markus Wolf that detailed the value of Hall's information: "The materials deal with vital information concerning the basic organization of signals intelligence (sigint) collection by the United States in peace and in war, specific plans for the European theater of operations, and the specific role of West Berlin in the enemy's electronic warfare."[15] An HVA sigint expert cited by Wolf claimed that Hall's information "consists of some of the most important American signals intelligence directives. . . . The contents expose basic plans of the enemy for signals intelligence collection for the next decade."[16]

The sheer volume of top-secret documents Hall provided was overwhelming. In his autobiography Wolf said that East German analysts began complaining that they could not keep pace with the flow of information from Hall and his handlers asked him to slow down to avoid discovery.[17]

The US government acknowledged in general terms the damage caused by Hall in a court affidavit on the case, asserting that the spy had passed "voluminous classified national defense information concerning signals intelligence projects."[18] Hall had compromised the United States' most sensitive sigint operations against the Soviet Union and Warsaw Pact and had betrayed offensive electronic capabilities that would have provided the United States and NATO with a distinct advantage in the event of an armed conflict. His espionage allowed the Soviet bloc to develop countermeasures that not only reduced US intelligence gathering but could have also resulted in the loss of American lives in wartime.

The sigint secrets that Hall passed, in fact, may have contributed to the unfortunate death of one US military officer. Violent confrontations between the United States and the Soviet Union occurred in the early days of the Cold War but had largely ceased in the 1950s. One exception, however, was the killing of Major Arthur Nicholson by a Soviet sentry in northern Germany in March 1985. Nicholson worked in the US Military Liaison Mission, which was operated under joint US–Soviet authority. Though the mission's ostensible task was to serve as a liaison, both sides exploited it for intelligence gathering on each other.

Before the tragic incident, another member of the mission had surreptitiously photographed the interior of a Soviet tank in a brief moment unguarded by sentries. The operation was discussed at a meeting of intelligence collectors from various military units in Berlin. Hall represented his unit at the meeting and later admitted that he had passed the information about shoddy security to the Soviets. Nicholson was on a visit to a Soviet tank warehouse when he was killed.[19] Hall's tip-off may well have sparked increased Soviet security and provoked the itchy trigger finger that shot Nicholson. Hall claimed he initially felt that his report may have been responsible for the death, but he shrugged off his guilt and continued spying.

Jeffrey Carney

The East Germans enjoyed an abundance of spy riches on US sigint collection. Hall's information was supplemented by another spy, Jeffrey Carney, an air force sergeant assigned from 1982 to 1984 to the Electronic Security

Command in Berlin.[20] Born in Cincinnati in 1963, Carney was fascinated with Germany from an early age. He enlisted in the air force when he was seventeen years old and demonstrated a keen aptitude for languages. He became fluent in German and was trained as a communications specialist before his assignment to Berlin.

Carney was a rare exception among US enlisted military who primarily spied out of financial motives. He was a homosexual and constantly feared that he would be discovered and drummed out of the service. Gradually, his resentment against the air force festered as he became convinced that his sexual orientation would never be accepted. In October 1983, the young airman became so distraught that he took the Berlin subway, the U-Bahn, into the eastern sector to defect.[21] His HVA contacts convinced him to remain in place as a spy, and eventually he viewed them as friends sympathetic to his sexual orientation.[22]

East German knowledge of the army's sigint operations and capabilities from Hall was now matched by similar secrets about the air force. Six months after he agreed to spy, Carney was transferred back to the United States as an instructor at Goodfellow Air Force Base in Texas. He was still able to obtain top-secret information on air force electronic intercept plans and capabilities, including a sophisticated program to disrupt Soviet air-to-ground communications, which he passed to the HVA during trips to Mexico.[23]

In 1985, Carney defected to East Germany. Revelations in the "Year of the Spy" plus his own upcoming polygraph test in a routine reinvestigation were taking their psychological toll on the troubled airman. According to HVA chief Markus Wolf, the final impetus for his defection occurred when Carney found his lover dead with a plastic bag over his head in the bathtub of their apartment and, forever paranoid, he was convinced that US intelligence was responsible and was on the verge of dealing him the same fate.[24] He traveled to Mexico City, where the HVA smuggled him out to Cuba and then on to East Berlin.

Since Benedict Arnold defected to the British during the Revolutionary War, American spies who have sought refuge in the land of their spymasters have been sorely disillusioned about their decision, and Carney was no exception. The East Germans provided him with financial support, but despite his espionage contributions to the Soviet bloc, they still distrusted him and frowned on his homosexual lifestyle.

Carney ultimately became a victim of the dramatic historical changes at the end of the 1980s. After East Germany collapsed and was absorbed into West Germany, Carney became a subway conductor and lived a hidden existence in a Berlin suburb. But his anonymity did not last for long. One of his HVA handlers betrayed him to the media in exchange for quick cash, and West German intelligence notified the US authorities. In April 1991, agents of the US Air Force Office of Special Investigations apprehended and whisked him off to the United States to stand trial.

Carney confessed to his espionage and, after his court-martial at Andrews Air Force Base, he was sentenced in December 1991 to thirty-eight years in prison. He was released after serving eleven years of his sentence and, as a convicted felon, could only find odd jobs to survive.

Summing Up

Carney and Hall spied for the East Germans for a combined total of ten years, while Clyde Conrad passed secrets to the Hungarians for fourteen years. Another American spy, however, far surpassed all three of them together by spying for more than three decades for another communist adversary. For most of that time, he spied alone inside the CIA, where James Angleton spent years in a feverish hunt for Soviet moles. Ironically, Angleton was looking in the wrong place.

The Spy for China

LARRY WU-TAI CHIN

There is no place where espionage is not used.

SUN TZU, The Art of War, *147*

For millennia, Sun Tzu's emphasis on the importance of espionage has been a pillar of Chinese military and political strategy. His advice about using spies everywhere would be applied relentlessly in the United States in the last quarter of the twentieth century. During that period, Chinese intelligence flooded the United States with students, scientists, businessmen, and émigrés from all walks of life to harvest America's political, economic, and scientific secrets. The Chinese espionage tradition in the United States had its roots in the spying of a Chinese-born American who worked in the most overt part of the CIA and who spied for more than three decades for the PRC.

Larry Wu-tai Chin's espionage for the Chinese Communist regime lasted longer than that of any known American spy. He spied throughout decades that witnessed dramatic upheavals in China, the Great Leap Forward, the Cultural Revolution, the Sino/Soviet split, and the power struggles following Mao Zedong's death. He spied throughout decades of similar upheaval in the United States, the Vietnam conflict, the 1960s' revolution, Watergate, and the tensions of US–Soviet rivalry. Espionage was a key cornerstone of that rivalry, and US spy catchers focused considerable effort on ferreting out Soviet bloc spies inside the US government. James Angleton alone spent years searching for Soviet moles inside the CIA. Although Angleton was skeptical of the rift between the Soviet Union and China, he never appeared to worry about a Chinese spy in the CIA.

Born in Beijing in 1922, Chin studied English and journalism at Yenching University in the Chinese capital. Because of his language abilities, he took a break from his university studies in 1943 and was hired as an interpreter, first at the British Military Mission and then at the US Army's liaison office in China. After finishing his degree, he worked as an interpreter at the US consulates in Shanghai and Hong Kong.

In his college years, Chin had been a vocal supporter of close ties between the United States and China. Moreover, by the time Mao Zedong launched his communist revolution against Chiang Kai-shek's government, Chin had already become a trusted employee of the US government. In 1948, a fellow student introduced Chin to a Chinese intelligence officer who played on his ego and patriotism, flattering him about his knowledge of the United States and claiming that China needed someone with his unique insights to forge bonds with the post–World War II superpower.[1] The ploy worked, and Chin agreed to find a job in the US government where he would have access to secrets he would share with the land of his birth.

When the Korean War broke out, Chin was frequently dispatched to South Korea by the Department of State to interview Chinese prisoners of war. He passed his communist spymasters' locations of prisoner of war camps in South Korea and questions put to the captured Chinese prisoners. He also gave them the names of the prisoners of war who answered those questions, who undoubtedly met untimely deaths once they were repatriated after the war. Although Chin's passage of these secrets occurred three decades before his trial, his spying during wartime became one of the major espionage charges against him: "Here was a clear act that damaged the national security of the United States in the midst of a military conflict. Americans were dying and Larry was spying."[2]

In 1952, just three years after the Chinese communist revolution, Chin was hired to work as a translator by the CIA's Foreign Broadcast Information Service (FBIS).[3] FBIS was unique among CIA units because its primary task had little to do with secrets. FBIS was the US government's wire service, the equivalent of Reuters or the Associated Press, and was solely dedicated to monitoring, recording, and analyzing foreign press and broadcast media.

At the CIA, FBIS officers scanned the foreign press and snipped out articles of national security interest for translation. FBIS also established offices overseas and erected its radio antennas in friendly countries to capture television and radio broadcasts around the globe. Its overseas branches were run by CIA employees with security clearances who supervised linguists skilled in both English and their native languages who could provide timely and accurate translations of daily news around the world. The foreign employees were screened for security purposes but were authorized no clearances or access to secret information.

Chin was one of those foreign translators when he began work at FBIS's Okinawa field station in 1952. At most, he could relate to his Chinese handlers specific news items of interest to the CIA throughout his eight years at the FBIS site. The Chinese, however, were patient and could wait for Chin to eventually burrow more deeply into the CIA. In 1961 he emigrated to the United States, and he became a naturalized US citizen in 1965. After five more years working at an FBIS site in California, he was transferred to FBIS headquarters in Virginia. By then he was no longer one of the CIA's foreign translators but a full-fledged employee with a top-secret security clearance.

At CIA headquarters, one branch of FBIS specialized in producing classified analyses of the news media, and its analysts required access to the full array of CIA finished intelligence to do their job. FBIS officers were also involved in classified projects on an ad hoc basis. FBIS included some of the most talented, native-born linguists in the CIA, and occasionally these experts would be asked to translate documents from top spies in foreign governments to ensure timeliness and accuracy.

Chin became an FBIS analyst in 1970, a job that gave him access to the CIA's finished intelligence. Like his fellow spies Clyde Conrad and John Walker, Chin received glowing performance appraisals from his superiors, one of whom praised him as "one of the ablest Chinese linguists in the branch and the entire division."[4] As a result, Chin was among those tabbed to do sensitive translations of reports from some of the CIA's Chinese sources, and, like Karl Koecher, he betrayed these agents to his handlers.

Chin was equally appreciated by his Chinese spymasters. From the late 1960s until his retirement in 1981, Chin traveled regularly to Toronto, Hong

Kong, and London to pass reams of classified documents to his handlers.[5] When he retired, he received medals for his career achievements from both the CIA and the Chinese Ministry of State Security. He had entered the exclusive club of spies rewarded by both the betrayers and the betrayed.[6]

Chin's motivation to spy for the Chinese evolved during his long career. At first he agreed to spy out of a naive dual loyalty, whereby sharing American secrets would foster understanding between the United States and the land of his birth. The Chinese, however, shared the Soviets' belief that money reinforced the loyalty of even the most ardent patriots. During his long career, he received payments from the Chinese that qualified him as one of the $1 million American spies.

Chinese spy payments stoked Chin's love of gambling, and he gradually lost thousands of dollars while vacationing at Las Vegas casinos. Although it is impossible to estimate the amounts that Chin frittered away at the gaming tables, FBI investigations surfaced evidence of assets that appeared excessive for someone living on a government pension. By the time of his arrest in 1985, the FBI estimated that Chin had $564,000 in bank accounts, including $200,000 in one Hong Kong bank. He also had real estate investments worth about $700,000 in Virginia, Maryland, and his beloved Las Vegas.[7]

After retiring in 1981, Chin continued to do contract translation for the CIA. In 1982, he traveled to Beijing, where top officials of the Ministry of State Security feted him at a banquet and paid him a $50,000 bonus.[8] Chin had obeyed Chinese guidance on tradecraft so scrupulously that he spied undetected for more than three decades and could now enjoy retired life. But his days were numbered.

In the end, Chin met the same fate as many American spies: He was unmasked by a Chinese intelligence officer who defected to the United States. According to an FBI affidavit submitted to the court at Chin's trial, an "extremely sensitive source of proven reliability . . . provided information regarding an intelligence agent of the People's Republic of China identified as '2542.'" Although this source did not know the true name of the Chinese agent, he passed enough information about him to the FBI to narrow the search to Chin.[9]

The FBI confronted Chin in 1985. After the debacle of the Koecher investigation, the FBI had learned from its mistakes. Agents did not browbeat, threaten, or hint at offers of immunity during their interview of Chin. As in the Pelton case, FBI agents carefully walked Chin through a recounting of his activities. Chin was stunned by the wealth of detail the FBI had amassed about his spying. Still, he asked the FBI agents if they were bluffing about his alleged espionage. The agents proceeded to name Chin's Chinese handler and to give the dates and details of his contacts with the Ministry of State Security. Chin knew he was trapped. Only someone deep inside Chinese intelligence could have related those details to the FBI.

Without admitting to espionage, Chin himself raised the possibility of working for the FBI as a double agent to wriggle out of his increasingly hopeless situation. It was too late. Larry Wu-tai Chin, sixty-three years old, ready to retire comfortably on hundreds of thousands of dollars from espionage, was arrested on November 22, 1985.

In February 1986, Chin went on trial for seventeen counts of espionage and income tax violations. Because he had confessed to spying for the Chinese, he and his attorneys decided that his only defense was to emphasize his lofty ideological motives for handing American secrets to the Chinese for more than thirty years. His noble mission was merely the improvement of US–Chinese relations. "If this information was brought to the attention of the Chinese leadership," he argued on the witness stand, "it might break the ice and start to turn from hostility to friendship. I wanted [Premier] Chou en-Lai to see it."[10]

Chin's supposedly noble service as a self-styled intermediary was also a lucrative calling, but he explained his abundant assets as the product of sound investment and luck at the casinos, even though he had consistently been a loser at the tables. In one admission at the trial, he claimed that the Chinese paid him $180,000 for a report about President Richard Nixon's intention to normalize relations with the PRC. According to Chin, this was the only classified document he ever gave to China, and the payment was merely a by-product of his alleged diplomatic efforts.[11]

The jury rejected Chin's self-serving defense. After a few hours of deliberation, the judge read the guilty verdict as Chin's wife and three children wept in the courtroom. Two weeks after the verdict, Chin asked his prison guard to put a clean plastic trash bag in the garbage can in his cell. He slid the plastic bag over his head, bound it tightly with shoelaces from a new pair of sneakers, and lay quietly on his cot until death came.

Chin's suicide prevented debriefings that could have illuminated the full extent of the damage he had done to US national security. According to testimony at his indictment, Chin "reviewed, translated, and analyzed classified documents from covert and overt human and technical collection sources which went into the West's assessment of Chinese strategic, military, economic, scientific and technical capabilities and intentions."[12] The volume of documents is difficult to gauge, but, according to one report, thirty translators labored full time for three months to process the documents Chin had delivered.[13] Considering the length of time Chin spied for the Chinese, there was undoubtedly little raw intelligence and analysis in CIA hands that the Chinese had not seen.

Chin's arrest was a wake-up call not only to the CIA but to the entire US government about the threat of Chinese espionage. Chinese spying had been largely neglected in the decades when American spies predominantly worked for the Soviet bloc. The Chin case was a harbinger of espionage to come. By the dawn of the twenty-first century, Chinese intelligence collection against the United States would eclipse Russian espionage efforts.

The Chin case awakened America to spying by other nations besides Russia. Communist China, of course, had long been an adversary of the United States, but revelations of spying by US allies would shock the American public far more. A day before Chin's arrest, one of the most controversial spies since the Rosenbergs was arrested for espionage. He had spied not only for an American ally but also for a country that depended on the United States for its very existence.

The Spy for Israel

JONATHAN POLLARD

It's likely he will never see the light of day again.

JOSEPH DIGENOVA, *US district attorney, on Jonathan Pollard's sentence; quoted by Kessler,* Spy vs. Spy, *319*

Nothing symbolized the "Year of the Spy" as much as the week before Thanksgiving 1985. As Americans prepared for their annual late-November feast, three spies were arrested within a period of five days and paraded through federal courts to be charged with espionage. Ronald Pelton had spied for the Soviet Union and was sentenced to life in prison. Larry Wu-tai Chin spied for the PRC and committed suicide before his sentencing.

The third spy was Jonathan Pollard. Unlike his fellow spies in the dock that week, Pollard had betrayed his country for the relatively short period of eighteen months. Unlike them, his case did not fade into obscurity but remains controversial even today. Pollard, unlike Pelton and Chin, had not spied for an enemy but for Israel, America's most stalwart ally in the Middle East. Israel was more than an ally, however. The beleaguered country depended on the United States for its economic and military security. In the year Pollard was arrested, Israel received $1.5 billion in emergency aid to combat a severe economic crisis and an equivalent amount in military assistance.

As a close ally, Israel also received US intelligence on areas of mutual interest. Pollard, however, did not believe that America was sharing enough and decided on his own to right the imbalance. As a counterterrorist analyst for the US Navy, he had access to top-secret materials across the intelligence community and delivered suitcases full of these materials to the Israeli government.

Like so many other American spies, Pollard hardly fit the James Bond image. Resembling a swarthier version of the actor Alan Arkin with puffier cheeks, he was short and squat, had a receding hairline, and wore black, horn-rimmed glasses. He was born in Galveston, Texas, in 1954 but moved to Indiana when his father, a research microbiologist, was hired by the University of Notre Dame. His parents were fervent US patriots and also instilled in their children an appreciation for their Jewish religion and culture. During a family trip to Europe, Pollard's parents took their young son to Dachau, where the horrific memories of the Holocaust made him vow silently that this kind of brutality would never happen again.

Pollard later graduated from Stanford University with a degree in political science, but his flourishing academic career withered after that. In rapid succession he dropped out of Notre Dame Law School and then from Tufts University's Fletcher School. He had been fascinated in his youth by spy novels and military tales, so he then decided to apply for the CIA but was rejected. Finally, in 1979 he landed a job as a junior analyst for the US Navy monitoring foreign ships' movements around the globe. In 1984, he was assigned to the navy's new Antiterrorism Alert Center, which had been established in response to the deadly attack against the US Marine Corps barracks in Beirut.

Pollard had been not only an extremely bright and somewhat bookish child but also a small and frail one. Because of this unlucky blend, he was bullied and taunted by his classmates at school yet found escape in stories of the adventures of soldiers and spies.[1] He soon immersed himself so deeply into these adventures that he began living out his fantasies to overcome his insecurity. As the line between fantasy and reality increasingly blurred, he became a compulsive yet extremely bungling liar.

After his arrest, college classmates were interviewed and related some of his outlandish yarns. At Stanford, he had claimed that his father and he escaped Czechoslovakia when his father's CIA job was exposed. At other times, he had bragged that he was a colonel in the Israeli Army or a Mossad agent and once had even addressed a telegram to himself as "Colonel Pollard."[2] He had also boasted that he had killed an Arab while on guard duty at an Israeli kibbutz. No one took any of these implausible tales seriously, and they simply dismissed Pollard as a crackpot.

Pollard's penchant for tall tales persisted in his professional life and soon had more serious consequences as he relied on lies to cover simple mistakes or enhance his career prospects. Once, when he appeared late for an interview about transferring to another navy analyst job, he explained his tardiness with a bizarre story about his wife's kidnapping by the Irish Republican Army.[3] On another occasion, he sought approval from his superiors to cultivate a South African military attaché. He actually did know the South African, but, to improve his chances for the navy's blessing, he told his superiors that he had lived in Pretoria when his father was the CIA representative there. As a result of his easily disproved story, Pollard's clearance was downgraded, prompting him to file a grievance to regain the higher level of access.

Pollard's fascination with espionage went beyond spinning bizarre yarns. Like a child with shiny new toys to show off to his playmates, he volunteered snippets of classified information to a row of foreigners. Before he spied for Israel, he tried to boost his image by sharing secrets with the South African attaché, an Australian naval officer, two investment advisers, and a journalist, Kurt Lohbeck, who reported extensively on Afghan freedom fighters.[4]

Pollard's imaginary spy life distracted him from more mundane chores, especially the management of his personal finances. He was constantly late with rent payments and barely escaped eviction from his Washington apartment. He also neglected payments on a loan from the Navy Federal Credit Union, which prompted a notification to his superiors.[5] Yet despite his habitual lies, questionable contacts with foreigners, and financial difficulties, he was given back his top-secret clearance and promoted through the analyst ranks. He slipped through the cracks—or, rather, the yawning abyss of US Navy security—without anyone raising an eyebrow. The failure was no surprise—after all, John Walker had been committing espionage inside the navy for years. Like Walker, Pollard had received glowing performance evaluations, but his recurrent problems were never included in his personnel file or conveyed to new superiors when he changed positions within the navy.[6]

As a naval analyst, Pollard participated in intelligence exchanges with the Israelis and believed the United States was holding back on information critical to the survival of the Jewish state. US intelligence had provided Israel with satellite reconnaissance photography at critical times in the past, especially before the commando raid to rescue hostages at Entebbe Airport in Uganda. After Israeli jets bombed Iraq's Osirak nuclear reactor in June 1981, the United States limited the sharing of some intelligence, especially reconnaissance photos, fearing that its information could facilitate attacks against other Middle Eastern targets and provoke a wave of anti-Americanism in an already-unstable region.

Pollard's resentment against the US decision ignited the volatile mixture of motives that drove him to spy. His espionage was a fatal cocktail of every major motive that has impelled human beings to spy for centuries. He was in financial straits. He was fascinated with the thrill of spying. He was a mediocre man with a grossly inflated ego and yearning for praise and acceptance. He was ideologically sympathetic to a foreign power, and this sympathy provided the final motive that would drive him into espionage: revenge.

Through a mutual friend, Pollard arranged a meeting with Avi Sella, a legendary Israeli pilot involved in the Osirak bombing. Sella was on the US lecture circuit raising funds for Israel bonds while pursuing a degree in computer science at Columbia University. Once Sella heard from the friend that Pollard was a naval intelligence officer, before the meeting he decided to get a green light from Yosef Yagur, a friend who also happened to be the science counselor at the Israeli Embassy in Washington.

The daring fighter pilot and the paunchy analyst met at the Washington Hilton on May 29, 1984. Pollard volunteered to provide secrets to Israel so readily that Sella suspected his lunch partner was a provocation designed to entrap him.[7] Still, Sella arranged a follow-up meeting with Pollard to get a sample of his wares.

Sella reported the surprising outcome of the lunch to Yagur. Although Yagur was officially the embassy's science counselor, he was really an officer of LAKAM, an intelligence organization barely known, even in Israel. LAKAM, an acronym for Lishka Lekishrey Mada, was the Israeli Defense Ministry's Office of Scientific Liaison. The drab bureaucratic name masked a spy unit charged with acquiring scientific and technical secrets. In the past LAKAM had reportedly acquired the blueprints for France's Mirage jetfighter and had stolen secrets to aid the development of Israel's nuclear capability.[8]

In 1984, LAKAM was led by Rafi Eitan, one of Israel's legendary intelligence officers. Eitan had fought in the Jewish Underground in Palestine during World War II and had joined the Mossad in 1951. Among his many exploits in the Mossad, Eitan participated in the kidnapping of Adolph Eichmann, the infamous Nazi organizer of the Holocaust, off the streets of Buenos Aires in 1960. Eitan's close friend, Ariel Sharon, became Israeli defense minister in 1981 and tabbed him to run LAKAM.

Eitan was a first-class field operative but an unsuitable headquarters bureaucrat.[9] He focused more on intelligence operations than the political context in which they occurred, and this proved fatal in the Pollard case. Pollard's tantalizing offer had been reported to both LAKAM and the Mossad, which was aware of Pollard from intelligence exchanges and had dismissed him as an eccentric kook. Eitan, however, craved secret information and decided to test Pollard's mettle.

Over the next eighteen months, Pollard rummaged through intelligence community databases and amassed stacks of classified documents for biweekly deliveries to his LAKAM handlers. As an authorized courier, he was able to spirit documents out of his office without suspicion. He packed his briefcase to the brim every day, and three times a week he drove to a car-wash where he stuffed the contents into a bulky suitcase. Every other Friday he lugged the bulging suitcase to an Israel Embassy employee's apartment, where LAKAM officers photocopied top-secret materials and returned them to him on Sunday. During his brief spying career, Pollard passed the Israelis more than 1 million pages of secret information.[10]

In return for the mounds of documents, Pollard's spymasters funded trips for him and his fiancée, Anne Henderson, to Europe and Israel, where he was entertained by Eitan and other top LAKAM officers. On a lavish trip to seven cities in Europe, Pollard and his fiancée stayed at posh hotels, dined in gourmet restaurants, and capped off the grand tour by getting married in Venice.[11] The Israelis had already spotted Pollard $3,000 for an engagement ring on a previous trip to Paris, so funding the honeymoon was the least they could do for their ace spy and his betrothed.

LAKAM also paid Pollard $1,500 a month for his suitcases stuffed with American secrets, a figure they soon upped to $2,500. To ensure a long-term spying relationship, LAKAM then deposited $30,000 for him in a Swiss bank account, which would be supplemented with annual payments of $30,000 for the next nine years, when he could "retire" from his spy career.[12] Soon the newlyweds were dining at fine restaurants in the nation's capital—Jonathan Pollard was finally living the glamorous life of a spy that he had only imagined in his sweeping fantasies.

Ironically, the increasing number of arrests in the "Year of the Spy" caused Pollard's downfall. Pollard had easily eluded routine US Navy security procedures, but eventually his superior became concerned that he was reviewing documents unrelated to his duties as a counterterrorist analyst on the Americas and the Caribbean. While the superior began to monitor his employee more closely, one evening another colleague was suspicious when he spotted Pollard hauling a huge batch of documents from their navy facility.[13] The colleague, sensitized by the recent arrest of John Walker and other spies, reported the incident. Pollard's superior decided to investigate and was shocked to find that his analyst had signed out dozens of documents on the Middle East that were not in his office and that were unrelated to his duties as a counterterrorist analyst on the Americas and the Caribbean.[14]

The NIS was notified and called in the FBI. On November 15, 1985, FBI surveillance cameras in Pollard's office filmed him cramming sixty documents into his briefcase in less than five minutes. FBI and NIS agents confronted him in the parking lot once he carried the documents out of the building, and their chat set off an avalanche of events that would engulf Pollard and his wife.

The compulsive but stupid liar in Pollard took over. He first claimed that he was ferrying the documents to a navy colleague, which NIS agents quickly established was false. Agents requested his consent to search his residence, where Pollard had also squirreled away piles of classified materials. He refused but also asked to call his wife because she was expecting him home. Using a prearranged code, he tipped off his wife to destroy the documents in their apartment. Anne Pollard understood the message and rushed madly to gather the papers into a large suitcase. She dragged the heavy suitcase downstairs to throw the contents into a dumpster in the alley, only to spot a suspicious car there which she believed was FBI surveillance targeted against them.

Anne Pollard was partially right. In a bizarre twist of the "Year of the Spy," the cars were, indeed, from the FBI; but the agents were there to watch the apartment of Ronald Pelton's girlfriend, who also lived in the neighborhood.[15] So many spies were operating at the time that they were bumping into each other and their spy hunters. Anne Pollard was obviously unaware of the FBI's true purpose, but frightened out of her wits, she decided on another plan that would only strengthen the case against her husband.

Anne implored her neighbor to bring the bag to the Four Seasons Hotel, where she would retrieve it and then destroy the contents. But the hastily developed plan went awry when Anne and the neighbor missed each other. The neighbor lugged the suitcase back home, where he and his wife wondered why Anne had said there were some classified government documents in it. The wife called her father, who happened to be a naval officer, and he notified the NIS. The stash of secret documents was in NIS hands the next day to bolster the mounting evidence of Pollard's espionage. The Pollards ran into more bad luck when Jonathan, believing that Anne had destroyed the material, thought he had weathered the storm and acceded to the request for a search of his residence. The federal agents found over sixty documents in his home that Anne had missed in her haste.

At this point, Pollard was only guilty of mishandling classified information. The next day, he was summoned back for more interviews and a polygraph test. As always, he tried to worm his way out of the predicament with another lie. Pressed by NIS agent Ronald Olive, Pollard made a major blunder by admitting that he had passed some classified documents to the journalist Kurt Lohbeck. Once he confessed to the unauthorized passage of secrets, the case was no longer a matter of mishandling classified material but one of possible espionage.[16]

Pollard also failed the polygraph test and was told to come back the next day for more questioning. By then he had alerted the Israelis to his plight and was ready to be rescued by them. After all, Eitan had assured Pollard he would take care of him and also claimed he doubted the US would ever take any action against him given the bilateral relationship.[17] To his surprise, no one from LAKAM contacted him with an escape plan. He finally called the Israeli Embassy to request asylum and was told to come in only if he could elude FBI surveillance.[18] He finally told FBI agents that he had to take his wife to the Washington Hospital Center for medical treatment the next day. FBI surveillants trailed him to the appointment and then on a suspiciously winding route through the streets of the nation's capital.

According to NIS agent Olive, no one suspected that Pollard was spying for the Israelis until that morning.[19] Pollard's circuitous journey ended within sight of the blue Star of David emblazoned on the white flag flying over the Israeli Embassy. As the embassy gates opened to let another car in, Pollard zoomed his Mustang right in behind it. Now on Israeli territory, the Pollards breathed a sigh of relief.

Their relief was only momentary. In spite of his frantic pleading, Israeli security politely but firmly advised Pollard that he had to leave. Once outside the gates and back on US territory, Pollard's car was blocked by the horde of FBI surveillants that had swooped in to surround the embassy. On November 21, 1985, Jonathan Pollard was arrested for espionage right on the doorstep of his spymasters' embassy.

A day later, the FBI arrested his wife Anne. As a side dollop to spying for the Israelis, Pollard had filched a few documents about China to give her so she could have an edge in winning a contract with the Chinese Embassy for her public relations firm.

The Pollards were arrested in "the speediest international major espionage case ever worked."[20] Pollard had been caught less than two weeks after the initial tip-off from a coworker. The arrest was in large part the result of the efficiency of the NIS and an FBI squad seriously overworked by a flood of other cases. But the arrest also resulted from the colossal failure of Pollard's handlers in LAKAM.

LAKAM's inadequate tradecraft and inattention to basic security measures destined the Pollard operation to failure from the outset. LAKAM may have stolen jetfighter blueprints and nuclear secrets, but it proved incapable of running a risky spy operation under the nose of its major ally.

Espionage against an ally is often riskier than spying on an enemy. Spy catching is an expected and even commonplace by-product of hostile relations, but the exposure of a spy for an ally can jeopardize otherwise-healthy bilateral relations. US–Israeli relations may have been too vital to each other's security for the Pollard case to have a significant impact. At the same time, a few angry congressmen could have made the difference on votes of interest to the Israelis. A few resentful Pentagon officials could have delayed the shipment of key military equipment. Considering the high stakes, the Pollard operation should have been run with the highest standards of tradecraft.

Instead, LAKAM took unnecessary risks. LAKAM undoubtedly was lulled into a false sense of confidence because the FBI, occupied with Soviet bloc and Chinese spies, paid little attention to Israeli activities. Israel did not figure in the FBI's criterion country list, which specified the nations presenting the greatest espionage threats. Pollard also supplied LAKAM with quarterly FBI counterintelligence summaries that undoubtedly indicated that Israeli diplomats in the United States were under little scrutiny. However, the Pollard operation was too dicey to rely on that lulling information.

LAKAM ignored basic tradecraft procedures from the outset. Avi Sella may have been a heroic pilot, but he was not a trained intelligence officer and he could have been recognized when meeting Pollard because of his high profile on the lecture circuit. Nevertheless, even though LAKAM quickly substituted Yosef Yagur as Pollard's handler, Sella remained active in the operation. As the FBI closed in on Pollard, it was Sella who the Israeli spy called for help.

LAKAM also jeopardized the operation by allowing and even encouraging Pollard's vacuum cleaner approach to gathering secrets. Although LAKAM did provide Pollard with guidance on specific issues of intelligence interest, pressuring him to shovel documents week after week into a suitcase only exposed their spy to avoidable risks and ultimately compromised the operation. Delivery of the documents to an apartment in the heart of the nation's capital further aggravated the problem. Considering the number of times Pollard visited the apartment, he could have been spotted by an acquaintance as he entered or exited the building.

The Israelis could have met Pollard less frequently and tasked him to provide only the most important documents in which they were interested rather than amassing stacks of paper. He could have photographed the documents at home, returned them the next day, and passed the information in less unwieldy form to his handlers. Instead of biweekly visits to the apartment of an Israeli embassy official in the heart of Washington, Pollard could have passed rolls of film at remote spots outside the city or even in dead drops, the impersonal communication method used so effectively by the KGB throughout the Cold War.

LAKAM also never advised Pollard to prepare suitable cover stories if spotted in the apartment building. More important, he was never prepared with an explanation for lugging large batches of documents from work. Instead, when he was eventually confronted, he simply devised one implausible story after another and each time dug himself more deeply into a hole of easily disproved lies. If he had been armed with a mildly convincing explanation, he might have been merely slapped on the wrist for mishandling classified materials instead of arrested for espionage.

LAKAM did warn Pollard about flaunting his newfound wealth and resisted his demands for higher payments that could have attracted attention. At the same time, his handlers gave him cash to fund inordinately expensive European trips. He paid for five-star hotels and gourmet dining with his credit cards, leaving a traceable record of expenses far beyond the means of a midlevel government analyst on vacation. Pollard himself later complained about "the money I couldn't recycle, the trips I couldn't explain, the hotels we were told to stay in which were clearly beyond our means, the credit cards he [Eitan] insisted we use despite the obvious disadvantages, and the volume of material he wanted that had me running around the city like a chicken with its head cut off."[21]

The Israelis also failed to provide Pollard with a detailed exfiltration plan. Rescuing a spy who is already under suspicion is extremely difficult even with such a plan, but an attempt to devise one on the fly is doomed from the outset. After Pollard's alert, Yagur madly tried to get a response from Rafi Eitan about rescuing his spy but, despite the spymaster's earlier assurances, only received "a wishy-washy reply."[22] Yagur, Avi Sella, and two other LAKAM officers were simply ordered to hightail it out of the United States immediately. Pollard was abandoned. By then it was already too late. Perhaps the Israelis had made a political decision that saving Pollard would only exacerbate the spy scandal; perhaps Eitan had never intended to exfiltrate him if he fell under suspicion. Whatever the case, the Israelis' abandonment of Pollard sent a chilling message to potential spies: If you are thinking about spying for Israel, think twice. You will be left alone, out in the cold, to fend for yourself. If this message was not chilling enough, the Israeli government's subsequent actions would thoroughly discourage any potential spies. The Israelis not only abandoned their top spy but also helped to condemn him.

Pollard's arrest was splashed across headlines around the country and ignited a furor over Israeli duplicity. The White House and Congress issued harsh protests, and Secretary of State George Shultz demanded explanations from Prime Minister Shimon Peres. The Israelis tried to wriggle out of the scandal by claiming that the Pollard case was a rogue operation, a thin veil to save face that few believed. To further curb the political fallout, Peres promised to cooperate with the US investigation.

In response to Peres's offer, the United States sent an interagency team to call the Israelis' bluff. The Israelis stonewalled and were less than fully cooperative. Still, they did provide sufficient information to strengthen the case against Pollard. During his spying days, Pollard had passed more than a thousand documents to LAKAM. The Israelis only returned a paltry fraction of the documents, but that was enough to provide conclusive proof of his espionage. As the journalist Wolf Blitzer noted in his account of the case, "They [the Israelis] did something that was truly unprecedented in the annals of covert intelligence operations—they made available evidence to convict their own agent."[23]

The Israelis betrayed Pollard, and he in turn betrayed them. Despite its alleged cooperation on the case, Israel had concealed Avi Sella's part in the operation. Embittered by Israel's abandonment, Pollard revealed Sella's role, and the United States responded angrily by issuing indictments for Sella and the other Israelis involved in the case. Although the Pollard operation was supposedly unauthorized, the rogues were never disciplined. On the contrary, Sella was later promoted to brigadier general and given command of a key air force base. After LAKAM was disbanded as a result of the case, Rafi Eitan was named head of a government-owned chemical company but was later shuffled off to a more obscure job. The old spy, however, did not merely fade away; in 2006 he was elected to the Israeli parliament. Years after Pollard's arrest, Eitan belied his own government's claim that Pollard was a rogue operation: "All my actions, including Pollard, were done with full knowledge of those in charge."[24]

The Pollards and the US government reached a plea agreement. Jonathan pled guilty to one count of conspiring to deliver national defense information to a foreign power, and Anne admitted guilt as an accessory to possession of classified materials. DOJ promised not to recommend a life sentence for Jonathan's espionage in return for his cooperation, an issue that would become crucial to the outcome of the case.

On March 4, 1987, the Pollards appeared in court for sentencing. Judge

Aubrey Robinson pronounced the words that would spark more than two decades of controversy over the case: "I commit the defendant to the custody of the Attorney General or his authorized representative for life."[25] Anne was sentenced to two concurrent five-year terms. The Pollards were shocked about the severity of Jonathan's sentence, especially because they believed they had a deal with the government. The DOJ recommendation against a life sentence, however, was not binding on the judge.

Various factors influenced the harsh sentence: the sheer volume and importance of the information given away, Pollard's hollow claims of remorse in court, and perceptions of his continuing allegiance to Israel. The icing on the cake was perhaps an interview Pollard granted to Blitzer, who wrote an article based on the meeting that appeared in the *Washington Post* three weeks before the sentencing. The navy ruled that the interview was a violation of Pollard's plea agreement because he spoke with the journalist without prior authorization.

In the article Blitzer claimed that Pollard was not a bungler, as he had been portrayed in the media, but an Israeli master spy.[26] The article provided the public with a glimpse into the damage done by Pollard. Pollard, as Blitzer claimed, had pinpointed the location of Palestine Liberation Organization (PLO) headquarters in Tunisia and had supplied the Israelis with information on the Tunisian air defense system.[27] Armed with that information, Israeli jetfighters decimated the PLO compound and killed more than sixty members of the organization on October 1, 1985, just a month before Pollard's arrest. Delicate negotiations between the United States and Tunisia on the PLO were ruined, and US relations with other moderate Arab nations suffered a serious setback. Pollard's spying had proven that America's concerns about Israeli misuse of its intelligence were well founded.

The million pages of secrets that Pollard had passed to Israel went far beyond the PLO and Tunisia and covered a broad spectrum of military and political information about Middle Eastern countries and about Soviet weapons systems that were or might be supplied to Arab states in the region.[28] Eitan specifically asked Pollard for the highly sensitive Radio Signal Notations (RASIN) manual on signal intelligence collection. LAKAM later told Pollard the manual had aided them in monitoring communications between the Soviet General Staff in Moscow and its military assistance group in Syria, one of the Israelis' primary intelligence targets.[29] Just as the information that John Walker passed to the KGB might have tipped the balance in the Soviets' favor in the event of a war, the volumes of US information betrayed by Pollard would give Israel significant advantages in any Middle Eastern conflict.

There was, however, one critical difference. In spite of superpower tensions, the United States and Soviet Union were not on the brink of open warfare. Israel, however, had proven itself a militant aggressor, willing to take the offensive against its regional enemies whenever an attack would serve its interests. Because of these concerns, the United States selectively shared intelligence with Israel. Now Pollard's betrayal had undermined that policy by giving Israel the information needed to upset the fragile stability in the volatile Middle East.

The one topic that was of little interest to the Israelis was terrorism.[30] Apparently, the Israelis were unimpressed with US intelligence on the issue or believed that their own formidable counterterrorist capabilities were sufficient. Still, considering the brutal attacks against Israelis around the world, it seems inconceivable that they would not want any tidbits of information from the American treasure trove to which Pollard was privy. Ironically, because Israel had suffered so much at the hands of terrorists, Pollard's theft of counterterrorist secrets could have earned his handlers some sympathy in the United States.

The extensive damage done by all Pollard's gifts to Israel was outlined in a classified memorandum from Secretary of Defense Caspar Weinberger to Judge Robinson, which undoubtedly played a role in the decision to impose a harsh sentence.[31] Weinberger was personally outraged by Pollard's treachery and, in an unclassified supplement to his memorandum, provided stark comments that were sure to further sway the judge's assessment of the spy's damage to national security: "It is difficult for me, even in the so-called Year of the Spy, to conceive of greater harm to national security than that caused by the defendant in view of the breadth, the critical importance to the United States, and the high sensitivity of the information he sold to Israel."[32]

Pollard's life sentence sparked a wave of appeals and protests that have continued to the present and have rivaled the lingering controversy over the Rosenbergs' espionage. Although the Soviets worked far behind the scenes to orchestrate propaganda against the Rosenbergs' execution, the

Israelis, who had initially betrayed Pollard, openly badgered US government officials to lighten his sentence.

Since Pollard's conviction in 1987, Israeli prime ministers have personally appealed to US presidents for clemency, but every appeal has been rejected. In 1998, Prime Minister Benjamin Netanyahu even publicly admitted that the government was aware of the operation and acknowledged that Pollard had been its spy, even though four of his predecessors had claimed otherwise. But this humbling confession fell on deaf ears in America, and Pollard remained in prison. In the same year, the Israelis made yet another appeal to President Bill Clinton just as they were negotiating with the Palestinians at the Wye Plantation in Maryland. George Tenet, the CIA director who was doing double duty as an intermediary between the two sides, told Clinton that he would be forced to resign if Pollard were freed. Clinton again rejected the Israeli appeal.[33]

Throughout his time in prison, Pollard's own efforts have only harmed his case and alienated him from his family and friends. In 1990, he divorced his wife Anne and, in a prison ceremony, married Esther Seitz, a messianic supporter of the "Free Pollard" movement. Pollard was also granted Israeli citizenship in 1995. His family tried to dissuade him from the move because they believed it would harm his chances for a pardon. Pollard angrily severed ties with them.

Pollard trumpeted the injustice of his punishment from inside his prison cell. He fashioned himself as a Jewish patriot who did no harm to America and was sentenced to life because of anti-Semitic forces in the US government. His more vocal advocates, who organized rallies and collected funds for his legal fees, also raised the ugly specter of anti-Semitism as the insidious reason for locking him away for life.

The critical issues for Pollard's defenders revolved around the inordinately harsh punishment he received for spying for a close ally. Even those who were less strident about charges of anti-Semitism believed that Pollard had been singled out for harsh punishment primarily because he spied for Israel: "He was punished in a way that no one spying for an ally had ever been punished before."[34] The United States, they argued, was outraged that an ally like Israel had deceived its main benefactor. The United States could not punish Israel because of larger strategic equities, so it punished Pollard instead. His defenders buttressed this argument by noting the subtle distinction between spying *against* the United States and *for* Israel. In their view, Pollard was guilty of espionage for Israel but had done no harm to US interests. American espionage law, however, recognizes no such subtlety.

A key argument in Pollard's defense was the comparatively lighter sentences given to other Americans who spied for US allies. Other Americans who have spied for friendly countries, in fact, have received disproportionately lenient sentences in comparison with Pollard. Even some who betrayed secrets to the Soviets, like Clayton Lonetree, have not been condemned to a lifetime in prison. This argument, however, ignores one glaring difference between Pollard and these spies. The staggering amount of information Pollard gave away single-handedly provided an often independent-minded ally with advantages that could have been used for military actions in the Middle East inimical to American strategic interests.

The political context of the era also contributed significantly to Pollard's fate, just as it had in the Rosenbergs' case. The Decade of the Spy had shocked and infuriated the government and the American public. In that context, arrested spies stood little chance of leniency. In the 1980s, more spies were sentenced to life imprisonment than in any decade in American history. Pollard was hardly singled out to spend the rest of his days behind bars—John Walker, his brother Arthur, Jerry Whitworth, Ronald Pelton, and Clyde Conrad met the same fate. Larry Wu-tai Chin could have received the same sentence if he had not committed suicide, and Edward Lee Howard would have undoubtedly joined the rest in prison for life if he had not fled to the USSR. Pollard's punishment might have been different if he had spied in another decade when the accumulated weight of espionage cases was not as overwhelming as in the 1980s.

Supporters of Jonathan Pollard still champion his cause today. A website, Justice for Jonathan Pollard (www.jonathanpollard.org), is devoted to securing his release and catalogues every aspect of his case, from alleged judicial flaws to conspiratorial anti-Semitic maneuvers that condemned him to life in prison. The website also announces rallies, letter campaigns, and other organized efforts to win clemency for their favorite victim. Although Pollard gradually faded into obscurity in the United States, his case still remains a controversial political issue in Israel. The Israelis even linked the Pollard case with the Middle East peace process in 2010. Israeli officials suggested that, in exchange for Pollard's release, they would continue a moratorium on construction of new West Bank settlements, a flashpoint in negotiations with the Palestinians.[35]

This tactic failed, but Pollard's supporters were undeterred. An intensive lobbying campaign organized by David Nyer, a twenty-five-year-old social worker in New York, resulted in a wave of appeals for a presidential pardon from members of Congress and former senior government officials.[36] Thirty-nine members of Congress joined an appeal championed by Representative Barney Frank, and the parade of luminaries included former secretaries of state Henry Kissinger and George Shultz, former attorney general Michael Mukasey, former CIA director James Woolsey, and the former chairmen of congressional intelligence committees Senator Dennis DeConcini and Representative Lee Hamilton.[37]

Encouraged by this support, Netanyahu, after assuming the prime minister post for a second time, broke precedence with his predecessors in January 2011 by making a public rather than a quiet appeal to the White House. Although admitting that Israel's actions in the Pollard case were "wrong and wholly unacceptable," Netanyahu emphasized the argument constantly voiced by Pollard's supporters regarding the disproportionate sentence.[38]

Opponents of a Pollard release were as intense as the spy's supporters. In the past, seven former secretaries of defense, four directors of naval intelligence, and senior congressional leaders have strongly argued against a pardon.[39] In the end, the Obama administration did not issue the pardon.

Pollard may yet see the light of day, however. According to NIS agent Ronald Olive, an obscure twist in the law guarantees the release of a person sentenced to life for certain crimes, among them espionage, after thirty years in prison.[40] At the same time, Israeli law reportedly stipulates that captured Israeli agents are entitled to continue receiving their salary at a double rate while they are imprisoned. Pollard will be a senior citizen by the time he has served thirty years in jail, but after that he may retire very comfortably in Israel on a nest egg from his brief time as a spy.

Pollard and the other major spies of the 1980s gradually faded from the American public's memory by the end of the decade. By that time, other dramatic events had shattered the world order in ways that would have a major impact on spying against America. In many ways, espionage would change radically. But in some ways, it would remain the same.

PART **V**

ESPIONAGE AND THE NEW WORLD ORDER: THE 1990s

The End of the
Cold War and
US Counterespionage

We have slain a large dragon. But we live now in a jungle with a
bewildering variety of poisonous snakes. And, in many ways,
the dragon was easier to keep track of.

CIA director **JAMES WOOLSEY** *at his Senate confirmation hearing, February 1993,
US Central Intelligence Agency; "Woolsey, Testimony at Confirmation Hearing."*

On the eve of the 1990s, hundreds of East and West German citizens chipped away at the Berlin Wall until they opened a gaping hole in the most visible symbol of the Cold War division of Europe. Within two years after the Berlin Wall fell, the communist regimes in Eastern Europe were toppled, Germany was reunified, and the Soviet Union ceased to exist. The superpower conflict that defined the world order for almost half a century was over.

Still, peace had not come. The "snakes" referred to by Woolsey had crawled out of the jungle in hot spots around the globe. During the 1990s, the United States deployed troops against warlords in Somalia and dictators in Iraq, Serbia, and Haiti. Terrorism gradually replaced the Soviet Union as the greatest threat to national security. A shadowy terrorist group known as al-Qaeda (Arabic for "the Base") sprouted from the jihadist forces that had fought the Soviets in Afghanistan and attacked Americans both at home and abroad. In 1993, al-Qaeda fanatics exploded a car bomb in the garage of New York's World Trade Center; and five years later, al-Qaeda's cohorts bombed US embassies in Kenya and Tanzania.

This new geopolitical order and these new threats were not the only dramatic changes of the decade. Globalization—the burgeoning economic and cultural interdependence of the world's peoples and corporations—was accelerated by revolutionary developments in telecommunications as the World Wide Web was born and the internet enabled instant communications around the globe. By 1994. one-third of American homes had a personal computer, and by the end of the decade an estimated 50 million Americans surfed the internet.

These revolutionary advances also changed spying against America. In the globalized economy, corporate information became as important to a nation's security as military or political secrets. America, the only remaining superpower when the dust of the Cold War settled, was the primary target. According to a survey by the American Society for Industrial Security, in 1996 alone the loss or compromising of American proprietary information cost more than $2 billion a month, a figure that doubled the following year.[1]

America's primary economic competitors had been its staunchest allies in the Cold War struggle against the Soviet Union. No longer facing a Soviet threat, these allies stole corporate secrets to gain advantages in the international marketplace. French intelligence routinely broke into hotel rooms in Paris to steal corporate secrets from the computers and suitcases of American businessmen.[2] Ronald Hoffman, a scientist at the Science Applications International Corporation, moonlighted by selling classified software to four Japanese companies. In response to this increasing wave of corporate theft, Congress passed the Economic Espionage Act in 1996, which made the theft or misappropriation of trade secrets a criminal offense.

The internet age also affected espionage against America. Some of the spies in the 1990s were computer savvy and used that knowledge to facilitate the acquisition and transmission of secrets to their handlers. At the same time, the computer revolution also benefited spy catchers. The development of data mining and link analysis software allowed investigators to sift through mounds of information rapidly and establish connections that might quickly narrow the list of potential espionage suspects.

These developments still did not deter Americans from spying, although incidents of known espionage decreased in the 1990s. According to DOD's PERSEREC study, twenty Americans began spying during the decade, only one-third the number during the Decade of the Spy.[3] With the Cold War over, new trends in espionage also emerged. The vast majority of Cold War spies had come from the military, but in the 1990s only one-quarter of those arrested for espionage came from its ranks. The military had learned a painful lesson from the espionage cases of the Cold War. All the services that had suffered from spies in their midst had vastly improved the lax security that had enabled John Walker, Clyde Conrad, and others to betray secrets for years.

As in the past decade, a growing number of spies in the 1990s passed secrets to US allies and were sometimes motivated more by divided loyalties than by money. According to the PERSEREC study, half the spies arrested in the 1990s claimed that dual allegiance impelled them to cooperate with foreign powers, a trend that reflected the increasing impact of globalization.[4] As PERSEREC analysts noted, "The traditional concept of national allegiance born in an era of nation-state politics breaks down in the global economy."[5]

One example of a spy with divided loyalties was Steven Lalas, a Greek American who spied for the Greek government for sixteen years and was arrested in May 1993. He was recruited by a Greek military officer while he was in the US Army in 1977, but his spying career blossomed when he later worked as a Department of State communicator. From 1991 to 1993, he was assigned to Athens, where he had direct access to the US Embassy's secret correspondence with Washington on bilateral relations with the Greek government. He had also passed to the Greeks classified documents on US strategy in the Balkans and assessments of Greek policy in the former Yugoslavia. Although his dual loyalty may have driven him to espionage, he also received a tidy sum of $20,000 from the Greeks during his Athens posting.[6]

A twist on divided loyalty was the case of Albert Sombolay, a naturalized American born in Zaire who enlisted in the US Army in 1985. In 1990, Sombolay, while serving in an artillery unit in Germany, volunteered to spy for Iraq and Jordan out of loyalty not to either country but to the Arab cause in general. The Iraqis never responded to his offer, but Sombolay passed infor-mation about military deployments to Jordan, one of America's strongest allies in the Middle East. Sombolay was arrested in 1991 and sentenced in a court-martial to thirty-four years of hard labor.[7]

Sombolay's case reflects the potentially imminent damage from military spies. At a time when US forces are spread around the globe in peacekeep-ing missions and fighting insurgents in Afghanistan, a spy in the ranks can provide information about military plans and tactics that can cost Ameri-can lives. Considering the level of America's military commitment around the world, an effective counterespionage policy is as essential to the protec-tion of the armed forces as body armor and gas masks.

Despite these new trends in espionage, the end of the Cold War did not herald the end of Russian spying against America. When Boris Yeltsin defied hard-line coup plotters against the Gorbachev government in August 1991, jubilant crowds of Muscovites hauled down the towering bronze statue of Felix Dzerzhinsky in Lubyanka Square in front of KGB headquarters. Dzerzhinsky, who established the Bolsheviks' first internal security service, the Cheka, to spread their iron rule over Russia, was the father of the KGB, the omnipotent instrument of Communist Party policy that had combined the functions of the American CIA, FBI, NSA, and other law enforcement and intelligence agencies. His statue may have come down in 1991, but his spirit would soon rise from the ashes.

After the collapse of the Soviet Union, the KGB was dissolved, and its functions were dispersed to a host of new, separate agencies. Foreign intel-ligence collection was delegated to the Foreign Intelligence Service (SVR, the acronym for Sluzhba vneshney razvedki in Russian), where it has remained until the present. The more controversial internal security responsibilities went through a rockier transformation and were assigned to a row of newly minted organizations that were disbanded and renamed in rapid succession.

Finally, this merry-go-round of name changes and reorganizations ended in April 1995, when President Yeltsin created the Federal Security Service (FSB, the acronym for Federal'naya sluzhba bezopasnosti in Russian). Before long the FSB began to recover not only its lost pride but also some of the former powers of the KGB. In 1998 Vladimir Putin, a former KGB offi-cer, was tabbed by Yeltsin to head the FSB; within two years he was elected

Russia's president, a testimony to the restored influence of the country's internal security service. Putin escalated the FSB's budgets and personnel numbers, and an emboldened FSB soon began trumpeting the dangers of foreign espionage in the strident language of the Soviet era.

The SVR also clung to its communist past. The government may have changed the name from the KGB First Chief Directorate to the SVR, but it was unable to change the world outlook of its officers. Like their FSB counterparts, SVR officers were nurtured on the belief that Russia was surrounded by enemies on all sides and that the West, led by the United States, was bent on destroying their way of life. Soviet communism may have ceased to exist, but the threat from the West had not.

Russia also faced domestic threats similar to those faced by the United States: the ballooning influence of organized crime and terrorism within its own borders. The collapse of the Soviet Union had rekindled nationalist passions that had been dampened by Soviet repression. Now rebels in Chechnya sought their independence through increasingly violent attacks against Russian targets. All these emerging threats required domestic and foreign intelligence services capable of adjusting their Cold War strategies. Instead, the SVR, much like the FSB, still considered the United States to be the "main enemy," the KGB's official designation for its Cold War adversary.

When the SVR was created after the abolition of the KGB, the service was still actively running spies inside the US government. One of these spies had worked deep inside the inner sanctum of the CIA, and his arrest would have a crippling impact on the agency into the next century.

Aldrich Ames and
His Impact on the CIA

Thanks to Ames, we all but shut down CIA operations in Moscow.

VIKTOR CHERKASHIN, *one of Aldrich Ames's*
KGB handlers; Cherkashin, Spy Handler, *4*

On February 21, 1994, the vast majority of CIA employees were shocked to see one of their colleagues, Aldrich Ames, on the television news, in handcuffs, flanked by men in FBI blue jackets who pushed him into an unmarked car. The headline emblazoned on the screen read SOVIET SPY ARRESTED. Spies in the US government abounded in the 1980s. But a CIA veteran at the center of Soviet operations? Inconceivable. Yet the inconceivable had now happened.

A small circle of CIA officers knew that Ames would be arrested.[1] For almost a decade, they had wrestled with a gnawing problem: America's best spies inside the Soviet government, one after the other, had been caught and executed by the KGB in the mid-1980s. At the height of the Cold War, when information from these spies was crucial for President Ronald Reagan's clash with the Soviet Union, they had been picked off in rapid succession by the KGB and eliminated. Edward Lee Howard was unaware of most of the spies, so his treachery could not explain the losses.

Clayton Lonetree and another US Marine Corps guard may have let the KGB into the US Embassy in Moscow, but this explanation was also discarded after an exhaustive review of CIA documents in Moscow.[2]

The mystery was finally solved. All along, it had been one of the CIA's own. Aldrich Ames spied for the Soviet Union and then for the Russian Federation for nine years. He volunteered to spy for the Soviet KGB in April 1985, in the midst of the "Year of the Spy." Two months later, he betrayed the names of every major Soviet spy working for the CIA. If he had quit spying that very day, he would have still justified the assessment of his espionage by then–CIA deputy director Robert Gates: "There is no doubt that the Agency's greatest counterintelligence failure and perhaps operational failure during the last half of the Cold War was Ames's treason and his work as a Soviet mole in the heart of CIA's clandestine service."[3]

In return for his treachery, Ames was the highest-paid American spy of the Cold War (the highest-paid *known* spy, that is). He was not only one of five in the $1 million club; he stood alone in the $2 million ranks, with a hefty $2.5 million in cash payments and KGB accounts by the time of his arrest. He earned twice as much money as John Walker in half the time.

"Rick" Ames, as he was known among his colleagues, was born in the rustic town of River Falls, Wisconsin, in May 1941. His parents were both teachers—his father, Carleton, was a history professor; and his mother, Rachel, was a teacher in the local high school. Carleton's specialty was Asia, and in the formative years of the CIA he was enlisted by the agency to serve a tour in Southeast Asia. Carleton Ames, however, proved to be a heavy-drinking, plodding officer who received less-than-glowing appraisals of his performance. Unfortunately, most of his children inherited his unlucky genes. Three of his four children, including Rick, developed drinking problems.[4]

Rick Ames enrolled in the University of Chicago in 1959 to pursue dual interests in international relations and drama. Drawn more by the Bohemian life of the theater, he flunked out of college. In 1962, he followed his father's footsteps into the CIA and eventually earned a degree by studying nights at George Washington University. He was then accepted into the clandestine service and, after training, he was assigned overseas to conduct espionage operations in Istanbul and then in Mexico City.

Before his first tour in Turkey, Ames married a fellow CIA employee, Nancy Segebarth, but the marriage was already on the rocks by the time he met Maria Del Rosario Casas Dupuy on his tour in Mexico City. Rosario, a cultural attaché in the Colombian Embassy, had been recruited by one of Ames's colleagues to provide information on Soviet bloc diplomats in the Mexican capital. By the time Ames's tour ended, he and Rosario were in love and, in 1983, he separated from his wife. Rosario quit the Colombian government and returned to the United States to live with Rick, who was assigned to CIA headquarters until his divorce was settled and, in keeping with agency regulations, Rosario became a US citizen.

Ames, who had specialized in the Soviet target, was assigned as chief of the branch in the Soviet Division which was responsible for monitoring worldwide Soviet operations from a counterintelligence perspective to ensure they were run securely.[5] The job was one of the most critical in the CIA's spy service, and only a few officers at CIA headquarters were privy to the full scope of these operations and knew the identities of America's spies inside the Soviet government. Rick Ames sat in this small circle. If the KGB had drafted a wish list of spies to run in the entire CIA, the chief of this counterintelligence branch would have been among the top ten.

In many ways, Ames was suited for the job. A bookish and somewhat tweedy professorial type, he had shown little of the social skills and street smarts required of an effective recruiter and handler of spies in his first two overseas tours. Supervisors had noted in performance appraisals that he was clearly more suitable for desk jobs at headquarters, where he could apply his analytic skills.[6]

While in the headquarters job, Ames's financial problems worsened daily. Burdened by debts from a costly divorce, he also faced Rosario's demands for a lifestyle to which she had grown accustomed as a Colombian diplomat overseas. The accumulating financial pressures were overwhelming him to a degree that, he later admitted, had "embarrassed and potentially humiliated" him.[7] Sometime in late 1984 or early 1985, he later confessed, the idea of using his unique access to cure his financial ills dawned on him.

During his time in the job, Ames developed a relationship with a joint FBI–CIA unit targeting Soviet officials in the United States. The joint unit sanctioned Ames's proposal to cultivate Sergey Chuvakhin, a diplomat in the Soviet Embassy, which gave him perfect cover to initiate an espionage relationship with the Soviets. In April 1985, before a scheduled meeting with Chuvakhin, Ames screwed up his courage with a few vodkas, the alcoholic tactic that had fortified him in so many critical moments in the past. As luck would have it, Chuvakhin failed to show for their appointed meeting, and Ames walked a few blocks from their meeting site to the Soviet Embassy. Once inside, he mumbled to a security guard a few comments about Chuvakhin's no-show, but at the same time he passed a note for delivery to the KGB resident. In the note Ames identified himself and provided the identities of two Soviet double agents and a CIA phone directory listing with his name.[8]

At this point Ames, like many other American spies, rationalized his actions. He asked for a quick $50,000 in exchange for the information, which, he reasoned to himself, was of little national security value because the agents in question were provocations already working for the KGB. A month later, Ames received the money.

As Ames leafed through the greenbacks, he realized that this KGB payment did not have to be the last one. In his unique position in the CIA, he also realized that he was in danger once he identified himself to the KGB. He was among the handful of officers who knew that the CIA had riddled the KGB and GRU with penetrations. One of them might learn about his approach and betray him to the CIA. He was trapped in a vicious circle. The more he gave the KGB, the greater the risk that a Soviet spy could tell the CIA about a major leak. To protect himself, Ames decided that he would have to betray the Soviets who could endanger him.[9]

On June 13, 1985, Ames met Chuvakhin at Chadwick's, a quiet bar tucked away below a freeway in Washington's fashionable Georgetown neighborhood. From the KGB's perspective, Ames's initial information, a phone list and a couple of double agents, had whetted their appetite but had not proven conclusively that he was a genuine CIA volunteer. Chuvakhin was ordered to continue the overtly "diplomatic" dialogue in the event Ames's approach was an FBI trap to ensnare a KGB officer in Washington.

During the lunch Ames proved to the KGB beyond any doubt that he was genuine. He quietly slipped Chuvakhin a bag full of documents that would condemn to death the West's most important spies inside the Soviet Union.[10] Among the names in the bag were Dmitriy Polyakov, the GRU general who had spied for the CIA inside the senior ranks of the Soviet military for more than two decades, and Oleg Gordievsky, the high-ranking KGB resident in London who had passed secrets to the

British for years. Ames also betrayed a dozen more Soviet sources working for the CIA and FBI, including Valeriy Martynov and Sergey Motorin, two KGB officers in Washington who had been recruited by the joint FBI–CIA unit.[11]

The bag of secrets was a counterespionage gold mine. No American had ever betrayed so many of his country's spies in a single meeting.

For almost nine years after that meeting, Ames continued to pass secrets to the KGB during an overseas assignment in Rome and tours at headquarters. A few months after the meeting, Ames married Rosario. While posted to headquarters, Ames, using the pretext of visiting his wife's family in Colombia, traveled to Bogotá and Caracas to meet his KGB handlers or communicated with them in Washington through an impersonal communications system of dead drops similar to that of John Walker. In about 1992, Rosario accidentally discovered the KGB's notes, which her careless husband had squirreled away instead of destroying. Unlike Barbara Walker, Rosario overcame her initial shock and never objected to Rick's spying, especially because its fruits bought her the luxury goods she craved.

The Soviets themselves almost compromised their prize spy. Ames's gold mine of information about the vast extent of CIA espionage was a bitter pill to swallow. The Politburo was so outraged at the massive hemorrhage of secrets that its knee-jerk reaction was to arrest and punish the traitors en masse. According to Viktor Cherkashin, the officer who handled the Ames case in Washington, KGB chief Alexander Kryuchkov pushed the proposal for mass arrests out of blind ambition.[12]

No matter who was responsible for the idea, KGB professionals were undoubtedly horrified. Karl Koecher had been arrested the year before and, just a month before Ames betrayed the CIA network, John Walker had been finally neutralized after eighteen years of spying for the KGB. The US government was highly sensitized to espionage, and the arrest of so many Soviet agents could alert it to a mole in the CIA and endanger a source who could continue to pass secrets for years. This time the KGB might not be able to withstand an Angletonian molehunt that could pinpoint Ames.

The KGB presumably argued for other options: arrest and execute some, arrest others and force them to tell the CIA they had retired or switched jobs, string out the operations for years to prevent any CIA suspicions. They undoubtedly proposed to let the spies continue contact with the CIA to feed disinformation and identify more CIA officers and modus operandi in the process that could ferret out other spies. All their arguments fell on deaf ears.

There is no indication that the outraged Soviet Politburo thought about anything but retribution. These Soviet leaders never asked themselves why more than a dozen of their most qualified professionals in the intelligence services and the military spied for the enemy. They never asked why these members of the elite, who traveled abroad and lived a far more comfortable lifestyle than the average Soviet citizen, risked their lives in a tightly controlled dictatorship to betray secrets to the USSR's sworn enemy. If they had asked those questions, the aged fossils in the Politburo might have found some answers to prevent the crumbling of their empire. Instead, they dismissed the CIA spies as traitorous aberrations rather than symptoms of a cancer eating away at the body politic. Punishment of the spies was little more than a band-aid on the sucking chest wound of Soviet communism.

Faced with an intransigent Politburo, the KGB took elaborate measures to protect Ames. It threw out red herrings, tidbits of disinformation cleverly designed to divert the CIA away from the possibility of a mole in its midst.[13] As one example, a shadowy Soviet volunteer dubbed "Mr. X" popped up in East Berlin to tell the CIA that its communications had been compromised.[14] KGB hallway gossip and other reports were carefully fed to the CIA claiming that gross tradecraft blunders in Moscow or security lapses by the agents themselves had tipped off KGB supersleuths. The unmasking of Lonetree, a minor spy in the KGB pantheon, and the possibility that marine guards may have let the KGB into the Moscow Embassy afforded the Soviets an unexpected opportunity to further muddle the issue for the CIA.

The KGB red herrings succeeded in distracting the CIA. CIA director William Casey tasked former director of operations John Stein to conduct an independent investigation of the compromises.[15] Although Stein's final report could not be found, according to subsequent recollections, he had suggested that a technical breach may have been responsible and that no common denominators existed among the cases. Each, perhaps, bore the "seeds of its own destruction"—that is, perhaps a mistake by a CIA officer in Moscow who had failed to spot a surveillant; perhaps an error by the agent, who had been overzealous in photographing a document in his office; perhaps spending beyond his means and inviting suspicion.

Besides that, by the late 1980s the CIA leadership was preoccupied with other issues, especially the Iran-Contra scandal that would plague the last years of the Reagan administration and result in the indictments of senior CIA officials. Soon the compromises receded into the past and were largely forgotten. Arrests of Soviet agents eventually petered out. Ames had been granted an overseas assignment to Rome and, though he continued to spy for the KGB, he no longer had access to the inner sanctum of CIA's Soviet operations. By the end of the decade, the Berlin Wall had fallen and the Soviet Union was in disarray. The mysterious spy arrests of the mid-1980s were merely pesky gnats swarming around the battlefield of a war now won, an unsolved puzzle from a bygone age.

A more fundamental issue was at the heart of the CIA's failure to pursue the compromises. Ultimately, like other Americans throughout the Cold War, and indeed throughout US history, the CIA suffered from the same disbelief that had plagued counterespionage in the past, a disbelief that one of its own could spy for the enemy. Still haunted by the legacy of Angleton's witch hunt in the 1970s, the CIA was even less disposed than its sister agencies to suspect a spy in its midst.

As in other cases, the warning signs had already been present for years. Even if Rick Ames had not turned out to be a spy, his assignment to one of the most sensitive CIA positions was highly questionable based on his performance alone. Although he displayed occasional flashes of competence, he was a mediocre officer. He received some scathing performance evaluations throughout his career, which had undoubtedly added a dollop of revenge and resentment to his financial motives for spying. His superior in Turkey labeled him as "unsuited for the life of an operations officer overseas."[16] By 1990, Ames was a senior officer with considerable experience in Soviet operations but was still ranked third from the bottom by a promotion panel.[17]

Ames had also inherited his father's drinking genes. Drinking, however, was an occupational hazard in the espionage world. Long nights cultivating foreigners for recruitment in smoke-filled bars and other haunts in foreign capitals were fueled by alcohol. Ames, however, exceeded even the CIA's relaxed standards. He had passed out in drunken stupors at CIA social events and was driven home once by security guards.[18] Similar incidents plagued him throughout his career, not only in the CIA but even in his espionage contacts with the Russians, where he was often drunk and forgot basic information about meeting times and places.

Besides drinking, Ames committed numerous gaffes throughout his career. After dozing on a subway in New York, he left a briefcase on the seat full of classified information.[19] Fortunately, a Polish émigré found the bag and, after glancing at the documents, returned it to the FBI. Ames also used a safe house in New York for a tryst with Rosario, still his girlfriend at the time, a clear violation of basic security regulations. During a routine reinvestigation, Ames's colleagues in Rome also noted that he frequently left his safe open at night.[20]

Not every poor performer is a spy. Ames may have ranked third from the bottom on an employee evaluation list, but there were two others below him. Neither one turned out to be a spy. Besides his mediocre record, however, he also displayed a number of glaring espionage indicators. If anyone at the CIA had paid a modicum of attention to these indicators, he might have been caught before 1994.

One of the ironies of the case was that Ames, a trained CIA operations officer with considerable experience in Soviet operations, practiced horrendous tradecraft and ignored elemental security procedures. Some spies prove to be far more adept at espionage than they are at their real jobs. Ames was not. He was as lazy, sloppy, and careless at spying as he was at his CIA job.

Ames made only feeble attempts to conceal his growing payments from the KGB. By the time he returned from his tour in Rome, his colleagues began to notice that he was sporting Italian designer suits and had had all his teeth capped, a vast improvement after a lifetime of chain smoking. He also parked a brand new Jaguar at CIA headquarters every day and allowed his avaricious wife to indulge in expensive purchases on the couple's credit cards. When Ames was arrested, Rosario reportedly had five hundred pairs of shoes in her closet, a collection probably only rivaled by that of Imelda Marcos.[21]

Ames was amassing about $30,000 a month in credit card bills, a princely sum for a midlevel government bureaucrat. His most dimwitted expenditure was to pay $540,000 in cash for a new house in suburban northern Virginia and to spruce it up with another $100,000 in improvements.[22] To avoid any suspicion, he could have easily taken a mortgage on the house, as most Americans would do. Instead, he explained that his newfound wealth came from the largesse of his rich Colombian in-laws.

Ames's misuse of money was not his only careless mistake. He had a solid pretext to meet his Soviet handlers so he could pass them CIA secrets. In Washington he was supposedly cultivating the Soviet diplomat Sergey Chuvakhin for recruitment, and later in Rome he was doing the same with Alexander Khrenkov, another Soviet official. Ames was required to report all these contacts and record the results of his meetings. But he neglected to report many of them, primarily out of sheer laziness. When he was chided by a supervisor in Rome about his failure to report the Khrenkov meetings, Ames angrily replied that he would pay for the meetings himself so he would not have to be bothered with the reporting.[23] The incident aroused suspicion and would later figure in the mounting body of evidence against him. CIA officers did not have casual social relationships with KGB officers, and Ames was admitting to a superior that he intended to violate regulations. Spying always entailed unavoidable risks, but Ames continually took unnecessary ones. He could have easily fabricated reports about the meetings to stave off any suspicion.

Ames's laziness resulted in other tradecraft blunders. Spies routinely destroy their materials or hide them in specially crafted concealment devices to prevent accidental discovery or withstand any officially sanctioned searches that might arise. A sloppy pack rat, Ames left his correspondence with the Soviets lying around his house or routinely threw incriminating notes away in the garbage.

Yet despite his endless series of basic tradecraft errors, Ames spied unhindered for nine years because of the CIA's disbelief. One CIA officer, however, was convinced that there was a mole within. Paul Redmond, the deputy chief of CIA counterintelligence in the early 1990s, revived the mole hunt and assigned a small team of crack investigators led by veteran analyst Jeanne Vertefeuille to discreetly start the search.[24] In the summer of 1991, he also alerted the FBI about the revived investigation and promised to share with them full details about the compromise of the Soviet network.

The FBI had its own interest in the compromises because its two sources inside the KGB residency in Washington, Vladimir Martynov and Sergey Motorin, were among those who had been executed. The FBI had independently run its own investigation, code-named ANLACE, to find the cause of the compromises but had gotten nowhere.

Redmond's team focused on CIA employees who knew about the compromised Soviet agents and began winnowing out possible suspects. Ames was among them and stood out because of his lavish lifestyle. As in the Clyde Conrad case, Redmond's investigators followed the money and the team gradually uncovered the trail of financial evidence that Ames had left in his wake—the cash payment for his house, credit card bills amounting to $455,000, and several bank deposits of less than $10,000 to avoid Internal Revenue Service reporting requirements. Sandy Grimes, one of the key CIA investigators, compared the dates of the deposits with the dates of his reported meetings in Washington with Chuvakhin. Ames's deposits were all made within a few days after meeting the Soviet.[25] By the end of 1992, Rick Ames was the leading spy suspect.

The FBI arrayed the full investigative resources at its disposal against Ames, whose lazy carelessness finally came home to roost. Covert searches of his house and trash surfaced spy notes he had written to the Soviets, other incriminating texts left on his printer ribbon, and more notes on his computer. He had entered the computer age and transmitted notes to the KGB on diskettes. His computer skills, however, were rudimentary. The KGB's notes to him on diskettes were written in WordPerfect 5.1, a format that automatically creates its own backup files.[26] FBI experts easily found the damning evidence on Ames's computer.

Once he became the leading suspect, Ames was shuffled off to a job at CIA's Counternarcotics Center, where he had little access to information about Russian operations.[27] His job mainly involved multilateral intelligence cooperation among countries in the Black Sea region to combat narcotics trafficking. Russia was one of the countries involved in the project and Ames was scheduled to travel to Moscow on an official visit in February 1994. Although Ames seemed oblivious to the intense investigation swirling around him, the FBI and CIA could not risk him getting wind of it and seeking asylum with his Russian handlers. Another Edward Lee Howard would devastate both agencies.

On February 21, the day before Ames was scheduled to leave for Moscow, he was suddenly summoned to CIA headquarters regarding last-minute preparations for the trip. It was a federal holiday and there was little traffic as he drove on the quiet, tree-lined streets near his home in Arlington, Virginia. A few blocks from his home, he edged up to a stop sign and found his path blocked by a car. Another car zoomed in behind him, and Mike Donner, a towering, brawny FBI agent, jumped out of the car and arrested Rick Ames. Rosario was arrested at their home soon after.

Rick and Rosario had a five-year-old son who, like the Rosenbergs' sons, could have been faced with a parentless life. Ames was offered a plea bargain—admit his guilt and cooperate fully about his espionage activities, and in return Rosario would receive a more lenient sentence. Although the CIA and FBI knew that Ames had betrayed its top Soviet agents, they could only gauge the full extent of his damage by debriefing him in detail about all the information he had passed to the KGB for nine years. Fearing for his son's welfare, Ames agreed. He was sentenced to life imprisonment, and Rosario was sentenced to five years.

Ames was not the first CIA spy to be arrested; nor would he be the last. Unlike David Barnett, William Kampiles, and Edward Lee Howard, Ames was still on active duty with the CIA when he was arrested. He had also spied for far longer than any other CIA spy working for the Soviets but, much more important, he had far more access than other CIA spies. He was at the heart of the agency's most closely guarded counterintelligence secrets: the operations and recruitments of agents in the camp of America's main adversary. Ames was the KGB's lifelong dream and the CIA's nightmare—the perfect spy who could neutralize the entire CIA espionage apparatus against the Soviet Union worldwide.

Besides the incalculable human tragedy of the betrayed agents' fate, the damage done by Ames was extensive from an intelligence perspective. The network he compromised included a broad spectrum of sources in the Soviet intelligence services, foreign policy, and the military. The damage, however, went far beyond past cases. His treachery sent a chilling message to anyone who was either a CIA spy or considering a recruitment offer. Even if CIA officers claim that your security is their top priority, they cannot guarantee it. No matter how closely held your identity may be, there could be someone else like Ames ready to betray you. Ames's treachery could cast a pall over the CIA's efforts to recruit new spies and acquire intelligence about the Russian Federation.

Ames's arrest was followed by revelations that the CIA had given policy-makers intelligence from Soviet double agents in operations that may have been devised with Ames's advice. A panel tasked with studying the double agents believed that the tainted intelligence may have led to costly overestimates by DOD of Soviet weapons programs. The panel's report was another damaging blow to the CIA—not only had Ames poisoned the CIA's ability to recruit new sources, but its main consumers in the US government had also lost confidence in its intelligence.[28]

Still, Ames proved that spies rarely change history. Despite the extensive damage he did, despite the loss of an entire network of Soviet spies, his espionage had no impact on the outcome of the Cold War. The Soviets may have stopped the leak of their secrets thanks to him, but the other overwhelming problems afflicting the Soviet empire ultimately caused its downfall.

Although Ames's espionage had little impact on the superpower rivalry of the Cold War, his treachery devastated the CIA. The firestorm of criticism crippled the nation's primary intelligence organization for years to come. Because of the CIA's failure to acknowledge the possibility of a spy in its midst, some in the media portrayed the Directorate of Operations as a crusty, smug elitist network of old boys blinded by their hermetically sealed culture. Harsher critics portrayed the clandestine service as simply bungling clowns, and the CIA became grist for the humor mill of late-night comics and political cartoonists.[29] Past CIA scandals for the most part painted an image of a spy service transgressing its authorities in some cases, perhaps overzealous in pursuing its mission, but nonetheless swashbuckling and ruthlessly efficient. The Ames case, however, revealed that the CIA, which is "often portrayed as a wily covert manipulator of global events, is in fact a tired bureaucracy."[30]

The timing of the Ames arrest also exacerbated the damage to the CIA. After the downfall of the USSR in 1991, both the media and Congress raised questions about the mission of the CIA in a post–Cold War world. Senator Daniel Moynihan had even called for the abolition of the CIA and transfer of its duties to the Department of State. After decades of Cold War struggle, Americans were also weary and ready to reap the peace dividend of victory. In response, Congress had already called for deep cuts in the CIA's budget and personnel.

These CIA critics believed that the Ames case only justified their argument. In the late 1980s, the heyday of Ames's espionage, the Soviet Union was in its death throes, outgunned militarily and outstripped economically by the United States. But the Soviet Union had not been outspied. In the view of the CIA critics, Ames's treachery revealed that the only area of Soviet predominance had been in the intelligence arena. If the Cold War was eventually won without the CIA, emasculated as it was by a long-undetected spy within, who needed it in a post–Cold War world? Not only was the CIA an anachronism to these critics; it had also proven to be incompetent and ineffective.

Very few commented on the opposite side of the coin. Aside from Ames, other CIA officers around the globe had obtained the enemy's secrets from dozens of penetrations in the Soviet government and the Soviet bloc throughout the Cold War. For years as he ascended to the general ranks, Dmitriy Polyakov provided secrets of the Soviet military that were considered an invaluable contribution to US understanding of the strategy, tactics, and intentions behind the Soviet threat.[31] Colonel Ryszard Kuklinski, a Polish military intelligence officer, provided the CIA with "thousands of pieces of key information about the Warsaw Pact" and reported first hand information on Soviet and Polish government plans regarding the imposition of martial law in Poland.[32] Before their compromise by Ames, over a dozen KGB and GRU officers stationed around the globe revealed Soviet intelligence operations against US national security interests.[33] The hard work of all the CIA officers involved in these operations, their dedication and successes, were unfortunately overshadowed by Ames's treachery and lost in the congressional and media furor over the case.

One of the more humiliating episodes for the CIA in this uproar was a visit paid to Ames in jail by the chairmen of the congressional intelligence committees, Senator Dennis DeConcini and Representative Dan Glickman. Like other American spies before him, Ames tried to mask the greed motivating his espionage with more high-minded political motives, claiming that the CIA was a self-serving sham that deceived the American people.[34] Incredibly, DeConcini and Glickman solicited Ames's views about his own espionage and the role of intelligence in the post–Cold War world, which only gave the confessed spy a forum to join other critics in lambasting his former employer. "It was," CIA director James Woolsey said, "a little bit like taking John Gotti as an authority on the FBI."[35]

The House and Senate intelligence committees chaired by Glickman and DeConcini conducted investigations that condemned the CIA for its handling of the Ames case. The CIA's inspector general, Fred Hitz, also issued a scathing report. After reviewing it, Woolsey dubbed the Ames case "a systemic failure of the CIA; . . . a failure in management, accountability, in judgment, in vigilance."[36] Hitz's report laid responsibility for the debacle on twenty-three senior CIA officers, including former CIA directors William Casey, William Webster, and Robert Gates.

Woolsey chose to reprimand eleven current and retired senior officers. Although he also wanted to institute some major counterintelligence changes at the CIA, calls by critics for more radical reform eclipsed his attempts. Senator DeConcini was adamant about stripping the CIA's traditional overseas counterintelligence responsibilities and giving them to the FBI. But even FBI director Louis Freeh argued against the inefficiency of that proposal.[37] Others in the FBI, however, were less forgiving. Even after the embarrassing Howard escape, the CIA had continued to withhold key counterespionage information from the FBI, and senior FBI officials fought hammer and tongs over the Ames case to ensure that such a situation would never happen again.[38] Finally, both the executive and legislative branches stepped into the fray and ordered the squabbling children to play nicely in the sandbox.

In the 1995 intelligence authorization bill, Congress enacted into law a provision that not only the CIA, but every government agency, would be required to notify the FBI in a timely manner of any indication that classified information may have been disclosed to a foreign power without authorization.[39] This meant that the CIA did not have to suspect one of its employees was a spy to meet the legal threshold for notifying the FBI; the mere indication that classified information had been passed would now require notification. The compromises of CIA agents in the mid-1980s would have met that threshold and required immediate notification to the FBI.

The White House introduced its own reforms. In May 1994 President Bill Clinton issued a presidential directive establishing the National Counterintelligence Center to coordinate activities more effectively among agencies involved in counterintelligence, particularly the FBI and CIA.[40] The galling part of the directive for the CIA was a mandate that the chief of counterespionage at the agency would now be a senior FBI agent. Some in the CIA considered the directive a presidential reprimand for the Ames case. For its punishment, the CIA would now be forced to endure the FBI looking over its shoulder, digging into its files, and making decisions about possible espionage cases.

The CIA would have far more serious concerns to worry about because of Ames. Ultimately the Ames case was the most devastating in CIA history, crippling the agency and discrediting it in the eyes of the American public. The Ames case convinced an already-skeptical Congress to slash the CIA's budget and staff; created mistrust in its intelligence, the very heart of its mission; and raised self-doubt in the agency itself about its mission and its effectiveness. The CIA nose-dived in a tailspin from which it had not recovered before September 11, 2001, when the nation most needed the best spy service possible.

Ames's arrest had solved the mystery of the Soviet agents compromised in the 1980s. But there had been other operations compromised to which Ames had no access. In one case, the FBI and CIA were quietly investigating suspicions in 1989 that Felix Bloch, a high-ranking State Department officer, was a Soviet spy. FBI agents monitoring Bloch's phone conversations were shocked as they listened to an anonymous call tipping him off to the investigation.[41]

Ames had not the slightest idea about the Bloch investigation. After a decade marked by the arrests of major spies, the FBI and CIA were now accustomed to the possibility of moles within the intelligence community. And now the possibility existed that there may have been another Soviet mole buried inside US intelligence. The CIA had been crippled by the Ames case; revelation of a second spy could be the final nail in its coffin. Still, a small cadre of CIA and FBI officers collaborated quietly for years after Ames's arrest to narrow down possible suspects in the CIA. In the end, they were looking in the wrong place.

The Spy in the FBI

ROBERT HANSSEN

My security concerns may seem excessive. I believe experience has shown them to be necessary. I am much safer if you know little about me. Over time I can cut your losses rather than become one.

ROBERT HANSSEN, *in a letter to his KGB handlers, July 1988,*
quoted by Rafalko, Counterintelligence Reader, *4:111*

Throughout the Cold War, the FBI had proven less vulnerable to penetration than its sister agencies, but it too had suffered damage from Soviet espionage. In 1984, Richard Miller—an overweight, slovenly, and bumbling FBI agent in Los Angeles—had an affair with Svetlana Ogorodnikova, a Soviet émigré who recruited him for the KGB.[1] Miller was lured by the dual thrills of spying and romance, but he was also motivated by the extra money that would come in handy to support his family of eight children. Financially strapped, he initially sold Amway products from his car before he discovered the more lucrative side job of a spy.[2] He turned out to be as inept a spy as he was an FBI agent and was nabbed early in the operation. He was sentenced to twenty years in prison for his ham-handed spying and became the first FBI agent convicted of espionage.[3]

In the late 1990s, the intensive search for a mole besides Ames resulted in the capture of another FBI agent. Edward Earl Pitts had worked in FBI counterintelligence in the New York field office in the 1980s. Pitts experienced financial problems from the high cost of living in New York. To overcome them, he volunteered to spy for the KGB in 1987 and passed them FBI information for five years. Pitts's espionage for the Russians ended after he was reassigned to the FBI's Legal Division in Washington, where he had little access to information of interest to his spymasters.[4]

The FBI decided to run a sting operation against Pitts because he was no longer spying for the Russians. An FBI agent with native Russian recontacted him, ostensibly to renew the spy relationship. Pitts took the bait and began passing more classified information until the FBI had enough evidence to arrest him in December 1996.[5] Pitts pled guilty and was sentenced to twenty-seven years imprisonment after promising full cooperation about his spying activities. Pitts, however, had no access to the unexplained compromises. The second spy had to be someone else.

A small team at the FBI and CIA trudged ahead in the search for the elusive second spy.[6] By White House mandate, CIA counterespionage officers in the hunt were now supervised by a senior FBI agent. The first years of the new arrangement were occasionally marked by bitter clashes and flared tempers. The conflict was, in many ways, cultural. FBI and CIA officers working together in the same close quarters belonged to the same religion, counterespionage, but were from radically different sects. The CIA jealously guarded the secrets from its agents, even when that information related to the FBI's job of prosecuting spies. The FBI, conversely, needed to use evidence in an open court, even if that evidence came from CIA sources that could be compromised.

Time heals all wounds, and it eventually did so in the scarred FBI–CIA relationship. Besides the FBI chief of CIA counterespionage, other FBI agents were assigned on tours to the CIA, and soon CIA officers were working in FBI offices. The rotational policy, jokingly dubbed the "hostage exchange" program, gradually increased understanding and cooperation between the two onetime rivals. Although there were still occasional skirmishes over turf, FBI and CIA officers were cooperating on espionage cases as never before. Working in the same office, sharing similar stories about government service over a beer, traveling through the same rush hour traffic, the officers found there was more that united than divided them.

The one unfortunate by-product of this cooperation is that both sides developed a mindset about the spy hunt.[7] Like the CIA before Ames, the

FBI was culturally resistant to the notion that an FBI agent could be the major spy they sought. FBI spy hunters believed the second mole was in the CIA, and CIA officers shared the same theory. The CIA had already experienced two major Soviet spies in its midst, Howard and Ames, and in 1996 yet another, Jim Nicholson, an operations officer with no access to the unexplained compromises, was arrested for espionage. Given this spate of spies, the second mole just had to be a CIA officer.

The joint FBI–CIA team finally focused on a suspect at the CIA, Brian Kelley, a longtime counterintelligence officer who had joined the CIA after a career in the US Air Force and matched some of the leads the FBI and CIA had developed over the years.[8] Most damning of all, however, the CIA suspect was an expert on Soviet illegals and had worked directly on the Felix Bloch case. Bloch, who had been deputy chief of the US Embassy in Vienna, had been photographed in Paris while meeting a mysterious Finn named Reino Gikman.[9] Kelley had been instrumental in determining that Gikman, in fact, was actually a Soviet illegal.

Before the FBI could develop the case against Bloch, he received a coded warning by phone that Gikman and he were in danger.[10] The media then got wind of the Bloch investigation. The public was treated to nightly news clips of Bloch under surveillance by FBI agents, who in turn were trailed by TV cameramen. Bloch was fired by the Department of State, but without solid evidence, which the FBI could no longer obtain after the media exposure, any prosecution was out of the question. The FBI was furious and bent on finding the spy who had tipped off its prey.

The FBI deployed its full array of investigative resources against Kelley but found not a shred of proof that he was a Russian spy. After three years of investigating the CIA suspect, the FBI was back to square one.

Just as prospects of finding the second spy dimmed, the budding alliance between the FBI and CIA bore fruit. Because of the ingenuity and cooperation of a team of officers from both agencies working on the mole hunt, the FBI managed to acquire two critical pieces of evidence: an audiotape of a conversation between the spy and a KGB officer, and a trash bag in which the spy had concealed documents for his handlers.[11] Hopefully, both the voice on the tape and the fingerprints on the bag would at last identify the culprit.

Many involved in the case expected that they would hear Brian Kelley's voice on the tape conspiring with his Russian handler. But as a senior FBI counterintelligence officer listened to the tape, he suddenly got up, ripped the earphones off his head, and threw them down on the desk. He recognized the voice immediately, and it did not belong to Kelley. At the end of 2000, the director of the FBI's National Security Division visited the CIA to reveal the latest findings on the mole hunt and told the CIA's chief of counterintelligence and top official on Russian operations that the FBI now knew the identity of the spy.[12] Like Kelley, the spy knew about the Bloch case. The spy actually lived in the same Vienna, Virginia, neighborhood as Kelley. The spy, however, was FBI agent Robert Hanssen.

The two senior CIA officers inwardly breathed a sigh of relief. If the voice on the tape had belonged to one of their colleagues, the CIA might not have survived another major spy scandal. Now it would be the FBI's turn to bear the searing heat of public criticism. CIA director George Tenet wisely told the CIA not to gloat—its turn could come again at any time. Besides, the damage done by a spy, no matter where he or she worked, was a defeat for the United States, not just the FBI.

On February 18, 2001, seven years after Rick Ames's arrest, Robert Hanssen left the twenty-second package of secrets for the Russians in the woods of a public park near his home. After he left the park, his colleagues in the FBI arrested him. At the time of the arrest, the FBI knew that Hanssen was a spy but still had no idea of the many secret lives their fellow agent led.

Hanssen lived a life of many different compartments whose activities and values clashed with each other. On the surface, his upbringing and career reflected a straight-laced, conservative government bureaucrat and family man. He was born in 1944 into the middle-class family of a Chicago police officer. He married Bonnie Wauck, a devout Catholic from Chicago, in 1968 and converted to Catholicism. After graduating from Knox College in Galesburg, Illinois, he earned an MBA in accounting from Northwestern University in 1971. He joined the FBI in 1976 after brief stints as a certified public accountant and a Chicago police officer. After his first assignment to the FBI's office in Indianapolis, he spent the remainder of his career in Soviet counterintelligence posts in New York and Washington.

From childhood, Hanssen had been haunted by a legacy that afflicted many of America's most notorious spies. A shy and withdrawn child, he was not the son that his father, Howard Hanssen, a hardboiled Chicago cop, had wanted to sire. The elder Hanssen humiliated and physically and emotionally abused Robert from childhood through his adult years. Howard would swaddle his son in blankets and whirl him about the room until the boy vomited.[13] Once, while his son was lying on the floor, Howard hoisted him up so brutally that Robert urinated on himself. The abuse continued into Robert's teenage years. His father bribed a motor vehicle examiner to fail his son on a test for his driver's license. Even when Robert was an adult, his father would tell friends and neighbors that his son would never amount to anything. Robert never fought back; ultimately, his wife Bonnie threatened to ban Howard Hanssen from their home if he continued to ridicule his son.

Hanssen followed in a long line of other American spies who suffered in childhood because of flawed fathers. Benedict Arnold's father was dragged by his mother from New Haven taverns and his business failed. Arnold swore he would never be poverty-stricken again. John Walker's father was also a drunkard who was unable to support his family and lost their house. John Walker also vowed he would never be poor again. Rick Ames's father was a drunk and plodding, mediocre performer at work. Rick followed in his footsteps. Clayton Lonetree's father had been a stern disciplinarian who, like Hanssen's father, squashed his son's self-esteem. Throughout American history, fathers shaped the characters of many children who grew up to spy against their country.

The abuse and humiliation by Hanssen's father heightened his son's awkward nervousness and self-consciousness. He yearned to belong, to be accepted, something his father had refused him. In the rough-and-tumble, macho world of FBI agents, however, Hanssen could not fit in. Fellow agents dubbed him "Doctor Death" because of his black suits, mumbling speech, and morose, almost creepy demeanor. Because he had been rejected from one exclusive club, he embraced another.

After his conversion, Hanssen became a devout, archconservative Catholic. He joined Opus Dei, a strict Catholic organization that stresses the incorporation of the spiritual into the member's professional, social, and family life. On the surface, Hanssen appeared an exemplary Catholic and Opus Dei member. He went to Mass almost every day, fathered six children whom he raised as Catholics, and proselytized at work about Catholicism. He preached to his colleagues about his beliefs and chastised them for extracurricular transgressions like frequenting topless bars.

Hanssen, however, was a multipolar personality, a Sybil of spies whose drives were often contradictory to each other. Although he carped at his colleagues about visiting topless bars, he went alone to strip clubs in Washington.[14] In one of these haunts, Hanssen befriended a stripper, Priscilla Sue Galey, and used his KGB cash to buy her a used Mercedes and fund her travel to meet him in Hong Kong, where he was conducting an inspection of the legal attaché's office. After his arrest, he claimed that he had sex with Galey, but she denied it.

Simultaneously attracted and repelled by the decadence Galey represented, Hanssen tried to wean her away from stripping. He even convinced her to observe him and his family attending Mass together at his local church. To improve her chances for repentance, Hanssen gave her an American Express card to use for gas and repairs for the Mercedes. When the credit card bills showed that Galey was buying cigarettes and luxury items, Hanssen angrily took away the card and ended their bizarre relationship.[15]

Hanssen's sexual interests ranged beyond topless bars and strippers to more kinky perversions. He may have outwardly seemed to be a strict Catholic observing the holy sacrament of matrimony but, in the privacy of his home, he posted lurid descriptions on the internet of his wife unclothed and having sex with him. But Hanssen was not content with online exhibitionism and indulged in even more perverse thrills at his wife's expense.

Hanssen's best friend was Jack Hoschouer, an army lieutenant colonel he had known since high school. The two pals got together often, and their male chats frequently turned to sex. Hanssen eventually did more than talk about sex with his friend Jack. He rigged up a closed-circuit video system in his house and persuaded Jack to watch him and Bonnie making love in their bedroom. Hanssen also suggested using a date rape drug on his wife so his friend Jack could have sex with her.[16]

The incidents reflected the tangled web of Hanssen's conflicting impulses, his yearning for male bonding, his need to prove his masculinity, his fascination with subterfuge, and his inner struggle between Catholic purity and lust. Sharing his wife with his friend was somehow the ultimate ritual of an exclusive club of which he and Hoschouer were the only members.

In 1979, Hanssen joined another exclusive club with its own secret rituals —the Soviet GRU. At the time, he was assigned to Soviet counterespionage in the FBI's New York field office. New York City was an expensive post for

FBI agents long before Earl Pitts moonlighted as a Soviet spy to supplement his government salary. Hanssen's family was growing and he was barely managing to make ends meet, so he volunteered to sell secrets to the GRU.[17] Like Rick Ames, Hanssen later claimed that his approach was originally intended as a onetime deal to score quick cash and pay some pressing debts. And like Ames, he protected himself by passing the name of an American penetration of the Soviet intelligence services who could betray him.

Hanssen was the first American spy to betray GRU general Dmitriy Polyakov, the most productive source on the Soviet military during the Cold War. For reasons still unknown, Polyakov was not arrested after Hanssen's revelation to the GRU. Whether the GRU refused to share the information with its KGB rivals or whether it dismissed the allegation against a high-ranking general is unknown. In the end, it did not matter. Ames eventually gave up Polyakov in his delivery of materials to the KGB in June 1985, and the Soviet general, by then happily retired, was arrested and executed.

Bonnie Hanssen discovered her husband one day furtively penning a note to his GRU paymasters. Suspecting that he had a girlfriend, Bonnie stewed. Hanssen reassured her by telling her most of the truth. He told his wife that he was swindling the Russians, trading useless information for the extra money the family sorely needed. The wives of some American spies acted in different ways when they learned of their spouse's espionage. Barbara Walker, afraid of a beating, simmered in silent anger for years. Rosario Ames shrugged it off and bought more shoes. Bonnie Hanssen called a priest. The priest, obliged by his vows to preserve the secrecy of his talks with Hanssen, persuaded the spy to stop and give his ill-gotten gains to charity.[18] Hanssen agreed, and by 1981 he had returned to a much less costly assignment at FBI headquarters in Washington, his spying days seemingly behind him.

But not forever. In October 1985, Hanssen volunteered again—this time to spy for the KGB. He mailed a letter, signed only "B," to a KGB officer with a sealed note inside for Viktor Cherkashin, the head of KGB counterintelligence at the Soviet Embassy.[19] He offered documents for $100,000 and ensured his own security again by naming three Soviets cooperating with the FBI—Sergey Motorin, Valeriy Martynov, and Boris Yuzhin. But this time his CIA counterpart, Rick Ames, had beaten him to the punch. Ames had sacrificed the same Soviets less than four months before Hanssen did.

Still, the KGB's foreknowledge of the three spies proved that their mysterious new volunteer was the genuine article.

For the next six years, Hanssen never identified himself and rebuffed KGB offers to meet him in another country. As a fellow intelligence officer from the other side, KGB defector Oleg Gordievsky, noted, "The most important component in his [Hanssen's} survival as a spy was his decision never to meet anyone from the KGB face-to-face."[20] The KGB's anonymous spy still passed them batches of documents not only from the FBI but also from every element of the US intelligence community. As 1991 drew to a close, Hanssen suddenly dropped contact with the Russians. He had begun spying for a country and an intelligence service that no longer existed, although the newly established SVR at first kept receiving his secrets and paying in spite of the collapse of the USSR. Still, defectors from the KGB were flocking to the West after the collapse, and one of them could tip off the FBI about the anonymous mole.

Hanssen decided not to take any chances and remained out of contact with the SVR for almost eight years. As the new millennium approached, Hanssen knew he would be obliged to retire in a few years. With six children, he needed money for their education and a nest egg for his twilight years, so he returned to the SVR trough. In the intervening years, Hanssen, who was more at home with gadgets than with people, had become a computer expert. He had even warned his supervisor at one point that FBI computers were vulnerable and proved it by hacking into his boss's account. Before recontacting the SVR, Hanssen surfed the FBI's Automated Case System, searching on his own name, locations of dead drop sites, and names of KGB counterintelligence officers so that he could ferret out any glimmers that he had come under suspicion.[21] He would continue to surf the FBI's internal computer system to test his security until he was arrested.

Hanssen's computer searches reassured him. Not only were his employers oblivious to his spying but they were investigating a CIA officer instead. He had hoodwinked the FBI, and now he could monitor its investigation of the person suspected of his own espionage. Sometime in the fall of 1999, he recontacted the SVR and resumed his career as a spy. In the course of this career, he would pass Russian intelligence twenty-six diskettes, twenty-seven letters, and twenty-two packages chock full of classified intelligence community secrets.[22] In return he received $600,000 in cash and diamonds and another $800,000 in an escrow account, into which, thankfully, he was unable to dip before his arrest. As a spy, he had joined another exclusive club—he was one of the nation's five known million-dollar spies.

Hanssen managed to enter that club by eluding FBI spy catchers for years. One of the reasons for his success was his meticulous attention to tradecraft. Unlike Ames, who carelessly ignored basic security precepts, Hanssen used his insider knowledge to protect himself from exposure. When he first volunteered to spy for the KGB, he knew his colleagues were not monitoring mail sent to KGB officers' homes and decided that his first contact could be safely made with a letter. His constant monitoring of FBI computer files would also alert him to any suspicions about his spying and any tactics or new technical innovations that could jeopardize his security.

Hanssen's tradecraft went well beyond these defensive measures. He reversed the traditional spy–handler relationship by controlling the operation himself from the start. Intelligence services normally prefer controlling their spies, giving them precise instructions for communications and guidance on security measures. Their job is to know the operating environment and security situation thoroughly and to warn their spies of hidden pitfalls. Spies, who are often operating in their own country, believe they know better where the dangers lie, but they often fail to see the security threats through the prism of the enemy, as intelligence services do. The intelligence officer, who faces these threats as a part of his daily life in a hostile country, is normally more aware of the security dangers than his spy.

Hanssen, however, was an insider in the agency that presented the major threat to the Russians. Although the Russians may have preferred to control the relationship, Hanssen left them little opportunity to do so. His principal security measure was concealing his identity from the Russians and refusing to meet them. Although he passed the Russians information from across the intelligence community, the accumulated weight of the counterintelligence information he provided must have convinced them that their anonymous spy worked for the FBI. And that information must have also convinced the Russians that he was better positioned to protect himself than they were.

The Russians used a similar communications plan with Hanssen as they had employed successfully with John Walker and Rick Ames. Because

Hanssen rejected their occasional suggestions for a personal meeting, the Russians relied solely on impersonal communications with an elaborate set of dead drop sites. Hanssen, however, was a full partner in developing the plan, and he convinced the Russians to use sites he selected and often carefully refined their proposals to communicate with him.

Thanks to Hanssen, the Russians owned the FBI's defensive playbook and knew in advance where the holes in the line were to run their offense. Hanssen influenced the Russians' modus operandi and enabled them to run other spies in the United States. As one example, Hanssen was fond of dead drops in public parks. The Russians believed that remote wooded areas were more secure for these exchanges but, based on Hanssen's preferences, they began using parks to exchange information with Ames.[23]

Hanssen also skirted one of the major pitfalls that trapped other American spies: the unexplainable rise in income. Ames paid little attention to hiding his spy wealth and even flaunted it. Hanssen, however, bought no new houses with cash or indulged in fancy sports cars. With six children to support, he simply filtered the money piecemeal over a period of years into the family budget. His only extravagant spending involved Priscilla Galey, a covert part of his life that he ran like a spy operation. To his colleagues and family, he displayed little of the trappings of excessive wealth that would have raised eyebrows.

Although Hanssen claimed that money was his primary motive for spying, the gold mine of information he supplied to the Russians could have earned him far more than he received. But, unlike Walker and Ames, he never pressed the Russians for higher payments. Money was only one of the jumbled and often contradictory motives that drove Hanssen into espionage. The money Hanssen earned from his spying surely had practical benefits for his family, enabling him to pay tuition and remodel his house, but it also satisfied more deep-seated emotional needs. The illicit cash Hanssen received to support his family proved that his father was wrong and that he could be a breadwinner.

Because Hanssen was rejected by his father, he craved acceptance by others, whether it was Opus Dei, the FBI, or simply the male fellowship with his high school friend. Ultimately, the KGB accepted Hanssen and gave him the self-esteem his father and the FBI had denied him. The KGB satisfied a host of his needs. Spying for the enemy allowed him the revenge he sought against those who had rejected him. Espionage also enabled him to live the fantasy life of a secret agent that he read about in the thrillers he devoured throughout his life. He was a fan of James Bond movies, to the point that he owned two Walther PPKs, Bond's weapon of choice.[24] Like Clark Kent changing into Superman in a phone booth, Hanssen the nerd bureaucrat transformed into Hanssen the master spy when he planted his packages full of American secrets in Virginia's public parks.

Espionage boosted Hanssen's wounded ego and convinced him that the world, or, that is, his father and the FBI, seriously underestimated his superior intellect. Like John Walker, he took secret satisfaction in outwitting colleagues who he believed were his inferiors and failed to recognize his vast talents. The KGB recognized this and stroked his ego by occasionally sending him personal notes of appreciation from Chairman Vladimir Kryuchkov himself. If the FBI did not appreciate his work, Hanssen had found someone who did.

Most of all, the relationship with the Russians gave Hanssen control. He was no longer the helpless child wrapped in a blanket and spun mercilessly around the room by his father until he got sick. The burdens of mounting bills to support his family no longer controlled him once he discovered an independent source of income from espionage. Even his Catholic faith did not control him—he could observe his marriage vows one day and frolic with strippers the next. And the FBI could not control him because he was digging every secret out of its files to supply its main adversary.

Even the KGB did not control him. He called the shots in the espionage relationship, from refusing to meet the KGB in person to selecting dead drop sites. He quit spying when he wanted and resumed on his own terms. Because he never met a KGB officer, he could cloak his social awkwardness in his letters to his handlers. He would pontificate and offer the KGB gratuitous advice; once he counseled his paymasters to apply Chicago Mayor Daley's particular brand of urban management in the Soviet Union. He would carp at the KGB regarding communications and chide them for mistakes. When a Russian intelligence officer, Stanislav Gusev, was arrested in a technical operation against the State Department, Hanssen wagged his finger at the Russians—he learned about the FBI operation and could have warned them if he had been given a faster way to communicate.[25]

The control Hanssen exercised also led to a "grandiose belief he could never be caught because he was too clever."[26] When he was finally arrested, he asked his fellow FBI agents "What took you so long?" Critics of the FBI in Congress and the media would ask the same question, especially as news of the information Hanssen had passed began to emerge. Hanssen had destroyed the nation's defenses against Russian espionage. With knowledge of the FBI's physical and technical surveillance, the Russians could operate unhindered on American soil.

Hanssen gave the Russians information on the FBI's complete double agent program, which saved them valuable time and effort meeting spies who were really controlled by the US government.[27] He told the Russians the names of their personnel targeted for recruitment by the FBI so they could be warned, watched, or sent back home. Like Ames, Hanssen sacrificed Soviet spies working for the United States to protect himself.

The damage done by Hanssen to NSA operations was particularly costly to the American taxpayer. Hanssen revealed to the Soviets a covert tunnel built under the Soviet Embassy in Washington to eavesdrop on communications.[28] Hanssen also told the Russians that NSA was reading Soviet satellite transmissions because of an exploitable glitch in Soviet communications, and he also disclosed the limitations of NSA's ability to capture other Soviet communications.[29] NSA would have to spend additional millions to overcome the countermeasures the Soviets would take because of these nuggets of top-secret information. According to longtime NSA observer James Bamford, Hanssen's betrayal "was one of the biggest blows to NSA since its founding."[30]

Hanssen's most serious betrayal was passing to the Russians the US plan to ensure the survival of the government in the event of a nuclear attack.[31] The United States was hardly on a war footing with the Russians after the collapse of the Soviet Union, but compromise of the plan required a massive overhaul that cost more taxpayer dollars. If the two superpowers had been on a war footing, the Soviets might have had another distinct advantage because Hanssen had also passed the KGB an assessment of Soviet knowledge of US nuclear capabilities.[32] Overall, Hanssen supplied his Russian handler with more than 6,000 pages of classified documents. In one exchange alone, he provided more than 500 pages of secrets.

Considering the damage done by Hanssen, John Ashcroft, the new attorney general, told an interviewer that he did not exclude the death penalty for Hanssen and reportedly was strongly in favor of the government pursuing this maximum punishment.[33] After the Ames case, Congress had amended the espionage laws to provide for the death penalty if a spy's information led to the execution of American sources. Conversely, CIA director George Tenet argued against the death penalty.[34] The intelligence community, Tenet believed, needed to know the full extent of the damage Hanssen had caused and would not secure his cooperation without a plea bargain.

Hanssen's attorney, Plato Cacheris, a dapper and articulate expert in espionage cases, was not about to bargain if the government insisted on pursuing the death penalty. Besides, DOJ would have a difficult prosecution under any circumstances. Espionage cases were still complicated by the government's need to introduce classified information in court that could compromise intelligence sources. Besides, the case for the death penalty might fail in court—when Hanssen betrayed the executed spies Motorin and Martynov, the crime was not punishable by death, and so the constitutional prohibition on ex post facto punishment could defeat the argument.

Tenet prevailed. The US government bargained with Cacheris for life imprisonment without parole in return for Hanssen's full cooperation. Hanssen was debriefed for months by intelligence community officials until the FBI was satisfied that he had cooperated. In May 2002 Hanssen was formally sentenced to life without chance of parole.

The FBI suffered the same blistering criticism for Hanssen as the CIA had experienced seven years before when Ames was arrested. Hanssen had taken far greater care than Ames to conceal his spying, but he had still made some blunders along the way that might have ended his espionage. Even though he never flaunted his wealth, his finances may not have withstood the scrutiny of a periodic reinvestigation. Though he was out of contact with the KGB, he approached a GRU officer cold in 1993 and identified himself as an FBI agent who collaborated with the Russians.[35] In 1986, he once used an FBI phone line to contact the KGB and took some unnecessary risks by repeatedly using the same dead drop site near his home and keeping spy notes and reminders in his handheld computer.

Despite these tradecraft gaffes, Hanssen evaded detection because of his insider knowledge and the FBI's inability to believe that one of its own could be a spy. In August 2003, DOJ's inspector general released a critical report on the FBI's failure to unmask Hanssen years earlier. The report noted numerous instances of Hanssen's mishandling of classified information and inadvertent disclosures of secrets to unauthorized persons.[36] The inspector general found systemic flaws in the FBI's internal security responsible for Hanssen's unhindered spying for years. Despite his access to counterespionage data, Hanssen, like many of his colleagues, had never been tested with a polygraph and was only subjected to a cursory reinvestigation once in his career. The same flaws were also noted in an independent report on FBI security programs by a commission chaired by William Webster, its former director.[37]

Among the most egregious flaws, however, was the lack of compartmentation in the FBI's computer system, which allowed Hanssen to roam at will through files that were not only highly sensitive but also totally unrelated to his immediate job responsibilities. Congressional critics also focused on this shortcoming and lambasted the FBI for the unrestricted access in its computer network. Ironically, after the tragic events of September 11, 2001, just seven months after Hanssen's arrest, these same critics would condemn the US intelligence community for its failure to share information.

One of the most critical oversights, according to the inspector general, was that "the FBI demonstrated a reluctance to consider itself as a possible source for a penetration in the absence of leads identifying a specific FBI target."[38] Like the CIA in the Ames case, like so many government agencies throughout American history, the FBI, though the primary agency in unmasking spies, had refused to think the unthinkable about one of its own.

The Hanssen case was a crushing blow to the FBI, the culmination of a row of scandals that plagued the bureau in the 1990s. In 1992, while attempting to arrest Randy Weaver, a right-wing militant fugitive holed up in a backwoods cabin near Ruby Ridge, Idaho, FBI agents shot and killed his wife. A year later, FBI agents in Waco, Texas, raided the compound of a violent religious sect, the Branch Davidians. Besieged cult members burned down the compound, resulting in the deaths of eighty of their compatriots, including a large number of children. Besides these accusations of excessive force in the two cases, the FBI was bashed for the wrongful arrest of Richard Jewell for the Atlanta Olympics bombing in 1996. Three months after Hanssen's arrest, FBI director Louis Freeh resigned. At the time of his resignation, a CBS poll revealed that public confidence in the FBI had plunged to 24 percent.[39] In addition to the other incidents, Hanssen's case had taken the same toll on the FBI as Ames's treachery had on the CIA.

Ames and Hanssen were not the only Russian spies arrested during that decade. Some of the other spies arrested in the 1990s had begun to betray secrets three decades earlier, when the collapse of the Soviet bloc seemed inconceivable. One spy caught in the 1990s, however, decided to offer his services to the Russians even after his colleague Ames had been arrested.

The Last Vestiges of Cold War Espionage

I feel like Rip Van Spy. I thought I had put this to bed many years ago and I never dreamed it would turn out like this.

ROBERT LIPKA, *former National Security Agency employee, at his 1997 sentencing for espionage during the 1960s; cited by Andrew and Mitrokhin,* The Sword and the Shield, *18*

Jim Nicholson

In 1997 CIA officer Jim Nicholson failed to heed the lessons of the past. At a time when CIA sensitivities were heightened to espionage after the Ames arrest, Nicholson decided to cure his ailing finances by approaching the SVR.

Rick Ames had only been arrested a few months before Nicholson volunteered to the Russians while he was stationed in Kuala Lumpur.[1] Up to that time, Nicholson had steadily progressed through the CIA operations officer ranks after overseas tours in Manila, Bangkok, Tokyo, and Bucharest. After fourteen years in the CIA, he had risen to the GS-15 level, just one step away from the senior executive ranks. But after a messy divorce that left him with alimony payments and three children to support, he landed in serious debt.

Nicholson was in the waning months of his Malaysia tour when he volunteered, so the Russians prepared for his reassignment by designing future plans to meet him outside the United States. Contact with Nicholson inside the United States was simply too risky after the Ames case.

Over the next two years, Nicholson made a series of trips to Asia to meet his Russian spymasters in the SVR. Amazingly, his financial needs blinded him to the same pitfalls that had ensnared Rick Ames. After his travels, Nicholson deposited his spy earnings in the bank, leaving a trail of evidentiary crumbs for counterespionage investigators.[2] The tracking of finances and foreign travel had proved critical in the Ames investigation; and now Nicholson, a trained intelligence officer, was blithely making the same blunders. The story of Ames's hefty bank deposits right after meeting a Soviet in Washington was not only legend in CIA corridors but also in the public domain. If Nicholson was to embark on the risky path of spying for the Russians, common sense would have dictated that he pore over the details of the Ames case to determine the traps that might catch him. Fortunately, he did not.

Nicholson was also blissfully unaware that the newly mandated cooperation between the CIA and FBI had closed gaps in the pursuit of spies. Investigators focused on his foreign travel patterns, searched frequent flyer records, and scoured his finances to establish a correlation between his trips and sizable bank deposits.[3] Evidence against Nicholson began to mount rapidly. Nicholson roamed through CIA databases and asked colleagues for information on Chechnya, a topic unrelated to his instructor duties. In the new spirit of cooperation between Russia and the United States, Russian intelligence officially informed its American counterparts that they were focusing on Chechnya, the rebellious republic that was launching terrorist attacks against the government.[4] Suspicions about Nicholson were soon confirmed. He was surveilled during a trip to Singapore in July 1996 and was observed getting into a car with Russian diplomatic plates.[5] After his return, Nicholson gave his son a new car, paid credit card bills, and put more money in the bank.

The FBI had all the evidence it needed. Jim Nicholson was arrested at Dulles Airport on November 16, 1996, as he was about to board a flight to Switzerland with classified documents in his carry-on bag. At the time of his arrest, Nicholson was the highest-ranking CIA officer convicted of espionage charges (his mediocre colleague, Rick Ames, was a GS-14). His most significant damage stemmed from his assignment as an instructor, where he had access to the identities of a fresh crop of young clandestine operations officers whose CIA affiliation was yet unknown. Nicholson, who served at the facility for two years, passed the Russians the names of hundreds of graduates of the training course.[6] The Russians not only knew the identities of the new officers but could also pass the names on to other intelligence services as trinkets of cooperation to gain goodwill and frustrate CIA operations.

Nicholson admitted that he had received $180,000 from the Russians for his secrets and pled guilty in March 1997. In exchange for his cooperation, he was sentenced to twenty-three and a half years in prison. He had only spied for two years thanks to the new collaboration between the CIA and FBI. Both agencies had experienced growing pains in adjusting to the new relationship, but eventually the cooperation that had been forced on them from outside became almost routine. Without that cooperation, Robert Hanssen and Jim Nicholson might have spied for many more years.

Nicholson's spying days, however, were not quite over. In an episode reminiscent of the John Walker family espionage business, Nicholson, like Walker, recruited his son to serve as his intermediary to renew contact with Russian intelligence. Nicholson had tried to enlist a cellmate about to be released to communicate with the Russians.[7] When that failed, he convinced his son Nathan, a US Army veteran, to courier messages to the Russians at overseas locations from June 2006 to December 2007.[8]

Although Nicholson clearly had no further access to secrets in prison, the Russians were undoubtedly interested in any information about his arrest to determine if a mole in their own service had betrayed him. The Russians paid Nathan $47,000 over the course of the overseas meetings, which Nicholson instructed him to distribute to family members.[9] The FBI, tipped off by the cellmate's information, monitored Nathan's travels and e-mail communications with the Russians and, upon his return from one trip, found a notebook about his activities and cash in his luggage.

Just twenty-six years old, Nathan Nicholson was arrested, and father and son were both indicted in January 2009. After pleading guilty and agreeing to testify against his father, Nathan was sentenced to five years' probation. His father also pled guilty, and eight more years were tacked on to his original sentence. Another incident of father and son espionage was over.

George Trofimoff

Another American spied for the Russians in the 1990s but, unlike Jim Nicholson, his espionage career had started a quarter of a century earlier. George Trofimoff, a US Army officer, began spying at the height of the Vietnam War when antiwar rallies and the hippie movement marked the public's opposition to the US government. Trofimoff's motives for spying, however, had nothing to do with Vietnam or opposition to the government. Like many of his military colleagues, he simply spied for the money.

Trofimoff was born in Germany in 1927 to Russian parents who had fled Soviet communism.[10] He joined the US Army in 1948 and became a naturalized American citizen in 1951. After his discharge in 1956, he remained an officer in the army reserves and worked as a civilian in army military intelligence until 1994. Like Clyde Conrad, Trofimoff was among the army civilian and military personnel who spent almost their entire careers among the sizable US military contingent in Germany.

During his boyhood Trofimoff developed a very close relationship with Igor Susemihl, another émigré who grew up to become a Russian Orthodox priest in Austria. Despite the Soviets' professed atheism, the KGB was not averse to enlisting a man of the cloth as a spy, and Susemihl was a recruited agent. Susemihl, the KGB spy, and Trofimoff, the US Army officer, were as close as brothers. Aside from this brotherly love, Trofimoff had also charged thousands on his new credit card and the bills were coming home to roost. In 1969 he accepted his "brother's" recruitment pitch to spy for the Soviets. He would spy for the Russians for twenty-five years, throughout the Cold War and after the collapse of the USSR, until he returned to America to retire in 1995.

At the time of his recruitment, Trofimoff was chief of the Joint Interrogation Center, a NATO facility staffed by German, French, British, and American military in Nuremberg. On frequent trips to Austria to meet his brotherly priest and KGB handlers, Trofimoff betrayed US military and intelligence community requirements, NATO's order of battle, and documents on NATO's knowledge of Warsaw Pact capabilities. By the time his quarter century of spying ended, he had received the Soviets' prestigious award, the Order of the Red Banner, and a payment amounting to 90,000 deutsche marks.[11]

Trofimoff eventually fell victim to the hemorrhage of KGB secrets after the collapse of the USSR. The KGB archives smuggled out by Vassili Mitrokhin did not list Trofimoff's name but included enough information about an army spy recruited by a Russian Orthodox priest to narrow down the suspects. The Germans tumbled to Trofimoff and Susemihl but dropped the investigation because they feared that the statute of limitations would expire.

Trofimoff breathed a sigh of relief and returned to the United States to live in peaceful retirement in Florida. The FBI, however, was not about to let the matter drop. Because Trofimoff had obviously retired from espionage, the FBI orchestrated a sting operation by dispatching a native Russian-speaking agent to his door. The agent claimed that he was an SVR officer tasked with settling remaining accounts, which was welcome news to the greedy Trofimoff. To justify his back payments, Trofimoff reeled off his many accomplishments to the phony SVR officer, incriminating himself in the process.[12]

Trofimoff was arrested in June 2000 and, then seventy-four years old, went on trial a year later. During the trial, Trofimoff claimed that he thought the FBI agent was a Russian Orthodox Church representative who wanted to give him money, so he played along with a false story about working for the KGB. This implausible tale did little for his defense.

Aside from Trofimoff's complete lack of credibility, the prosecution arrayed a row of expert witnesses against him that featured a star-studded cast of Cold War espionage. Clayton Lonetree, now a free man, and Boris Yuzhin, a former KGB officer who had narrowly escaped execution after he was betrayed by Ames and Hanssen, both testified about the KGB from their unique perspectives, one as a spy and the other as an intelligence officer. Oleg Kalugin, the KGB overseer of the Walker and Pelton cases in Washington, had now resettled in the United States and also testified about KGB operations.[13] The trial seemed like a gathering of Cold War adversaries at the funeral of one of their fallen comrades. The collective testimony of these expert witnesses convinced the jury. Trofimoff was found guilty and sentenced to life in prison.

George Trofimoff was a throwback to the bygone era of the 1930s and 1940s, when Russian émigrés spying for the KGB lured their fellow countrymen into espionage. His case illustrated that, no matter how long one has spied undetected, no matter how old a spy has become, and no matter how long ago a spy began to betray secrets, the FBI has a long memory.

Robert Lipka

The case of Robert Lipka proved the point even more. Like Trofimoff, Lipka began spying for the KGB in the 1960s but had lost his access thirty years before he was arrested. Born in Niagara Falls in 1945, he entered the army right after high school. After training as an intelligence analyst, he was assigned to NSA headquarters in 1964. Already spending beyond his means, he volunteered at the Soviet Embassy in Washington to spy for the KGB. Before long, he was photographing NSA documents and leaving rolls of film in dead drops just outside the nation's capital.[14]

Lipka left the army in 1967 and moved to Lancaster, Pennsylvania, to attend college. Although he had walked out of NSA with a stash of documents, he never had a clearance or access to classified information again. By 1967 his value to the KGB had been eclipsed by a new volunteer, John Walker, who was passing mounds of information about America's secret communications. Still, the KGB was always reluctant to abandon young spies who could reenter government service to steal more classified information. In 1968 an "illegal" married couple was dispatched to contact Lipka. The FBI was tipped off to the pair but was unable to discover who they had contacted on their mysterious trip to Pennsylvania.[15]

The lead went cold for more than two decades until defectors began flocking to the West with Soviet secrets in the waning days of the USSR. Mitrokhin's KGB archives listed Lipka's name, and Oleg Kalugin's published revelations about the KGB also included a description that fit Lipka's profile: "The young soldier was a 'walk-in' who came to us in the mid-1960s, explaining that he was involved in shredding and destroying NSA documents and could supply us with a wealth of material."[16] By the time Kalugin's book appeared, the FBI was already on Lipka's trail. Lipka, in the tradition of Walker, Ames, and Hanssen, had told his first wife Patricia about his spying activities. She had even been with him on a few occasions when he placed caches stuffed with NSA information and retrieved packages with Soviet cash left in the woods. In return for immunity from prosecution, Patricia confirmed Lipka's espionage and cooperated fully with the FBI.

By the early 1990s Lipka had been out of access and out of contact with the Soviets for more than two decades. The FBI again relied on the same false flag sting operation that had trapped Trofimoff.[17] Like Trofimoff, Lipka also thought he was owed more money from the Russians, so he was eager to engage the purported Russian intelligence officer who showed up on his Pennsylvania doorstep in December 1993. Lipka, however, was initially skeptical. The Russian did not know about Lipka's fascination with chess or his code name, "Rook." The Russian answered that Lipka's case had been transferred from the KGB to the GRU, a plausible explanation considering the post-Soviet turmoil in the intelligence services.

Checkmate. Like Trofimoff, Lipka babbled on to the FBI agent about his spying exploits to justify back pay. He was arrested in February 1996, and he pled guilty in May of the following year. Lipka was sentenced to eighteen years imprisonment and fined $10,000 for espionage he committed thirty years before.

Lipka was a fifty-one-year-old, middle-aged ex-spy when he stepped through the prison gates. He was the youngest known American to spy for his country since the child wonder Theodore Hall had betrayed atomic bomb secrets to the KGB in the 1940s. Both of them had eluded capture for years. Hall went to his death without spending a day in prison, but Lipka was eventually caught. His fate provides a gloomy warning for any spies who are still resting comfortable, their spying days over, safe in the belief that they are beyond the reach of the law. Their time may still come.

Kurt Stand, Theresa Squillacote, and James Clark

Three more Soviet bloc spies whose espionage started in the distant past were not resting in comfortable retirement when they were arrested in October 1997. Kurt Stand, his wife Theresa Squillacote, and James Clark had spied for East Germany since the 1970s.[18] Suddenly, the communist government they had served disappeared from the map and reunified with West Germany. The trained and experienced trio then tried to sell their skills to other communists.

Squillacote, Stand, and Clark were anachronisms, the fading embers of a fiery communist era a half century earlier when spies betrayed their country for an ideology. Their paths first crossed in the mid-1970s in the Communist Party chapter of the University of Wisconsin. Most campus leftists of the era had little sympathy for Soviet communism, but Kurt Stand was a true believer. Born in 1954, Stand was a "red diaper baby" whose father had joined the CPUSA after escaping Nazi Germany. Stand's father kept contacts with his communist friends back in the homeland, and in the early 1970s introduced his son to one of them, Lothar Ziemer, who was an officer of the HVA, the foreign intelligence arm of East Germany's Ministry of State Security.

Stand was still a teenager when Ziemer recruited him to spy for the cause. In 1976 Stand brought James Clark to East Germany, where Ziemer recruited him. In 1980 Stand then rounded out the ring by marrying and recruiting Theresa Squillacote, whose devotion to communism rivaled his own. The couple had two children, whom they named Rosa and Karl after two famous German socialist revolutionaries, Rosa Luxemburg and Karl Liebknecht. The trio was trained by the HVA in the art of espionage, secret writing, radio communications, and clandestine photography. All three were given fake British passports for their frequent trips to East Germany.

Despite all these East German efforts, the trio never developed much significant access to US government secrets. Kurt Stand became a regional representative of an international union of hotel and restaurant workers. Clark was more successful. He worked for a few years for the US Army at a weapons arsenal in Colorado, and he could also cadge classified tidbits from a few friends in the Department of State. He managed to pass to the East Germans classified information about US chemical warfare defenses and intelligence community analyses regarding the Soviet leadership, nuclear doctrine, and the Warsaw Pact military. When Clark was arrested, he was long gone from the army and working as a private investigator in Falls Church, Virginia.

Squillacote graduated from Catholic University Law School and was hired by the National Labor Relations Board, hardly a repository of national defense secrets. She did, however, later manage to land a job as an attorney on the more promising House Armed Services Committee. She tried to sweeten her access by applying for various jobs at DOD and in the intelligence community. Ironically, she was hired as a senior attorney to the deputy undersecretary of defense for acquisition reform just when East Germany had been relegated to the ash heap of history.

Squillacote, however, was persistent. Her devotion to communism had outlived the country for which she spied, so she sought other communists who could use the spy ring's skills. In 1995 she wrote a letter hinting at her espionage potential to the communist deputy defense minister in South Africa. She was elated when she received an encouraging reply and happily told her confederates. She then received a second positive letter but her hopes were soon to be dashed. The second reply had really been written by the FBI.

By the time Squillacote approached the South Africans, the FBI was already investigating her and her two comrades for espionage based on access to HVA records that were later revealed in court.[19] However, as in the Trofimoff and Lipka cases, the FBI was faced with the problem of catching the trio in the act of spying; but Squillacote had provided an opening with her veiled offer to South Africa.

Squillacote was emotionally vulnerable and came from a family with a history of clinical depression. FBI behavioral psychologists prepared an agent to pose as a South African intelligence officer and play to her delicate emotions. The ruse exceeded even the FBI's expectations. Squillacote began to trust the agent, and in October 1996 she gave him four secret DOD documents on her own initiative.[20]

Squillacote, Stand, and Clark were arrested in October 1997. Clark broke from the couple and agreed to plead guilty for the more lenient sentence of twelve years and seven months. In July 1998 Squillacote and Stand stood trial. The most damning evidence against the couple emerged from HVA files obtained by the US government, simple three-by-five cards with an agent's code name, basic job description, targets, and assessment of reliability. Matching cards listed the true names of the agents.[21] The prosecution presented the matching sets, which fit Squillacote, Stand, and Clark perfectly. The jury found them guilty, and Stand was sentenced to seventeen-and-a-half years and Squillacote to twenty-one years and ten months in prison.

The couple made a series of appeals for a new trial and demanded the suppression of certain evidence that they believed had been illegally introduced at their original hearing. All the appeals were rejected. Their case, however, did inspire a flurry of criticism vaguely reminiscent of the 1950s debate between liberals and conservatives. The FBI was criticized for exploiting Squillacote's clinical depression, and CBS's *60 Minutes* featured a segment implying that the trio's activities had little impact and that they were lured by the FBI to volunteer to the South Africans.

A small coterie of socialist supporters set up a "Friends of Kurt Stand and Theresa Squillacote" committee that hardly engendered the stormy protests surrounding the Rosenberg case. The couple's two children received some help from the Rosenberg Fund for Children, which had been established by one of the Rosenberg sons to aid the offspring of socialist parents persecuted for their political leanings.

Their espionage and their trial are largely forgotten today. The damage done by the three East German spies was minimal and eminently forgettable, and all three harked back to an era of ideological espionage and commitment to communism that had long disappeared in America. Squillacote, Stand, and Clark sit in prison today for serving a country and a cause that no longer exist. Their spying was the last gasp of a dying ideology in America, an ideology that went out not with a bang but with a whimper.

Cold War Legacies

As the twentieth century drew to a close, the Cold War gradually receded into the history books. In 1995 the Venona Project closed up shop, and the US government declassified KGB messages that ended debate over the guilt of accused Soviet spies. One of those accused, Alger Hiss, was ninety-one years old and still maintained his innocence in spite of the Venona revelations. He died a year later with few believing his claims of innocence.

The last known surviving Soviet spy of the pre–World War II era was exposed in Mitrokhin's voluminous archives. The KGB had recruited Melitta Norwood, a British citizen, in 1937 while she worked at a metals institute involved in atomic bomb development. When her espionage was revealed, she was a grandmotherly eighty-seven years old and was living peacefully in a London suburb. The youngest atom bomb spy, Theodore Hall, died at the end of 1999. Morris Cohen, the Soviet illegal who handled Hall with his wife, Lona, had died a few years before.

Soviet spies from later decades were still alive, and some of those arrested had already served their terms. The "Falcon and the Snowman" had reached middle age in their jail cells. Andrew Daulton Lee was released on parole in 1998, and Christopher Boyce in 2002. Clayton Lonetree, the first US Marine convicted of espionage, was freed in 1996 after eight years in the brig and testified about his background with the KGB at the trial of another Soviet spy, George Trofimoff. Meanwhile, John Walker, Ronald Pelton, and Rick Ames all continue to serve their life sentences in federal penitentiaries.

Robert Hanssen was the last major Russian spy arrested, but his capture by no means marks the end of Russian spying against America. On December 31, 1999, Vladimir Putin, whose values were shaped by a career in the KGB, was appointed acting president of Russia and elected to the post a few months later. One of his first comments after his presidential appointment was that "the potential of the special services will not just be maintained but increased." Before the presidency, Putin had run the FSB and reenergized the service with more money, manpower, and authorities. As president, he appointed a row of his former KGB cronies to key positions throughout the government and tasked Russian intelligence to pursue foreign secrets more aggressively. He was reelected to the presidency in 2012 and continues his enthusiastic support of Russian intelligence operations against the United States.

The honeymoon between post–Soviet Russia and the United States was over. After Hanssen's arrest, the US government expelled fifty Russian intelligence officers and the Russians retaliated by expelling Americans from the US Embassy in Moscow. Since that time, the Russians have gradually restored the intelligence officer ranks in the United States to Cold War levels. Their only job is to recruit spies against America.

The threat of Russian spying still remained but was eclipsed by espionage from enemies old and new in the first years of the twenty-first century.

PART **VI**

ESPIONAGE
IN THE NEW
MILLENNIUM

New Threats, Old Threats

The United States is almost certainly one of the top intelligence priorities for practically every government on the planet. . . . But it is not only major nation-states which employ aggressive intelligence services. Terrorist groups . . . also conduct intelligence operations within the United States.

Silberman-Robb Commission on US counterintelligence, quoted in
"Commission on the Intelligence Capabilities of the United States," 486

Because of the actions of American spies during the Cold War, the US Navy's nuclear submarine fleet was vulnerable, America's secret military communications had been read, and NATO's defense plans for Europe and the US government's plan to survive a nuclear attack were in enemy hands. Yet fortunately, because the Cold War never erupted into an armed conflict, the United States always had time to take countermeasures and recover from the damage done by those spies.

But after September 11, 2001, America no longer had that time. Throughout the Cold War, neither side had attacked the other's homeland. But in a single hour on 9/11, terrorists had murdered almost 3,000 innocent civilians. The al-Qaeda attacks on the World Trade Center and Pentagon marked the beginning of a new war that would directly affect intelligence collection and counterintelligence.

The US intelligence community and law enforcement agencies immediately began to devote enormous resources to combating terrorism after the

9/11 attacks. The CIA and FBI, in particular, shifted large numbers of officers from other duties to pursue any lead that might uncover another terrorist attack. Counterespionage was understandably a lower priority than counterterrorism. In the post-9/11 world, a spy in the US government filching secret documents from a safe hardly rivaled the threat from a terrorist hatching a plot to detonate a nuclear bomb in a major US city.

Spying against America, however, did not stop. According to NCIX, 140 foreign intelligence services now spy against the United States.[1] The emerging trends of the 1990s also became more acute in the new century. Economic espionage rose sharply and, according to the White House Office of Science and Technology, now costs US companies an estimated $100 billion a year in lost sales.[2] The early years of the twenty-first century also witnessed Americans spying more because of divided loyalties than money. The most dramatic new trend, however, was the arrest of more Americans accused of spying not for Russia but for the PRC.

By the dawn of the twenty-first century, China's economy had become the fastest-growing in the world. In the late 1970s China shifted from a Soviet-style centralized economy to free market capitalism while adhering to the political tenets of communism. This decision would have a stunning impact not only on China but also on the rest of the world. After the reforms, China's gross domestic product skyrocketed to an annual rate of almost 10 percent. According to a 2012 Congressional Research Service report, economic experts believe that China could "overtake the US as the world's largest economy in a few years."[3]

China has used this newfound wealth to accelerate an unprecedented military buildup of high-technology weaponry, missiles, and naval warships, motivated in part by the potential threat of conflict with the United States over Taiwan. Ironically, China funded this expensive military effort from its trade with the United States. The United States is China's largest overseas market, and, according to the Office of the US Trade Representative, in 2012 America incurred its highest trade deficit with China, a hefty sum of $282 billion.[4]

Despite its overflowing coffers, China was still unable to buy restricted military technology on the open market, so it launched an intensive espionage campaign to acquire America's industrial and military secrets. Chinese espionage presented a challenge to American counterspies, who had been conditioned by a half century of ferreting out Soviet bloc spies in the US government. In the odd symbiosis of superpower rivalry, the US and Russian intelligence services mirrored each other in their approach to espionage. The CIA and the KGB both accepted volunteers for spying, scouted potential spies in each other's governments, probed for their vulnerabilities, and recruited them based on ideological affinity, greed, resentment, or other motives. Both services handled their spies the same way, meeting furtively in foreign capitals or exchanging information using dead drops, secret radio communications, and other clandestine methods. The FBI and its KGB internal security counterparts also hunted for each other's spies the same way, monitoring the opposition's intelligence officers on their home turf and investigating suspects exhibiting well-known indicators of espionage.

Chinese intelligence, conversely, operated with a different set of rules that frustrated traditional spy-catching efforts. In a rare glimpse into a country's intelligence gathering modus operandi, two veteran Chinese intelligence officers published a guidebook on the espionage methods that the PRC uses to obtain technological secrets. Although the authors revealed no real secrets, they did provide some insight into the philosophy behind Chinese intelligence collection.

According to the authors, the Chinese acquire 80 percent of their intelligence from overt sources but must rely on truly clandestine spying for the remaining 20 percent.[5] The Chinese authors revealed that four thousand intelligence organizations throughout China collect intelligence.[6] The organizations are, in fact, not intelligence agencies but institutes and business enterprises that independently pursue information for their specific needs. In an American equivalent, a branch of the National Aeronautics and Space Administration or a group of scientists from the Los Alamos National Laboratory would collect information without coordinating their efforts with US intelligence agencies. The coordination issues among these thousands of organizations must be daunting, but such a dispersed collection effort also presents an equally challenging problem for counterspies. Even if the FBI or CIA had a source in the heart of China's premier intelligence services—the civilian Ministry of State Security and the military intelligence wing of the People's Liberation Army—that source might be unaware of the broad spectrum of Chinese espionage against the United States.

China also played to its natural strengths to steal secrets: a population of more than a billion that facilitates the deployment of a vast army of intelligence collectors, each an expert in his or her own scientific field, to elicit tidbits of information. In this "grains of sand" approach, the huge number of collectors pours those grains into huge buckets that enable the Chinese to piece together the mosaic of Western technological advances.

The PRC's task was facilitated by the establishment of diplomatic relations with the United States in 1979, after which Chinese businessmen, students, and scientists visited America's shores in droves, and their American counterparts flocked to China in equal numbers. By 2004 more than 100,000 Chinese students were pursuing higher education in American schools and 27,000 official delegations of all stripes visited their American counterparts every year.[7]

The Chinese developed a template that was repeated for every US delegation visiting China, especially those involved in scientific exchanges. After a lengthy flight from the United States, visitors were regaled with a sumptuous banquet with several courses of exotic national dishes and generous rounds of toasts with mao tais, a potent Chinese cocktail. With their defenses battered by jet lag, stomachs bloated by food, and senses dulled by liquor, the wobbly American guests endured a relentless barrage of questions under the guise of polite dinner table chatter. Before long, some of the visiting Americans divulged secrets. This Chinese tactic was hardly traditional espionage, but it yielded bucketsful of intelligence grains.

Another strength of the PRC was the sizable overseas Chinese community, the members of which could be called on, despite the PRC's communist bent, to help the homeland. Given their shared heritage, Chinese intelligence already had an advantage in cultivating overseas Chinese. Chinese Americans were and continue to be particularly attractive targets because they make up an estimated 15 percent of America's research-and-development sector and some are involved in critical defense-related industries.

Besides the normal routine of dinners laced with generous portions of alcohol, Chinese Americans are greeted with more personal appeals. PRC intelligence officers stroke the ego of their Chinese American counterparts, appeal to their common heritage, and gradually hope to persuade some of them to share a morsel or two of classified information to help the homeland. The approach is framed in seemingly innocent terms—just a few questions to help China and, of course, in no way intended to harm the target's adopted country. The Chinese intelligence services exploit these sympathies because, as longtime FBI China analyst Paul Moore notes, "China focuses on recruiting Chinese Americans just because that's what it does best. Even if its intelligence methodologies against Chinese Americans work only occasionally, they work much better than Chinese approaches made to people of other ethnic backgrounds."[8]

The Chinese intelligence services could cast their nets widely and catch the occasional fish who was willing to share tidbits of information. As a result, the Chinese did not need to resort to probing potential spies for the financial or other vulnerabilities that had provided fertile ground for the Soviet bloc's intelligence agencies in decades past. These casual sources left no trail of bloated bank accounts or exhibited suspicious behavior on which American counterspies focused to pursue espionage suspects. "This means," as Moore notes, "that there are rarely the 'smoking guns' that we have in other cases of espionage—the unexplained bank deposits, the video-tapes of a suspect leaving items in a hollow rock in the park. . . . Even if it can be shown that the suspect provided information, it is likely to remain unclear whether this was deliberate or inadvertent."[9]

Despite the success of these methods, the Chinese intelligence services were still stealing that remaining 20 percent of secrets by using traditional espionage methods. The case of Larry Wu-tai Chin, as the first decade of the new millennium proved, was the rule and not the exception. The most controversial case of potential Chinese espionage touched the very core of America's national defense: the inner workings of its nuclear weapons capabilities.

Chinese Nuclear Espionage and the Wen Ho Lee Case

This is going to be just as bad as the Rosenbergs.

Comment by **PAUL REDMOND,** *former chief of CIA counterintelligence, on media revelations of Chinese nuclear espionage, cited by Stober and Hoffman,* Convenient Spy, *196 (In addition to Stober and Hoffman's balanced study, two other books approach the case from decidedly different perspectives: Wen Ho Lee's own defense is in his autobiography,* My Country versus Me; *for a radically different view of the case, Notra Trulock, the Department of Energy chief of counterintelligence who first focused on Lee, provides his account in* Kindred Spirit.*)*

Paul Redmond's comments were echoed by others shocked to read in the *New York Times* on March 6, 1999, that China had stolen America's nuclear secrets from the Los Alamos National Laboratory, a pillar of weapons research in the Department of Energy's (DOE) nationwide research-and-development network. Over the next eighteen months, the investigation of the main suspect in the case of Chinese nuclear theft would be muddled by bitter political partisanship, interagency squabbles, tangled legal arguments, and the ugly specter of racial prejudice.

At the center of this maelstrom was Wen Ho Lee, a slight, gray-haired Chinese American scientist at Los Alamos who stood accused of betraying America's most precious national defense secrets. Lee's path to Los Alamos was typical of many other Chinese American scientists working at national laboratories. He was born to a family of farmers in Taiwan in 1939 at the height of Japan's occupation of the island. After studying engineering at a Taiwanese university, Lee emigrated to America and received a PhD in engineering from Texas A&M University. Lee became an American citizen in 1974 and was hired as a specialist in hydrodynamics at the Argonne National Laboratory and then at Los Alamos.

When Lee began work at Los Alamos in 1978, the United States and China had launched an exchange program between their nuclear scientists. The reciprocal visits were designed for the mutual benefit of both nations, but China ultimately gained the most from the program. In 1988 the Chinese tested a neutron bomb, an enhanced radiation weapon designed to destroy human beings but leave infrastructure intact. The bomb's warhead was based on America's W-70, the most advanced warhead in its arsenal at the time. An espionage investigation regarding possible theft of the warhead design focused on Guo Bao Min, a Chinese American scientist at Lawrence Livermore National Laboratory.[1]

Like Wen Ho Lee, Guo had studied engineering first in Taiwan and then in the United States before working at Livermore. In 1979, he was in contact with Chinese scientists under the exchange program and afterward was discovered checking materials out of Livermore's library about topics outside his job responsibilities. The FBI investigation, code-named Tiger Trap, resulted in Guo's firing by Livermore but DOJ decided there was insufficient evidence to prosecute Guo.

In December 1982, Lee called Guo out of the blue to offer his help. Lee told Guo that he had contacts in Taiwan and perhaps he could discover who had accused the Livermore scientist. Guo dismissed his offer and hung up. Unbeknownst to Lee, FBI agents tapping Guo's phone heard the strange conversation and opened an investigation on him.[2]

Instead of allaying FBI suspicions, Lee initially denied that he had called Guo, a pattern of deception that would characterize his entire case. After finally admitting that he had made the call, he also confessed that he was in contact with Taiwanese scientists and had sent them Los Alamos materials. Although the materials were unclassified, they were subject to Nuclear Regulatory Commission export controls, and thus Lee should have sought authorization before dispatching them to the Taiwanese.[3] However, Lee's offense did not meet the threshold for prosecution and the FBI closed the investigation.

Lee, however, later aggravated his security problems. Lee and his wife Sylvia, who also worked at the lab, frequently met visiting Chinese scientists, and they also traveled twice to China on official visits in the late 1980s. In 1988, on his second trip, Lee was unexpectedly visited in his hotel room by two of his Chinese hosts. One of them, Hu Side, was considered the father of Chinese nuclear physics and was then head of China's equivalent of Los Alamos. Hu immediately began questioning Lee about nuclear bomb detonation. Six years later, Hu visited Los Alamos and warmly embraced Lee at a reception for his delegation. A bystander overheard the head of China's nuclear weapons program thanking Lee for his help with nuclear codes, a series of mathematical formulas that simulate the activity inside an exploding weapon.[4]

Lee never advised Los Alamos security about the incident, as he was required to do on posttrip reports.[5] He only admitted his contact with Hu ten years later, when he was given a polygraph test. His failure to report, however, did not make him a spy. Some scientists at the national labs were notoriously slipshod about security, either out of contempt for restrictions on the free exchange of ideas or out of sheer absentmindedness.

Lee, however, raised far more suspicion with another security violation. From 1988 on, Lee, an inveterate packrat, copied codes and files from his classified computer and downloaded them onto an unclassified Los Alamos network.[6] By 1993, his downloading activity was spotted by an internal computer audit system called Network Anomaly Detection and Intrusion Reporting (NADIR), but the red flags were never passed to DOE's Counterintelligence Office at the lab or the FBI. This oversight reflected the abysmal state of security at DOE's national labs, where lapses like Lee's were frequent but routinely ignored. In 1995, however, the CIA obtained startling information from a Chinese walk-in that would jolt the government out of its complacence about DOE security and turn the spotlight back onto Wen Ho Lee.[7]

The walk-in illuminated a mystery that had baffled the US government three years earlier, when the Chinese detonated a new bomb on the first try at Lop Nur, a test facility in northwestern China. American scientists were astounded because they had experimented more than a dozen times before the US version detonated. The walk-in provided the CIA with a document on China's nuclear modernization plans that explained the mysterious Chinese success. The document included secret information about the W-88 Trident D-5 warhead, the most sophisticated one in America's nuclear arsenal, and other US warheads.[8] According to some scientists, the theft of the W-88, which had been developed at Los Alamos and deployed on the US Navy's Trident missile, "saved the Chinese a decade or more of development time."[9] What the Rosenbergs, Fuchs, and Hall had done for the Russian bomb, an undetected spy had now done for the Chinese.

The DOE Counterintelligence Office, headed by Notra Trulock, a former NSA official, immediately began an internal investigation. Trulock compiled a list of possible suspects at Los Alamos based on three criteria: access to W-88 information, travel to China, and past security problems. Wen Ho Lee fit all three criteria to a tee and became Trulock's primary suspect. The DOE inquiry, dubbed "Kindred Spirit," set off a chain reaction of investigative missteps and interagency squabbles that would plague the Wen Ho Lee case for the next four years.[10]

DOE passed its conclusion to the FBI, which also focused on Lee, even though DOE had only investigated its own labs and not other agencies in the US government with access to W-88 information. DOE also failed to advise the FBI that a team of nuclear scientists at the lab were divided about China's new weapon. Before the walk-in revealed that the W-88 secret was in the PRC's hands, some scientists had already become convinced that the Chinese had developed their bomb with the aid of espionage; others, however, believed that they could have developed it without outside help.

Because Wen Ho Lee was at Los Alamos, the FBI assigned the case to a single overworked agent in its Albuquerque office. The FBI's counterespionage resources were already stretched thin—after the end of the Cold War, three hundred special agents had been reassigned from spy cases to violent crime investigations.[11] Besides that, the FBI pursued the investigation with less urgency after agents were advised of a new twist in the case—the CIA had now concluded that the Chinese walk-in was a double agent under the control of the PRC.[12]

Despite the conclusion, nuclear experts insisted that the material on the W-88 was genuine. Whether the walk-in was a double agent or not was irrelevant—his information included Chinese bomb designs clearly based on the W-88. Somewhere there was a spy.

The FBI intensified its investigation in August 1997 by preparing an affidavit to submit to the FISA court for surveillance coverage. Applications for FISA coverage were first reviewed and approved by DOJ's Office of Intelligence Policy and Review (OIPR). Attorneys in OIPR thought Lee's security lapses were insufficient to justify the warrant and blocked submission of the affidavit. A scathing review of the Lee case in 2001 led by an experienced DOJ espionage lawyer, Randy Bellows, faulted OIPR for mistakenly applying standards for FISA coverage that were higher than necessary in national security cases.[13] At the same time, the Bellows report criticized the FBI for accepting DOE's belief that Lee was a spy. US government agencies were entangled in knots that they had tied themselves.

By 1998, the Lee investigation became a political football in partisan infighting about President Bill Clinton's China policy. Just a year before, allegations had surfaced that China had contributed funds to Clinton's reelection campaign. A California businessman, Johnny Chung, admitted to DOJ that the thousands of dollars he had contributed to the Democratic National Committee had actually come from China's People's Liberation Army. Two other contributors—Mochtar Riady, who was CEO of the Indonesian conglomerate Lippo Group, and his son James, and another Indonesian political fundraiser, Ted Sioeng—were also alleged to have links to Chinese intelligence.

The Republican majority in Congress went on the offensive. The Senate held hearings on China's influencing of US elections, and in June 1998, the House of Representatives voted overwhelmingly to form a special committee to investigate technology transfer to China. The committee, headed by Representative Chris Cox, issued a blistering report in May 1999 claiming unequivocally that China had advanced its nuclear weapons program because of aggressive espionage and administration neglect. The political message of the report was trumpeted by Republican critics—the Clinton administration was downplaying and even ignoring nuclear espionage to avoid offending China and cramping its pro-China trade policies. Although some nuclear experts questioned the amount of progress China could make with its stolen American secrets, the Cox Committee report still hit like a bombshell.

The White House countered by pointing to Presidential Decision Directive 61, President Clinton's February 1998 mandate to improve the woeful state of security in DOE and its national labs. The White House also tasked PFIAB to study DOE security, and the PFIAB's final report was searing in its criticism: "The dysfunctional nature at the heart of DOE has too often resulted in the mismanagement of security in weapons-related activities and a lack of emphasis on counterintelligence. . . . DOE represents the best of America's scientific talent and achievements but it has also been responsible for the worst security record on secrecy that the members of this panel have ever encountered."[14]

Given the political firestorm over Chinese nuclear espionage, the Wen Ho Lee investigation suddenly gathered momentum and sparked more high-level interest. Just as the Cox Committee was putting the finishing touches on its report at the end of 1998, Lee traveled to Taiwan. The FBI had still not found a shred of evidence against him. With little left in its bag of investigative tricks, the FBI agreed to a DOE suggestion to give Lee a polygraph test after his trip.

Lee passed the polygraph test, but for the first time revealed his 1988 contact with Hu Side in a Beijing hotel room. The confession was enough justification for DOE to move Lee temporarily out of his classified position to a less sensitive one. Terrified that his job was in jeopardy, Lee managed to regain access to his classified computer account and sneak back into his old office to delete files he had downloaded over a ten-year period. In a few weeks, he managed to "erase evidence of perhaps the most massive computer security violation in Los Alamos history."[15]

In March 1999, the *New York Times* broke the story of Chinese espionage at Los Alamos. Even the slim hope of a covert FBI investigation of Lee was now dashed by the flurry of stories that began to emerge in the media. As a last-ditch effort, the FBI confronted Lee in a hostile interview after the *Times* story appeared, but he continued to deny any accusation of espionage. But his career at DOE was over. On March 8, two days after his session with the FBI, he was fired by Los Alamos for failing to report foreign contacts, failing to safeguard secrets, and deceiving lab officials about security issues.[16] An FBI search of his house surfaced instructions he had scribbled about making back-up tapes, which led to the discovery of his extensive downloading of files. Meanwhile, DOE's audit system, NADIR, had been recording this activity since 1993 unbeknownst to the FBI and DOE counterintelligence.

Lee's downloading of files raised suspicions of his espionage to a fever pitch. His explanation that he had moved the files to protect them from computer crashes seemed lame, especially because there had been no such catastrophes at the lab. Some in Congress began labeling Lee "the spy of the century," and pressure for his arrest was mounting.[17] Although the FBI case against him was flimsy, Attorney General Janet Reno and FBI director Louis Freeh decided that they needed to act to fend off the criticism.

On December 10, 1999, just short of his sixtieth birthday, Wen Ho Lee was arrested. He was charged with fifty-nine counts of mishandling classified information. The majority of the charges stemmed from the Atomic Energy Act, some of which carried a maximum penalty of life imprisonment. Lee, however, was not charged with passing the secrets of the W-88 warhead because the FBI still had no evidence to support the claim.

At bail hearings the government argued successfully that Lee was a flight risk and danger to national security. He was denied bail and held in solitary confinement for nine months while opposing attorneys prepared their case and filed motions. Meanwhile, Asian Americans began to rally to his cause and collect money for his defense. The ugly specter of racial prejudice began to cloud the case as some Asian Americans compared Lee's plight to the internment of Japanese Americans during World War II.[18] Their protests were joined by scientists who disputed the value of the information Lee had allegedly mishandled. In June 2000 Lee's supporters organized a massive National Day of Outrage in Albuquerque and other American cities.

Aside from the protests, the government's case suddenly began to crumble. An FBI agent had testified at the bail hearing that Lee had borrowed a computer from a colleague ostensibly to get a résumé but that his real purpose was to download files, a clear indication of his intent to deceive. A closer review of the colleague's testimony by Lee's defense team revealed that Lee had told him the truth. At a third bail hearing in August 2000, the defense confronted the FBI agent, who claimed that his earlier testimony had been mistaken.

The defense also challenged government claims about the intelligence value of Lee's downloaded files. At the first bail hearing, Stephen Younger, the associate director of Los Alamos's nuclear weapons program, testified that "the codes and databases that were downloaded represent a complete nuclear weapons design capability, everything that you would need to install that capability in another location, everything." Younger summed up his explosive testimony with a frightening alert. The codes could, "in the wrong hands, change the global strategic balance; . . . they represent the gravest possible security risk to the United States."[19]

Younger's riveting testimony undoubtedly contributed to the decision to incarcerate Lee without bail. Other scientists, however, privately grumbled that Younger's assessment was a gross exaggeration because, in their view, possession of the codes alone was a far cry from the ability to build a nuclear weapon. At a subsequent hearing, Lee's lawyers summoned their own expert witness to rebut Younger's contention. Harold Agnew, an eminent nuclear physicist who had directed Los Alamos from 1970 to 1979, debunked Younger's claims: "I disagree with the statement that, if the People's Republic of China . . . obtained the codes at issue here, it 'would change the global strategic balance.' . . . If the People's Republic of China had already obtained these codes, . . . it would have little or no effect whatsoever on today's nuclear balance; . . . no nation would ever stockpile any device based on another nation's computer codes."[20]

Judge James Parker, who presided over Lee's bail hearings, issued a memorandum that whittled away the government's case. According to the memorandum, FBI testimony about Lee's deceit had been discredited and Lee's downloads now appeared less damaging than DOJ had led the court to believe. Besides, the government had no evidence on the key issue of Lee's intent. The judge's message was clear—the prosecution's case was in tatters, and the government would lose in court.

DOJ and Lee's attorneys cobbled a plea bargain. Lee pled guilty to one felony count of mishandling classified information and agreed to cooperate with FBI debriefers, and his sentence for the crime was 277 days, the time he had already served in his Santa Fe jail cell. At the sentencing, Judge Parker stunned the courtroom by lambasting the government's weak case and criticizing the top officials of the agencies involved: "They have embarrassed our entire nation and each of us who is a citizen of it." In a highly unusual gesture, Parker ended by apologizing to Lee: "I sincerely apologize to you, Dr. Lee, for the unfair manner you were held in custody by the executive branch."[21] On September 13, 2000, Wen Ho Lee, who some had called the "spy of the century," was a free man.

Wen Ho Lee later sued the US government and five news organizations for violating his privacy by disclosing that he was under investigation for espionage. US law prohibits the government from releasing protected information from personnel records, but the furor over Chinese nuclear espionage inevitably led to the leak of Lee's identity to the press. Rather than face a trial where sources would have to be revealed, four of the five media outlets pursued a settlement out of court. In June 2006 the US government and the news organizations agreed to settle with Lee for $1.6 million.[22]

Lee's supporters also took a page from the Jonathan Pollard playbook. They created an online organization, WenHoLee.org (www.wenholee.org), in order to seek a presidential pardon for Lee's conviction on the single felony charge. Although his supporters pursue a pardon, the mystery remains unsolved. PRC official documents obtained by the CIA proved beyond any doubt that the Chinese had acquired secret information about American nuclear warheads. Until today, no spy has been arrested for passing the secrets of the W-88 to the PRC.

Spies for China

She's been a communist since the day she was born. Her bona fides are impeccable. I gradually converted her. She's now a rock-ribbed Republican.

FBI agent **JAMES J. SMITH** *on Katrina Leung, his Chinese spy,*
cited by Gertz, Enemies, *18*

Another Chinese spy case caused the FBI even more embarrassment than Wen Ho Lee. The Wen Ho Lee imbroglio resulted from interagency blunders by the US Department of Energy (DOE), DOJ, and the FBI, but the case of Katrina Leung, code-named "Parlor Maid," rested solely on the FBI's doorstep. Leung had been the FBI's prize Chinese source for eighteen years, until her role as a double agent working for the PRC was exposed. She had not only spied for the Chinese but also carried on longtime romances with not one but two FBI agents.

Espionage mixed with romance is a volatile brew that can dilute the objectivity and professionalism of the spy–handler relationship. During the Golden Age of Soviet espionage, the Soviets misread the depth of Elizabeth Bentley's love for her handler, Jacob Golos, and when the KGB wrested his spy network from her after his death, she turned on her spymasters and betrayed them to the FBI. Another offshoot of "falling in love with an agent" is the handler's blind rejection of glaring signs that his or her agent may be underperforming, providing inaccurate reports, or, worst of all, working for the other side.

Such was the case of FBI special agent James J. Smith, Katrina Leung's handler. Smith, known as "J.J." among his FBI colleagues, retired from the FBI in 2000 after a distinguished thirty-year career. He spent most of that career in Los Angeles, where he headed the China squad and was widely regarded as the FBI's leading expert on Chinese espionage. That expertise was enhanced by Smith's handling of Parlor Maid for eighteen years.

Parlor Maid, Leung's code name, was a top FBI producer of intelligence on China during those years and an adviser on counterintelligence issues as well.[1] She was also Smith's lover throughout the years of their spy–handler relationship and after his retirement. Because of that romance, Leung enjoyed unusual access—Smith consulted her on FBI cases and showed her classified documents on China to seek her assessments of them, a flagrant violation of security regulations and basic spy tradecraft.[2] He also brought Leung to FBI parties and she videotaped his retirement reception, a security lapse even an amateur would avoid.

Smith first met Leung in 1982, when he interviewed her regarding her activities while working in a company suspected of illegal technology transfer to China.[3] Leung talked freely about her contacts back in Beijing and shared a wealth of useful information. Leung demonstrated potential to be a long-term oasis in the desert of US intelligence on China—she was young, vivacious, socially skilled, and well connected in China. Smith recruited her as a source and, a short time later, became her lover.

Leung had been active on China issues since her college days. She was born Chan Man Ying in Guangdong Province in China on May 1, 1954, and her upbringing was provided by a childless aunt who moved them to Hong Kong and then emigrated to the United States in 1970. In 1976, she graduated with a double major in architecture and engineering from Cornell University, where she participated in pro-China organizations. After receiving an MBA from the University of Chicago, she moved to California in 1980 to work for Sida International, a company that promoted trade with the PRC.

Before long, Leung and her husband, Kam, a medical company executive, became active in political fund-raising and began rubbing shoulders with southern California's political elite. She served on the board of the Los Angeles World Affairs Council alongside former secretary of state Warren Christopher; Disney's CEO, Michael Eisner; and former Los Angeles Dodgers owner Pete O'Malley.[4] More important, because of her fluent Chinese and connections to the government in Beijing, she began organizing banquets for visiting Chinese officials and soon served as a bridge on trade and other issues between high-level Chinese and California politicians.

Leung's high-level Chinese contacts and frequent trips to the PRC gave her unprecedented access to elicit information of interest to US policymakers. She was also active in the Chinese American community in southern California and was questioned by the FBI about various espionage cases. Among them was the investigation of the Lawrence Livermore National Laboratory scientist Guo Bao Min, the same suspect Wen Ho Lee had called to offer his help in 1982. The FBI investigation was run by Special Agent Bill Cleveland, another specialist on Chinese espionage who met Leung. In 1988 Cleveland and Leung began their own affair that lasted until 1999. Katrina Leung was not only cheating on her husband but also on her FBI handler. By the late 1980s tidbits of information emerged that she was also cheating the FBI.

In 1987, the FBI received information about a call by a female to the Chinese Consulate in San Francisco who was identified as Leung. Leung asked the consulate to call her back at a phone booth number, a hint that the conversation concerned more than ordinary business. The suspicious conversation was ignored by the FBI.[5] In an even more suspicious incident in April 1991, a female using a code name called a Ministry of State Security (MSS) officer in China.[6] The use of a code name alone raised FBI suspicions about the mysterious caller, who was discussing a visit to Beijing by two FBI agents, one of whom was her lover, Bill Cleveland.

Leung's call caused a stir at the FBI. If their prize agent was using code names with a known Chinese intelligence officer, the painful explanation might be that she was really an MSS spy and had been deceiving the FBI for almost a decade. Rather than conduct an independent review of the case, the FBI let Smith handle the thorny issue. Smith, after all, was the FBI's Chinese espionage expert, and agents around the country routinely deferred to him on Chinese matters. In May 1991, an angry Smith confronted Leung about the call and she admitted to him that she was passing information to the MSS.

Smith argued to the FBI that Parlor Maid was still a well-connected spy and that he could turn her away from the Chinese and ensure her future loyalty to the FBI. He would later admit that he was frightened that the revelation of Leung as a Chinese spy would surface their affair, clearly something he wanted to conceal from the FBI and his family. The FBI deferred to Smith again and let him continue running Leung as a source.

Leung continued to spy for China despite Smith's efforts, and more hints of her double-dealing surfaced in the 1990s. In 1992, a source claimed that a Chinese double agent named "Katrina" was working for the FBI, and in 2000 another source fingered Leung as an MSS agent.[7] Despite the glaring indicators of Leung's deceit, the assistant director of FBI counterintelligence waved off the reports as "sources pointing fingers at each other."[8]

The compromise of sensitive US government technical operations led to an FBI investigation that, by the end of 2001, narrowed down the list of possible suspects to Leung.[9] The FBI built the case against Leung for a year before interviewing her. In December 2002 she admitted to FBI agents that, during meetings with Smith at her home, she had surreptitiously snatched classified documents from her lover's briefcase and photocopied them. She also admitted her MSS code name and the identity of her handler and confessed that she had passed to Chinese intelligence the information that she filched from Smith. And, Leung admitted, she did have an affair with her FBI handler for eighteen years.[10]

Under separate questioning by the FBI, Smith reluctantly confirmed their affair and admitted that he had probably shared too much information with Leung over the years.[11] Cleveland also admitted his own affair with Leung, but he apparently confined his dealings with her only to sex and so he was not accused of violating any laws.

Katrina Leung and J. J. Smith were arrested on April 9, 2003. Leung was charged with unauthorized access, retention, and copying of national defense information; lying to federal investigators; and tax evasion because she had not reported as income the $1.7 million she had received from the FBI over the years. Smith was charged with gross negligence in handling classified information and lying during his FBI reinvestigation. As a long-time FBI agent, Smith knew the stumbling blocks to successful prosecution of national security cases and used the "graymail" tactic to wriggle out of a trial.[12] He requested classified documents for his defense, which, if revealed during court proceedings, might compromise the information. The maneuver worked, and Smith was allowed a plea bargain that released him on three years' probation and a $10,000 fine.

The FBI was more interested in locking up a Chinese spy and wanted Smith's cooperation against Leung for the plea bargain. DOJ wanted to ensure that Leung could not receive any help from Smith to aid her defense, so the terms of Smith's plea agreement stipulated that he was prohibited from sharing any further information relating to the case with Leung or her attorneys. The stipulation, however, backfired. The federal judge in Leung's case ruled that her constitutional right to a witness needed for her defense had been violated by Smith's plea agreement. The judge dismissed the case.[13]

DOJ filed an appeal, but, realizing that the case was dying, US attorneys scrambled to negotiate an agreement with Leung.[14] On December 16, 2005, Leung pled guilty to two counts: lying to federal authorities and tax evasion.[15] She was released on three years' probation, and in return she agreed to cooperate with FBI debriefers about her spying for the Chinese, pay a $10,000 fine, and perform 100 hours of community service.

The Leung case left another blot on the FBI's reputation. First one of its own, Robert Hanssen, had been unmasked as a major Russian spy; and now another, J. J. Smith, had violated basic security relations in dealing with agents by his illicit affair with Katrina Leung. The romance led Smith to gloss over red flags in the case and enable a Chinese spy to continue duping the FBI for years. Smith, however, was not solely responsible for the disaster. According to the DOJ inspector general's review of the case, Smith had never been challenged by a row of supervisors in the field and at FBI headquarters about suspicious anomalies in the Leung operation.[16]

The inspector general's review of the case emphasized the FBI's failure to conduct "asset validation" of its sources.[17] By the time of the report, the FBI itself realized the need for sweeping changes in its approach. In an interview FBI counterespionage chief David Szady admitted "that the Leung case highlighted the FBI's need to better control its informants, to check the information they provide."[18]

In the spy trade asset validation is simply a system of measures to establish the reliability and veracity of sources.[19] Some form of this validation is used in many walks of life. Lawyers use it with witnesses before putting them on the stand, police use some form of validation to check out their informants, and corporations apply due diligence before collaborating with or buying a company to ensure that their investment is sound.

Asset validation not only in the FBI but also in the entire intelligence community was roundly criticized in the March 2005 report to the president by the Silberman-Robb Commission, which reviewed US intelligence capabilities regarding weapons of mass destruction.[20] The commission singled out one Iraqi source, code-named Curveball, whose information on Saddam Hussein's biological warfare capabilities was reported by DIA and formed part of the body of data supporting the existence of Iraqi weapons programs. Curveball turned out to be a fabricator, and the commission deemed DIA's disregard of agent validation "a major failure in operational tradecraft." [21]

The FBI's disregard of asset validation in the Leung operation prevented any independent review from resolving the anomalies in the case. As a result, Leung was able to funnel the FBI's requirements back to the Chinese so they would know the information the United States had about the PRC and the gaps in its knowledge. On a strategic level, that information could have enabled China to shape its policy based on US perceptions. On a tactical level, the information could have also assisted Chinese counterespionage in discovering spies in its government.

Because Leung was controlled by the MSS, the intelligence she provided to the FBI may have been shaped by the Chinese either to deceive the United States or influence its policy toward the PRC. During the 1940s, the assistant secretary of the Treasury, Harry Dexter White, was a top policymaker and KGB spy, but the Soviet positions he advocated in Franklin D. Roosevelt's inner circle were either in line with America's own or were flatly rejected. Leung hardly enjoyed White's influence, although some of her reports were ostensibly from high-level Chinese officials. Many of those reports were undoubtedly woven into analytic pieces with heaps of other information, further complicating any assessment of the influence she may have exerted on US policy. One thing, however, is certain. Katrina Leung, aka Parlor Maid, was "a Chinese spy who got away."[22]

Leung was run by the MSS as a classical double agent operation, unlike China's unorthodox spying methods to collect tidbits of intelligence from hordes of visiting targets. Another classical operation to collect that covert 20 percent of intelligence involved a spy ring in the US defense industry.

The Mak Family

The story of the Mak spy ring resembles a Chinese version of the Walker family espionage business. Two brothers, their wives, and one of their sons were charged with conspiracy to export US defense information. At the heart of the ring was Chi Mak, an engineer for Power Paragon, a southern California company and subsidiary of the L-3 conglomerate, one of the largest government defense contractors in America.

Although the United States had been plagued by spies among defense contractors since the 1950s, the number had dwindled to a trickle after the end of the Cold War. Tightened security measures were now mandated in government contracts and, faced with the loss of multi-million-dollar deals, the industry met and sometimes exceeded the government's strict standards. The industry had been mostly riddled with Soviet bloc spies during the Cold War, but it had also become an attractive target for China to accelerate its military modernization.

Chi Mak was ideally placed to contribute to the PRC's program. He was born in 1940 in Guangzhou and in the 1960s moved with his wife Rebecca Liu to Hong Kong, where he began spying on American ships on their way to Vietnam. Chi and Rebecca emigrated to the United States and became American citizens in 1985. An electrical engineer by profession, Chi Mak was hired by Power Paragon and received a security clearance in 1996. Initially, he traveled to Hong Kong to deliver the company's naval secrets to his brother, Tai Mak, who worked for Chinese military intelligence and who carried the information to the mainland.

In 2001, Tai Mak and his wife, Fuk Heung, emigrated to the United States, where they received permanent resident alien status. Tai Mak settled near his brother in California and found a job as a broadcast engineer for a Chinese TV station. The move enhanced the security of their spying operation. Chi Mak was able to avoid raising suspicions by frequent overseas trips, and his brother Tai instead served as the courier of Power Paragon's naval information between the United States and China.

The FBI opened a full investigation on the Mak family in 2004. In February 2005, FBI agents pieced together ripped-up papers from Chi's trash that revealed a shopping list of Chinese intelligence requirements on an array of US Navy secrets, including early warning systems, submarine propulsion technology, missile-launching procedures, destroyer technology, and shipboard communications.[23] FBI coverage of Chi's home and office then revealed that he was sending e-mails to his home with classified information and loading his briefcase with compact disks from work. At home, Chi downloaded the work e-mails and transferred the secret materials to other disks, which he then brought to his brother's house.[24]

In October 2005, the FBI learned of imminent plans by Tai Mak and his wife to travel to China. At the same time, surveillance of Chi Mak showed that he was loading information on disks regarding the Quiet Electric Drive project at Power Paragon. Chi was the lead engineer on the project, which developed a silent propulsion system for US Navy warships.[25] Chi had presumably betrayed other information about the project in the past, but the US Navy believed the system was too valuable to allow any more disks to fall into Chinese hands.

On October 28 the FBI arrested Tai Mak and his wife at Los Angeles International Airport as they were about to embark on another spy trip to China. A search of Tai's carry-on bag surfaced the disks with Power Paragon's information. Chi Mak and his wife Rebecca were arrested at their home the same day. Although Tai Mak refused to cooperate with the FBI, Chi admitted that he had passed Power Paragon materials to China but denied passing any classified information.

Unfortunately for the United States, he was telling the truth. Despite the wealth of US Navy information Chi had given China, none of it was classified.

Power Paragon's materials developed for the navy were considered sensitive proprietary information subject to export controls, but in court the unclassified documents did not meet the espionage threshold regarding injury to US national security interests. As a result, the government could not indict the Maks for espionage and had to settle for lesser charges of theft and transporting stolen property.[26]

In June 2006, a new indictment included Tai Mak's son Billy, a University of California, Los Angeles, student who had assisted his father in encrypting the stolen information. Then, in October, a federal grand jury added new charges to the indictment of the five spy ring members, including conspiracy to export US defense information.[27] Because the Power Paragon documents were unclassified, US attorneys had to thumb through statutes to find some basis for prosecuting the Mak ring.

The information Chi Mak admitted passing to the Chinese may not have been classified but would certainly have helped the Chinese in the event of a naval conflict with the United States. Among other items, Chi provided information about Aegis, an advanced antimissile system deployed on a broad spectrum of the navy's warships.[28]

Chi Mak was found guilty in May 2007 and sentenced to twenty-four-and-a-half years in prison. The other members of the family spy ring also pled guilty; his brother Tai was sentenced to ten years imprisonment, Chi's wife to three years, Tai's wife to three years probation, and Tai's son Billy to eleven months.

Dongfan Chung

The Mak family was only half of a PRC spy network in the United States that was eventually unmasked. At Chi Mak's trial the FBI testified that, during the search of the defendant's home, agents discovered a letter revealing that he also served as an intermediary between the Chinese and another engineer, Dongfan Chung, who worked on the space shuttle for the Boeing Corporation.[29] The pair was further linked to a shadowy Chinese military intelligence officer only identified as "PRC official 'A'" in court affidavits.[30]

Chung almost rivaled Larry Wu-tai Chin in the longevity of his espionage career. Like Chin, Chung was born in China and spied for the land of his birth for almost three decades. He emigrated to the United States in 1962, acquired US citizenship, and worked first for Rockwell International and then for the Boeing Corporation on the West Coast for thirty years. In about 1979 he volunteered to spy for the PRC by sending a letter to a Chinese professor claiming that he was "regretful for not contributing anything" to his homeland and offering to provide information.[31] Over the course of his lengthy spy career, in response to specific questions from his PRC handlers, Chung provided a wealth of aerospace and aircraft information, including twenty-four B-1 bomber manuals and documents related to Delta-IV rockets to launch manned space vehicles, the C-17 Globemaster cargo plane, F-15 fighter planes, helicopters, and the space shuttle.[32] Unbeknownst to his employers, Chung also traveled to China on several occasions to give lectures on space shuttle technology and meet his spy handlers.[33]

Chung was arrested for economic espionage and other charges in February 2008. During the investigation, the FBI found in his residence a staggering 250,000 pages of Boeing documents on restricted aircraft technology.[34] The long-serving, seventy-three-year-old spy was convicted in a trial and sentenced to fifteen years and eight months in prison.

Tai Shen Kuo, Gregg Bergersen, Yu Xin Kang, and James Fondren

A subset of PRC official "A"'s network was arrested 3,000 miles away on the East Coast the same day as Chung. This subset included a spy, his handler in the United States, and a courier. The spy handler was Tai Shen Kuo, a native of Taiwan who had become a US citizen and spent three decades in New Orleans importing furniture from the PRC. Kuo was a respected member of the New Orleans business community and had even received a gubernatorial appointment to a state overseas trade commission. His business involved frequent travel to China, where in the 1990s he was enlisted by PRC official "A" to seek out potential spies with access to US defense information.[35]

Kuo fulfilled his task by meeting and cultivating Gregg Bergersen, a US Navy veteran and weapons systems analyst at the Defense Security Cooperation Agency, the Pentagon unit responsible for implementing America's foreign arms sales. Kuo lured Bergersen into espionage by holding out the carrot of a lucrative joint consulting partnership on defense matters. Bergersen was actively seeking a postretirement income source, partly to support his gambling habit. Kuo twisted the hook in further by funding his spy's trips to Las Vegas and supplying him with cash for bets at casino tables. In return, Bergersen provided information on US military sales to Taiwan and communications security issues.[36]

In a classic false flag operation, Kuo convinced Bergersen that his information was supplied to Taiwan. Just as John Walker had deceived his subsource Jerry Whitworth that the latter's information ended up in Israeli hands, Kuo enabled Bergersen to rationalize the impact of his espionage because he believed that he was spying for a US ally. Bergersen, however, realized that the unauthorized recipient of stolen secrets is a moot point. He knew he was still committing a crime. During a meeting with Kuo in a rental car, Bergersen nervously begged his handler not to reveal him as the source of information he was passing on US arms sales to Taiwan. "If it ever fell into the wrong hands, . . . then I would get fired for sure," he told Kuo. "I'd go to jail . . . because I violated the rules."[37]

To provide further security and efficiency to the operation, the Chinese posted a courier to New Orleans to receive the materials from Kuo and deliver them directly to PRC official "A" in China. Yu Xin Kang, a thirty-three-year-old legal permanent resident alien, had met Kuo in China and had become his lover. Kuo's enthusiasm for the cause was undoubtedly heightened by the proximity of his mistress living in New Orleans, and, from a security perspective, Kang's courier duties enabled Kuo to make less frequent and potentially alerting trips to see his spymaster in China.

Bergersen soon pled guilty to charges of conspiracy to disclose national defense information and was ultimately sentenced to 57 months in prison. Kang received a lighter sentence of eighteen months, and Kuo was sentenced to 188 months and a $40,000 fine.[38] Kuo originally came to the United States to study at Nicholls College in Louisiana on a tennis scholarship and later became a tennis pro at a New Orleans country club. He is reportedly teaching tennis to his fellow inmates in prison.[39]

On the day Kuo and Bergersen were arrested, Kuo was staying at the home of another one of his DOD contacts in Virginia, James Fondren, a former US Air Force colonel. Among Kuo's possessions at the time of his arrest was an unclassified copy of a DOD document titled "The National Military Strategy of the United States of America 2008." Fondren had given Kuo the document.

Fondren had retired in 1996 and established Strategy, Inc., a consulting business whose only client was Kuo. In 2001 Fondren returned to the Pentagon as the deputy director of the Washington office of the US Pacific Command. Back with access to classified information, Fondren supplied Kuo and PRC official "A" with "opinion papers" on China, a thinly veiled method to slip secrets to the Chinese in return for payments.[40] Financially motivated, Fondren received from $350 to $800 for each paper. Like Bergersen, Fondren was led to believe that the information he provided on US military activities and policy in the Pacific region was passed to Taiwan.[41] Fondren became the tenth member of PRC official "A"'s ring to be unmasked. He was arrested on May 13, 2009. Four months later he was tried and convicted, and in January 2010, he was sentenced to three years in prison.

The ten arrests reflect the depth and breadth of Chinese espionage against the United States and the increasing efforts of the FBI and other security agencies to combat it. The arrests, however, also demonstrate that the Chinese, like their Russian counterparts, commit costly errors in tradecraft that can be exploited by US counterespionage.

During the heyday of Soviet espionage in the 1930s and 1940s, many of the Americans collaborating with the USSR knew the identities of their fellow spies, socialized with them, and talked openly on telephone lines about their espionage activities. By the time Soviet intelligence officers tried to impose stricter tradecraft on these networks, defectors from the cause had revealed entire rings to the FBI.

Identification of PRC official "A"'s network was not on this scale, but the tradecraft mistakes were similar. Chi Mak's lapse in retaining compromising materials led to Dongfan Chung. Also, once Tai Shen Kuo, the principal agent of his ring, was identified, his contacts with Bergersen, Kang, and Fondren yielded sufficient evidence to the FBI to arrest and prosecute them. Although unmasking the vast extent of Chinese espionage in the United States is a daunting task, the arrests prove that Chinese tradecraft is far from perfect and that mistakes can be exploited to neutralize their American spies.

The arrests also reflect a relatively new phenomenon in PRC espionage in the United States. The majority of Chinese espionage cases involved Chinese Americans induced by PRC intelligence to contribute to the homeland like Larry Wu-tai Chin, Katrina Leung, Peter Lee, Guo Bao Min, and the Mak family. However, Bergersen and Fondren were not Chinese American and were motivated purely by financial motives. PRC intelligence may predominantly target Chinese Americans but does not rely on them exclusively for US secrets.

Ronald Montaperto

Bergersen and Fondren were not the first non–Chinese Americans to spy for the PRC. Another example was Ronald Montaperto, an academic expert on China. After teaching at Indiana University and the Army War College, he joined DIA in the early 1980s and held a number of positions as a China analyst. He later left DIA to work at the China Analysis Center of the National Defense University and then headed the US Pacific Command's Asia-Pacific Center for Security Studies in Hawaii.

Montaperto wrote several studies on China and developed a reputation as a leading commentator on the PRC's military. As evidenced in his comments in a 1996 panel discussion, he advocated a decidedly benign view of the threat from the PRC: "China is years away from being in a position where the combination of capabilities and intentions would be such that they would pose a threat to US vital interests or the interests of our friends and allies."[42]

In 1982, while at DIA, Montaperto was tabbed to participate in a program to promote interaction between DIA's China analysts and military attachés from the PRC stationed in Washington. After the program ended, Montaperto continued his contact with two of the Chinese attachés but did not fully report his meetings as required by DIA regulations.[43]

During those contacts, Montaperto shared secret and top-secret information with his military attaché friends for almost a decade. The FBI began to focus on Montaperto in 1991. In an interview with FBI agents, he admitted continuing contact with the Chinese attachés and orally passing them classified information, although he could not recall exactly what material he had shared with them. Montaperto left DIA and the investigation was dropped.[44]

The case remained dormant until 2003, when the FBI ran a version of its sting tactic against Montaperto, this time without an agent posing as a foreign intelligence officer. Montaperto was offered a position in an ostensible DIA project that would require a polygraph test. Montaperto agreed and, under further questioning, he admitted again to passing classified information to the Chinese. This time, however, he remembered that he had shared with the attachés US intelligence on Chinese military sales in the Middle East.[45]

A search of Montaperto's residence turned up classified documents on China that he had hoarded. On June 21, 2006, he pled guilty to a single count of illegal retention of classified documents. As in the Mak case, the charge was far less serious than espionage. Montaperto's case epitomized the typical difficulties of investigating and prosecuting Chinese espionage. Unlike Soviet espionage cases, there were no dead drops, no minia-ture cameras, no unexplained wealth or mysteriously fattened bank accounts. Even with Montaperto's admissions, the difficulty of pinpointing specific documents and classified information he gave away eroded the prosecution's ability to prove serious damage to US national security interests.

The prosecution's case was also complicated by friends and supporters of Montaperto who rallied to his cause. His supporters were not the com-munists who defended the Rosenbergs, the Jewish groups that protested Pollard's life sentence, or the Asian Americans who marched for Wen Ho Lee. They were former and current US government intelligence and mili-tary officials that criticized the FBI and defended Montaperto, who they believed was accused based on mere technicalities about mishandling clas-sified information.[46]

This time, the high-level support worked. A federal judge sentenced Montaperto to a mere three months in prison, although the accused had admitted to more than sixty contacts with Chinese military intelligence officers and to passing top-secret US government information to the PRC. In issuing the sentence, the judge noted the "very serious charge" but con-fessed that he had been swayed toward more lenient punishment because of the letters and support from intelligence and military officials.[47]

Chinese Seeding Operations

A later revelation of another non-Chinese spy working for the PRC demon-strated that Chinese intelligence pursued seeding operations to infiltrate young Americans into positions of access. Glenn Duffie Shriver, a Michigan college student, went to China three times between 2001 and 2004 to study its language and culture. While in Shanghai in 2004, he responded to an advertisement to write a paper on United States–China relations. The sponsors were in reality Chinese intelligence officers who recruited Shriver to seek employment in the Department of State or CIA.[48] After failing State's foreign service exam, Shriver tried his luck applying to the CIA's National Clandestine Service. During the screening process, he admitted his collaboration with the PRC and was arrested in June 2010. He pled guilty to conspiring to provide secrets to the PRC and was sentenced to four years in prison.

The importance of the seeding operation to the Chinese was highlighted by the amount of money paid to Shriver; he received $70,000 for his application efforts, even though he had no access to a single secret. If Shriver had succeeded, the PRC's investment would have yielded bucketsful of those grains of sand that the Chinese had so painstakingly acquired through other espionage operations.

As in the Shriver case and the earlier case of the Soviets' Cambridge Five, universities remain priority targets for the seeding operations of intelligence services. Cuban intelligence learned the value of these operations well from its KGB ally and exploited it to infiltrate spies into America's national security apparatus for years.

Spies for Cuba I

ANA BELEN MONTES

All the world is one country. . . . I obeyed my conscience rather than the law.

ANA BELEN MONTES'S *statement at her sentencing, quoted by*
Counterintelligence Centre, "Unrepentant Ana Montes Sentenced"

With rare exceptions, the end of the Golden Age of Soviet espionage marked the end of the era of the purely ideological spy in America. Even those who later professed to spy for lofty motives—like Larry Wu-tai Chin, who wanted to build trust between America and China, and Jonathan Pollard, who wanted to help Israel—were handsomely paid for stolen secrets.

There were, however, a few exceptions. A few of the Chinese Americans who passed secrets to China were never paid and gave away information to help the land of their birth. Other exceptions were Kurt Stand, Theresa Squillacote, and James Clark, throwbacks to the era of America's flirtation with communism.

The most exceptional ideological spy of them all, however, was not caught until September 21, 2001. Just ten days after the al-Qaeda terrorist attacks in the United States, Ana Belen Montes, a senior DIA analyst and Cuban specialist, was arrested by the FBI for espionage. She had spied for sixteen years for Cuban intelligence and, aside from expenses, had not received a dime for betraying classified information. As the Counterintelligence Centre noted in its summary of Montes's espionage, the case "shows men aren't the only spies, Russia is not the only threat, and people don't always spy for money."[1]

Throughout Castro's reign, Cuba's intelligence service, the Dirección General de Inteligencia (DGI), was trained and funded by the KGB. The DGI was a KGB surrogate in the developing world and aggressively targeted American interests worldwide, but no major Cuban spy had been caught until Montes was arrested.

In 1998, the FBI rounded up an entire DGI network, dubbed the Wasp Network (in Spanish, la Red Avispa), that was tasked to spy on military installations and infiltrate Cuban American groups in southern Florida.[2] The trial of the Wasp Network remains controversial today. Five of the ten arrested spies in the network were convicted (five made plea agreements, and an additional four fled to Cuba to escape arrest). The sentence, however, was appealed because of accusations that the jury could not render an unbiased verdict in the heavily anti-Castro Miami venue of the trial. An appeals court panel overturned the conviction, but the full court subsequently upheld the original verdict. The continued imprisonment of the Cuban Five, as they have become known, continues to spark an international furor over the alleged injustice of their imprisonment, and their cause is advanced by a dedicated group of protesters, the National Committee to Free the Cuban Five.

The Cuban government has admitted the intelligence affiliation of the Wasp Network but claims that, after antiregime bombings in Havana, the spies were only penetrating anti-Castro groups that might plan future terrorist activities on the island. Despite this claim, the Wasp Network attempted to infiltrate US military installations in Florida. None of the Cubans in the network had any direct access to US secrets, and the closest any of them came to national security information was physical descriptions of facilities and counting planes at air bases.

Ana Montes was a different matter. During her sixteen-year spying career, she rose through the DIA ranks to become the senior analyst on Cuba and one of the intelligence community's leading experts on the hostile island nation just miles from American shores.

Based on her family history, Montes seemed an unlikely spy candidate. No other known American spy has come from a family so steeped in government service. Montes, whose parents were of Puerto Rican heritage, was born in February 1957 on a military base in Germany, where her father was stationed as a US Army psychiatrist. After her father left the army, he moved the family first to Topeka and then to Baltimore, where he set up a lucrative medical practice. There her mother worked as a federal investigator for an antidiscrimination agency. Her brother and sister both worked for the FBI. Her brother was working in the FBI's Atlanta field office when she was arrested, and her sister was in the Miami office, where, ironically, she took part in the Wasp Network investigation.[3] All the children, however, experienced a troubled childhood. Just as American spies ranging from Benedict Arnold to Robert Hanssen suffered because of the flaws of their fathers, Ana Montes and her siblings were reportedly bullied by their temperamental father to the point that her mother divorced him.[4]

Nevertheless, Montes followed her father's example and joined the family tradition of federal service. She graduated from the University of Virginia in 1979, worked briefly at DOJ, and then joined DIA in 1985. While working in the government, she studied at Johns Hopkins University's School of Advanced International Studies for a master's degree, which she received in 1988.

Montes began spying for Cuba sometime in 1984, while working at DOJ and studying at Johns Hopkins.[5] The best insight into her motives was her own statement at her sentencing. "All the world is one country," she told the federal judge." "I obeyed my conscience rather than the law. I believe our government's policy towards Cuba is cruel and unfair, profoundly unneighborly, and I felt morally obligated to help the island defend itself from our efforts to impose our values and our political system on it. We have displayed intolerance and contempt towards Cuba for most of the last four decades."[6]

Unlike other Americans who proclaimed similar lofty motives for their espionage, Montes sincerely spied for purely idealistic motives and this enabled her to steal secrets undetected for sixteen years. She never drove expensive sports cars, never lived in a fancy house, never spent extravagant amounts on luxury items, and never left a trail of unexplained wealth that would spark the interest of her coworkers or security investigators.

Besides her modest lifestyle, Montes appeared to be a workaholic wallflower. She was single and had a boyfriend, but rarely spent more than a few minutes at office parties. Coworkers described her as quiet, competent, and all business, to the point of striking some of them as aloof and even prickly at times. This extremely low profile allowed her to burrow deeply into the heart of US intelligence about Cuba.

After working as an analyst on Nicaraguan and Central American issues in her early DIA career, Montes was assigned to the Cuban account in 1992. Given her knowledge of the subject, she rapidly ascended through DIA's analyst ranks. In 1993 she was chosen to participate in the CIA's exceptional analyst program and traveled to Havana to interact with the Cuban military. She eventually sat on interagency boards where intelligence community specialists formulated assessments on Cuba. As a result, she had almost unfettered access to intelligence and policymaking across the entire US government. She was "the queen of Cuba within the US intelligence community."[7]

Throughout this distinguished career, Montes's apparent lack of a social life enabled her to devote her off-duty hours to spying. Because the United States was a hostile operating environment for the Cubans, they handled Montes with strict tradecraft measures. She met occasionally with her Cuban handlers to pass computer diskettes loaded with US secrets, but she was also in contact with the DGI through an impersonal communications system that included predesignated calls from pay phones and encrypted radio messages that she decoded with special software on her laptop computer.[8] She scrupulously followed the DGI's instructions, proving that she was as meticulous at spying as she was at analyzing Cuban affairs at DIA.

But even the most disciplined spies make mistakes. Continual leaks of information regarding Cuba, technical operations gone awry, and possible Cuban foreknowledge of US activities all raised concerns of a Castro spy inside the intelligence community.[9] Scott Carmichael, who would be the lead army counterintelligence officer in the Montes case, had investigated her earlier after receiving reports that she may have been suspiciously seeking sensitive information, but ultimately he found no concrete evidence. He later pressed the FBI to open an investigation on Montes, who was inside the small interagency circle with broad access to intelligence community information on Cuba. She presented an investigative challenge because her unblemished work performance and low-key lifestyle left no trail of the typical telltale signs of espionage. The FBI's persistence, however, paid off. During a court-approved surreptitious entry into Montes's apartment in May 2001, FBI agents uncovered clandestine communications instructions buried in her laptop computer. Although she was normally a painstakingly careful spy, she had forgotten the Cubans' warnings to erase their messages from the laptop's hard drive.[10]

Despite her scrupulous attention to detail, Montes was an intelligence analyst, not a trained clandestine operations officer. FBI agents surveilling her from May 2001 until her arrest in September observed her making calls from pay phones after traveling winding routes that seemed designed for her to determine if anyone was trailing her.[11] The FBI knew that she owned a cell phone, which made the frequent pay phone calls suspicious, and her apparent maneuvers to detect surveillance only heightened their concerns. Montes, untrained as she was, never noticed that the FBI was following her.

The September 11, 2001, terrorist attacks accelerated the case against Ana Montes. The US government was taking no chances after the most devastating attack on American soil since Pearl Harbor, and Cuba's cozy relations with state supporters of terrorism jangled nerves already frayed by worry about another attack.[12] Because of her job duties, Montes was on the verge of learning the post-9/11 invasion plans for Afghanistan.[13] She had to be stopped before she gave information to Cuba that might be passed on to a rogue state that supported terrorism. FBI agents arrested her in her DIA office at Bolling Air Force Base on September 21, just ten days after hijacked airliners smashed into the World Trade Center and Pentagon.

Montes pled guilty to conspiracy to commit espionage in March 2002. In October she stood impassive and still unrepentant in court as Judge Ricardo Urbina somberly told her "if you don't love your country, at least you should do it no wrong."[14] Because she had agreed to cooperate and share details about her espionage activities, she was sentenced to twenty-five years in prison instead of a life term.

Only comprehensive debriefings of Montes unearthed the full extent of the damage from her spying for Cuba. Even initial glimmers into the secrets she gave away were alarming: identities of undercover intelligence officers, a highly compartmented intelligence collection project, and US defense contingency planning for Cuba—to name but a few of the losses.[15] As a DIA analyst on El Salvador and Nicaragua in the late 1980s, she undoubtedly passed information that Cuba shared with its communist counterparts in both countries. A Green Beret military adviser was killed in an attack on a Salvadoran army compound visited by Montes only weeks before. As Scott Carmichael notes in *True Believer*, his insider's account of the case, "the death of American warfighters is the ultimate measure of a spy's depravity.[16]

Even without a complete damage assessment, Montes's broad access alone suggested that she kept the Cubans up to date on US intelligence activities against Cuba and details of policy deliberations about relations with Fidel Castro. Foreknowledge of US policy enabled Cuba to shape its policies at the most critical period since Castro's 1959 Revolution. When Montes began working on Cuba at DIA in 1992, Castro's perennial benefactor, the Soviet Union, had just ceased to exist and its demise spelled the end of the financial and military support that had kept the Cuban regime afloat.

Just when Cuba was beginning to feel the first economic pangs of Russian abandonment, Democrat Bill Clinton was elected president after twelve years of Republicans in the White House. Castro undoubtedly envisioned the change in administration as an opportunity to chip away at America's long-standing policy of isolating Cuba and to end its trade embargo. With the Cold War over, two bedrocks of that policy, Cuba's alliance with the Soviet Union and its ability to export revolution, were shattered, and rumblings about rapprochement with Castro were heard from some quarters. The insider's knowledge of US policy debates that Montes provided to Cuba enabled the Castro regime to shape its own policies to encourage opposition in America to the US government's isolation of the island nation.

Montes was not only positioned to inform Cuba about US policy but also may have been able to shape the policy herself through her contributions to intelligence estimates. In 1998, for example, Montes was the primary drafter of a DOD assessment that discounted any serious Cuban threat to the United States and downplayed intelligence about the regime's development of an offensive biological warfare capability. Then-secretary of defense William Cohen judged the report too rosy about the Cuban threat and heavily emphasized the biowarfare threat when he delivered the final report to Congress.

Castro himself publicly lauded the new assessment as a "serious report by objective people."[17] Castro, of course, had reason to crow—the not-so-objective author of the report was the most well-placed American spy in the history of his regime. The significance of Montes's influence, however, is questionable, and her lulling report illustrates the dubious advantages of spies as agents of influence.

A single spy rarely exercises critical impact on the policy of its target. Although Montes shaded intelligence to downplay the Cuban threat, her draft report was reviewed by superiors and colleagues before submission to the secretary of defense. None of those DIA colleagues have proven to be Cuban spies, and some of them undoubtedly shared Montes's views to varying degrees. Cuba, after all, did pose a significantly decreased military threat to the United States after the Cold War. After the flow of arms and oil from the USSR ended, the Cuban government was barely able to fuel its aging, rickety buses to transport workers to their grossly underpaid jobs on the island, much less wage war against anyone. Montes's report ultimately had little impact on reversing policy on behalf of her masters, the true measure of an agent of influence. Despite her efforts, Castro's empire was then and still remains under a trade embargo, impoverished and steadily crumbling.

However, two potentially dangerous threats to the United States still linger in Cuba: its biological warfare capability and its relationship with state supporters of terrorism. Cuba remains on the Department of State's list of countries that support terrorism; and Castro, until his health failed, had been repeatedly photographed while warmly embracing the leaders of state supporters of terrorism like Iran, North Korea, and Syria. The danger of Cuba exporting biological weapons to terrorists or providing them with a safe haven in Cuba could cost American lives in the war on terrorism. The threat of Cuba passing information from American spies to terrorists or their supporters could be equally catastrophic, and for that reason Ana Belen Montes was quickly arrested after 9/11.

Montes was not the only senior-level spy in the US government working for the Cubans. A husband-and-wife team spied for Fidel Castro almost twice as many years as Montes and continued spying undetected for six years after her arrest.

Spies for Cuba II

KENDALL AND GWENDOLYN MYERS

When I heard they were arrested, I felt like they had arrested Santa Claus
and the Easter Bunny.

LARRY MACDONALD, *an acquaintance of the Myerses, who lived at the marina in Maryland
where the Myerses docked their boat; quoted by Sheridan and Wilber,
"DC Couple's Disdain"*

Walter Kendall Myers would have looked more appropriately dressed in a
tweed coat and khaki trousers than in the blue prison jumpsuit he wore to
his indictment on charges of conspiracy to commit espionage. His wife,
Gwendolyn, likewise would have been more suitably attired in a sunflower
dress than the matching prison suit she wore as she sat next to her husband
in the courtroom. Kendall—seventy-two years old; tall at six feet, six inches;
bespectacled; white-haired; and mustachioed—resembled the Donald
Sutherland of his later movie career and appeared more like an elderly
blueblood or distinguished professor than an accused prisoner.[1]

Kendall Myers, in fact, was both. On April 15, 1937, he was born into a
Washington society family that counted among its forbears a number of
notable Americans. His father, a cardiac surgeon, was a distant relative of
President William Howard Taft, and his mother was the daughter of Gilbert Grosvenor, a longtime director of the National Geographic Society, and
granddaughter of Alexander Graham Bell, the inventor of the telephone.
Myers had the typical schooling of one born to such lineage, attending a

private boarding academy in Pennsylvania, graduating from Brown University, and then obtaining a doctorate in European history from Johns Hopkins University, the same institution where Ana Montes studied. He also did a stint in the US Army where, fluent in Czech, he monitored intercepts of the Soviets' Eastern European ally.

Myers's subsequent career was a blend of academia and government service. He taught European studies at his alma mater, the Johns Hopkins School of Advanced International Studies (SAIS), later worked as a contract instructor at the Department of State's Foreign Service Institute, and eventually became a full-time staff employee with a security clearance working on European matters in State's Bureau of Intelligence and Research (INR).

His life was not without turmoil. In 1974, after ten years of marriage, he separated from his wife, a fellow student at Brown and later a microbiologist who obtained sole custody of their two young children.[2] A year later, he lost control of his car on a Washington street and killed a teenage girl and seriously injured two of her friends. He was convicted of reckless driving but received only three years of unsupervised probation, a light sentence that some attributed to his family connections.[3]

In the late 1970s Myers met Gwendolyn Steingraber through mutual friends. Gwendolyn's background was markedly different from the urban, patrician milieu of Kendall Myers. She was born in Sioux City, Iowa, and raised in rural South Dakota, and she later volunteered to work for George McGovern's presidential campaign and then for liberal Senator James Abourezk. She would later work for the senator in Washington, where she walked the Capitol corridors with fellow aides such as Tom Daschle, future Senate majority leader, and Peter Rouse, who was later President Obama's acting chief of staff. Along the way she was twice divorced and had four children from her first marriage of eighteen years.

Despite their different backgrounds, Kendall and Gwendolyn were attracted to each other by their common belief in liberal causes. The couple lived together and moved to South Dakota, where Gwendolyn got a job through Abourezk at the state's Public Utilities Commission, while Kendall worked on a book about British prime minister Neville Chamberlain that he never finished.[4] The Myerses also adopted a lifestyle reminiscent of the 1960s, espousing and marching for various causes such as legalized abortion, solar energy, and the end of uranium mining. At one point, the police even raided their home and seized marijuana plants that the pair was growing in their basement.[5]

Just before their move to South Dakota, in December 1978, Kendall Myers spent two weeks in Cuba, a trip that proved to be the turning point in his and Gwendolyn's lives. Kendall was significantly impressed by his tour of the communist island, which had been arranged by a Cuban official at the United Nations whom they had met in Washington. Six months later, the same official traveled to South Dakota to visit the Myerses and recruited them to spy against the United States.[6]

Kendall Myers's mixed career in government and academe and his liberal views made him an ideal candidate for an approach by the Cubans. Jose Cohen Valdes, a former Cuban intelligence officer who had defected to the United States, noted that "Cuban intelligence views US universities as important centers to influence US policy and recruit persons who can provide critical information to the Cuban regime or influence US government officials."[7] At the time of his recruitment, Myers had been a professor at Hopkins's SAIS and was already a contract employee of the State Department.

As Valdes further notes, Cuban intelligence, like other services, pursues targets that it can seed into government national security agencies and direct toward jobs with access to information of priority interest to the Castro regime.[8] In Kendall Myers's case, his Cuban recruiter urged him to seek staff employment at the State Department or the CIA.[9] Enthused over their newfound cause, the Myerses relocated back to Washington. Kendall returned to the Foreign Service Institute but was eventually hired as a staff employee with a security clearance at State's INR, where he had broad access to classified information across the intelligence community. The couple married in 1982 to ensure that he would have no problem obtaining a security clearance. Undoubtedly coached by their Cuban handlers, they also scrupulously avoided any discussions of Cuba with friends and acquaintances.

Upon their return to the nation's capital, the Myerses embarked on a spying career for Cuba that lasted almost three decades. They were a mom-and-pop espionage shop, the Cubans' version of the Rosenbergs, slavishly devoted to Castro's communist cause, though their betrayal went undetected far longer than that of the two Soviet spies. The importance of their spying contribution was illustrated by a clandestine visit to Cuba around New Year's Day 1995, when they spent four hours enthralled in conversation with Cuban leader Fidel Castro.[10]

Kendall and Gwendolyn Myers, like Ana Montes, were throwbacks to a bygone era of ideologically motivated espionage. In a 1978 diary entry revealed later in court affidavits, Kendall waxed poetic about his trip to the communist island and lauded Castro's brilliance and charisma, calling him "one of the greatest leaders of our time," who had helped the Cubans "to save their souls."[11] Gwendolyn was equally mesmerized by Cuba, and the couple's newfound job as spies cemented their marriage bonds even more powerfully.

The Cubans employed tradecraft with the Myerses similar to that used with Montes. Initially, as the Myerses later revealed, they frequently met with their Cuban handlers in New York. But for security reasons, they subsequently traveled to various locations throughout South America and Europe for personal meetings. They also passed information to the Cubans in Washington through the traditional espionage method of brush passes, where spy and handler momentarily pass by each other and exchange materials. Gwendolyn later admitted that her favorite brush pass was the quick transfer of shopping carts in a grocery store.[12]

The Cubans also supplemented these personal contacts with coded email messages and encrypted short-wave radio communications.[13] In the Myerses' case, their radio communications provided the first lead to their spying. According to court affidavits in the case, the FBI collects messages sent by Cuban intelligence and had intercepted some particularly tantalizing ones between Havana and a Cuban intelligence officer that pointed to the existence of a spy in the US government.[14] Even if a transmission is determined to be a message about espionage, however, the spies cannot be readily fingered because the Cubans, like any professional intelligence service, use code names to mask their identities.

Although the Myerses were not identified in the Cuban messages, references in them matched specific information about the couple. In one instance, Havana urged the handler to express concern about a tumor in the shoulder of "Agent E-634." Nine days later, Gwendolyn underwent surgery to remove a shoulder tumor.[15] The similarity could have been a mere coincidence, but another Havana message around the same time instructed the handler to reconnoiter the area around the intended new residence of a spy. A month after the message, the Myerses moved to a new home. The correlations were sufficient to make the Myerses suspects warranting a broader investigation. In the course of the investigation, the FBI found that the Myerses owned the same brand of short-wave radio as Montes, a seemingly insignificant point but a tradecraft lapse by the Cubans that contributed to the mounting evidence of their espionage.

Kendall retired from the State Department in October 2007. In the previous year, he had sparked a diplomatic flap by publicly blasting the US–UK special relationship as a "one-sided" myth in which President George W. Bush had shabbily treated his British counterpart Prime Minister Tony Blair by drawing him into the Iraq war.[16] His comments caused an uproar in the United Kingdom and prompted the State Department to issue a disclaimer that Myers had spoken as an academic and not as a US government representative. The incident undoubtedly raised the eyebrows of his superiors at State and, coupled with his clandestine activity for Cuba, led to his decision to retire.

The Myerses firmly intended to spend their twilight years on their yacht and began sailing extensively. No longer with access to secrets, Kendall and his wife had not met the Cubans since a 2006 session in Guadalajara. But Kendall and Gwendolyn still harbored their three-decades-long affection for Castro's Cuba. In April 2009, he warmly welcomed the Cuban intelligence officer who approached him in front of his alma mater, Hopkins's SAIS, to rekindle their relationship, and his wife joined him for a meeting with the Cuban later that evening.

The Cuban intelligence officer, however, was actually an FBI undercover source. The FBI had resorted to the sting technique that had worked with other spies in the past like Robert Lipka and George Trofimoff. The Myerses fell for the ruse, which exceeded even the FBI's hopes for ensnaring the two spies. Over the course of three meetings in hotel rooms that month, Kendall and Gwendolyn reminisced about their cooperation with Cuba and regaled the FBI undercover source with stories of their activities—everything from details of their recruitment, their meetings abroad, sessions with Fidel Castro, and communications to his theft of information and smuggling classified documents from his office.[17] The meetings went beyond nostalgia over past services rendered; the purported Cuban asked and Kendall Myers agreed to provide information on the Summit of the Americas in 2009 and on executive branch personnel involved in US policy toward Latin America. Although admitting that they were "burned out" by their espionage, Kendall affirmed that he and his wife "would like to be a reserve army . . . ready when needed."[18]

The Myerses agreed to meet the Cuban again, but the fourth meeting never took place. During their meetings with the undercover source, they had discussed living in Cuba and had claimed that "our idea is to sail home," and they were planning a sailing trip to the Caribbean later that year with no set date to return. The FBI had to move before the pair might defect to Cuba and escape justice. Kendall and Gwendolyn Myers were arrested on June 4 as they entered the Capital Hilton Hotel in Washington to meet their new Cuban friend. The three-year-long hunt for a Cuban spy, conducted jointly by the FBI and State's Diplomatic Security, was over.[19]

Three days after the arrest, Fidel Castro, who years before had praised a DOD assessment on Cuba to which his spy, Ana Montes, had contributed, leaped to the defense of the accused couple in a Cuban blog. Although denying that he had met them and not confirming their espionage, Castro claimed that "I can't help but admire their disinterested and courageous conduct on behalf of Cuba."[20]

The evidence against the Myerses, presented with a vast amount of detail in court affidavits, appeared insurmountable, especially thanks to the couple's loquacious revelations to the FBI undercover source. Both pleaded guilty, Kendall to charges of conspiracy to commit espionage and wire fraud, and Gwendolyn to conspiracy to gather and transmit national defense information. Kendall was sentenced to life imprisonment, and Gwendolyn to eighty-one months in jail. At the sentencing Judge Reggie Walton noted that "Cuba is no beacon of liberty. I see no sign of remorse. You are proud of what you did."[21] Kendall Myers's own statement at the sentencing proved him right: "Our overriding objective was to help the Cuban people defend their Revolution."[22]

As in the Montes case, comprehensive debriefings of Myerses would be required to assess the full extent of the damage from their espionage, but a sample of their betrayal was provided in court affidavits. Between August 2006 and October 2007, little more than a year of the Myerses' three decades of spying, Kendall viewed and presumably passed to his handlers more than two hundred classified reports related to Cuba.[23] Considering that his access to secrets began with his assignment to State's INR in 1988, he undoubtedly passed the Cubans materials from a few thousand classified documents or more. Because his work at State primarily concerned Europe, he did not enjoy the same access as Montes did, but the longevity of his espionage allowed Castro's intelligence service to corroborate some of her information and confirm that she continued to be a bona fide agent and had not been compromised and doubled back to deceive the Cubans.

The Myerses' case, along with the arrest of China spies in recent years and the July 2010 unmasking of a dozen Russian illegals operating in the United States, certainly alerted the public to the fact that espionage against the nation was thriving. But as the tenth anniversary of the tragic events of September 11, 2001, approached, the primary threat to US national security was still terrorism. A disturbing aspect of this threat was espionage on behalf of terrorists bent on destroying the American way of life.

Espionage and the War on Terrorism

I wish to desert from the US Army. I wish to defect from the United States.
I wish to join al-Qaeda, train its members, and conduct terrorist attacks.

National Guardsman **RYAN ANDERSON** *on an FBI videotape,*
quoted by Counterintelligence Centre, "Ryan Anderson"

The thought of a spy or saboteur working for terrorists inside the US military or anywhere in the US government is chilling. Ryan Anderson, fortunately, offered his services not to terrorists but to FBI agents engaged in a sting operation against the young guardsman.

Anderson seemed like the baby-faced boy next door. He was raised in Everett, Washington, a city about twenty-five miles north of Seattle whose official website boasts that it is "an All-American city" with the second-largest marina on the West Coast and "some of the best salmon and steelhead fishing in the world."[1] The son of a schoolteacher, Anderson followed the typical path of many young boys in Everett during the 1990s, attending a Lutheran church with his parents, graduating from a local high school, and then attending Washington State University, where he studied Middle Eastern history.

Anderson was so attracted to the Middle East that he converted to Islam before earning his college degree in 2002. After graduation, he joined the Army National Guard and was stationed at Fort Lewis in his home state.

Sometime before the scheduled deployment of his unit to Iraq in late 2003, the boy next door was lured by extremist fundamentalism and transformed into "Johnny Taliban," as he was later dubbed by the media.[2]

The few classmates and teachers who remembered Anderson from his student days claimed that he frequently adapted his personality to gain acceptance by various cliques.[3] While in the Washington National Guard, he tried to join a far more dangerous clique than those of his school days. He began roaming through extremist chat rooms on the internet under the alias "Amir Abdul Rashid" to contact al-Qaeda, claiming that "I share your cause."

Thankfully, no one from al-Qaeda contacted Anderson, but his notes attracted the attention of a concerned citizen, Shannen Rossmiller, a judge in Montana who surfed jihadist websites on her own initiative to seek any hints of impending terrorist attacks. She baited Anderson with a phony exchange of e-mails and, shocked when he admitted that he was a National Guardsman, she immediately contacted the Department of Homeland Security, which in turn called the FBI.

The army and the FBI identified Anderson and launched a sting operation.[4] In late January 2004, FBI agents posing as jihadists met with the unsuspecting Anderson. The budding terrorist, who was a tank crewman in the National Guard, not only told them that he wanted to attack America but also offered sketches of army tanks and information about tanks, weapons, and vulnerabilities of armor deployed in Iraq. He was arrested in February 2004 on five counts of attempting to aid the enemy and providing intelligence to a terrorist network. Although his defense counsel claimed that he suffered from mental disorders, the twenty-seven-year-old guardsman was convicted at a court-martial and sentenced to life imprisonment without possibility of parole. Anderson was an immature, delusional, and, fortunately for the United States, hopelessly inept volunteer who was caught before he could inflict harm against American troops in Iraq. His case, however, was not an isolated incident.

Paul Raphael Hall

In 2001 Paul Raphael Hall of Phoenix, a convert to Islam who went under the name Hassan Abu Jihaad, served as a signalman second class aboard the naval destroyer USS *Benfold* operating in the Middle East. Just a few months after the al-Qaeda bombing of the USS *Cole* in Yemen, Abu Jihaad communicated with a well-known website run by Azzam Publications, a prominent recruitment and propaganda arm for extremists. Azzam was headed by Babar Ahmad, a British citizen of Pakistani origin who was under investigation by the British authorities.

During a search of Ahmad's London residence, the British discovered e-mail correspondence regarding movements of the aircraft carrier battle group that included the *Benfold* together with information about potential vulnerabilities of the ships to terrorist attack.[5] The British passed the information to the US authorities, whose investigation surfaced Abu Jihaad as a likely suspect. The FBI used an undercover source acquainted with Abu Jihaad to gather additional evidence.[6] Abu Jihaad was arrested in March 2007 and sentenced to ten years each on counts of transmitting classified information and material support to terrorism. On appeal, a judge subsequently overturned the conviction on material support to terrorism because of technicalities inherent in the legal statutes, but the conviction on the other count stood and Abu Jihaad is serving his ten-year sentence.[7]

Ali Mohammed

Ryan Anderson and Abu Jihaad were not alone. A half dozen similar cases have been documented and discussed by Daniel Pipes in his article "Pentagon Jihadis."[8] The most disturbing case involved Ali Mohammed, a former major in the Egyptian Army who was recruited by Ayman al-Zawahiri into the Egyptian Islamic Jihad before the radical group merged with al-Qaeda.

Perhaps more than any other case, Ali Mohammed illustrated the potential danger of terrorist infiltration in the US government. In September 1985, Mohammed traveled to the United States and married an American, which subsequently facilitated his acquisition of US citizenship. A year later, he enlisted in the US Army and became a supply sergeant but, due to his background, was primarily assigned as an instructor on Middle Eastern issues at the John F. Kennedy Special Warfare School in Fort Bragg, North Carolina. He also used his considerable military experience to provide weapons and explosives training to terrorists who were later responsible for exploding a truck bomb in the World Trade Center in 1993.

After his honorable discharge from the army in 1989, Mohammed moved to the forefront of al-Qaeda operations based on his military skills and US experience. He personally orchestrated Osama bin Laden's moves to safe havens in Sudan and then Afghanistan and trained the al-Qaeda leader's bodyguards. He then provided military training to al-Qaeda in Afghanistan and to Somali tribesmen before the October 1993 tragedy depicted in the film *Blackhawk Down*, in which eighteen US soldiers were killed. In 1998, Mohammed advanced even further in al-Qaeda when he played a key role in planning the bombing of US embassies in Kenya and Tanzania.[9]

Ali Mohammed was arrested in 1998 and sentenced to life imprisonment for his role in the bombing of US embassies in Africa, but his case serves as a stark example of the potentially catastrophic threat from terrorist spies, who present more imminent dangers than their Cold War counterparts.[10] During the Cold War, American counterespionage often failed to catch the spies who penetrated almost every agency of the US government. Until these Soviet spies were discovered, they passed secrets that could have shifted the balance in a war with the Soviet Union. The Soviets would have enjoyed significant military advantages armed with the knowledge of the US Navy's capabilities from the Walker spy ring and NATO's battle plan for Europe from retired army sergeant Clyde Conrad, to name just two. Fortunately, the United States never went to war, and the Soviets never had the opportunity to fully exploit the advantages gained from their Cold War spies. Once those spies were unmasked, the United States had time to adopt countermeasures to offset the damage from American secrets in the hands of the USSR.

Now, however, America is at war and no longer has the time to develop countermeasures against terrorist espionage. Terrorists, whether from al-Qaeda or other terrorist groups bent on destroying the American way of life, could exploit information from their spies to pinpoint the security vulnerabilities of potential targets, gauge America's knowledge of terrorist tactics, and ultimately use that insider information to launch attacks.

Al-Qaeda's commitment to spectacular attacks on US soil imparted a new sense of urgency to America's counterespionage mission. Imagine a Robert Hanssen in the FBI or an Aldrich Ames in the CIA spying for a terrorist group, compromising American sources who could warn of an impending attack. Imagine a Karl Koecher, an illegal infiltrating the CIA not for the Czechs but for a rogue state like Iran or North Korea, worming his way into a job translating reports from key agents reporting on those nations' links with terrorists. Imagine a Jonathan Pollard not working for Israel but for Hezbollah, crawling through intelligence community databases, providing a terrorist group with information about the vulnerabilities of America's ports and nuclear power plants. The damage that could be done by a terrorist infiltrator with the access of these past spies could be catastrophic.

The best way to neutralize terrorists' espionage is to penetrate their ranks, just as the CIA and FBI have done over the years by recruiting their own spies in state-sponsored intelligence services. Terrorist groups, in fact, operate like these intelligence services. Terrorists spy before they terrorize. They case and observe their targets. They collect intelligence information about their enemy's vulnerabilities from elicitation and from publicly available sources. They vet potential recruits with rigorous screening procedures.

Like intelligence officers, terrorists also practice tradecraft. Materials discovered in al-Qaeda safe houses in Afghanistan and other countries include training manuals on espionage tradecraft, such as identification of clandestine meeting sites and dead drop locations, techniques to recruit sources, and tracking and reporting on targets and clandestine communications.[11]

Terrorists also prepare their operatives to live cover, the art of blending seamlessly into a target society, with intensity that Soviet illegals would have envied. In an al-Qaeda safe house in Afghanistan, US forces found handwritten notes with guidance on how to operate under cover, including tips on travel in alias, documents to carry, even down to minute details about the proper underwear to don in a foreign land.[12]

For al-Qaeda terrorists, living one's cover even has the sanction of Islamic doctrine. Some of the September 11, 2001, hijackers were believed to be adherents of Takfiri wal Hijra, an extremist offshoot of the Muslim Brotherhood spawned in the 1960s, which claims that the Koran advocates integration into corrupt societies as a means of plotting attacks against them. According to Takfiri precepts, terrorists can play the infidel to gain access to the enemy's targets and violate Islamic laws, provided the goal justifies the otherwise forbidden behavior. Some of the 9/11 hijackers wore expensive jewelry and sprayed themselves with cologne at US airports, believing that these Western habits would shield them from the scrutiny given orthodox Muslims. The immersion of all nineteen hijackers into American society tragically illustrated the gruesome effectiveness of living cover down to the smallest detail.

Because terrorists operate like intelligence services do, they also infiltrate spies into their target societies. A manual seized in a raid of al-Qaeda disciples in Manchester includes an entire section with details on recruiting spies, clear evidence of the importance of espionage for jihad extremists.[13] Some of these terrorist infiltrators have already been exposed. One al-Qaeda recruit, Iyman Faris, a naturalized American citizen, exploited his job as a truck driver to plan sabotage of bridges and derailment of trains across the United States.

Al-Qaeda also recruits its members among natives of Western countries to blend into target societies. In testimony to the US Senate in September 2010, Michael Leiter, director of the National Counterterrorism Center, emphasized the increased al-Qaeda efforts to recruit Americans and their growing involvement in plotting attacks.[14] Jose Padilla, a thug from a Chicago gang, epitomized this type of al-Qaeda recruit. After converting to Islam in prison, a breeding ground for terrorist recruitment, Padilla was trained in al-Qaeda camps to launch a "dirty bomb" attack and could maneuver in American society without the scrutiny given those of Middle Eastern background.[15]

Terrorist spies can work in almost any profession that provides the access to prepare for an attack—a cafeteria worker picking up snippets of information in a mess hall; a crossing guard checking out school bus schedules; or, as the exposure of a plot against John F. Kennedy Airport in New York in 2007 demonstrated, an airline employee with motive and access to inflict significant damage.[16] But the most important spies of all that terrorists would hunt are from the US government, especially its intelligence community.

Considering their unsavory backgrounds, the al-Qaeda recruits mentioned before would presumably have failed to pass muster if they sought jobs in US intelligence. John Walker Lindh, dubbed the "American Taliban" after his capture in Afghanistan, was of a different mold. He came from an affluent northern California suburb, had no criminal record, and had decent academic credentials. His knowledge of Arabic and travel in the Middle East may have made him an attractive candidate for US intelligence. Ryan Anderson's résumé—a degree in Middle Eastern history and military service—likewise might have won him at least an interview for a job in the national security arena. Others with similar experience yet with healthier psychological profiles than Lindh and Anderson could be—or may already have been—recruited by terrorists to infiltrate the US government.

America has fortunately not suffered irreparable harm from spies throughout its history. Spies, to be sure, have caused significant damage that has cost American lives and millions of taxpayer dollars to develop countermeasures that could have been used to build new schools, roads, and hospitals to improve America's quality of life. Now, however, the United States perhaps confronts one of the greatest espionage challenges in its history. The information from a single terrorist spy could enable devastating terrorist attacks resulting in mass casualties.

One of the methods terrorists could use to attack the United States is sabotaging vital computer networks. In February 2012, FBI director Robert Mueller noted that cybercrimes, including cyberespionage, will pose the greatest threat to the United States.[17] Both the US government and industry have already been victims of this newest form of espionage, and advances in information technology will undoubtedly escalate the threat in the future.

Cyberespionage

A clever computer programmer in the immediate future will unleash electron-based "cyberagents" to recover more vital information in a day than a thousand fictional James Bonds could recover in a lifetime.

KEITH MELTON, *intelligence historian, "Spies in the Digital Age"*

According to a report from the NCIX on cyberespionage, when FBI agents arrested Boeing engineer Dongfan Chung in 2008, they discovered 250,000 pages of US government documents squirreled away in his home, roughly the equivalent of four, four-drawer filing cabinets.[1] Jonathan Pollard, who provided Israel with an estimated 1 million pages of documents during his spying career, packed satchels full of materials, smuggled them out of his office, and stuffed them into a suitcase for delivery to his handlers. Pollard first came under suspicion when a fellow employee noticed him lugging batches of documents from his office building and reported the incident, which led to an investigation and the spy's arrest. (Pollard's story is recounted in detail in chapter 16.)

As these examples illustrate, the storage and transmission of secrets are risky elements of espionage and can lead to a spy's demise. In the past, intelligence services have surmounted these obstacles by using various devices, such as microdots or miniature cameras to film documents, but even these methods entail risk. Now, however, government secrets, like much of the world's information, reside more in computers than in locked cabinets or vaults. Advances in computing technology are ideally suited to espionage and have significantly reduced the risk of clandestine communications. Spies like Pollard and Chung can now transmit larger volumes of computer data at higher speeds by means of smaller and thus easily concealed devices.

As the NCIX report notes, the bulk of materials found in Chung's house could easily fit on a cheap compact disk.[2] The same documents could be downloaded as well to a small flash drive or memory card capable of storing large amounts of information, then hidden in an innocuous-looking file on a computer and instantly transmitted by a spy to his handlers. The storage capacity of these portable devices will continue to increase exponentially in the future. At some point, a spy may be able to download the complete holdings of entire agencies into such devices.

Aside from the threat from insiders, remote cyberintrusions eliminate the foibles of the human spy—his risky downloading of information at his job, forensic audits of his computer usage, or simple mistakes that could lead to detection.[3] These remote intrusions are commonly described with the term "hacking," that is, the unauthorized access to and manipulation of information systems. In the early days of hacking in the 1970s, young electronic engineers and computer scientists applied their skills to mischief making or small-scale theft.

By the end of the 1980s, early evidence of computer hacking for espionage had surfaced. A cabal of West German hackers approached the KGB to sell the fruits of its computer penetrations to steal defense and technology information from US government computer systems. Clifford Stoll, a researcher at the Lawrence Berkeley National Laboratory, discovered an unauthorized user on the lab's network and doggedly tracked the hacker until he was finally identified and arrested by the German authorities. Stoll kept a daily log of his activities and documented the hunt in *The Cuckoo's Egg*, one of the early landmark studies of cyberespionage.[4]

Computer hacking contributed significantly to a dramatic increase in economic espionage. The digital theft of US trade secrets has resulted in substantial commercial losses to both large and small companies in a broad spectrum of industries. Accurate financial losses are difficult to calculate. As the NCIX report notes, estimates range widely, from $2 billion to $400 billion.[5] The victims often do not even know that their proprietary information has been stolen; in other cases, companies are reluctant to report computer intrusions out of concern for reputational damage. And companies use different criteria to estimate losses, which also contributes to the wide-ranging estimates. Despite the lack of exact estimates, the losses are sizable and cost corporations—and, ultimately, consumers—billions of dollars.

The NCIX report was the first comprehensive and publicly blunt admission by the US government that the PRC is the major perpetrator of cyberespionage to steal American military, economic, and technological information. This allegation was based on considerable evidence. In the past decade at least 760 US companies have been targets of computer attacks originating in China.[6] In 2010, six out of seven cases of economic espionage involved China; estimates of losses in these cases included $100 million worth of insecticide research from Dow Chemical, $400 million worth of chemical formulas from DuPont, and $600 million of proprietary data from Motorola.[7] Aside from the financial losses, Representative Mike Rogers, chairman of the House of Representatives' Intelligence Committee, noted that cybertheft against one large US company resulted in the elimination of jobs: "Those are 10,000 jobs that would be in this economy, that would employ Americans, that are gone because of Chinese economic espionage."[8]

China's computer attacks are not limited to the theft of trade secrets from US companies. According to US Air Force estimates, by 2007 Chinese hackers had drained from 10 to 20 terabytes of information from US government computer networks.[9] A year later, intrusions into government systems had already risen by 40 percent.[10] The attacks have targeted a broad spectrum of agencies, including the national laboratories, the State and Commerce departments, and members of Congress.[11]

A large number of attacks, however, are aimed at DOD and defense contractors involved in classified military weapons projects. As one example, in April 2009 computer penetrations of a $300 billion US Air Force project for the latest-generation fighter jet, the Joint Strike Fighter, were traced back to internet protocol addresses in China.[12] In January 2013, the Defense Science Board, a DOD senior advisory group of government and military experts, noted in an unclassified version of a report on cyber threats to military defense that "DOD and its contractor base ... have sustained staggering losses of system design information incorporating years of combined knowledge and experience."[13] Although the report did not single out China, in a May

2013 report to Congress, the Pentagon publicly acknowledged the country as a major source of cyberespionage to acquire US military technology. [14]

China's cyberespionage against the US military is not just an isolated tool used to collect intelligence. Computer network exploitation, in fact, is integral to the country's overall economic and military vision for the future. As noted in the Northrop Grumman report to the US–China Economic and Security Review Commission, Chinese military strategists "view information dominance as the precursor for overall success in a conflict" and are conducting a long-term campaign to collect intelligence to achieve this goal.[15] The operations also allow the Chinese to compensate for their relative technological backwardness in developing advanced weapons systems. China's computer attacks against US economic targets are also rooted in national policy. In 2010 the Chinese National People's Congress adopted its new five-year economic plan, which lists seven priority industries for development, all of which parallel the leading targets of computer attacks against US and Western corporations.[16]

Despite these coincidences, China routinely denies accusations of cyberespionage, and indeed the anonymity of cyberspace complicates efforts to identify with certainty the perpetrators of attacks. However, according to the Northrop Grumman report, "government efforts to recruit from among the Chinese hacker community and evidence of consulting relationships between known hackers and security services indicates some government willingness to draw from this pool of expertise."[17] This allegation was based on extensive research into the open source information available in China, Western scholarship, and forensic analyses of computer attacks against US systems.

Northrop Grumman's research surfaced a consulting relationship between the Shanghai Public Security Bureau, one of the country's internal security organs, and Peng Yinan, the founder of a Chinese hackers' group called Javaphile.[18] In addition, the Third Department of the People's Liberation Army—the military's cryptographic service, which is responsible for leading China's cyber efforts—has also recruited talented computer specialists and hackers for its program.[19] Another indicator of Chinese government involvement surfaced in January 2010, when Google publicly accused China of a cyberattack to steal its source code. This attack was traced back to servers at two schools in China, one of which, the Lanxiang Vocational School in Shandong Province, trains computer scientists for the military.[20]

This assessment was further reinforced in February 2013, when Mandiant, a cybersecurity company, issued a report with a comprehensive analysis of a widespread cyberespionage activity characterized as "Advanced Persistent Threat 1 (APT1)," which has stolen terabytes of data from a broad range of industries in at least 141 organizations in English-speaking countries. Mandiant experts traced the attacks back to four large networks in an area of Shanghai, where a PLA signals intelligence unit is located.[21] Although all these examples may not provide absolute confirmation of the Chinese government's involvement in cyberespionage, it strains credulity that it would not use every possible means to achieve its economic and military policy goals.

Although China may be the foremost attacker of US computer systems, NCIX also singled out Russia for its cyberespionage.[22] Russia enjoys a long tradition of excellence in mathematics and has spawned some of the world's leading computer hackers, some of whom have been involved in high-profile cybercrimes. One Russian mathematician, Vladimir Levin, was arrested and sentenced to three years in a Florida prison for the electronic transfer of at least $12 million from Citibank accounts to his own.[23] A Russian computer programmer, known only by his moniker "A-Z," developed software that enabled the digital theft of identity data; a gang of German criminals used the program to steal $6 million from banks in the United States, the United Kingdom, Spain, and Italy.[24]

These are but two of many examples of cybercrime originating in Russia. As in the China case, the anonymity of cyberspace complicates confirmation of Russian intelligence agencies' involvement in cyberespionage. The US government, however, through its NCIX report, took the step of publicly naming the Russian government as a major perpetrator of cyberespionage: "Russia also is seen as an important actor in cyber-enabled economic collection and espionage against other countries, albeit a distant second to China."[25]

As one example of its cyberespionage, Russian intelligence is strongly suspected of penetrating the military systems of Georgia to collect information both before and during its attack against the country in August 2008. The Georgians sent troops into South Ossetia to establish control of the rebellious region that had declared its autonomy. The Russians supported the separatists and retaliated against Georgia, winning a swift victory within a few days.

Russia's conflict with Georgia surfaced another aspect of cyber operations, cyberwarfare, that is, the penetration of information systems not for espionage but for sabotage. As the Northrop Grumman report notes, the talents for penetrating a computer to collect intelligence are the same as those for conducting offensive actions in wartime.[26] In August 2008, the Russians were suspected of disrupting the computer communications of the Georgian government and military to reduce its ability to resist the attack and brought down civilian websites to instill panic in the populace. The attack was considered the first "integration of offensive cyber operations into political-military strategy."[27]

In a similar hypothetical scenario in the United States, cyberattacks could be launched by terrorists to destroy vital infrastructure systems, including the banking industry, telecommunications, electrical grids, and air traffic control. Most experts, however, believe that, though terrorists use the internet for propaganda and recruiting purposes, they are by no means close to developing this offensive capability.[28]

The potential for cyberwarfare on a grand scale is still under debate. Some former US government officials have painted an apocalyptic picture of a nation decimated by cyberattacks from capable adversaries. Others, however, believe that these nightmare scenarios are overblown and that adversaries such as China and Russia would not risk jeopardizing bilateral economic interests or inviting massive retaliation against their own systems.[29] Conversely, some argue that increasing allegations regarding the United States' offensive cyber operations against its adversaries could provoke retaliatory attacks against the nation's information systems. No one, however, disputes the threat of cyberespionage.

Cyberespionage will continue to increase in the future. Security industry experts expect "the number of cyberespionage attacks to increase . . . and the malware used for this purpose to become increasingly sophisticated."[30] The proliferation of new technologies will provide even more opportunities for cyber spies. According to the NCIX report, the number of portable devices such as laptops and smartphones that connect to the internet will increase from about 12.5 billion in 2010 to 25 billion in 2015 and will create more endpoints that cyber spies can target to steal secrets.[31] New technologies such as cloud computing, which lower costs by eliminating the need for companies to buy and maintain their own computer servers, will enable users to access information anywhere on the globe. Although reducing costs, this development could also facilitate the theft of US government and corporate secrets.

Another form of computer attack that experts also expect to increase in the future is "hacktivism," the politically motivated penetration of information systems to manipulate data or degrade service.[32] The experts' forecast is based on the stunning successes of hacktivists in recent years. Hacktivists have shut down the websites of major corporations and have acquired customer data and published it online to protest against the companies' activities. As one example, Anonymous, a loose collective of hacktivists operating around the globe, temporarily shut down the websites of Master-Card, Visa, PayPal, and others in 2010.[33]

The Anonymous attacks on the financial services corporations were launched to retaliate against them for severing ties with WikiLeaks and its associates. WikiLeaks, led by the Australian internet activist Julian Assange, bills itself as a nonprofit media organization that provides an anonymous means for sources to leak information to the public. Although many hacktivist attacks do not concern espionage, some, like WikiLeaks, target government secrets not to pass them surreptitiously to foreign powers but to reveal them publicly in the interests of ensuring freedom of information.

In 2010, WikiLeaks made headlines with its public release of US military field reports from the wars in Iraq and Afghanistan. Later that year, WikiLeaks' most explosive revelation was its possession of 251,000 messages concerning the US Department of State's correspondence with American embassies around the world. In November WikiLeaks collaborated with major media organizations to begin releasing these messages to the public.[34]

This release sparked a furor. Among other items, the State Department's cables revealed negative assessments of heads of state and other senior foreign government officials and comments shared in confidence by foreign interlocutors with US embassy officials around the world, often on issues of critical interest to US policy. Senior US government officials, including Secretary of State Hillary Clinton, expressed outrage and sharply condemned WikiLeaks for chilling diplomatic efforts and endangering the lives of Americans and cooperative foreigners.[35] Subsequent comments by government officials, however, suggested that the damage to overall national security may have been less than originally assessed.[36]

The WikiLeaks controversy provoked a debate on a range of issues regarding the balance between the public's right to know and the preservation of secrecy in the interests of national security. As some have argued, the information released would restrain potential foreign interlocutors in the future from honest discussions with American officials. Others supported the release, claiming that the US government routinely overclassifies information that the public in a democratic society needs to formulate an understanding of its nation's foreign policy. Media organizations that cooperated with WikiLeaks were also criticized for publicizing unsubstantiated and insufficiently analyzed information.[37]

The debate also focused on the sources of WikiLeaks' treasure trove of government data, who were portrayed as either courageous whistleblowers or vile traitors. One of the possible sources, US Army private first class Bradley Manning, had been arrested in May 2010 on suspicion of passing restricted material to WikiLeaks. He faced twenty-three charges, including aiding the enemy, which is punishable by death under military law. In February 2013, Manning pled guilty to charges of mishandling classified material but not to more severe federal charges against him. A number of groups hailing his whistleblowing, such as the Bradley Manning Support Network, have sprung to his defense and have organized rallies and petitions to gain his release.[38]

Manning is not an isolated case. In June 2013, Edward Snowden, a former CIA and NSA employee and defense contractor, sparked a furor by publicly claiming responsibility for leaking to the media details of sensitive NSA collection programs designed to combat terrorism. Like Manning, Snowden belongs to the "new breed of radical technophiles" bred in the internet age of complete freedom of information who advocate transparency and privacy as bedrocks of a democratic society.[39]

The WikiLeaks affair and the exposure of NSA collection secrets have established a new benchmark in cyberespionage. WikiLeaks has already spawned similar hacktivist groups dedicated to revealing classified US government and commercial proprietary information, and the exposure of secrets will most certainly increase in years to come. The prosecution of offenders, even if they are caught in the shadowy realm of cyberspace, will be complicated. Among the charges against Manning was violation of the Espionage Act.[40] Although he was not accused of spying for a foreign power, the law forbids delivery of national defense information to "persons not entitled to receive it," not just other nations. Whistleblowing is viewed by the public far less negatively than spying for a nuclear-armed nation hostile to the United States. When the "persons not entitled" to information under the Espionage Act are media outlets and social advocacy groups claiming to act in the public interest, jurors may be less inclined to convict. Although a *Time* poll indicated that 53 percent of Americans believed NSA leaker Snowden should be prosecuted, 43 percent of the age group ranging from 18 to 34 thought he should not, and a petition to the White House demanding a pardon for Snowden received 60,000 names in only three days, signs that indicate that support for hacktivists may only increase in the future.[41]

At the heart of all these issues is the US government's future ability to secure vital information systems against intrusions. To combat cyberoffensive operations, the US government developed a plan, "The National Strategy to Secure Cyberspace," which was launched by the George W. Bush administration in 2003 and expanded on in its "Comprehensive National Cybersecurity Initiative" in 2008.[42] In May 2009, President Barack Obama declared America's digital infrastructure a "strategic national asset" and issued a new cybersecurity initiative that built on the 2008 plan.[43] In the White House's budget proposal for 2014, the president advocated increased spending to protect US computer networks from cyberattacks.

The US government agencies involved in national security have also established cybersecurity units dedicated to tackling the issue. The FBI created a separate cyber division and also heads the National Cyber Investigative Joint Task Force, which includes a number of intelligence community agencies. The Department of Homeland Security (DHS) established the National Cybersecurity and Communications Integration Center, which houses the US Computer Emergency Readiness Team, the operational arm of DHS's cyberdefense. Finally, DOD, which was criticized in a Government Accountability Office (GAO) report for its fragmented approach to the issue, created a separate US Cyber Command in June 2009 to ensure a focal point for the coordination of cyber operations and defense.[44]

During the past decade, all these efforts have been plagued by a number of problems documented in a series of GAO reports, including limited resources, competing priorities, a shortage of technically qualified personnel, and a debate on legal issues regarding interaction with critical private-sector industries.[45] One of the difficulties has been the divided responsibility in the US government for overall cybersecurity. DOD, which includes NSA, the nation's premier cyberagency, is responsible for military networks, whereas DHS must assure the security of the nation's federal civilian and private-sector infrastructure. Although the two agencies have signed an agreement to cooperate more closely, some observers note that secrecy concerns still preclude the full sharing of information, and disputes over jurisdiction and authority remain an issue.[46]

Another controversial issue concerns the historical friction between civil liberties and national security requirements. Although General Keith Alexander, the head of NSA and the US Cyber Command, has assured lawmakers on this score, privacy advocates and civil libertarians still fear that any expanded role for the military in domestic cyber issues will lead to further government intrusion into citizens' lives.[47] Congressional legislation on cybersecurity under debate includes a provision that enables companies to share personal data on their customers with the government. The information can only be shared for national security purposes, but the American Civil Liberties Union and other groups believe that the law provides few safeguards against the government's abuse of privacy rights.

The counterespionage wheel appears to have come full circle. Turf battles over authority plagued the nation's ability to thwart espionage from the Civil War until the end of the twentieth century. Likewise, the tension between civil liberties and national security, which will always be an issue in a democratic society, made Americans suspicious of counterespionage, and at times civil rights were abused in its name. As technology increasingly heightens the threat of cyberspying, now is the time to learn the historical lessons of espionage against America and resolve these issues before it is too late.

Conclusion

No counterintelligence official can guarantee our nation will
never suffer another incident of treason or espionage.

Office of the National Counterintelligence Executive,
National Counterintelligence Strategy of the United States, 2009, *3*

In 2001, the National Counterintelligence Executive replaced the National
Counterintelligence Center, which had been established in 1994 after the
Ames spy case to improve coordination and collaboration in the US government on a range of counterintelligence activities, including the insider
threat from spies. After more than two centuries, the hundreds of American
spies, especially in the Cold War, had gradually made some believers of
those traditionally skeptical and suspicious of the threat of espionage
against the nation.

The establishment of NCIX also represented progress in overcoming the
turf battles and institutional rivalries that have plagued America's counterespionage efforts since the nation's birth. Among these rivals, the FBI and
CIA now collaborate more closely on espionage than ever before in their
respective histories. Besides these two agencies, the intelligence community at large is also gradually building a cadre of professionals devoted to
counterespionage. These professionals no longer fit the stereotype of a
James Angleton poring over files in dimly lit offices searching for clues to
spies. Rather, as one CIA analyst noted, "Spy hunting takes experienced

analysts, operations officers, technical specialists, lawyers, financial investigators, law enforcement officers, and psychologists, all working as a team."[1] Analysts play an especially critical role in determining the secrets that America's adversaries seek and the methodologies they use to recruit spies and plumb them for information.

In spite of these improvements, the warning in the *National Counterintelligence Strategy* still holds true. Although American secrets may be remotely stolen through cyberespionage, no search engine or software can divine the plans and intentions of the US government better than an insider spy, and America's adversaries will continue to seek—and find—them. The same array of motives that impelled the Americans discussed here to spy will persist, and the conflicting loyalties in this era of increased globalization will remain a new motive for some to rationalize their passage of secrets to other nations.

Counterespionage professionals will be challenged to find these spies because of advances in technology and new threats from a broader set of adversaries. As discussed in the previous chapter, the revolution in computer technology has enabled the cyber theft of America's government and commercial information. These advances have also facilitated the practice of espionage itself. As a former CIA officer noted, "Digital technology changed virtually every process in the creation, storage, transmission, and securing of secrets. . . . Secrets by the gigabyte can be almost instantly copied onto storage devices smaller than a stick of gum."[2]

That same technology facilitates espionage in ways that average Americans are unaware of and, undoubtedly, may not believe, just as their forbears were reluctant to recognize indicators of spying. For example, the availability of personal database information can significantly facilitate an intelligence service's spotting and assessing of potential spies.[3] The proliferation of social media networks also provides similar opportunities. The electronic barrier between interlocutors inherent in these social networking sites is ideally suited for deception and is routinely exploited by criminals and predators using false identities with their targets. Users routinely post personal information that can also be exploited by foreign intelligence services to identify areas of supposed mutual interest, develop relationships in the anonymity of cyberspace, and identify vulnerabilities and thus potential motives to commit espionage.

Although these adversaries include traditional intelligence services like the Russian and Chinese agencies that have spied against the United States for years, spy hunters now confront a far broader spectrum of threats from hostile states and groups. One example of a growing insider threat is particularly disturbing. In the decade since the 9/11 attacks, the US military has broadened its overseas deployment to volatile areas like Afghanistan, Yemen, and Somalia, where it trains and cooperates with local forces in the hunt for terrorists. Unfortunately, a series of attacks by Afghan military and intelligence officers against NATO forces have highlighted the insider threat to US troops. The terrorists who have infiltrated the ranks of the Afghan security forces spy before they attack, using their insider status to conduct reconnaissance and choose the best times and methods for optimal destruction. These insider attacks will undoubtedly spread to the other countries where the United States is engaged and will require increased counterespionage vigilance to ensure the safety of the nation's troops.

The threat of corporate espionage that mushroomed after the Cold War will continue to increase not only through increasing cyber theft of proprietary secrets but also by more traditional means. As one example of an emerging corporate threat, in its National Counterintelligence Strategy, the NCIX emphasizes as one of its primary mission objectives the assurance of the supply chain. The globalization that creates conflicting loyalties has also resulted in partnerships between US and foreign companies that can facilitate espionage by adversaries seeking access through supply chains to US technological advances and other intellectual property. For example, one of the most popular electronic devices in the world, Apple's iPod, has 451 parts made in several different countries.[4] "Such outsourcing," as one observer noted, "although efficient and cost effective, leaves Apple open to foreign industrial espionage at critical stages of design."[5]

These are but a few of the emerging espionage threats to US national security. Though spying will not stop, NCIX believes that the US counterespionage community must assure the American people that "we have measurably increased the rigor of our system of national intelligence and have put in place systems, practices, and procedures that make foreign penetration more difficult to accomplish and easier to detect."[6] Achievement of this objective will not only require convincing the remaining skeptics of the dangers of the espionage threat but also assuring that the balance between national security needs and civil liberties is maintained.

As Jennifer Sims and Burton Gerber suggest, the United States does not have to enter into "Faustian bargains" to ensure its security at the expense of civil liberties.[7] The intelligence community, in concert with Congress and the executive branch, must assure the American people that measures to eliminate the threat of espionage will be applied solely to protect national security and for no other reason. The threat to the nation demands it.

Notes

Introduction

1. Sulick, *Spying in America.*
2. Lloyd, *Guinness Book of Espionage,* 9.
3. Weinstein and Vassiliev, *Haunted Wood.*
4. For further information on the Venona Project, see Benson and Warner, *Venona;* Haynes and Klehr, *Venona: Decoding Soviet Espionage;* Romerstein and Breindel, *Venona Secrets;* and West, *Venona.*
5. Redmond, "America Pays the Price."
6. The requirement is included in the Intelligence Authorization Act of 1995, HR 4299, 103rd Congress, Section 811, (c) (A): "The head of each department or agency within the Executive branch shall ensure that the Federal Bureau of Investigation is advised immediately of any information, regardless of its origin, which indicates that classified information is being, or may have been, disclosed in an unauthorized manner to a foreign power or an agent of a foreign power." http://thomas.loc.gov/cgi-bin/query/F?c103:5:./temp/~c103 2llk3Y:e103236:.
7. Andrew and Gordievsky, *KGB,* 529.
8. Herbig and Wiskoff, *Espionage,* 21. This excellent study covers 150 espionage cases and provides an array of statistics regarding motivations and other factors to determine trends that may help security investigators spot potential spies. The book will be referred to hereafter as the PERSEREC study.
9. Brenner, "Strategic Counterintelligence."
10. Herbig and Wiskoff, *Espionage,* 69.

11. US Central Intelligence Agency, "Woolsey, Testimony at Confirmation Hearing."
12. Gertz, *Enemies,* 6–7; Sims, "Democracies and Counterintelligence," in *Vaults, Mirrors & Masks,* ed. Sims and Gerber, 2. See also Wise, *Tiger Trap,* 6: "China has in many ways become America's chief rival."
13. Cited by Church, "Justice."
14. Nasheri, *Economic Espionage,* 59.
15. Sun Tzu, *Art of War,* 148.
16. In some cases, where the identities of America's penetrations of foreign intelligence services have been discussed in publicly available sources, their role in unmasking American spies will be discussed here. In more recent espionage cases of which I am aware through my government service, the identities of sources must remain secret. The author not only has a legal restraint in discussing classified information but also a moral obligation to those agents since the CIA makes commitments to protect their security. If the discussions of some cases appear to gloss over the exposure of an American spy, I am fulfilling those obligations to protect sources—but even without those details, the stories are still compelling.
17. Cherkashin and Feifer, *Spy Handler,* 54.
18. For a comprehensive treatment of Weisband and Hall, see Sulick, *Spying in America,* pt. 4, chap. 2, and pt. 5, chap. 3.
19. Herbig and Wiskoff, *Espionage,* 8.
20. Ibid., 9.
21. Ibid., 9–10.
22. Eig, "Classified Information Procedures Act."
23. The history of Venona by John Earl Haynes and Harvey Klehr provides a list of 349 spies, some identified by name and others, still unidentified, by code name that were surfaced in the project. The authors also include a list of 170 more Soviet spies of the era who were identified by other sources; Haynes and Klehr, *Venona,* 339, 371. Since that publication, the Center for Counterintelligence and Security Studies has compiled a list of 541 sources; Center for Counterintelligence and Security Studies, "American Agents." Population statistics are from http://kclibrary.lonestar.edu/decade40.html.
24. FBI Uniform Crime Reporting Statistics.
25. Office of the National Counterintelligence Executive, "Foreign Spies Stealing," 9.
26. US Department of Justice, Office of the Inspector General, "Federal Bureau of Investigation's Ability," 2.
27. Constantin, "2012 Will See Rise."
28. Smith, "Cyber-Threats Pose 'Existential Threat.'"

Chapter 1

1. Zinn, *People's History of the US,* 436.
2. For further information on Abel, see Rafalko, *Counterintelligence Reader,* 3:49–51; and Bernikow, *Abel.*
3. Andrew and Mitrokhin, *Sword and the Shield,* 146.
4. Ibid., 148.

5. For further information on Hayhanen, see Rafalko, *Counterintelligence Reader,* 3:51–55.
6. Ibid.
7. Ibid., 175.
8. Andrew, *For the President's Eyes Only,* 212–13.
9. According to a book published in Russia, Smith was the first CIA officer recruited by the KGB; Kolpakiki, *Vneshnyaya razvedki Rossii,* 70. Another former CIA officer, Tennent Bagley, believes that Smith might have compromised Pyotr Popov and speculates that Smith may have also assisted the KGB in recruiting another mole in the KGB; Bagley, *Spy Wars,* 69–79. Bagley is a staunch believer that KGB defector Yuriy Nosenko was a double agent dispatched to prove that the Soviets had no involvement with John F. Kennedy's assassin, Lee Harvey Oswald, which is discussed in further detail in chapter 6.
10. Ibid.
11. Rositzke, *CIA's Secret Operations,* 68–69.
12. The Polyakov case is discussed in comprehensive detail by Sandra Grimes and Jeanne Vertefeuille, *Circle of Treason,* 26–54. The case is also treated by Wallace and Melton, *Spycraft,* location 2269–2398; and Earley, *Confessions of a Spy,* 231–37.
13. Polyakov's naming of American spies is discussed by Grimes and Vertefeuille, *Circle of Treason,* 27; Earley, *Confessions,* 233; and Wallace and Melton, *Spycraft,* 113. See also Mangold, *Cold Warrior,* 229–30; and Wise, *Nightmover,* 61–62.

Chapter 2

1. For a detailed account of the Drummond case, see Rafalko, *Counterintelligence Reader,* 3:183–84; and Huss and Carpozi, *Red Spies,* 215–39.
2. Grimes and Vertefeuille, *Circle of Treason,* 27.
3. Rafalko, *Counterintelligence Reader,* 3:183.
4. "Master Spies."
5. Herbig and Wiskoff, *Espionage,* 17.
6. For further details, see Rafalko, *Counterintelligence Reader,* 3:185–86.
7. Andrew and Gordievsky, *KGB,* 461.
8. Ibid.
9. Ibid., 462.
10. Ibid.
11. Ibid.
12. Ibid.
13. Andrew, *For the President's Eyes Only,* 216.
14. Barker and Coffman, *Anatomy,* 16. The study by Barker and Coffman is the most comprehensive treatment of the Mitchell and Martin case, and this section draws heavily from their observations.
15. "Security Practices in the National Security Agency," cited by ibid., 99. See also Bamford, *Puzzle Palace,* 180.

16. Bamford, *Puzzle Palace,* 181.
17. Barker and Coffman, *Anatomy,* 25.
18. Andrew and Mitrokhin, *The Sword and Shield,* 178–79.
19. Mitchell and Martin, "Text of Statement."
20. Andrew and Mitrokhin, *Sword and the Shield,* 179.
21. Bamford, *Puzzle Palace,* 197.
22. Rafalko, *Counterintelligence Reader,* 3:58.
23. Andrew and Gordievsky, *KGB,* 459.
24. NSA's handling of the Mitchell and Martin case was roundly criticized in "Security Practices in the National Security Agency," cited by Barker and Coffman, *Anatomy,* 83–123.

Chapter 3

1. Zinn, *People's History,* 491.
2. Whittaker Chambers served as a courier for the Soviet intelligence services until he became disillusioned with communism because of Stalin's pact with Hitler and purges of the Soviet military and other institutions. He later appeared at congressional hearings and publicly identified a number of Americans spying for the Soviets. Judith Coplon was a DOJ employee who spied for the Soviets and provided them with counterintelligence information. Although she was arrested and convicted in two court trials, she never spent a day in jail because the convictions were overturned and never reversed during the long appeals process. For further information on Bentley, Chambers, and Coplon, see Sulick, *Spying in America.*
3. Suter, "Military Mutinies.'"
4. Lewes, *Protest,* 92.
5. US Senate, *COINTELPRO.*
6. Kalugin, *Spymaster,* 84, 192–93.
7. Rafalko, *Counterintelligence Reader,* 3:191–92.
8. Earley, *Confessions,* 329.
9. Tully, *Inside the FBI,* 67–68.
10. See *United States of America v. Ronald Humphrey; United States of America v. Truong Dinh Hung,* 61–62. Yung Krall discussed her work as a double agent for the CIA in the second half of her autobiography, *Thousand Tears.*
11. Herbig and Wiskoff, *Espionage,* 9.
12. Ibid., 10.
13. Tully, *Inside the FBI,* 69.
14. Ibid., 61.
15. Ibid., 63.

Chapter 4

1. Zinn, *Twentieth Century,* 557.
2. *United States of America v. David Henry Barnett,* cited by Rafalko, *Counterintelligence Reader,* 3:167. See also Barron, *KGB Today,* 232.

3. The HABRINK program is discussed in detail in *United States of America v. David Henry Barnett*, cited by Rafalko, *Counterintelligence Reader*, 3:166–76.
4. Ibid., 173.
5. In an ironic tragedy of Cold War espionage, the source, Vladimir Piguzov, was compromised a decade later by CIA mole Aldrich Ames. Piguzov's compromise is discussed by Bearden and Risen, *Main Enemy*, 198; and his role in unmasking Barnett is discussed by Wise, *Nightmover*, 103–4, and by Weiner, Johnston, and Lewis, *Betrayal*, 74.
6. Rafalko, *Counterintelligence Reader*, 3:168.

Chapter 5

1. Herbig and Wiskoff, *Espionage*, xiii.
2. Barron, *KGB Today*, 197.
3. Ibid.
4. Zacharski comment to the author.
5. Allen and Polmar, *Merchants*, 394.
6. Ibid., 395.
7. The CIA unclassified damage assessment was submitted to the Senate Permanent Subcommittee on Investigations and is discussed by Barron, *KGB Today*, 203.
8. Rafalko, *Counterintelligence Reader*, 3:254.
9. Senate Permanent Subcommittee on Investigations report cited by Barron, *KGB Today*, 203.
10. Testimony cited in "Caught Unawares," 46.
11. "Wary of Critics," *New York Times*, August 19, 1994.
12. Allen and Polmar, *Merchants*, 396.
13. Ibid, 177.
14. Ibid., 181.
15. Ibid., 179–80.
16. Rafalko, *Counterintelligence Reader*, 3:264.
17. Allen and Polmar, *Merchants*, 180.
18. The FBI testified about the Polish agent's information at Harper's trial. The CIA's Polish agent is discussed by Rafalko, *Counterintelligence Reader*, 3:264; and in "Partners in Espionage," 57.
19. Allen and Polmar, *Merchants*, 183.
20. Rafalko, *Counterintelligence Reader*, 3:264.
21. Allen and Polmar, *Merchants*, 198.
22. Ibid., 199.
23. Rafalko, *Counterintelligence Reader*, 3:265.
24. Ibid.
25. Lindsey, *Falcon*.
26. Rafalko, *Counterintelligence Reader*, 3:179.
27. Allen and Polmar, *Merchants*, 405.
28. Ibid.
29. Lindsey, *Falcon*, 133–34.

30. Ibid., 138–39.

31. On January 21, 1980, Boyce escaped from prison by hiding in a drainage hole for hours and using a jerry-rigged ladder and clippers to cut through barbed wire. After nineteen months as a fugitive, he was caught and returned to prison. He was released on parole in 2003; Lee had already been released on parole in 1998. See Hoover, "In an Audacious Escape."

32. For further information on the Kampiles case, see Allen and Polmar, *Merchants*, 202–3; Barron, *KGB Today*, 229–32; Rafalko, *Counterintelligence Reader*, 3:186; and Tully, *Inside the FBI*, 41–67.

33. Tully, *Inside the FBI*, 47.

34. Barron, *KGB Today*, 230.

35. Tully, *Inside the FBI*, 46.

36. Thanakos testified at Kampiles's trial about his approach. The episode is recounted by Tully, *Inside the FBI*, 42–43.

37. Bokhan's role is discussed by Bearden and Risen, *Main Enemy*, 29–30; and Earley, *Confessions*, 120. Bokhan was later compromised by CIA spy Aldrich Ames, but he had already managed to flee to safety in the West before he could be arrested.

38. Transcript of Trial, *United States of America v. William Kampiles*, cited by Tully, *Inside the FBI*, 51.

39. The CIA suffered a barrage of criticism for giving a newly hired analyst access to such secret programs. But the criticism turned to outrage when information surfaced in court that, aside from Kampiles's copy of the manual, more than a dozen other copies were missing and unaccounted for. CIA security suddenly appeared to rival the laxity of defense contractors.

40. Tully, *Inside the FBI*, 50.

Chapter 6

1. For details on the recruitment of the five, see Andrew, *Defend the Realm*, 168–74.

2. Rafalko, *Counterintelligence Reader*, 3:112.

3. Martin, *Wilderness*, 68. Along with Martin's critical examination of the Angleton period, other comprehensive studies of the era are those by Rafalko, *Counterintelligence Reader*, 3:109–18; Epstein, *Legend*; Epstein, *Deception*; Wise, *Molehunt*; Mangold, *Cold Warrior*; and Bagley, *Spy Wars*.

4. Riebling, *Wedge*, 138.

5. Rafalko, *Counterintelligence Reader*, 3:113–14.

6. Martin, *Wilderness*, 106.

7. Rafalko, *Counterintelligence Reader*, 3:113.

8. Bagley, *Spy Wars*, 11–12.

9. Ibid., 3:114.

10. FBI report of March 5, 1964, in "Investigation of the Assassination of President John F. Kennedy," Hearings, US House of Representatives, Hearings, Select Committee on Assassinations, cited by Wise, *Molehunt*, 152.

11. Mangold, *Cold Warrior*, 183.

12. Rafalko, *Counterintelligence Reader,* 3:114.
13. Psychologist interview with Mangold, *Cold Warrior,* 182.
14. US Senate, Select Committee on Intelligence, "Assessment of the Aldrich Ames Espionage Case," paragraph B2; Bearden and Risen, *Main Enemy,* 175–76, 197–98; Earley, *Confessions,* 198–200.
15. Mitrokhin and Andrew, *Sword and the Shield,* 186, 368. According to Bagley, a Soviet KGB source had earlier advised the CIA about plans for assassinating Nosenko, but the source turned out to be a double agent and, in Bagley's view, the information was designed to convince the CIA of Nosenko's credibility (*Spy Wars,* 164–65).
16. Bagley, *Spy Wars.*
17. Robarge, "James Angleton Phenomenon."
18. For further information on Orlov, see Wise, *Molehunt,* 205–19; and Martin, *Wilderness,* 159–60.
19. Mangold, *Cold Warrior,* 246.
20. Ibid.
21. Mangold, *Cold Warrior,* 263.
22. Ibid., 300.
23. Rafalko, *Counterintelligence Reader,* 3:116.
24. Colby and Forbath, *Honorable Men,* 364.
25. For further details, see Rafalko, *Counterintelligence Reader,* 3:110. Angleton's mail monitoring program seems contradictory. For a CIA officer who thought the Soviets were capable of grand conspiracies, it seems hardly credible that they would entrust important information to ordinary mail, which they would assume the United States monitored as they did in the USSR. Apparently such was the case, as suggested by a CIA inspector general's assessment that the intelligence from the opened letters was "meager." Martin, *Wilderness,* 71.
26. Mangold, *Cold Warrior,* 317.
27. Ibid, 110.
28. The author attended these sessions when he was a young officer in the early 1980s.
29. Robarge, "James Angleton Phenomenon." See also Hood, Nolan, and Halpern, *Myths Surrounding James Angleton.*

Chapter 7

1. "American Cultural History 1980–1989."
2. Ibid.
3. Herbig and Wiskoff, *Espionage,* 11.
4. Kessler, *Spy in the Russian Club,* 30, 72.
5. Ibid., 119.
6. Ibid., 159.
7. Herbig and Wiskoff, *Espionage,* 76.
8. For a brief synopsis of the case, see *Espionage and Other Compromises,* 56.
9. Herbig and Wiskoff, *Espionage,* 51.

10. The other two, Aldrich Ames of the CIA and Robert Hanssen of the FBI, are discussed in part V.

Chapter 8

1. Earley, *Family,* 13. In addition to Earley's book, other comprehensive studies of the Walker spy ring are Rafalko, *Counterintelligence Reader,* 3:233–35; Barron, *Breaking the Ring;* Blum: *I Pledge Allegiance;* Hunter, *Spy Hunter;* and Kneece, *Family Treason.* Hunter was the lead FBI investigator on the Walker case; he accused Blum of "inaccuracies" in the latter's book on Walker and noted that Earley's study was the most accurate; Hunter, *Spy Hunter,* 191, 210.
2. Earley, *Family,* 173; Hunter, *Spy Hunter,* 164.
3. Hunter, *Spy Hunter,* 195.
4. Pincher, *Traitors,* 97.
5. Walker, *My Life,* 21.
6. Sale, *Traitors,* 184.
7. Ibid., 191.
8. Andrew and Mitrokhin, *Sword and the Shield,* 205.
9. Rafalko, *Counterintelligence Reader,* 3:233.
10. Kalugin, *Spymaster,* 85.
11. Rafalko, *Counterintelligence Reader,* 3:233.
12. Hunter, *Spy Hunter,* 207.
13. Ibid., 187.
14. Barron, *Breaking the Ring,* 59.
15. Sale, *Traitors,* 184.
16. Earley, *Family,* 135.
17. Experts cited by Allen and Polmar, *Merchants,* 333.
18. Whitworth's correspondence with the FBI is detailed by Allen and Polmar, *Merchants,* 172.
19. Rafalko, *Counterintelligence Reader,* 3:235.
20. Earley, *Family,* 211.
21. Rafalko, *Counterintelligence Reader,* 3:235.
22. Allen and Polmar, *Merchants,* 149.
23. Earley, *Family,* 178.
24. Ibid., 263.
25. Rafalko, *Counterintelligence Reader,* 3:235–36.
26. Whitworth trial transcript cited by Allen and Polmar, *Merchants,* 249.
27. Earley, *Family,* 14.
28. Hunter, *Spy Hunter,* 188–89.
29. Earley, *Family,* 109–10.
30. Ibid., 368.
31. Walker, *My Life,* 312.
32. Ibid., 103.
33. Ibid., 156.
34. Ibid., 162, 339.
35. Rafalko, *Counterintelligence Reader,* 3:233.

36. Studeman affidavit cited by Church, "Justice," *Time.*
37. Kalugin, *Spymaster,* 84.
38. Sale, *Traitors,* 248.
39. Rafalko, *Counterintelligence Reader,* 3:234.
40. Ibid.
41. Cited by Miller, *Spying,* 489.
42. Hunter, *Spy Hunter,* 176.
43. Ibid., 208–9.

Chapter 9

1. Yurchenko's defection is discussed by Rafalko, *Counterintelligence Reader,* 3:233; and Bearden and Risen, *Main Enemy,* 70–83.
2. Wise, *Nightmover,* 128.
3. Rafalko, *Counterintelligence Reader,* 3:268, 276–77. See also Bearden and Risen, *Main Enemy,* 77–78.
4. Gates, *From the Shadows,* 363.
5. Bearden and Risen, *Main Enemy,* 146
6. Earley, *Confessions,* 186.
7. "Spy Who Redefected."
8. Bearden and Risen, *Main Enemy,* 123–24.
9. Ibid., 100–101, 325.
10. Richelson, *Century,* 393–94.
11. The FBI interviews with Pelton are detailed by Allen and Polmar, *Merchants,* 257–63; and Kessler, *Spy vs. Spy,* 246–59.
12. Miller, *Spying,* 489.

Chapter 10

1. For an in-depth review of the Tolkachev operation, see Royden, "Tolkachev." See also Wallace and Melton, *Spycraft,* location 2394–2745.
2. Royden, "Tolkachev," 18.
3. Rafalko, *Counterintelligence Reader,* 3:268. See also Riebling, *Wedge,* 355.
4. Howard, *Safehouse,* 51. Howard's book is a largely self-serving account designed to disprove the espionage charges against him. Howard submitted the manuscript to the CIA for approval, as required for all current and former CIA employees. Because he was living in Russia, his manuscript was undoubtedly reviewed and approved by the KGB, making Howard the only CIA author with a book approved by both Cold War superpowers.
5. Allen and Polmar, *Merchants,* 382. See also Wise, *Spy,* 111–13.
6. Wise, *Spy Who Got Away,* 119.
7. Bearden and Risen, *Main Enemy,* 87.
8. Ibid., 113.
9. The JIB technique is described in detail by Wallace and Melton, *Spycraft,* location 2617–44; and Bearden and Risen, *Main Enemy,* 116–17.
10. Gates, *From the Shadows,* 363.

11. Cited by US Senate, Select Committee on Intelligence, "Assessment of the Aldrich Ames Espionage Case," paragraph B1.
12. Gates, *From the Shadows*, 364.
13. Howard discusses his time in Budapest and Sweden in *Safehouse*, 195–201, 223–26.
14. For further discussion of the compromises, see Bearden and Risen, *Main Enemy*, 156–58.
15. Ibid., 301–2.

Chapter 11

1. Bearden and Risen, *Main Enemy*, 199.
2. Barker, *Dancing with the Devil*, 110. Two other books have been written about the Lonetree case: Kessler, *Moscow Station;* and Headley, *Court-Martial*. Headley was the chief investigator for Lonetree's defense team, and his viewpoint is clearly prodefendant. Headley argues that Lonetree was denied his rights and duped by government agencies into believing he would be a double agent after confessing his crimes.
3. Kessler, *Moscow Station*, 15.
4. Allen and Polmar, *Merchants*, 79.
5. Rafalko, *Counterintelligence Reader*, 3:272; Bearden and Risen, *Main Enemy*, 201–202.
6. Earley, *Confessions*, 221.
7. Andrew and Gordievsky, *KGB*, 529.
8. Although John Walker spied in the navy, he was already a retired civilian when the FBI was tipped to his spying by his wife, and thus the FBI was the responsible law enforcement agency to investigate his activities. Although the FBI had jurisdiction in the investigation, it coordinated with the NIS because Walker's son Michael was on active duty in the navy when he was arrested for conspiring with his father.
9. Allen and Polmar, *Merchants*, 82–83; Kessler, *Moscow Station*, 211–15, 259.
10. For further details on the NIS handling of the case, see Headley, *Court-Martial*, 48–64.
11. Bearden and Risen, *Main Enemy*, 301–2.
12. Barker, *Dancing with the Devil*, 164.
13. Kessler, *Moscow Station*, 165.

Chapter 12

1. Sulick, *Spying in America*, 253–63.
2. Kessler, *Spy vs. Spy*, 51.
3. Petersen, *Widow Spy*, location 1801.
4. For further background on the TRIGON case, see ibid., chaps. 9–12, locations 2473–3265; Bearden and Risen, *Main Enemy*, 10–11; and Earley, *Confessions*, 55–58. For details on Koecher's compromise of the case, see Earley, *Confessions*, 72–73.

5. Bearden and Risen, *Main Enemy*, 10. For comprehensive details of the poison pill issue, see Petersen, *Widow Spy*, locations 1895–1903, 2348–2411.
6. Kessler, *Spy vs. Spy*, 302–3. Kessler traveled to Prague to meet the Koechers a year after they returned home and conducted more than sixty hours of interviews with the couple.
7. Kessler, *Spy vs. Spy*, 295. Karl disputed some of the allegations about the couple's wife-swapping activities but never denied that they indulged, and Kessler also interviewed others who had participated in the orgies and knew the Koechers well.
8. Andrew and Mitrokhin, *Sword and the Shield*, 201.
9. The Czech source is discussed by Earley, *Confessions*, 73; Andrew and Mitrokhin, *Sword and Shield*, 201; and Kessler, *Bureau*, 235.
10. Earley, *Confessions*, 73. See also Kessler, *Bureau*, 240.
11. Kessler, *Bureau*, 242.
12. "Accused Czech Spy Says He Was on the US Side." See also Werner, "US Weighs Moves."
13. Kessler, *Bureau*, 243.
14. Karl Koecher surfaced in the headlines in a bizarre tale in 1999 related to the death of Princess Diana. Koecher emerged as an associate of a shadowy American who tried to sell documents allegedly proving that British royalty had assassinated the princess.

Chapter 13

1. Herrington's book, *Traitors among Us*, is the most comprehensive treatment of Conrad's spying and provides an insider's look into the development of the case since Herrington supervised the investigation as head of US Army counterintelligence in Europe. Herrington's study deals primarily with the Conrad case but also reviews other US Army spies, including James Hall, who is discussed in chapter 14.
2. Herrington, *Traitors among Us*, 399.
3. Ibid., 102.
4. Ibid., 82.
5. Ibid., 104.
6. Sale, *Traitors*, 11.
7. Williams, *Damian*, location 1130.
8. Ibid., location 1402.
9. Sale, *Traitors*, 13.
10. Herrington, *Traitors among Us*, 108–11.
11. Ibid., 84–85
12. Ibid., 89–90.
13. Ibid., 92.
14. Ibid., 105.
15. Williams, *Damian*, location 1347.
16. Ibid., location 1473.

17. The three options are discussed in detail by Herrington, *Traitors among Us,* 203–4.
18. Ibid., 387.

Chapter 14

1. Macrakis, *Seduced by Secrets,* location 1857.
2. Herrington, *Traitors among Us,* 251–55.
3. Ibid., 256. As in the Conrad case, Colonel Herrington also supervised the Hall investigation and his first-hand account is the most comprehensive study of the case to date.
4. Ibid., 260.
5. Ibid., 275–76.
6. Ibid., 279.
7. Ibid., 282.
8. Wolf maintained in his autobiography that Yildirim introduced several potential spies in the US military to the HVA. Wolf, *Man without a Face,* 327.
9. Ibid., 328.
10. Herrington, *Traitors among Us,* 328.
11. Macrakis interview with Hall, *Seduced by Secrets,* location 1937.
12. Koehler, *Stasi,* location 3295; Herrington, *Traitors among Us,* 324.
13. Koehler, *Stasi,* 3295.
14. Macrakis, *Seduced by Secrets,* location 2225.
15. Herrington, *Traitors among Us,* 333,
16. Ibid., 334.
17. Wolf, *Man without a Face,* 329.
18. *United States of America v. James W. Hall III,* Application for Certain Search Warrants.
19. Herrington, *Traitors among Us,* 336–38.
20. *Espionage and Other Compromises,* 21.
21. Ibid.
22. Macrakis, *Seduced by Secrets,* location 1995.
23. Wolf, *Man without a Face,* 331.
24. Ibid.

Chapter 15

1. The approach is discussed in detail by Hoffman, *Spy Within,* 134–44. Hoffman's book is the most comprehensive study of the Chin case to date. Other sources date Chin's recruitment to earlier in his academic career, possibly in 1943 or 1945; but it appears that Chin did not actively undertake espionage work until 1948.
2. Ibid., 155.
3. In 2005, FBIS was incorporated into the newly formed Open Source Center, which is tasked to collect and analyze information from overt sources for the intelligence community.

4. Hoffman, *Spy Within*, 50.
5. Rafalko, *Counterintelligence Reader*, 3:257.
6. Volkman, *Spies*, 157.
7. *United States of America v. Larry Wu-tai Chin, Affidavit for Search Warrant;* Allen and Polmar, *Merchants*, 376; Volkman, *Spies*, 156.
8. Ibid., 377.
9. *United States of America v. Larry Wu-tai Chin, Affidavit for Search Warrant.* This source is also discussed in *Espionage and Other Compromises*, 9; Hoffman, *Spy Within*, 19–41; Richelson, *Century*, 395–96; and Kessler, *Spy vs. Spy*, 233.
10. Chin's court testimony is cited by Allen and Polmar, *Merchants*, 375.
11. Kessler, *Spy vs. Spy*, 239.
12. *United States of America v. Larry Wu Tai Chin aka Chin Wu-tai*, Indictment, cited by Richelson, *Century*, 348.
13. Hoffman, *Spy Within*, 196.

Chapter 16

1. Olive, *Capturing Jonathan Pollard*, 2. Olive was the Naval Investigative Service agent directly responsible for the Pollard investigation and provides a unique insider's account of the case. Whereas Olive believes Pollard was a damaging spy aptly punished for his crime, other books argue the injustice of his sentence: Goldenberg, *Hunting Horse;* and Mark Shaw, *Miscarriage of Justice.* Shaw presents his arguments about legal flaws in the case, and Goldenberg delves into the policy issues behind Pollard's sentence. Another detailed account of the case is by Wolf Blitzer, *Territory of Lies.* US government documents on the case include *United States of America v. Jonathan Jay Pollard,* Indictment; *United States of America v. Jonathan Jay Pollard,* Government's Memorandum in Aid of Sentencing; and *United States of America v. Jonathan Pollard,* Supplemental Declaration of Caspar L. Weinberger.
2. Richelson, *Century of Spies*, 398.
3. Olive, *Pollard*, 34.
4. Allen and Polmar, *Merchants of Treason*, 355.
5. Olive, *Pollard*, 61.
6. US Central Intelligence Agency, "Jonathan Pollard Espionage Case," 6.
7. *United States of America v. Jonathan Pollard,* Indictment, paragraph 17.
8. Blitzer, *Territory of Lies*, 10.
9. Ibid., 11–12.
10. Olive, *Pollard*, ix; *United States of America v. Jonathan Pollard,* Indictment, paragraph 20c.
11. *United States of America v. Jonathan Pollard,* Indictment, paragraph 18.
12. Ibid., paragraph 21.
13. *United States of America v. Jonathan Pollard,* Governments Memorandum in Aid of Sentencing, 5.
14. Ibid., 4–5.
15. Olive, *Pollard*, 136. Olive's account is the first that reveals Anne Pollard's spotting of the FBI surveillance on Pelton.

16. Allen and Polmar, *Merchants of Treason*, 365.
17. US Central Intelligence Agency, "Jonathan Pollard Espionage Case," 43.
18. *United States of America v. Jonathan Pollard*, Governments Memorandum in Aid of Sentencing, 34.
19. Olive, *Pollard*, 170.
20. Ibid., 191.
21. Blitzer, *Territory of Lies*, 178
22. Ibid., 150.
23. Ibid., 296.
24. Richelson, *Century of Spies*, 403.
25. Olive, *Pollard*, 231.
26. Blitzer, "Pollard: Not a Bungler."
27. Pollard's passage of this information is also discussed by Olive, *Pollard*, 217–18.
28. US Central Intelligence Agency, "Jonathan Pollard Espionage Case," 9, 22, 55.
29. Ibid., 38, 57, 82.
30. Ibid., 56.
31. The journalist Seymour Hersh provided a comprehensive review of the extensive damage of Pollard's espionage regarding the compromise of technical collection systems, especially those of NSA, and also discussed the possibility that Israel may have traded some of Pollard's information to the Soviets in exchange for allowing Russian Jewish scientists to leave the USSR. Hersh, "Traitor."
32. *United States of America v. Jonathan Pollard*, Supplemental Declaration of Caspar L. Weinberger.
33. Tenet, *At the Center*, 68–72.
34. Goldberg, *Hunting Horse*, 58.
35. Kershner, "Israel Plans Public Appeal."
36. Stein, "Hidden Hand."
37. Stein, "Kissinger."
38. Greenberg, "Netanyahu Calls for Release."
39. Best and Mark, "Jonathan Pollard."
40. Olive, *Pollard*, 258–59. Under US law at the time of Pollard's sentencing, a person sentenced to life imprisonment was presumptively entitled to parole after thirty years in prison. The US government, however, still has the right to oppose the parole.

Chapter 17

1. Poteat, "Downside," 13.
2. Schweizer, "Our Thieving Allies."
3. Herbig and Wiskoff, *Espionage*, 68.
4. Ibid., 69.
5. Ibid., 72.
6. Rafalko, *Counterintelligence Reader*, 3:412.
7. Ibid., 413–14.

Chapter 18

1. The activities of the unit are discussed by US Senate, Select Committee on Intelligence, "An Assessment of the Aldrich Ames Espionage Case and Its Implications for US Intelligence" (hereafter SSCI, "Assessment"); and US Department of Justice, Office of the Inspector General, "Review of the FBI's Performance in Uncovering the Espionage of Aldrich Hazen Ames." For further information on the Ames case, see Bearden and Risen, *Main Enemy;* Wise, *Nightmover;* Weiner, Johnston, and Lewis, *Betrayal;* Earley, *Confessions;* Adams, *Sellout;* and Maas, *Killer Spy.* Other US government documents with information on the case include *United States of America v. Aldrich Hazen Ames,* Affidavit in Support of Warrants for Arrest and Search and Seizure Warrants; US Central Intelligence Agency (CIA), "Unclassified Abstract of the CIA Inspector General's (IG) Report on the Aldrich H. Ames Case"; and CIA, "Statement of the Director of Central Intelligence on the Clandestine Services and the Damage Caused by Aldrich Ames."

2. Bearden and Risen, *Main Enemy,* 301–2.

3. Gates, *From the Shadows,* 17.

4. Weiner, Johnston, and Lewis, *Betrayal,* 168.

5. Grimes and Vertefeuille, *Circle of Treason,* 166; SSCI, "Assessment," paragraph B3.

6. CIA, "Unclassified Abstract," 3:325; SSCI, "Assessment," paragraph A2.

7. Wise, *Nightmover,* 113.

8. Ames's contacts with Chuvakhin are detailed by SSCI, "Assessment," B1.

9. Ames comments on this to investigators after his arrest are provided by CIA, "Unclassified Abstract," 3:328–29.

10. After his arrest Ames claimed he provided this treasure trove of information at the June 13 lunch with Chuvakhin, but he could have been mistaken and it might have been earlier. As Sandy Grimes, one of the primary CIA investigators on the case, noted, one of the agents Ames admitted betraying, Oleg Gordievsky, was recalled to Moscow and interrogated in May, which could suggest Ames provided all the names at an earlier meeting with Chuvakhin. Grimes and Vertefeuille, *Circle of Treason,* 169–70.

11. In one of the tragic ironies of superpower espionage, Ames was tapped to meet and escort Soviet defector Vitaliy Yurchenko when he landed in the United States. When Yurchenko decided to return to the Soviet Union, one of his Soviet escorts was Valeriy Martynov. The KGB used the escort duty as a pretext to send Martynov home, where he was interrogated and executed as a result of Ames's betrayal.

12. Cherkashin, *Spy Handler,* 190.

13. SSCI, "Assessment," paragraph B2. See also Adams, *Sellout,* 141, 148–49.

14. For further details, see Earley, *Confessions,* 197–98; Bearden and Risen, *Main Enemy,* 190–91; and Grimes and Vertefeuille, *Circle of Treason,* 103.

15. SSCI, "Assessment," paragraph B2. Also see Bearden and Risen, *Main Enemy,* 164–65; Grimes and Vertefeuille, *Circle of Treason,* 99.

16. SSCI, "Assessment," paragraph A2; Clarridge, *Spy for All Seasons,* 121.

17. CIA, "Unclassified Abstract," 3:326.
18. SSCI, "Assessment," paragraphs A2–A3.
19. CIA, "Unclassified Abstract," 3:328.
20. Ibid.
21. Kessler, *Bureau*, 376.
22. SSCI, "Assessment," introduction.
23. SSCI, "Assessment," paragraph B2; Earley, *Confessions*, 242–43.
24. Vertefeuille and her colleague Sandy Grimes provide a first-hand account of the Ames investigation; see Sandra Grimes and Jeanne Vertefeuille, *Circle of Treason*.
25. CIA, "Unclassified Abstract," 3:323; Grimes and Vertefeuille, *Circle of Treason*, 142–43.
26. Earley, *Confessions*, 317.
27. SSCI, "Assessment," paragraph B2.
28. For more information on the damage assessment, see CIA, "Statement of the Director of Central Intelligence," 3:314–32.
29. Bearden and Risen, *Main Enemy*, 529.
30. Wise, *Nightmover*, 315.
31. Grimes and Vertefeuille, *Circle of Treason*, 44–45.
32. CIA Center for the Study of Intelligence, "Preparing for Martial Law," 4.
33. The agents are discussed throughout Bearden and Risen, *Main Enemy*, and listed by Earley, *Confessions*, 143–44.
34. Weiner, Johnston, and Lewis, *Betrayal*, 263.
35. Cited by Earley, *Confessions*, 334.
36. Cited by Weiner, Johnston, and Lewis, *Betrayal*, 284.
37. Riebling, *Wedge*, 449–50.
38. See US Department of Justice, Office of Inspector General, "Review of the FBI's Performance in Uncovering the Espionage Activities of Aldrich Hazen Ames," paragraph IIIa.
39. The precise language in the Intelligence Authorization Act of 1995, HR 4299, 103rd Congress, Section 811, (c) (A), is as follows: "The head of each department or agency within the Executive branch shall ensure that the Federal Bureau of Investigation is advised immediately of any information, regardless of its origin, which indicates that classified information is being, or may have been, disclosed in an unauthorized manner to a foreign power or an agent of a foreign power." http://thomas.loc.gov/cgi-bin/query/F?c103:5:./temp/~c1032llk3Y:e103236.
40. The center has since been renamed the National Counterintelligence Executive.
41. Rafalko, *Counterintelligence Reader*, 4:105.

Chapter 19

1. Rafalko, *Counterintelligence Reader*, 3:272–73.
2. Verbitzky, *Sleeping with Moscow*, 13.
3. Ibid., 7.

4. For further details on the case, see *United States of America v. Earl Edwin Pitts,* Affidavit in Support of Criminal Complaint, 3:364–66.
5. Ibid.
6. The work of the joint unit is discussed in detail by US Department of Justice, Office of the Inspector General, "Review of the FBI's Performance in Deterring, Detecting and Investigating the Espionage Activities of Robert Philip Hanssen," paragraphs III C1–C3.
7. The mindset issue is discussed in detail in ibid., paragraph III C 2.
8. Kelley was placed on administrative leave by the CIA during his investigation. Once Hanssen was identified, Kelley resumed his career and became one of the intelligence community's leading instructors on counterintelligence. After retirement he continued to teach in both the government and academic institutions until his sudden death from a heart attack on September 19, 2011. For further details about the investigation, see ibid., paragraph III C 2.
9. Rafalko, *Counterintelligence Reader,* 4:123.
10. *United States of America v. Robert Philip Hanssen,* Affidavit in Support of Criminal Complaint, paragraph V 104–5.
11. The evidence is discussed in ibid., paragraphs IV.49.B, IV.49.G., V.67, VI.A.140–41, C.145.
12. The author was the Russian Operations official who met the FBI official. The division was responsible for clandestine operations and counterintelligence in Russia, Eastern Europe, and the former Soviet republics.
13. Vise, *Bureau and the Mole,* 8. Other books on Hanssen include Havill, *The Spy Who Stayed Out in the Cold;* Schiller, *Into the Mirror: The Life of Master Spy Robert Hanssen;* Wise, *Spy;* and Shannon and Blackman, *Spy Next Door.* US government documents on the case include the following: *United States of America v. Robert Philip Hanssen,* Affidavit in Support of Criminal Complaint; Federal Bureau of Investigation, "Statement of FBI Director Louis J. Freeh"; US Department of Justice, Office of the Inspector General, "Review of the FBI's Performance"; and US Department of Justice, "Review of FBI Security Programs."
14. Havill, *Spy,* 101.
15. Ibid., 147–48.
16. Wise, *Spy,* 259.
17. US Department of Justice, Office of the Inspector General, "Review of the FBI's Performance," paragraph III B 1.
18. Havill, *Spy,* 57.
19. Details of Hanssen's approach are provided in *United States of America v. Robert Philip Hanssen,* Affidavit in Support of Criminal Complaint, paragraphs V 50–55.
20. Gordievsky, "What Makes the Double Agent Tick?"
21. *United States of America v. Robert Philip Hanssen,* Affidavit in Support of Criminal Complaint, paragraph VI.G 161–63.
22. Rafalko, *Counterintelligence Reader,* 4:102–3.
23. Ibid., 4:103.

24. Havill, *Spy: The Inside Story*, xxi.
25. Rafalko, *Counterintelligence Reader*, 3:113; *United States of America v. Robert Philip Hanssen*, Affidavit in Support of Criminal Complaint, paragraph V 131.
26. Wise, *Spy: The Inside Story*, 274.
27. For further details on the information Hanssen passed the KGB and SVR, see Rafalko, *Counterintelligence Reader*, 4:105.
28. Herbig and Wiskoff, *Espionage*, 74.
29. Rafalko, *Counterintelligence Reader*, 4:105. See also Wise, *Spy: The Inside Story*, 285, and Kessler, *Bureau*, 444.
30. Cited by Wise, *Spy: The Inside Story*, 285.
31. Rafalko, *Counterintelligence Reader*, 4:123; Herbig and Wiskoff, *Espionage*, 74.
32. Rafalko, *Counterintelligence Reader*, 4:119; *United States of America v. Robert Philip Hanssen*, Affidavit in Support of Criminal Complaint, paragraph V 114.
33. Wise, *Spy: The Inside Story*, 262–64.
34. The disagreement was widely reported in the media. See Novak and Shannon, "Ashcroft"; Johnston and Risen, "How FBI Turncoat Struck the Deal"; and Oswald, "Ashcroft Will Not Budge."
35. Hanssen's tradecraft errors are detailed by US Department of Justice, Office of the Inspector General, "Review of the FBI's Performance," paragraph III B 4.
36. Ibid.
37. US Department of Justice, "Review of FBI Security Programs."
38. US Department of Justice, Office of the Inspector General, "Review of the FBI's Performance," paragraph III C.
39. Wise, *Spy: The Inside Story*, 249.

Chapter 20

1. *United States of America v. Harold J. Nicholson*, Affidavit in Support of Complaint, Arrest Warrant and Search Warrants, cited by Rafalko, *Counterintelligence Reader*, 3:354–63. Also see *United States of America v. Harold J. Nicholson*, Statement of Facts in Support of Plea Agreement.
2. A detailed breakdown of Nicholson's travels correlated with bank deposits is included in the Nicholson Affidavit in Rafalko, *Counterintelligence Reader*, 3:357.
3. Ibid., 354–63.
4. Ibid., 357, 360.
5. Ibid., 358.
6. Ibid., 360.
7. *United States of America v. Harold Nicholson and Nathaniel Nicholson*, Application and Affidavit for Search Warrant.
8. Ibid., paragraphs 32–45.
9. Pincus, "Imprisoned Ex-CIA Officer."
10. A summary of Trofimoff's espionage and the complete affidavit of charges against him (*United States of America v. George von Trofimoff*) are given by Rafalko, *Counterintelligence Reader*, 4:93–101. For a full account of the Trofimoff story, see Byers, *Imperfect Spy*.

11. Trofimoff Affidavit, cited by Rafalko, *Counterintelligence Reader*, 4:94, 4:100.
12. Details of the sting operation are provided by Rafalko, *Counterinteligence Reader*, 4:94.
13. Kalugin was later sentenced to fifteen years hard labor by a Russian court for his book about the KGB and testimony in the Trofimoff case.
14. Lipka's espionage activities are presented in *United States of America v. Robert Stephan Lipka*, cited by Rafalko, *Counterintelligence Reader*, 3:347–50.
15. Rafalko, *Counterintelligence Reader*, 3:349; Kessler, *Bureau*, 385.
16. Kalugin, *Spymaster*, 83.
17. Details of the sting operation are included in the Lipka complaint cited by Rafalko, *Counterintelligence Reader*, 3:349–50.
18. For further details of the case, see Rafalko, *Counterintelligence Reader*, 4:189–202.
19. For the details of the HVA records, see Rafalko, *Counterintelligence Reader*, 4:189, 194.
20. Ibid., 193–94.
21. Ibid., 194.

Chapter 21

1. Brenner, "Strategic Counterintelligence."
2. Cited by Poteat, "Downside," 13.
3. Morrison, "China's Economic Conditions."
4. Office of the US Trade Representative, "China."
5. Zhongwen and Zongxiao, *Sources and Techniques*, summarized by Rafalko, *Counterintelligence Reader*, 4:54–58.
6. Ibid., 55.
7. Interagency Opsec Support staff, *Intelligence Threat Handbook*.
8. Moore, "How China Plays the Ethnic Card."
9. Moore, "China's Subtle Spying."

Chapter 22

1. "The Cox Report," cited by Rafalko, *Counterintelligence Reader*, 4:26.
2. US Senate, "Report on the Investigation of Espionage Allegations against Dr. Wen Ho Lee," cited by Rafalko, *Counterintelligence Reader*, 4:59.
3. Ibid.
4. Another Chinese American scientist was also targeted in a Beijing hotel room visit. Peter Lee (no relation to Wen Ho) was a laser expert first at Los Alamos and then Livermore laboratories. During a 1985 visit to Beijing, Chinese scientists used their typical approach to Chinese Americans by asking for his help on a few scientific questions. Lee cooperated and later admitted to the FBI that he had passed the Chinese information. He pled guilty and was sentenced to a year in a halfway house, community service, and a $20,000 fine. Rafalko, *Counterintelligence Reader*, 4:3.

5. "Cox Report," 60. Information about Lee's contact with Hu Side is also included in *United States of America v. Wen Ho Lee,* Affidavit in Support of Search Warrant.

6. Ibid., 61. A description of the files Lee moved is included in the *United States of America vs. Wen Ho Lee,* Indictment, paragraphs 16–22.

7. "Cox Report," 25–26, 61–62.

8. Ibid., 25.

9. Gertz, *China Threat,* 149.

10. The missteps in "Kindred Spirit" are documented in "Cox Report," 59–74.

11. US Department of Justice, "History of the FBI."

12. "Cox Report," 62.

13. US Department of Justice, "Attorney General's Review Team on the Handling of the Los Alamos National Laboratory Investigation."

14. "Rudman Report," cited by Rafalko, *Counterintelligence Reader,* 4:343, 346.

15. Stober and Hoffman, *Convenient Spy,* 180.

16. Ibid., 204.

17. Ibid., 243.

18. Ibid., 270.

19. Testimony of Stephen Younger, Detention Hearing in the Case of *United States of America v. Wen Ho Lee,* cite by Rafalko, *Counterintelligence Reader,* 4: 58.

20. *United States of America v. Wen Ho Lee,* Declaration of Dr. Harold M. Agnew.

21. Stober and Hoffman, *Convenient Spy,* 330.

22. Farhi, "US, Media Settle."

Chapter 23

1. Details of Leung's access and cooperation with the FBI are included in "Review of the FBI's Handling and Oversight of FBI Asset Katrina Leung," paragraph 4B.

2. *United States of America v. Katrina Leung,* Affidavit in Support of Complaint and Arrest Warrant for Katrina Leung, March 2003, paragraphs 14–22; and "Review of FBI's Handling," paragraphs 4C–4F.

3. "Review of FBI's Handling," paragraph 4B.

4. Wildmuth, "Arrest of GOP Fundraiser."

5. "Review of FBI's Handling," paragraph 4B.

6. Ibid.

7. Ibid., paragraph 4C.

8. Ibid., paragraph 4.

9. Ibid., paragraphs 4B, 5.

10. Leung's admissions are included in *United States of America v. Katrina Leung,* Affidavit, paragraphs 22A–22F.

11. Smith's admissions are included in *United States of America v. James J. Smith,* Affidavit, paragraphs 25A–25F, 26B.

12. Gertz, *Enemies,* 46.

13. *United States of America v. Katrina Leung,* Order Granting Defendant Motion to Dismiss.

14. Gertz, *Enemies,* 47.
15. US Department of Justice, "Statement of the US Attorney on the Guilty Pleas."
16. "Review of FBI's Handling," paragraph 4C.
17. Ibid., paragraph IV.
18. Gertz, *Enemies,* 52–53.
19. Asset validation regarding the Iraq weapons issue is discussed in detail in "Commission on the Intelligence Capabilities of the United States," 558–68.
20. Ibid., 558. The commission recommended the adoption of improved asset validation members for the entire intelligence community (568).
21. Ibid.
22. Gertz, *Enemies,* 20.
23. *United States of America v. Chi Mak,* Affidavit, paragraph VI.C.19.
24. Ibid.
25. Ibid., paragraph VI.A.19.
26. Gertz, *Enemies,* 58–59; Wise, *Tiger Trap,* 216.
27. *United States of America v. Chi Mak et al.,* Second Superseding Indictment.
28. Brenner, "Strategic Counterintelligence."
29. The FBI testimony is cited by Wise, *Tiger Trap,* 216–18.
30. Wise identified PRC official "A" as Lin Hong, a senior intelligence officer of China's People's Liberation Army; Wise, *Tiger Trap,* 220–26. See also Counterintelligence Centre, "Espionage Cases: Tai Shen Kuo."
31. *United States of America v. Dongfan "Greg" Chung,* paragraph 22.
32. Ibid., paragraphs 2–10.
33. Ibid., paragraphs 21D, 22J.
34. Office of the National Counterintelligence Executive, "Foreign Spies Stealing."
35. *United States of America v. Tai Shen Kuo, Gregg William Bergersen, and Yu Xin Kang,* Affidavit in Support of Criminal Complaint, paragraph 8.
36. Ibid., paragraphs 32–33.
37. Ibid., paragraph 54.
38. US Department of Justice, "New Orleans Man Sentenced."
39. Arrillaga, "How a Networking Immigrant Became a Spy."
40. *United States of America v. James Wilbur Fondren Jr.,* Affidavit in Support of Criminal Complaint, paragraph 13.
41. *United States of America v. James Wilbur Fondren Jr.,* Indictment. See also *United States of America v. James Wilbur Fondren Jr.,* Affidavit, paragraph 13.
42. "China Opening the Door to the East."
43. *United States of America v. Ronald N. Montaperto,* Statement of Facts, paragraph 4.
44. Gertz, *China Threat,* 36–37.
45. *United States of America v. Ronald N. Montaperto,* Statement of Facts, paragraphs 6–8, 10.
46. Gertz, "Intelligence Analyst Probed."
47. The sentence is discussed by Aronoff, "Spying-for-China Scandal."
48. *United States of America v. Glenn Duffie Shriver,* Statement of Facts, paragraphs 2–5.

Chapter 24

1. Counterintelligence Centre, "Unrepentant Ana Montes Sentenced."
2. For further details on the ring, see Rafalko, *Counterintelligence Reader,* 4:206–14.
3. Montes's family is discussed by Johnson, "She Led Two Lives."
4. Popkin, "Ana Montes."
5. Carmichael, *True Believer,* 55. Carmichael, who was a lead investigator on the case at DIA, provides the most comprehensive treatment of Montes's espionage to date. His insider's account also provides rare insight into the difficulties faced by counterespionage officers as they try to investigate a suspect without alerting him or her to the investigation. See also *Espionage and Other Compromises,* 39.
6. Carmichael, *True Believer,* 133.
7. Ibid., 57.
8. Montes's communications with the Cubans are detailed in *United States of America v. Ana Belen Montes,* Affidavit in Support of Criminal Complaint, paragraphs II.A.11–19, II.B.20–22.
9. Carmichael, *True Believer,* 29.
10. *United States of America v. Ana Belen Montes,* Affidavit in Support of Criminal Complaint, paragraphs II.A.14–19.
11. Ibid., paragraphs III.38–45.
12. *Espionage and Other Compromises,* 39.
13. Carmichael, *True Believer,* viii.
14. Counterintelligence Centre, "Unrepentant Montes."
15. *United States of America v. Ana Belen Montes,* Affidavit in Support of Criminal Complaint, paragraphs III.32–36.
16. Carmichael, *True Believer,* 163.
17. Radosh, "Castro's Top Spy."

Chapter 25

1. Harnden, "Spying for Fidel."
2. Ibid.
3. Ibid.
4. Ibid.
5. Ibid.
6. *United States of America v. Walter Kendall Myers,* Criminal Complaint, paragraph 29.
7. Jose Cohen Valdes, *El Servicio de Inteligencia Castrista,* 2. Translation of the Spanish text is by the author.
8. Ibid., 14–15.
9. *United States of America v. Walter Kendall Myers,* Criminal Complaint, paragraph 31.
10. Ibid., paragraph 43.
11. Ibid. paragraph 30.

12. Ibid., paragraph 43.
13. Ibid., paragraphs 34, 37, 44–51. Also see *United States of America v. Walter Kendall Myers and Gwendolyn Steingraber Myers,* Indictment, paragraph 63 bb.
14. *United States of America v. Walter Kendall Myers,* Criminal Complaint, paragraphs 44–46.
15. Ibid., paragraphs 47–48.
16. Thompson, "Couple's Capital Ties."
17. *United States of America v. Walter Kendall Myers,* Criminal Complaint, paragraphs 39–43.
18. Ibid., paragraph 43.
19. Crowley, "Arrest."
20. "Alleged Cuban Spies Given Praise."
21. Counterintelligence Centre, "Espionage Cases: Walter Kendall Myers."
22. Cratty, "Former State Department Official Sentenced."
23. *United States of America v. Walter Kendall Myers,* Criminal Complaint, paragraph 68.

Chapter 26

1. "Everett, Washington USA."
2. Malkin, "Trailing Attempted Espionage."
3. Counterintelligence Centre, "Ryan Anderson."
4. *Espionage and Other Compromises,* 3.
5. *United States of America v. Hassan Abu Jihaad, aka Paul R. Hall,* Criminal Complaint, paragraphs 15–16.
6. Ibid., paragraph 32.
7. *United States of America v. Hassan Abu Jihaad,* Memorandum of Decision.
8. Pipes, "Pentagon Jihadis."
9. Ali Mohammed confessed to his involvement in the activities presented here under questioning by the FBI, as indicated in the DOJ complaint in *United States of America v. Ali Mohammed.*
10. Much of the Ali Mohammed case is still shrouded in mystery. The investigative journalist Peter Lance and others claim that, after his discharge from the Egyptian Army, Mohammed volunteered to the CIA to spy on radicals in Hamburg mosques but was dropped after the agency discovered he was a double agent who informed Hezbollah of his mission. Lance also maintains that Mohammed was an FBI informant for years and that the FBI and DOJ missed indications of impending terrorist attacks in their handling of the Mohammed case. See Peter Lance, *Triple Cross.* The DOJ attorneys in the Mohammed case and other terrorist prosecutions, Patrick Fitzgerald and Andrew McCarthy, have vehemently refuted Lance's allegations. See McCarthy, *Willful Blindness.*
11. Glasser, "Terrorist's Guide."
12. Ibid.
13. "Military Studies in the Jihad."
14. *Nine Years after 9/11.*

15. Sulick, "Al-Qaeda Answers."
16. Weidlich "Kennedy Airport Terror Plot."
17. Cowley, "FBI Director."

Chapter 27

1. Office of the National Counterintelligence Executive, "Foreign Spies Stealing" (hereafter NCIX report).
2. Ibid.
3. For a discussion of remote operations, see Wallace and Melton, *Spycraft*, location 8737–46.
4. Stoll, *Cuckoo's Egg*.
5. NCIX report, 4.
6. Riley and Walcott, "China-Based Hacking."
7. Information from a briefing by a senior US intelligence official cited by Nakashima, "In a World of Cybertheft."
8. *National Public Radio,* "China's Cyber Threat."
9. Krekel, "Capability."
10. US Department of Justice, Office of the Inspector General. "Federal Bureau of Investigation's Ability to Address the National Security Cyber Intrusion Threat," 2.
11. Rogin, "Top 10 Chinese Cyber Attacks."
12. Gorman, Cole, and Dreazen, "Computer Spies."
13. Defense Science Board, "Resilient Military Systems," 3.
14. US Department of Defense, "Annual Report," 36.
15. Krekel, "Capability," 7.
16. Riley and Walcott, "China-Based Hacking."
17. Krekel, "Capability," 45.
18. Ibid., 46–48.
19. Ibid., 47.
20. Metzl, "China."
21. Mandiant, "APT1," 2–3.
22. NCIX report, 28.
23. Heintz, "Look at Russian Hacking."
24. Acohido, "Meet A-Z."
25. NCIX report, 20.
26. Krekel, "Capability," 8.
27. Haddick, "This Week at War."
28. Hersh, "Online Threat."
29. The arguments are presented in ibid. Two of the officials Hersh cites are Michael McConnell, former director of national intelligence, and Richard Clarke, former national security adviser for counterterrorism.
30. Constantin, "2012 Will See Rise."
31. NCIX report, 14.
32. Acohido, "Cyberattacks."
33. McMillan, "Anonymous."

34. Birnbaum, "WikiLeaks."
35. US Department of State, "Secretary Clinton."
36. Thiessen, "Stop Downplaying the WikiLeaks Damage."
37. Marvin Kalb, cited by Kitfield, "WikiLeaks."
38. The support group's website is www.bradleymanning.org. Other groups are Free Bradley, StandwithBrad.org, and I Am Bradley Manning.
39. Scherer, "Geeks Who Leak."
40. As a US Army member, Manning is subject to the Uniform Code of Military Justice. He is accused of violating Article 134, which incorporates civilian statute Title 18 USC 793 of the Espionage Act.
41. Scherer, "Geeks Who Leak."
42. US President, "National Strategy to Secure Cyberspace." President Bush's initiative was issued as "National Security Presidential Directive 54."
43. US President, "Comprehensive National Cybersecurity Initiative."
44. US Government Accountability Office, "Defense Department Cyber Efforts."
45. US Government Accountability Office, "Information Security"; US Government Accountability Office, "Critical Infrastructure Protection"; US Government Accountability Office, "Defense Department Cyber Efforts."
46. Hersh, "Online Threat."
47. US Department of Defense, "Nominee Urges Government."

Conclusion

1. Ehrman, "Toward a Theory," 17.
2. Wallace, "Time for Counterespionage," in *Vaults, Mirrors & Masks,* ed. Sims and Gerber.
3. Wallace and Melton, *Spycraft,* location 8746–62.
4. Varian, "IPod Has Global Value," *New York Times,* June 28, 2007.
5. Rishikof, "Economic and Industrial Espionage," in *Vaults, Mirrors, & Masks,* ed. Sims and Gerber, 200.
6. Office of the National Counterintelligence Executive, *National Counterintelligence Strategy,* 3.
7. Sims and Gerber, "Way Ahead," in *Vaults, Mirrors, & Masks,* ed. Sims and Gerber, 285.

Bibliography

"Accused Czech Spy Says He Was on the US Side." *Washington Post,* November 30, 1984. https://secure.pqarchiver.com/washingtonpost_historical/ access/124175362.html?FMT=AI&FMTS=ABS:AI&date=Nov+30%2C+1984&a uthor=&desc=Accused+Czech+Spy+Says+He+Was+on+the+U.S.+Side.

Acohido, Brian. "Cyberattacks Likely to Increase This Year." *USA Today,* January 11, 2012. www.usatoday.com/tech/news/story/2012-01-08/hacktivism-lulzsec-anonymous/52489606/1.

——. "Meet A-Z: The Computer Hacker behind a Cybercrime Wave." *USA Today,* August 5, 2008. www.usatoday.com/tech/news/computersecurity/2008-08-04-hacker-cybercrime-zeus-identity-theft_N.htm.

Adams, James. *Sellout: Aldrich Ames, the Spy Who Broke the CIA.* New York: Penguin, 1995.

Albright, Joseph, and Marcia Kunstel. *Bombshell: The Secret Story of America's Unknown Atomic Spy Conspiracy.* New York: Random House, 1997.

"Alleged Cuban Spies Given Praise from Castro." *Huffington Post,* July 9, 2009. www.huffingtonpost.com/2009/06/08/alleged-cuban-spies-given_n_212429. html.

Allen, Thomas G., and Norman Polmar. *Merchants of Treason: America's Secrets for Sale.* New York: Dell, 1988.

Ambler, Eric. *The Light of Day.* Black Lizard Edition, 2004. New York: Vintage Books, 1962.

"American Cultural History 1980–1989." Lone Star College, http://kclibrary. lonestar.edu/decade80.html.

Andrew, Christopher. *Defend the Realm: The Authorized History of MI-5.* New York: Alfred A. Knopf, 2009.

———. *For the President's Eyes Only: Secret Intelligence and the American Presidency from Washington to Bush.* New York: Harper, 1995.

Andrew, Christopher, and Oleg Gordievsky. *The KGB: The Inside Story of Its Foreign Operations from Lenin to Gorbachev.* London: Sceptre, 1991.

Andrew, Christopher, and Vasili Mitrokhin. *The Sword and the Shield: The Mitrokhin Archive and the History of the KGB.* New York: Basic Books, 1999.

Aronoff, Roger. "Spying-for-China Scandal." *Accuracy in Media,* October 20, 2006. www.aim.org/media-monitor/spying-for-china-scandal/.

Arrillaga, Pauline. "How a Networking Immigrant Became a Spy." Associated Press, May 8, 2011.

Bagley, Tennent H. *Spy Wars: Moles, Mysteries and Deadly Games.* New Haven, CT: Yale University Press, 2007.

Bamford, James. *The Puzzle Palace: Inside the National Security Agency, America's Most Secret Intelligence Organization.* New York: Houghton Mifflin, 1982; New York: Penguin, 1983. Citations refer to the Penguin edition.

Barker, Rodney. *Dancing with the Devil: Sex, Espionage and the U.S. Marines—The Clayton Lonetree Story.* New York: Simon & Schuster, 1996.

Barker, Wayne, and Rodney Coffman. *Anatomy of Two Traitors: The Defection of Bernon F. Mitchell and William H. Martin.* Laguna Hills, CA: Aegean Park Press, 1981.

Barron, John. *Breaking the Ring.* Boston: Houghton Mifflin, 1987.

———. *KGB: The Secret Work of Soviet Secret Agents.* New York: Readers Digest Press, 1974; New York: Bantam Books, 1974.

———. *KGB Today: The Hidden Hand.* London: Hodder & Stoughton, 1984; London: Coronet, 1985. Citations refer to the Coronet edition.

Bearden, Milton, and James Risen. *The Main Enemy: The Inside Story of the CIA's Final Showdown with the KGB.* New York: Random House, 2003.

Benson, Robert L., and Michael Warner. *Venona: Soviet Espionage and the American Response 1939–1957.* Washington, DC: National Security Agency and Central Intelligence Agency, 1996.

Bentley, Elizabeth. *Out of Bondage.* New York: Devin-Adair, 1951.

Bernikow, Louise. *Abel.* New York: Simon & Schuster, 1970; New York: Ballantine, 1982.

Best, Richard, and Clyde Mark. "Jonathan Pollard: Background and Considerations for Presidential Clemency." Congressional Research Service Report for Congress, January 31, 2001. www.fas.org/irp/crs/RS20001.pdf.

Birnbaum, Ben. "WikiLeaks Releases State Department Cables." *Washington Times,* November 28, 2010. www.washingtontimes.com/news/2010/nov/28/wikileaks-releases-state-reports/?page=all.

Blitzer, Wolf. "Pollard: Not a Bungler but Israel's Master Spy." *Washington Post,* February 15, 1987.

———. *Territory of Lies: The Rise, Fall and Betrayal of Jonathan Jay Pollard.* New York: Harper & Row, 1990; orig. pub. 1989.

Blum, Howard. *I Pledge Allegiance: The Shocking True Story of the Walker Family of Spies.* New York: Pocket Books, 1987.

Bowman, M. E. "Collective Security v. Privacy." *Intelligencer* 14, no. 2 (Winter–Spring 2005): 39–47.

——. "The Drumbeats for Clemency for Jonathan Pollard Reverberate Again." *Intelligencer,* 18, no. 2 (Winter–Spring 2011): 7–12.

Brenner, Joel. *America the Vulnerable: Inside the New Threat Matrix of Digital Espionage, Crime, and Warfare.* New York: Penguin, 2011.

——. "Strategic Counterintelligence." Speech to American Bar Association Standing Committee on Law and National Security, March 29, 2007. www.ncix. gov/publications/speeches/ABAspeech.pdf.

Byers, Andy J. *The Imperfect Spy: The Inside Story of a Convicted Spy.* St. Petersburg, FL: Vandamere Press, 2005.

Carmichael, Scott. *True Believer: Inside the Investigation and Capture of Ana Montes, Cuba's Master Spy.* Annapolis, MD: US Naval Institute Press, 2007.

"Caught Unawares: The Case of William Bell and Marian Zacharski." *Security Awareness Bulletin* (US Department of Defense), no. 3 (June 1983): 43–51. http://books.google.com/books?id=2wNgbdnKuKAC&pg=PA43&lpg=PA43&d q=security+awareness+bulletin+caught+unawares&source=bl&ots=5hmX-JdH tf&sig=SorZPt6vhSu8VcRTVBFXjaRe7A0&hl=en&sa=X&ei=zVmhT_-vO4f28 wSxzsisCA&ved=0CE4Q6AEwAA#v=onepage&q&f=false.

Centre for Counterintelligence and Security Studies. "American Agents Working for the Soviets, 1930s–1950s." www.cicentre.com/?pages=cases_venona.

Charney, David L. "True Psychology of the Insider Spy." *Intelligencer,* 18, no. 1 (Fall–Winter 2010): 47–54.

Cherkashin, Viktor, and Gregory Feifer. *Spy Handler: Memoirs of a KGB Officer.* New York: Basic Books, 2005.

"China Opening the Door to the East." www.cdi.org/adm/936/transcript.html.

Church, George. "Justice for the Principal Spy." *Time,* September 8, 1986. www. time.com/time/magazine/article/0,9171,962236-1,00.html.

"CIA Head Lobbies against Death Penalty for Alleged FBI Spy," CNN, May 19, 2001. www.nytimes.com/2001/07/29/us/how-fbi-turncoat-struck-the-deal-that-spared-his-life.html?ref=robertphiliphanssen.

Clarridge, Duane. *A Spy for All Seasons: My Life in the CIA.* New York: Scribner, 1997.

Colby, William, and Peter Forbath. *Honorable Men: My Life in the CIA.* New York: Simon & Schuster, 1981.

Commager, Henry Steele, and Samuel Eliot Morison. *The Growth of the American Republic.* 6th ed. New York: Oxford University Press, 1969.

"Commission on the Intelligence Capabilities of the United States regarding Weapons of Mass Destruction: Report to the President of the United States." March 31, 2005.

Constantin, Lucien. "2012 Will See Rise in Cyberespionage and Malware, Experts Say." *PC World,* December 26,2011. www.pcworld.com/article/247008/2012_ will_see_rise_in_cyberespionage_and_malware_experts_say.html.

Cooper, H. H. A., and Lawrence J. Redlinger. *Catching Spies: Principles and Practices of Counterespionage.* Boulder, CO: Paladin Press, 1988. New York: Bantam Books, 1990.

Counterintelligence Centre. "Espionage Cases: Tai Shen Kuo." www.cicentre. com/?page=KUO_Tai_Shen.

———. "Espionage Cases: Walter Kendall Myers." www.cicentre.com/?page= MYERS_Kendall.

———. "Ryan Anderson." www.cicentre.com/?page=ANDERSON_Ryan.

———. "An Unrepentant Ana Montes Sentenced to 25 Years." www.cicentre. com/?page=montes_sentencing&hhSearchTerms=unrepentant+and+ana+and +montes.

Cowley, Stacy. "FBI Director: Cybercrime Will Eclipse Terrorism." *CNN Money*, March 2, 2012. http://money.cnn.com/2012/03/02/technology/fbi_ cybersecurity/index.htm.

Cratty, Carol. "Former State Department Official Sentenced to Life for Spying for Cuba." CNN, July 16, 2010. http://articles.cnn.com/2010-07-16/justice/spy. couple.sentenced_1_kendall-myers-cuban-agents-gwendolyn-steingraber-myers?_s=PM:CRIME.

Crowley, Philip J. "Arrest of Walter Kendall Myers." US Department of State Press Release, June 5, 2009. www.state.gov/r/pa/prs/ps/2009/06a/124404.htm.

Davis, James Kirkpatrick. *Spying on America: The FBI's Domestic Counterintelligence Program*. New York: Praeger, 1982.

Deacon, Richard. *The Chinese Secret Service*. London: Frederick Muller, 1974; London: Grafton, 1989.

Denning, Dorothy E. *"Industrial Espionage."* http://infosecuritymag.techtarget. com/articles/1999/aprilcover.shtml.

De Toledano, Ralph. *Seeds of Treason*. New York: Funk & Wagnalls, 1950; Orig. pub. Belmont, MA: Western Islands, 1965.

———. *Spies, Dupes and Diplomats*. New York: Duell, Sloan and Pearce, 1952; New Rochelle, NY: Arlington, 1967.

Devitt, Michael. "A Brief History of Computer Hacking." *MPA Media*. www. dynamicchiropractic.com/mpacms/dc/article.php?id=18078.

Dulles, Allen. *The Craft of Intelligence*. New York: Harper & Row, 1963; Guilford CT: Lyons, 2006. Citations refer to the Lyons edition.

Earley, Pete. *Confessions of a Spy: The Real Story of Aldrich Ames*. New York: G. P. Putnam's Sons, 1997.

———. *Family of Spies: Inside the John Walker Spy Ring*. New York: Bantam Books, 1988.

Ehrman, John. "Toward a Theory of CI—What Are We Talking about When We Talk about Counterintelligence?" *Studies in Intelligence* 53, no. 2 (June 2009): 5–20. www.cia.gov/library/center-for-the-study-of-intelligence/csi-publications/csi-studies/studies/vol53no2/pdfs/U-%20UnclassStudies% 2053-2.pdf.

Eig, Larry M. "Classified Information Procedures Act: An Overview." Congressional Research Service Report for Congress, March 2, 1989.

The Enemy Within: Terror in America—1776 to Today. Washington, DC: International Spy Museum, 2004.

Epstein, Edward J. *Deception: The Invisible War between the KGB and CIA*. New York: Simon & Schuster, 1989.

——. *Legend: The Secret World of Lee Harvey Oswald.* New York: Ballantine, 1979.

Espionage and Other Compromises of National Security: Case Summaries from 1975–2008. Monterey, CA: Defense Personnel Security Research Center, 2009.

Farhi, Paul. "US, Media Settle with Wen Ho Lee." *Washington Post,* June 3, 2006. www.washingtonpost.com/wp-dyn/content/article/2006/06/02/AR2006060201060.html.

Feklisov, Alexander. *The Man behind the Rosenbergs: By the KGB Spymaster Who Was the Case Officer of Julius Rosenberg, Klaus Fuchs, and Helped Resolve the Cuban Missile Crisis.* New York: Enigma Books, 2003.

Fink, Steve. *Sticky Fingers: Managing the Global Risk of Economic Espionage.* Lincoln, NE: iUniverse, 2003.

Gates, Robert. *From the Shadows: The Ultimate Insider's Story of Five Presidents and How They Won the Cold War.* New York: Touchstone, 1996.

Gaudin, Sharon. "Five Charged with Conspiracy to Export US Defense to China." *Information Week,* November 6, 2006. www.informationweek.com/news/showArticle.jhtml?articleID=193502101.

Gertz, Bill. *The China Threat: How the People's Republic Targets America.* Washington, DC: Regnery, 2003.

——. *Enemies.* New York: Crown, 2006.

——. "Intelligence Analyst Probed over Ties to a Spy for China." *Washington Times,* July 6, 2006.

Gilbert, James L., John P. Finnegan, and Ann Bray. *In the Shadow of the Sphinx: A History of Army Counterintelligence.* Fort Belvoir, VA: Department of the Army, 2005.

Glasser, Susan B. "A Terrorist's Guide to Infiltrating the West." *Washington Post,* December 9, 2001.

Goldenberg, Eliot. *The Hunting Horse: The Truth behind the Jonathan Pollard Case.* Amherst, MA: Prometheus Books, 2000.

Gordievsky, Oleg. "What Makes the Double Agent Tick?" *The Telegraph,* February 25, 2001. www.telegraph.co.uk/comment/4259821/What-makes-the-double-agent-tick.html.

Gorman, Siobhan, August Cole, and Yochi Dreazen. "Computer Spies Breach Fighter-Jet Project." *Wall Street Journal,* April 21, 2009. http://online.wsj.com/article/SB124027491029837401.html#printMode.

Greenberg, Joel. "Netanyahu Calls for Release of Spy for Israel Serving Life Sentence in US." *Washington Post,* January 4, 2011. www.washingtonpost.com/wp-dyn/content/article/2011/01/04/AR2011010403720.html.

Grimes, Sandra, and Jeanne Vertefeuille. *Circle of Treason: A CIA Account of Traitor Aldrich Ames and the Men He Betrayed.* Annapolis, MD: Naval Institute Press, 2012.

Haddick, Robert. "This Week at War: Lessons from Cyber War I." *Foreign Policy,* January 28, 2011. www.foreignpolicy.com/articles/2011/01/28/this_week_at_war_lessons_from_cyberwar_i.

Harnden, Toby. "Spying for Fidel: The Inside Story of Kendall and Gwen Myers." *Washingtonian,* October 5, 2009. www.washingtonian.com/articles/people/spying-for-fidel-the-inside-story-of-kendall-and-gwen-myers/.

Havill, Adrian. *The Spy Who Stayed Out in the Cold: The Secret Life of FBI Double Agent Robert Hanssen.* New York: St. Martin's Press, 2001.

Haynes, John Earl, and Harvey Klehr. *Venona: Decoding Soviet Espionage in America.* New Haven, CT: Yale University Press, 1999.

Haynes, John Earl, Harvey Klehr, and Alexander Vassiliev. *Spies: The Rise and Fall of the KGB in America.* New Haven, CT: Yale University Press, 2009.

Headley, Lake, and William Hoffman. *The Court-Martial of Clayton Lonetree.* New York: Henry Holt, 1989.

Heintz, Jim. "A Look at Russian Hacking." *ABC News,* November 20, 2011, http://abcnews.go.com/Technology/story?id=119291&page=1#.TxHln_Lsadl.

Helms, Richard. *A Look over My Shoulder: A Life in the Central Intelligence Agency.* New York: Random House, 2003.

Herbig, Katherine L., and Martin F. Wiskoff. *Espionage against the US by American Citizens 1947–2001.* Monterey, CA: Defense Personnel Security Research Center, 2002.

Herrington, Stuart. *Traitors among Us: Inside the Spy Catcher's World.* Novato, CA: Presidio Press, 1989; San Diego: Harvest, 1999. Citations refer to the Harvest edition.

Hersh, Seymour. "The Online Threat: Should We Be Worried about a Cyber War?" *New Yorker,* November 1, 2010. www.newyorker.com/reporting/2010/11/01/101101fa_fact_hersh.

——. "The Traitor: Why Pollard Should Never be Released." *New Yorker,* January 18, 1999. http://archives.newyorker.com/?i=1999-01-18#folio=026.

Heuer, Richards J. "Nosenko: Five Paths to Judgment." *Studies in Intelligence* 31, no. 3 (Fall 1987): 71–101.

Hoffman, Tod. *The Spy Within: Larry Chin and China's Penetration of the CIA.* Hanover, NH: Steerforth Press, 2008.

Holtzman, Michael. *James Jesus Angleton, the CIA and the Craft of Intelligence.* Amherst: University of Massachusetts Press, 2008.

Hood, William. *Mole.* New York: Ballantine Books, 1982; Washington, DC: Brassey's, 1993.

Hood, William, James Nolan, and Sam Halpern. *Myths Surrounding James Angleton: Lessons for American Counterintelligence.* Washington, DC: Consortium for the Study of Intelligence, 1994.

Hoover, Eleanor. "In an Audacious Escape, Unlikely Spy Christopher Boyce Goes Back into the Cold." *People Magazine,* February 25, 1980. www.people.com/people/archive/article/0,,20075889,00.html.

Hoover, J. Edgar. *Masters of Deceit.* New York: Henry Holt, 1958; New York: Pocket Books, 1961.

Horace. *The Complete Works of Horace,* edited by Casper J. Kraemer. New York: Modern Library, 1936.

Horton, Douglas. Quotation from *Quotations Book.* http://quotationsbook.com/quote/34365/.

Howard, Edward Lee. *Safe House: The Memoirs of the Only CIA Spy to Seek Asylum in Russia.* Bethesda, MD: National Press Books, 1995.

Hulnick, Arthur S. "The Ames Case: How Could It Happen?" *International Journal of Intelligence and Counterintelligence* 8, no. 2 (Summer 1995): 133–54.

Hunter, Robert W. *Spy Hunter: Inside the FBI Investigation of the Walker Espionage Case.* Annapolis, MD: Naval Institute Press, 1999.

Huntington, Samuel P. "The Democratic Distemper." In *The Crisis of Democracy: Report on the Governability of Democracies to the Trilateral Commission,* edited by S. P. Huntington, M J. Crozier, and J. Watanuki. New York: New York University Press, 1975.

Huss, Pierre J., and George Carpozi Jr. *Red Spies in the UN.* New York: Coward-McCann, 1965.

Interagency Opsec Support Staff. *Intelligence Threat Handbook.* June 2004. www.fas.org/irp/threat/handbook/foreign.pdf.

Jeffreys-Jones, Rhodri. *Cloak & Dollar: A History of American Secret Intelligence.* New Haven, CT: Yale University Press, 2002.

Johnson, Tim. "She Led Two Lives; Dutiful analyst, and Spy for Cuba." *Miami Herald,* June 16, 2002, A1.

Johnston, David, and James Risen. "How FBI Turncoat Struck the Deal That Spared His Life." *New York Times,* July 29, 2001. www.nytimes.com/2001/07/29/us/how-fbi-turncoat-struck-the-deal-that-spared-his-life.html?ref=robertphiliphanssen.

Juvenal. *The Sixteen Satires,* translated by Peter Green. New York: Penguin, 1992.

Kalugin, Oleg. *Spymaster.* New York: St. Martin's, 1994; London: Smith Gryphon, 1994. Citations refer to the Smith Gryphon edition.

Keegan, John. *Intelligence in War: Knowledge of the Enemy from Napoleon to Al-Qaeda.* New York: Alfred A. Knopf, 2003.

Kershner, Isabel. "Israel Plans Public Appeal to Ask US to Free a Spy." *New York Times,* December 21, 2010. www.nytimes.com/2010/12/22/world/middleeast/22mideast.html?scp=10&sq=JONATHAN%20POLLARD&st=cse.

Kessler, Ronald. *The Bureau: The Secret History of the FBI.* 2002. Reprinted. New York: St. Martin's Press, 2003.

———. *Escape from the CIA: How the CIA Won and Lost the Most Important KGB Spy Ever to Defect to the US.* New York: Pocket Books, 1991.

———. *Moscow Station: How the KGB Penetrated the American Embassy.* New York: Macmillan, 1989.

———. *The Spy in the Russian Club.* New York: Pocket Books, 1990.

———. *Spy vs. Spy: The Shocking True Story of the FBI's Secret War against Soviet Agents in America.* New York: Scribner's, 1988; New York: Pocket Books, 1989. Citations refer to the Pocket Books edition.

Kitfield, James. "WikiLeaks Collateral Damage." *National Journal,* December 16, 2011. www.nationaljournal.com/nationalsecurity/wikileaks-collateral-damage-0111216.

Kneece, Jack. *Family Treason: The Walker Spy Case.* New York: Stein and Day, 1986; New York: Paperjacks, 1988.

Koehler, John O. *Stasi: The Untold Story of the East German Secret Police.* Boulder, CO: Westview Press, 1999; Kindle edition.

Kolpakiki, A., and G. Prokhorov. *Vneshnyaya razvedki Rossii.* Moscow: Olma Press, 2000.

Krall, Yung. *A Thousand Tears Falling: The True Story of a Vietnamese Family Torn Apart by War, Communism, and the CIA.* Marietta, GA: Longstreet Press, 1995.

Krekel, Bryan. "Capability of the People's Republic of China to Conduct Cyber Warfare and Computer Network Exploitation: Prepared for the US-China Economic and Security Review Commission." Northrop Grumman Corporation, October 2009. www.uscc.gov/researchpapers/2009/Northrop Grumman_PRC_Cyber_Paper_FINAL_Approved%20Report_16Oct2009.pdf.

Lamphere, Robert. *The FBI-KGB War.* New York: Random House, 1986.

Lance, Peter. *Triple Cross: How bin Laden's Master Spy Penetrated the CIA, the Green Berets and the FBI—and Why Patrick Fitzgerald Failed to Stop Him.* New York: William Morrow, 2006; Kindle edition.

Latell, Brian. *Castro's Secrets: The CIA and Cuba's Intelligence Machine.* New York: St. Martin's Press, 2012.

Lee, Wen Ho. *My Country versus Me.* New York: Hyperion, 2001.

Lewes, James. *Protest and Survive: Underground GI Newspapers during the Vietnam War.* Westport, CT: Greenwood Publishing, 2003.

Lindsey, Robert. *The Falcon and the Snowman.* New York: Simon & Schuster, 1979.

Lloyd, Mark. *The Guinness Book of Espionage.* New York: DaCapo Press, 1994.

Loeb, Vernon, and Walter Pincus. "Guilty Plea, Release Leave Unresolved Questions in Lee Case." *Washington Post,* September 17, 2000.

Lum, Thomas, and Dick K. Nanto. "China's Trade with the United States and the World." Congressional Research Service Report for Congress. August 18, 2006. www.au.af.mil/au/awc/awcgate/crs/rl31403.pdf.

Lynn, William J. "Defending a New Domain: The Pentagon's Cyberstrategy." *Foreign Affairs,* September–October 2010. www.foreignaffairs.com/ articles/66552/william-j-lynn-iii/defending-a-new-domain.

Maas, Peter. *Killer Spy: The Inside Story of the FBI's Pursuit and Capture of Aldrich Ames, America's Deadliest Spy.* New York: Warner Books, 1995.

Macrakis, Kristie. *Seduced by Secrets: Inside the Stasi's Spy-Tech World.* New York: Cambridge University Press, 2008; Kindle edition.

Malkin, Michelle. "Trailing Attempted Espionage: Who Is Ryan Anderson, a.k.a. Amir Talhah?" *National Review Online,* February 13, 2004. www.nationalreview.com/comment/malkin200402130909.asp.

Mandiant. "APT1: Exposing one of China's Cyberespionage Units." February 2013. http://intelreport.mandiant.com/Mandiant_APT1_Report.pdf.

Mangold, Tom. *Cold Warrior: James Jesus Angleton—The CIA's Master Spy Hunter.* New York: Simon & Schuster, 1991.

Martin, David C. *Wilderness of Mirrors.* New York: HarperCollins, 1980; Guilford, CT: Lyons Press, 2003. Citations refer to the Lyons Press edition.

"Master Spies." International Spy Museum, www.spymuseum.com/pages/ agent-drummond-nelson.html.

Masters, Jonathan. "Confronting the Cyber Threat." *Council on Foreign Relations,* May 23, 2011. www.google.com/url?sa=t&rct=j&q=&esrc=s&source=web&cd=4 &ved=0CEMQFjAD&url=http%3A%2F%2Fwww.cfr.org%2Ftechnology-and-

foreign-policy%2Fconfronting-cyber-threat%2Fp15577&ei=pCETT_7YBZSltw
fBwuWGAg&usg=AFQjCNFbyFs5F3UxgLn2y5Nw7iuXi_IDbQ.

McCarthy, Andrew. *Willful Blindness: A Memoir of the Jihad.* New York: Encounter Books, 2008.

McMillan, Robert. "Anonymous Takes Down Visa.com in WikiLeaks Protest." *PC World,* December 8, 2010. www.pcworld.com/businesscenter/article/213024/anonymous_takes_down_visacom_in_wikileaks_protest.html.

Melton, H. Keith. "Spies in the Digital Age," January 19, 1999. http://cryptome.org/jya/melton.htm.

Metzl, Jamie. "China and Cyberespionage." *Asia Society,* August 2011. http://asiasociety.org/policy/strategic-challenges/china-and-cyberespionage.

"Military Studies in the Jihad against the Tyrants." www.thesmokinggun.com/archive/jihad12chap9.html.

Miller, Nathan. *Spying in America.* New York: Dell, 1989.

Mitchell, Bernon, and William Martin. "Text of Statement Read in Moscow by Two US Security Agency Workers." *New York Times,* September 7, 1960. http://query.nytimes.com/mem/archive/pdf?res=F40814F73B551A7A93C5A91782D8 5F448685F9.

Mogelever, Jacob. *Death to Traitors.* New York: Doubleday, 1960.

Moore, Paul D. "China's Subtle Spying." *New York Times,* September 2, 1999.

——. "How China Plays the Ethnic Card." *Los Angeles Times,* June 24, 1999. http://articles.latimes.com/1999/jun/24/local/me-49832.

Morison, Samuel Eliot. *The Oxford History of the American People 1869–1963.* New York: Mentor, 1972.

Morrison, Wayne M. "China's Economic Conditions." Congressional Research Service. June 26, 2012. http://www.fas.org/sgp/crs/row/RL33534.pdf.

Nakashima, Ellen. "In a World of Cybertheft, US Names China, Russia as Main Culprits." *Washington Post,* November 3, 2011. www.washingtonpost.com/world/national-security/us-cyberespionage-report-names-china-and-russia-as-main-culprits/2011/11/02/gIQAF5fRiM_story_1.html.

Nasheri, Hedieh. *Economic Espionage and Industrial Spying.* New York: Cambridge University Press, 2005.

National Public Radio. "China's Cyber Threat a High Stakes Game." November 27, 2011. www.npr.org/2011/11/27/142828055/chinas-cyber-threat-a-high-stakes-spy-game.

Nine Years after 9/11: Confronting the Terrorist Threat to the Homeland. Hearing before the US Senate Homeland Security and Government Affairs Committee, 112th Cong., September 22, 2010. Testimony of Michael Leiter, Director of the National Counterterrorism Center. www.dni.gov/testimonies/2010-09-22%20 D-NCTC%20Leiter%20Testimony%20for%20SHSGAC%20Hearing.pdf.

Novak, Viveca, and Elaine Shannon. "Ashcroft on the Spot." *Time,* May 28, 2001. www.time.com/time/magazine/article/0,9171,999968,00.html.

Office of the National Counterintelligence Executive. "Foreign Spies Stealing US Economic Secrets in Cyberspace." October 2011. www.dni.gov/reports/20111103_report_fecie.pdf.

———. *National Counterintelligence Strategy of the United States, 2009.* http://www. ncix.gov/publications/strategy/docs/NatlCIStrategy2009.pdf.

Office of the US Trade Representative. "China." www.ustr.gov/countries-regions/ china.

Olive, Ronald J. *Capturing Jonathan Pollard.* Annapolis, MD: Naval Institute Press, 2006.

Oswald, John. "Ashcroft Will Not Budge on Death for Spy Suspect." *New York Daily News,* May 21, 2001. http://articles.nydailynews.com/2001-05-21/ news/18177565_1_death-penalty-spy-agency-plea-deal.

"Partners in Espionage: James Harper and Ruby Schuler." *Security Awareness Bulletin,* US Department of Defense, no. 3 (June 1983): 53–60. http://books. google.com/books?id=2wNgbdnKuKAC&pg=PA43&lpg=PA43&dq=security+a wareness+bulletin+caught+unawares&source=bl&ots=5hmX-JdHtf&sig=SorZ Pt6vhSu8VcRTVBFXjaRe7A0&hl=en&sa=X&ei=zVmhT_-vO4f28wSxzsisCA& ved=0CE4Q6AEwAA#v=onepage&q&f=false.

Peterson, Martha. *The Widow Spy: My CIA Journey from the Jungles of Laos to Prison in Moscow.* Wilmington, NC: Red Canary Press, 2012; Kindle edition.

Philbrick, Herbert. *I Led Three Lives.* New York: Grosset and Dunlap, 1952.

Pincher, Chapman. *Traitors.* London: Sidgwick and Jackson, 1987; New York: Penguin, 1987. Citations refer to the Penguin edition.

Pincus, Walter. "Cold War Footnote: CIA Obtained East German Foreign Spy Files." *Washington Post,* November 22, 1998.

———. "Imprisoned ex-CIA Officer Pleads Guilty Again." *Washington Post,* November 9, 2010. www.washingtonpost.com/wp-dyn/content/article/2010/11/08/ AR2010110806311.html.

Pipes, Daniel. "Pentagon Jihadis." *New York Post,* September 29, 2003. www.danielpipes.org/1259/pentagon-jihadis.

Popkin, Jim. "Ana Montes Did Much Harm Spying for Cuba: Chances Are You Haven't Heard of Her." *Washington Post,* April 18, 2013. http://www. washingtonpost.com/sf/feature/wp/2013/04/18/ana-montes-did-much- harm-spying-for-cuba-chances-are-you-havent-heard-of-her/?hpid=z4.

Poteat, S. Eugene. "The Downside of Globalization: The Surge in Economic and Industrial Espionage." *Intelligencer* 15, no. 2 (Fall–Winter 2006–7): 11–18.

Powers, Richard Gid. *Broken: The Troubled Past and Uncertain Future of the FBI.* New York: Free Press, 2004.

———. *Secrecy and Power: The Life of J. Edgar Hoover.* New York: Free Press, 1987.

Powers, Thomas. *Intelligence Wars: American Secret History from Hitler to Al-Qaeda.* New York: New York Review of Books, 2002.

———. *The Man Who Kept the Secrets.* New York: Alfred A. Knopf, 1979.

Radosh, Ronald. "Castro's Top Spy." *Front Page,* March 29, 2002. http://archive. frontpagemag.com/readArticle.aspx?ARTID=24029.

Rafalko, Frank, ed. *Counterintelligence Reader.* 4 vols. Washington, DC: National Counterintelligence Center, 2001.

Raviv, Dan, and Yossi Melman. *Spies against Armageddon: Inside Israel's Secret Wars.* New York: Levant Books, 2012; Kindle edition.

Redmond, Paul. "America Pays the Price for Openness." *Wall Street Journal,* June 23, 2000. www.apfn.net/messageboard/7-09-3/discussion.cgi.46.html.

Richelson, Jeffrey T. *A Century of Spies: Intelligence in the Twentieth Century.* New York: Oxford University Press, 1995.

Riebling, Mark. *Wedge: The Secret War between the FBI and CIA.* New York: Alfred A. Knopf, 1994.

Riley, Michael, and John Walcott. "China-Based Hacking of 760 Companies Shows Cyber Cold War." *Bloomberg,* December 17,2011. www.bloomberg.com/ news/2011-12-13/china-based-hacking-of-760-companies-reflects-undeclared-global-cyber-war.html.

Rishikof, Harvey. "Economic and Industrial Espionage: Who Is Eating America's Lunch, and How Do We Stop It?" In *Vaults, Mirrors, and Masks: Rediscovering US Counterintelligence,* edited by Jennifer E. Sims and Burton Gerber. Washington, DC: Georgetown University Press, 2009.

Robarge, David. "The James Angleton Phenomenon." *Studies in Intelligence* 53, no. 4 (December 2009): 49–61. www.cia.gov/library/center-for-the-study-of-intelligence/csi-publications/csi-studies/studies/vol53no4/201ccunning-passages-contrived-corridors201d.html.

——. "Moles, Defectors and Deceptions: James Angleton and CIA Counterintelligence." *Journal of Intelligence History* 3, no. 2 (Winter 2003): 21–49.

Rogin, Josh. "The Top 10 Chinese Cyber Attacks (That We Know of)." *Foreign Policy,* January 22, 2010. http://thecable.foreignpolicy.com/posts/2010/01/22/ the_top_10_chinese_cyber_attacks_that_we_know_of.

Romerstein, Herbert, and Eric Breindel. *The Venona Secrets: Exposing Soviet Espionage and America's Traitors.* Washington, DC: Regnery, 2000.

Rositzke, Harry. *The CIA's Secret Operations: Espionage, Counterespionage and Covert Action.* New York: Reader's Digest Press / Thomas Y. Crowell, 1977.

Royden, Barry G. "An Exceptional Espionage Operation: Tolkachev, a Worthy Successor to Penkovsky." *Studies in Intelligence* 47, no. 3 (2003): 5–33.

Sale, Richard. *Traitors: The Worst Acts of Treason in American History from Benedict Arnold to Robert Hanssen.* New York: Berkley, 2003.

Scherer, Michael. "The Geeks Who Leak." *Time,* June 13, 2012.

Schiller, Lawrence. *Into the Mirror: The Life of Master Spy Robert P. Hanssen.* New York: HarperCollins, 2002.

Schweizer, Peter. "Our Thieving Allies." *New York Times,* June 23, 1992. www.fas. org/irp/congress/1992_cr/s920624-spy.htm.

Shannon, Elaine, and Ann Blackman. *The Spy Next Door: The Extraordinary Secret Life of Robert Philip Hanssen, the Most Dangerous FBI Agent in US History.* Boston: Little, Brown, 2002.

Shaw, Mark. *Miscarriage of Justice: The Jonathan Pollard Story.* New York: Paragon House, 2001.

Sheridan, Mary Beth, and Del Quentin Wilber. "DC Couple's Disdain for US Policies May Have Led to Alleged Spying for Cuba." *Washington Post,* June 7, 2009. www.washingtonpost.com/wp-dyn/content/article/2009/06/06/ AR2009060602245.html.

Sims, Jennifer E., and Burton Gerber, eds. *Vaults, Mirrors, and Masks: Rediscovering US Counterintelligence.* Washington, DC: Georgetown University Press, 2009.

———. "The Way Ahead." In *Vaults, Mirrors and Masks: Rediscovering US Counterintelligence,* edited by Jennifer E. Sims and Burton Gerber. Washington, DC: Georgetown University Press, 2009.

Smith, Gerry. "Cyber-Threats Pose 'Existential Threat,' FBI Warns." *Huffington Post,* January 12, 2012. www.huffingtonpost.com/2012/01/12/cyber-threats_ n_1202026.html?ref=mostpopular.

"Spy Who Redefected Shown on German TV." Associated Press, March 14, 1986.

Stein, Jeff. "The Hidden Hand in the Free-Pollard Campaign." *Washington Post,* January 5, 2011. http://voices.washingtonpost.com/spy-talk/2011/01/the_ hidden_hand_in_the_free-po.html.

———. "Kissinger: Release Israeli Spy Pollard." *Washington Post,* March 7, 2011. http://voices.washingtonpost.com/spy-talk/2011/03/kissinger_release_israeli_ spy.html.

Stober, Dan, and Ian Hoffman. *A Convenient Spy: Wen Ho Lee and the Politics of Nuclear Espionage.* New York: Simon & Schuster, 2001.

Stoll, Clifford. *The Cuckoo's Egg: Tracking a Spy through the Maze of Computer Espionage.* New York: Doubleday, 1989; London: Bodley Head, 1990.

Sulick, Michael. "Al-Qaeda Answers CIA's Hiring Call." *Los Angeles Times,* July 10, 2005.

———. *Spying in America: Espionage from the Revolutionary War to the Dawn of the Cold War.* Washington, DC: Georgetown University Press, 2012.

Suter, Keith. "Military Mutinies." *Global Directions,* 2, http://global-directions. com/Articles/Peace%20and%20Conflict/MilitaryMutinies.pdf.

Tenet, George. *At the Center of the Storm: My Years at the CIA.* New York: Harper-Collins, 2007.

Theoharis, Athan. *The FBI and American Democracy.* Lawrence: University of Kansas Press, 2004.

Thiessen, Marc. "Stop Downplaying the WikiLeaks Damage." *The American,* December 8, 2010. http://blog.american.com/2010/12/stop-downplaying-wikileaks-damage/.

Thompson, Ginger. "Couple's Capital Ties Said to Veil Spying for Cuba." *New York Times,* June 18, 2009. www.nytimes.com/2009/06/19/world/19spies. html?pagewanted=2&_r=1&ref=world.

Tolstoy, Leo. *Anna Karenina,* translated by David Magarshack. New York: New American Library, 1961.

Trulock, Notra. *Kindred Spirit: Inside the Chinese Nuclear Espionage Scandal.* San Francisco: Encounter Books, 2003.

Tully, Andrew. *Inside the FBI.* New York: Dell, 1980.

Tzu, Sun. *The Art of War,* translated by Samuel B. Griffin. New York: Oxford University Press, 1963.

United States of America v. Aldrich Hazen Ames. Affidavit in Support of Warrants for Arrest and Search and Seizure Warrants, US District Court, Eastern District of Virginia, February 1994. http://cryptome.org/jya/ames.htm.

United States of America v. Ali Mohammed. Guilty plea, US District Court, Southern District of New York, Criminal No. 98 Cr. 1023, October 20, 2000. http://cryptome.org/usa-v-mohamed.htm.

United States of America v. Ana Belen Montes. Affidavit in Support of Criminal Complaint, Arrest Warrant and Search Warrant, September 21, 2001. www.fas.org/irp/ops/ci/Montes_092101.pdf.

United States of America v. Ana Belen Montes. Indictment and Factual Proffer in Support of the Guilty Plea, US District Court for the District of Colombia, Magistrate No. 01-0568M-01, March 19, 2002. http://news.findlaw.com/hdocs/docs/montes/usmontesplea031902.pdf.

United States of America v. Chi Mak. Affidavit, US District Court, Central District of California, Criminal No. 05-M-394-ALL, October 31, 2005. www.4law.co.il/fbicn1.pdf.

United States of America v. Chi Mak et al. Indictment, US District Court, Central District of California, Criminal No. 05-M-394-ALL, November 15, 2005 .www.cicentre.com/resource/resmgr/spycase_docs/mak_chi_ind161105.pdf.

United States of America v. Chi Mak et al. Second Superseding Indictment, US District Court, Central District of California, Criminal No. 05-293(B)-CJC, October 25, 2006. www.4law.co.il/fbicn5.pdf.

United States of America v. Dongfan "Greg" Chung. Indictment, US District Court, Central District of California, No. SA CR-08-00024, February 6, 2008. www.justice.gov/opa/pr/2008/February/chung-indictment.pdf.

United States of America v. Earl Edwin Pitts. Affidavit in Support of Criminal Complaint, Arrest Warrant and Search Warrants, United States District Court, Eastern District of Virginia, Case No. 96-104, December 17, 1996. In *Counterintelligence Reader,* 3:365–66, edited by Frank Rafalko. Washington, DC: National Counterintelligence Center, 2001.

United States of America v. George von Trofimoff, Affidavit, United States District Court, Middle District of Florida, Tampa Division, Case No. 8:00-CR-197-7-24C. In *Counterintelligence Reader,* 4:95–101, edited by Frank Rafalko. Washington, DC: National Counterintelligence Center, 2001.

United States of America v. Glenn Duffie Shriver. Statement of Facts, US District Court for the Eastern District of Virginia, no. 1:10cr-00402-LO, October 22, 2010. http://jnslp.files.wordpress.com/2010/10/shriver_statement-of-facts.pdf.

United States of America v. Harold J. Nicholson. Affidavit in Support of Complaint, Arrest Warrant and Search Warrants, US District Court for Eastern District of Virginia, Alexandria Division, November 15, 1996. In *Counterintelligence Reader,* 3:354–63, edited by Frank Rafalko. Washington, DC: National Counterintelligence Center, 2001.

United States of America v. Harold J. Nicholson. Statement of Facts in Support of Plea Agreement, US District Court for District of Oregon, Portland Division, Case No. 09-cr-40-1-br, November 8, 2010. www.justice.gov/usao/or/Indictments/01182011_Statement%20of%20Facts.pdf.

United States of America v. Harold J. Nicholson. Statement of Facts in Support of Plea Agreement, US District Court for Eastern District of Virginia, Alexandria

Division, Criminal No. 96-448-A. www.cicentre.com/resource/resmgr/ spycase_docs/nicholson_harold_statement19.pdf.

United States of America v. Harold Nicholson and Nathaniel Nicholson. Application and Affidavit for Search Warrant, US District Court of Oregon, Criminal No. 08-MC-9276-A-E, December 11, 2008. www.cicentre.com/resource/resmgr/ spycase_docs/nicholson_aff11dec08.pdf.

United States of America v. Harold Nicholson and Nathaniel Nicholson. Indictment, US District Court, District of Oregon, No. CR-09-40-BR, January 27, 2009. www.cicentre.com/resource/resmgr/spycase_docs/nicholson_hn_indict_ jan09.pdf.

United States of America v. Hassan Abu Jihaad. Memorandum of Decision, United States District Court, District of Connecticut, No. 3-07CR57, March 4, 2009. http://jurist.law.pitt.edu/pdf/abujihaadhassan.pdf.

United States of America v. Hassan Abu Jihaad, aka Paul R. Hall. Criminal Complaint, United States District Court, District of Connecticut, Criminal No. 09-1384-cr, March 1, 2007. www.law.com/jsp/tal/PubArticleTAL.jsp?id=12024 77070850&slreturn=1.

United States of America v. James J. Smith. Affidavit, April 2002. www.fas.org/irp/ ops/ci/smith.html.

United States of America v. James W. Hall III. Affidavit, Application for Certain Search Warrants, US District Court, Southern District of Georgia, December 21, 1988. http://c.ymcdn.com/sites/www.cicentre.com/resource/resmgr/ spycase_docs/hall_james_aff1288.pdf.

United States of America v. James Wilbur Fondren Jr. Affidavit in Support of Criminal Complaint, US District Court for the Eastern District of Virginia, Alexandria Division, Criminal No. 1:09MJ327, May 11, 2009. www.cicentre. com/resource/resmgr/spycase_docs/fondren_j_23aug09.pdf.

United States of America v. James Wilbur Fondren Jr. Indictment, US District Court for the Eastern District of Virginia, Alexandria Division, Case No. 1:09-cr-00263-CMH, June 11, 2009. www.cicentre.com/resource/resmgr/spycase_ docs/fondren_indict_11jun09.pdf.

United States of America v. Jonathan Pollard. Government's Memorandum in Aid of Sentencing, US District for the District of Columbia, Criminal no. 02-8607, January 6, 1987. www.irmep.org/ila/pollard/01061987govt_memo_aid_ sentence.pdf.

United States of America v. Jonathan Pollard. Indictment, Criminal No. 86-0207, US District Court, District of Columbia, June 4, 1986. http://irmep.org/ila/ pollard/02171987US_opp_def_mot_for_evidence.pdf.

United States of America v. Jonathan Pollard. Supplemental Declaration of Caspar L. Weinberger, Secretary of Defense. Criminal No. 86-0207, US District Court, District of Columbia, March 3, 1987. www.irmep.org/ila/pollard/03041987 weinberger.pdf.

United States of America v. Katrina Leung. Affidavit in Support of Complaint and Arrest Warrant, March 2003. www.fas.org/irp/ops/ci/leung.html.

United States of America v. Katrina Leung. Indictment, US District Court, Central District of California, April 9, 2003. Usleung50803ind-1.pdf.

United States of America v. Katrina Leung. Order Granting Defendant Motion to Dismiss, US District Court, Central District of California, Criminal No. 03-434 FMC, January 6, 2005. http://ca.findacase.com/research/wfrmDocViewer. aspx/xq/fac.20050106_0000001.CCA.htm/qx

United States of America v. Larry Wu-tai Chin. Affidavit for Search Warrant, Eastern District of Virginia, Alexandria Division, November 22, 1985. www. cicentre.com/resource/resmgr/spycase_docs/chin_affidavit1185.pdf.

United States of America v. Larry Wu Tai Chin aka Chin Wu-tai. Indictment, United States District Court, Eastern District of Virginia, Alexandria Division, Criminal No. 85-00263-A, January 12, 1986.

United States of America v. Richard Miller. Affidavit, US District Court, Central District of California, October 1984. www.cicentre.com/resource/resmgr/ spycase_docs/miller_aff1084.pdf.

United States of America v. Robert Philip Hanssen. Affidavit in Support of Criminal Complaint, Arrest Warrant and Search Warrants, United States District Court, Eastern District of Virginia, February 20, 2001. www.fas.org/irp/ops/ci/ hanssen_affidavit.html.

United States of America v. Ronald Humphrey; United States of America v. Truong Dinh Hung. In "Executive Authority for National Security Surveillance," edited by William Banks and M. E. Bowman, www.wcl.american.edu/journal/ lawrev/50/banks.pdf?rd=1.

United States of America v. Ronald N. Montaperto. Statement of Facts, US District Court, Eastern District of Virginia, Criminal No. 1: 06cr257, June 2006. http:// montaperto.blogspot.com/2006_06_01_archive.html.

United States of America v. Tai Shen Kuo, Gregg William Bergersen, and Yu Xin Kang. Affidavit in Support of Criminal Complaint, US District Court, Eastern District of Virginia, Alexandria Division, No. 1: 08mj98, February 6, 2008. www.fas.org/irp/ops/ci/kuo-affidavit.pdf.

United States of America v. Walter Kendall Myers. Criminal Complaint, US District Court for the District of Columbia, No. 09-326-M-07, June 4, 2009. www. scribd.com/doc/16176377/US-v-Walter-Kendall-Myers-Criminal-Complaint.

United States of America v. Walter Kendall Myers and Gwendolyn Steingraber Myers. Indictment, US District Court for the District of Columbia, Criminal No. 09-150 (RBW/JMF), June 4, 2009. http://i.cdn.turner.com/cnn/2009/ images/06/05/myers.indictment.pdf.

United States of America v. Wen Ho Lee. Affidavit in Support of Search Warrant, US District Court, District of New Mexico. www.fas.org/irp/ops/ci/lowe_affidavit. html.

United States of America v. Wen Ho Lee. Declaration of Dr. Harold M. Agnew, May 27, 2000. www.fas.org/irp/ops/ci/agnew.html.

United States of America v. Wen Ho Lee. Indictment, US District Court, District of New Mexico, Criminal No. 99-1417, December 10, 1999. www.fas.org/irp/ops/ ci/docs/lee_indict.html.

US Central Intelligence Agency. "James Woolsey, Testimony at Confirmation Hearing, US Senate Select Committee on Intelligence, February 2, 1993. https:// www.cia.gov/library/center-for-the-study-of-intelligence/csi-publications/

books-and-monographs/directors-of-central-intelligence-as-leaders-of-the-u-s-intelligence-community/chapter_12.htm#_ftn1.

———. "Statement of the Director of Central Intelligence on the Clandestine Services and the Damage Caused by Aldrich Ames." December 7, 1995. In *Counterintelligence Reader*, 3:314–32, edited by Frank Rafalko. Washington, DC: National Counterintelligence Center, 2001.

———. "Unclassified Abstract of the CIA Inspector General's Report on the Aldrich H. Ames Case." In *Counterintelligence Reader*, 3:326, edited by Frank Rafalko. Washington, DC: National Counterintelligence Center, 2001.

US Central Intelligence Agency, Center for the Study of Intelligence. "Preparing for Martial Law: Through the Eyes of Col. Ryszard Kuklinski." Washington, DC: Central Intelligence Agency, 2009.

US Central Intelligence Agency. Foreign Denial and Deception Analysis Committee. "The Jonathan Pollard Espionage Case: A Damage Assessment." George Washington University National Security Archives. www.gwu.edu/~nsarchiv/ NSAEBB/NSAEBB407/

US Department of Defense. "Annual Report to Congress: Military and Security Developments Involving the People's Republic of China 2013," May 6, 2013. www.defense.gov/pubs/2013_China_Report_FINAL.pdf.

US Department of Defense, Defense Science Board. "Resilient Military Systems and Advanced Cyber Threats," January 2013. www.acq.osd.mil/dsb/reports/ ResilientMilitarySystems.CyberThreat.pdf

US Department of Defense. "Nominee Urges Government, Private Sector Cooperation." Press release. April 25, 2010. www.defense.gov/News/NewsArticle. aspx?ID=58772.

US Department of Justice. "Attorney General's Review Team on the Handling of the Los Alamos National Laboratory Investigation." May 2000. www.usdoj. gov/ag/readingroom/bellows.htm.

———. "New Orleans Man Sentenced to More Than 15 Years in Prison for Espionage Involving China." Press release. August 8, 2008. www.justice.gov/opa/ pr/2008/August/08-nsd-701.html.

———. "A Review of FBI Security Programs." Commission for the Review of FBI Security Programs, March 2002. www.fas.org/irp/agency/doj/fbi/ websterreport.html.

———. "Statement of the US Attorney on the Guilty Pleas Entered by Katrina Leung." Press release. December 16, 2005. www.justice.gov/usao/cac/ Pressroom/pr2005/173.html.

US Department of Justice, Federal Bureau of Investigation. "FBI Uniform Crime Reporting Statistics." www.ucrdatatool.gov/Search/Crime/State/ RunCrimeStatebyState.cfm.

US Department of Justice, Federal Bureau of Investigation, "History of the FBI," www.fbi.gov/about-us/history/brief-history.

US Department of Justice, Federal Bureau of Investigation. "Statement of FBI Director Louis J. Freeh on the Arrest of FBI Special Agent Robert Philip Hanssen." News release, February 20, 2001. www.fbi.gov/news/pressrel/ press-releases/veteran-fbi-agent-arrested-and-charged-with-espionage.

US Department of Justice, Office of the Inspector General. "The Federal Bureau of Investigation's Ability to Address the National Security Cyber Intrusion Threat." www.justice.gov/oig/reports/FBI/a1122r.pdf.

———. "A Review of the FBI's Handling and Oversight of FBI Asset Katrina Leung." May 2006. www.usdoj.gov/oig/special/s0605/final.pdf.

———. "A Review of the FBI's Performance in Deterring, Detecting and Investigating the Espionage Activities of Robert Philip Hanssen." August 2003. www.usdoj.gov/oig/special/0308/final.pdf.

———. "A Review of the FBI's Performance in Uncovering the Espionage Activities of Aldrich Hazen Ames." April 1997. www.justice.gov/oig/special/9704.htm.

US Department of State. "Secretary Clinton Delivers Remarks to the Press on Release of Confidential Documents." November 29, 2010. http://blogs.state.gov/index.php/site/entry/clinton_statement_2010_11_29.

US Government Accountability Office. "Critical Infrastructure Protection: Cybersecurity Guidance Is Available but More Should Be Done to Promote Its Use." December 2011. www.gao.gov/assets/590/587529.pdf.

———. "Defense Department Cyber Efforts: DOD Faces Challenges in Its Cyber Activities." July 2011. www.gao.gov/new.items/d1175.pdf.

———. "Information Security: Weaknesses Continue Amid Federal Efforts to Implement Requirements." October 2011. www.gao.gov/new.items/d12137.pdf.

US House of Representatives. *Final Report of the Select Committee on US National Security and Military/Commercial Concerns about the People's Republic of China*, HR Rep. 105-861. In *Counterintelligence Reader*, 4:4–58, edited by Frank Rafalko. Washington, DC: National Counterintelligence Center, 2001.

US President. "Comprehensive National Cybersecurity Initiative." March 2, 2010. www.fas.org/irp/eprint/cnci.pdf.

———. "National Security Presidential Directive 54." January 8, 2008. www.dhs.gov/xnews/releases/pr_1207684277498.shtm.

———. "National Strategy to Secure Cyberspace." February 2003. www.dhs.gov/xlibrary/assets/National_Cyberspace_Strategy.pdf.

US Senate. *COINTELPRO: The FBI's Covert Action Programs against American Citizens. Final Report of the Select Committee to Study Governmental Operations*, April 23, 1976. www.icdc.com/~paulwolf/cointelpro/churchfinalreportIIIa.htm.

US Senate, Committee on the Judiciary. "Report on the Investigation of Espionage Allegations against Dr. Wen Ho Lee." March 8, 2000. In *Counterintelligence Reader*, 4:59, edited by Frank Rafalko. Washington, DC: National Counterintelligence Center, 2001.

US Senate, Select Committee on Intelligence. "An Assessment of the Aldrich Ames Espionage Case and Its Implications for US Intelligence." November 1, 1994. www.fas.org/irp/congress/1994_rpt/ssci_ames.htm

Valdes, Jose Cohen. *El Servicio de Inteligencia Castrista y La Comunidad Academica Norteamericana* [Castro's Intelligence Service and the US Academic Community]. Institute for Cuban and Cuban-American Studies Monograph Series. Miami: University of Miami, 2002.

Varian, Hal. "An IPod Has Global Value." *New York Times,* June 28, 2007. www. nytimes.com/2007/06/28/business/worldbusiness/28scene.html.

Verbitzky, Anatole, and Dick Adler. *Sleeping with Moscow: The Authorized Account of the KGB's Bungled Infiltration of the FBI by Two of the Soviet Union's Most Unlikely Operatives.* New York: Shapolsky, 1987.

Vise, David. *The Bureau and the Mole: The Unmasking of Robert Philip Hanssen, the Most Dangerous Double Agent in FBI History.* New York: Grove, 2002.

Volkman, Ernest. *Espionage: The Greatest Spy Operations of the 20th Century.* New York: John Wiley & Sons, 1995.

———. *Spies: The Secret Agents Who Changed the Course of History.* New York: John Wiley & Sons, 1994.

Walker, John A. *My Life as a Spy.* Amherst, NY: Prometheus Books, 2008.

Wallace, Robert. "A Time for Counterespionage." In *Vaults, Mirrors and Masks: Rediscovering US Counterintelligence,* edited by Jennifer E. Sims and Burton Gerber. Washington, DC: Georgetown University Press, 2009.

Wallace, Robert, and H. Keith Melton. *Spycraft: The Secret History of the CIA's Spytechs from Communism to Al Qaeda.* New York: Dutton, 2008; Kindle edition.

Waller, J. Michael. "Espionage and National Security." *Insight on the News* 17, no. 13 (April 2, 2001). www.questia.com/library/1G1-72328684/espionage-and-national-security#articleDetails.

"Wary of Critics, Poland Sends Its Top Spy Back into the Cold." *New York Times,* August 19, 1994.

Weidlich, Thomas. "Kennedy Airport Terror Plot Suspect Found Guilty in Failed Bomb Attack." *Bloomberg News,* May 26, 2011. www.bloomberg.com/news/2011-05-26/kennedy-airport-terror-plot-suspect-found-guilty-in-failed-bombing-ttack.html.

Weiner, Timothy, David Johnston, and Neil A. Lewis. *Betrayal: The Story of Aldrich Ames, an American Spy.* New York: Random House, 1995.

Weinstein, Allen, and Alexander Vassiliev. *The Haunted Wood: Soviet Espionage in America; The Stalin era.* New York: Random House, 1999; New York: Modern Library, 2000. Citations refer to the Modern Library edition.

Werner, Leslie Maitland. "US Weighs Moves in Spy Case." *New York Times,* December 1, 1984. www.nytimes.com/1984/12/02/us/us-weighs-moves-in-czech-spy-casse.html?scp=14&sq=karl%20koecher&st=cse.

West, Nigel. *Venona: The Greatest Secret of the Cold War.* New York: HarperCollins, 1999.

West, Rebecca. *The New Meaning of Treason.* New York: Viking Press, 1964.

Wildmuth, John. "Arrest of GOP Fundraiser May Curtail Political Involvement." *San Francisco Chronicle,* April 12, 2003.

Williams, Danny L. *Damian and the Mongoose: How a US Counterespionage Agent Infiltrated an International Spy Ring.* Tucson: Wheatmark, 2011; Kindle Edition.

Winks, Robin. *Cloaks and Gowns: Scholars in the Secret War, 1939–1961.* New York: William Morrow, 1987.

Wise, David. "The Felix Bloch Affair." *New York Times Magazine,* May 13, 1990.

———. *Molehunt: How the Search for a Phantom Traitor Shattered the CIA.* New York: Random House, 1992; New York: Avon, 1994. Citations refer to the Avon edition.

———. *Nightmover: How Aldrich Ames Sold the CIA to the KGB for $4.6 Million.* New York: HarperCollins, 1995.

———. *Spy: The Inside Story of How the FBI's Robert Hanssen Betrayed America.* New York: Random House, 2002.

———. *The Spy Who Got Away: The Inside Story of Edward Lee Howard, the CIA Agent Who Betrayed His Country's Secrets and Escaped to Moscow.* New York: Random House, 1988.

———. *Tiger Trap: America's Secret Spy War with China.* New York: Houghton Mifflin, 2011.

Wolf, Markus. *Man without a Face: The Autobiography of Communism's Greatest Spymaster.* New York: Public Affairs, 1997.

Zhongwen, Huo, and Wang Zongxiao. *Sources and Techniques of Obtaining National Defense Science and Technology Intelligence.* Beijing: Kexue Jishu Wenxuan Publishing, 1991. The book is summarized in *Counterintelligence Reader,* 4:54–58, edited by Frank Rafalko. Washington, DC: National Counterintelligence Center, 2001.

Zinn, Howard. *A People's History of the US.* New York: HarperCollins, 1999; New York: HarperPerennial, 2003. Citations refer to the HarperPerennial edition.

———. *The Twentieth Century: A People's History.* New York: HarperCollins, 1998; New York: HarperPerennial, 2003. Citations refer to the HarperPerennial edition.

About the Author

Michael J. Sulick is a retired intelligence operations officer who from 2007 to 2010 was director of the Central Intelligence Agency's National Clandestine Service, where he was responsible for supervising the CIA's covert collection operations and coordinating the espionage activities of the US intelligence community. During his twenty-eight-year career, his assignments also included chief of CIA counterintelligence (2002–4) and chief of the CIA's Central Eurasia Division (1999–2002). He is also the author of *Spying in America: Espionage from the Revolutionary War to the Dawn of the Cold War.* He received a PhD in comparative literature from the City University of New York.

INDEX